Christianity
and Social Work

*Readings on the Integration of
Christian Faith and
Social Work Practice*

FOURTH EDITION

T. Laine Scales and Michael S. Kelly
Editors

The editors and publisher gratefully acknowledge permission to reprint or adapt material from the following works:

Excerpts from *Giving and Taking Help*, Revised Edition, by Alan Keith-Lucas, Editor: David Sherwood, © 1994, Excerpts Reprinted with permission of North American Association of Christians in Social Work.

Ethical integration of faith and social work practice: Evangelism by David Sherwood, *Social Work and Christianity*, Vol. 29 no. 1, pp. 1-12, © 2001, Reprinted with permission of North American Association of Christians in Social Work.

Figure from Physicians' and patients' choices in evidence-based practice. by R. B. Haynes, P.J. Devereaux, & G.H. Guyatt *British Medical Journal*, Vol. 324 , 1349-1350., © 2002. Reprinted with permission of BPJ Publishers LTD.

"Accepting a Trust So Responsible:" Christians Caring for Children at Buckner Orphan's Home, Dallas, Texas, 1879-1909, b. T. Laine Scales, *Social Work and Christianity*, Vol.38, no.3, pp. 332-55, © 2011, Reprinted with permission of North American Association of Christians in Social Work.

"To Give Christ to the Neighborhood:" A Corrective Look at the Settlement Movement and Early Christian Social Workers, by T. Laine Scales and Michael S. Kelly, *Social Work and Christianity*, Vol.38, no.3, pp. 356-76, © 2011 Reprinted with permission of North American Association of Christians in Social Work.

ISBN 978-0-9715318-7-1

CONTENTS

SECTION 2
CHRISTIANS CALLED TO SOCIAL WORK:
SCRIPTURAL BASIS, WORLDVIEWS AND ETHICS

INTRODUCTION TO THE 4ᵀᴴ EDITION.

T. Laine Scales and Michael S. Kelly

For this 4ᵗʰ edition of *Christianity & Social Work*, we found ourselves reflecting on the myriad ways our authors have shared their own "truths" in this new volume. The most ever-present aspect of truth for us as Christian social work scholars and teachers is our love for the clarity of Jesus as he shares his word and his belief that if we abide in his teachings, his truth shall make us free (John 8:32). Still, as any Christian (and any social worker, Christian or not) knows, discerning the "truths" and practice wisdom in our field can be a daunting task, particularly as we strive to practice in a fast-paced, multicultural world that seldom slows down long enough to let us hear that small, still voice declaring the truth of God's love for all the world's people. This book reckons, in its own way, with that necessity for stillness and reflection that all Christian social workers need to prepare for their professional journeys into the complex and ever-changing world of social work practice.

Our 4ᵗʰ edition builds on a solid foundation set by Dr. Beryl Hugen in the first edition, published in 1999. Attempting to create a completely new resource, Dr. Hugen found it difficult in those days to find enough writers to address the themes and topics important to our students and practitioners. Indeed, we seemed to be so busy practicing that we failed to share our work with one another. In the past decade, largely through NACSW's focus on publications, Christian social workers have been more intentional about sharing our "practice wisdom" in writing. Through the years, by carefully adding to that pioneering volume, we have tried to address the particular questions of Christian students, teachers, and practitioners by sharing our authors' humble truths with a busy and growing group of Christians in social work practice and education.

As of 2011, there were approximately 675 MSW and BSW programs in the U.S, and many are housed in religiously-affiliated colleges and universities. In addition, many Christians are educated within non-sectarian colleges and universities or practicing within both religiously-affiliated and secular agencies. As with previous editions, it is our intention to address the historical roots of Christians in social work and move our field into the future by employing a variety of perspectives by Christian authors. As multiple authors in this book will make clear, there is not *one* way to be a Christian social worker; rather it is our hope that the multiplicity of voices contained here will argue for how *many* ways there are to be a faithful Christian and effective social work practitioner.

1

We both work in Christian colleges, informed by our specific Christian traditions (Laine at Baptist Baylor, and Michael at Jesuit Catholic Loyola Chicago). As teachers and researchers we are eager to see more Christian social work scholarship that we can draw on to help prepare our students for careers as practitioners. We both came to the field, in part, because of the calling of our Christian faith and, while we certainly don't require the same religious commitment of our students, we want to speak to those who are attempting to integrate their faith experience with their social work preparation. We know from our own experiences that it can be a challenge to even raise the issues that are in these pages with student colleagues, faculty members, and supervisors. As you read these chapters, we hope you will feel energized and encouraged by the abundance of scholarship for Christian social workers: you are far from alone if you endeavor to become a social worker rooted in your own Christian faith experience.

As might be expected with any textbook entering its 4th edition, we were eager to make our new edition current and reflective of our readers' priorities. To that end, in 2009-10, we reached out to NACSW members and faculty who have read our book and used it in the classroom to solicit their input in an online survey. What they told us (maybe what you told us!) was illuminating and encouraging. The encouraging news was that many of our respondents said that they loved the book and used the chapters across the various core social work domains (Introduction to the profession, practice, HBSE, and policy) to bolster their course content. Many said they used our book as the focal text for their practice course, or used it as a companion volume for students throughout their BSW or MSW course work.

While it's always heartening to get good feedback, we remain evidence-based and data-driven in our approach to social work pedagogy. So we also wanted to know what content readers thought was missing or out of date. The survey data revealed some key areas that we're pleased to include in this new edition: more content on the Christian roots of social welfare history, examples of Christian-informed interventions focused on at-risk populations; an example of international social work practice from a Christian perspective; an argument for how Evidence-based Practice (EBP) must be informed by spiritual and religious values of both social work practitioners and their clients; an overview of social work in congregations, and a discussion of how Christian social workers can work ethically and sensitively with lesbian and gay clients. We're grateful to these new authors for offering their voices to the larger conversation of what it means to be a Christian social worker.

Connection to the Educational Policy Accreditation Standards

In organizing this 4th edition, we have carefully considered the *Educational Policy and Accreditation Standards* (EPAS) from the Council on Social Work Education. These standards shape the core content of social work curricula and this book engages the EPAS in each chapter. It is important for schools of social work to show how they prepare students to demonstrate specific competencies in social work practice. To help with this integration we have included Appendices with charts that guide readers toward potential connections. The first chart is organized according to the chapters of this book and the second chart is organized by the competencies of the EPAS. We hope these tools be a helpful guide for students and instructors. Now we will turn to the themes of each section.

SECTION 1
Christian Roots of the Social Work Profession

The proper role of Christianity in social work practice has been debated, but most admit that our historical roots are Judeo-Christian. Unfortunately an over-simplified version of the role of Judeo-Christian thought in U.S. social welfare history is recorded in social work textbooks. In addition, textbooks often oversimplify or distort the complex relationship between friendly visitors, settlement workers, and urban missionaries that served as a foundation for professionalizing social work. practice, perhaps the least contested relates to our historical roots.

As our authors explore in Section 1, the early history of social work is deeply rooted in our biblical mandate to love, in Christian faith, and in social action to express that faith. Unfortunately, rather than exploring these narratives and celebrating our historical roots, our profession has often glossed over, or in some cases, even rewritten that history into an oversimplified version in which Christians are not portrayed very favorably. We intend Section 1 to provide a supplement and a corrective to the typical social work textbooks that may not speak to the Christian social worker's desire to understand our historical roots in deeper ways. We thought it was fitting to begin the book and Section 1 with Mary Anne Poe's chapter, "Good News for the Poor," to remind us of the scriptural foundations that motivate many of us. Chapter 2, "To Give Christ to the Neighborhood" describes Baptist and Catholic settlement houses that expressed the faith of their founders and served as a gateway to professional social work. Timothy Johnson recounts a very important story of African American Christians in Chapter 3, "The Black Church as a Prism for Exploring Christian Social Welfare and Social Work." Laine Scales uses the Buckner Orphan's Home as a case study in Chapter 4 to highlight child welfare efforts of church-related agencies in the early 20th century. The first section ends with Tanya Brice's chapter, "Go and Sin No More," an example of the pioneering work of African American women of faith.

SECTION 2
Christians Called to Social Work:
Scriptural Basis, Worldviews and Ethics

Related to the Christian origins of our profession is our sense of calling into social work. Just as the earliest Christian volunteers sought to live out their faith through social action, today's Christian social workers listen to hear

God's calling upon their lives. Social work students continue to report being motivated by religious calling in serving their clients (Canda & Furman, 2009; Graff, 2007). As they listen, Christian social workers seek to understand their own worldviews, as well as the worldviews of others and to practice ethically while living out their calling. Section 2 provides readings to help us explore our callings and worldviews, first by reviewing scriptural bases for social welfare, then by challenging us to think deeply about our worldviews and ethics, and finally by examining the stories of other social work students and alumni who have been called. David Sherwood launches Section 2 with Chapter 6, "The Relationship Between Beliefs and Values in Social Work Practice: Worldviews Make a Difference," in which he challenges us to examine how worldviews influence our work. In Chapter 7, Beryl Hugen explores the idea of vocation in "Calling: A Spirituality Model for Social Work Practice." Julia Pryce explains the tradition of Catholic Social Teaching in Chapter 8 and challenges students and teachers to exercise "the preferential option for the poor" in "Social Work for Social Justice: Strengthening Practice with the Poor Through Catholic Social Teaching." We hope you will reflect upon your own journey toward social work as you read Chapter 9, "Journeys toward Integrating Faith and Practice: Students, Practitioners, and Faculty Share Their Stories," written by professors T. Laine Scales, Helen Harris, Dennis Myers, and Jon Singletary, who interviewed their students and alumni. In Chapter 10, Mary Anne Poe explores a biblical and theological foundation of social justice in "Fairness is Not Enough: Social Justice as Restoration of Right Relationships" and David Sherwood closes out Section 2 with Chapter 11 in his essay about professional ethics and our Christian faith as they come together in "Doing the Right Thing: A Christian Perspective on Ethical Decision-Making in Social Work Practice."

SECTION 3
Human Behavior and Spiritual Development in a Diverse World

While the larger issue of spirituality is well-studied in social work scholarship, we focus this section on an oft-neglected area of inquiry: how the Christian faith of social workers (and their clients) impacts the encounters inherent to social work practice. In Chapter 12, Hope Haslam Straughan reviews and critiques several theoretical perspectives on individual spiritual development. Jim R. Vanderwoerd, in Chapter 13, identifies several key biblical beliefs and values that provide a foundation from which to understand a Christian vision for 21st century social welfare, drawing on understandings of social structures rooted in neo-Calvinist understandings within Reformed Protestantism and Catholic Social Teaching. Alison Tan draws from both her own experience as a Christian in social work and an Evidence-Based Practice perspective to discuss what is known about how best to assist Lesbian Gay Bisexual and Transgender clients in Chapter 14. David R. Hodge and Crystal R. Holtrop present a variety of spiritual assessment tools useful in different social work practice settings in Chapter 15.

SECTION 4
Christians in Social Work Practice: Contemporary Issues

In the same way we offer alternative views to the narratives found in typical social work histories, in Section 4 we offer supplementary information about contemporary issues in social work practice. Christian social workers may view their clients and their work with particular lenses; through these specific world-views, and there is much diversity among individual Christian social workers. These chapters attempt to reckon with the need for social work practitioners (both secular and Christian alike) to reflect on the difference between merely good intentions and demonstrable competence. The new EPAS standards from the Council on Social Work Education (CSWE) make clear that it is necessary now for schools of social work to show how they prepare their students to demonstrate specific competencies in social work practice. We believe that the chapters in this section challenge readers to become more competent and evidence-informed in their approach to practice, as well as clear about how for many of us, being a Christian in social work is about more than just being competent. It's also (for Catholics like Michael Kelly) about building the kingdom of God right here, right now; for others it might be about recognizing that being a Christian in social work may make us susceptible to hubris and assuming that our good intentions are enough to help others, even if what we're offering them isn't what they asked for (as Patterson ably demonstrates in her discussion of the mixed blessing of Christian missions and international social work practice).

In Chapter 16, Helen Wilson Harris leads us on a journey into understanding the nature and approach to professional helping according to Alan Keith Lucas, and in particular, "one of his core ideas—that all good helping involves the skill-ful use of reality, empathy, and support—dimensions of the helping process that reflect the very nature of God." In Chapter 17, David Sherwood posits a limited and cautious perspective for the role of evangelism in social work practice. In Chapter 18, Diana Garland and Gaynor Yancey provide insights related to how congregations are growing as settings for social work practice with individuals, children, and families. NACSW Executive Director Rick Chamiec-Case details the diverse array of potential models for Christians looking to integrate their faith and social work practice identities in Chapter 19. And following those themes, Alison Tan and Michael S. Kelly, in Chapter , critique the "value-neutral" EBP model and propose ways to infuse religious and spiritual perspectives of practitioners and clients into contemporary EBP thinking. Elizabeth Patterson shares her own story of implementing anti-oppressive international social work practices in Romania as part of her international Christian social work practice in chapter 21. And finally, Ron Carr, a long-time practitioner with gangs in the Pacific Northwest, teams with Michael S. Kelly in Chapter 22 to share his experiences bringing a unique fusion of personal history, Christian calling, and evidence-informed practice to his work with street gangs.

Conclusion: Discerning our Truths with Humility

We come to conclude this 4th edition renewed in our conviction that Christianity and social work have a lot to offer us when they are brought together successfully. The chapters in this volume attempt to do just that, with a careful eye towards avoiding any absolute statements about what Christianity is or what social work is (or perhaps most of all, what they look like when they're brought together). Jesus taught us that the truth will set us free. We believe that God loves us enough to trust us to figure out those truths in our prayer lives, discussions with fellow social work colleagues, and lived experience with our clients. We offer this 4th edition of *Christianity & Social Work* to add to your experience as a Christian in social work and hope that you will discern some rich truths in the pages that follow.

References

Canda, E. R. & Furman, L.D. (2009). *Spiritual diversity in social work practice: The heart of helping (2nd Ed.)*. New York: Oxford University Press.

Graff, D.L. (2007). A study of baccalaureate social work students' beliefs about the inclusion of religious and spiritual content in social work. *Journal of Social Work Education, 43* (2), 243-256.

SECTION 1

CHRISTIAN ROOTS OF THE SOCIAL WORK PROFESSION

CHAPTER 1

GOOD NEWS FOR THE POOR: CHRISTIAN INFLUENCES ON SOCIAL WELFARE

Mary Anne Poe

For the United States of America, the wealthiest and most powerful country in the world, the question of what to do about the poor in our midst is a haunting question. How do the poor impact our economy and political system – our freedom and well-being – our rights and privileges? How does American prosperity affect the poor? The United States has to address the problem because of concern for the very ideals that are American. It also has to address the problem because widespread poverty leads inevitably to social unrest.

For Christians, the question of what to do about the poor raises even more critical concerns. How does God want the poor to be treated? What does the Bible say? What is our responsibility as individuals and as part of the church to our poor neighbors? How should Christians try to influence the political and economic systems?

Social welfare programs and policies are a response to questions that arise in each generation. Why should we care about the poor? How do we determine who deserves help and who does not? Should we attempt to change individual hearts or change social structures in order to alleviate poverty? Who is responsible for the poor? Programs and policies always reflect our values about the nature of poor people and our responsibility to them. What we do as a society about poverty, what programs and policies we develop, depends on how we answer these questions.

Like music in a symphony, there have been themes that recur in the relationship between programs and policies that serve the poor and the belief systems that inform them. The political, economic, and social contexts give shape to particular programs and policies that emphasize specific beliefs that vary in different historic periods. Political, economic, and social conditions interact with belief systems in unpredictable ways at various times to influence views of poverty (Dobelstein, 1986). This chapter highlights some of those themes as they have been experienced through history and how Christian faith and practice have intersected with the public arena to address needs.

Biblical Principles Regarding the Poor

The Bible records God's revelation to people and how humans have responded to God. The biblical record, taken as a whole, supports specific principles about what it means to be human and how humans should relate to God, to other people, and to the environment. Some of the fundamental premises in the biblical record set the stage for social welfare history. These basic premises have been described in more detail by others (Keith-Lucas, 1989; Sider, 2007), but generally include the following:

> Humans are created beings designed for relationship with others. They are interdependent.
> God is concerned for justice and right relationships among people.
> In these relationships humans can do great good or great harm.
> Humans have the ability and responsibility to choose, perhaps not their particular life circumstances, but how they will respond to their life circumstances.
> Humans have value and dignity.
> Work is a natural part of human nature and contributes to one's sense of worth and dignity.
> The ability to create wealth is a gift.
> Material and environmental resources should be shared. They do not "belong" to any one person or group. Stewardship is the human responsibility to share resources fairly.
> God has a special concern for those who are disadvantaged.

The earliest biblical records reveal distinctive guidelines for the care of the poor. The guidelines are shaped by the covenant relationship of a people with their God who represented love and justice. If God is Creator, then all human life should be treated with respect and care. This is a way to honor God. The guidelines apply not only to individuals and families, but also to the larger community and society.

The ancient Hebrew idea of charity, *tsedekah*, is directly related to the concept of justice (Morris, 1986). The helper benefited from the act of charity as well as the one receiving help. It was a reciprocal benefit that balanced relationships between people. In the Scriptures, God specified the need for interdependent relationships and charity as an aspect of this. The prophet Micah summed up this principle by stating, "He has showed you, O people, what is good. And what does the Lord require of you? To act justly and to love mercy and to walk humbly with your God" (Micah 6:8). God intended that society benefit by sharing resources among all its members in a just and equitable way.

The Old Testament law specified how the community should provide care and to whom. God's people were supposed to be hospitable to strangers and foreigners (Exodus 22:21; Hebrews 13:2). The Sabbath and Jubilee years restored property and maintained a more equitable distribution of resources (Leviticus 25; Exodus 21: 1-11; Deuteronomy 15: 12-18). Those with wealth were supposed to leave grains in the fields for the poor (Leviticus 19: 9-10; Ruth). Communities and families cared for widows and orphans (Deuteronomy 14: 28-29; 26:12). They were to offer kind treatment to slaves and debtors and provide a means for them to gain their freedom (Deuteronomy 15). Lenders were to make loans without charging interest (Exodus 22: 25; Deuteronomy 15: 1-11).

God is known for avenging the mistreatment of the weak (Psalm 9:8, 12, 16; 10: 17-18). The prophets railed against the people and nations that failed to behave mercifully and justly with the poor. They voiced words of judgment when the laws were ignored (Isaiah 59: 15; Ezekiel 34: 1-6; Amos 4: 1-3; Amos 5: 21-24; Zechariah 7: 8-14; Malachi 3:5). Those who could work were expected to do so, but the laws were aimed at the community and required the kind of compassion toward the poor that God himself had demonstrated. God's word strongly asserts that God is just and wants people to behave in a just and caring way toward one another, and especially toward the weak (Sider, 2007).

The New Testament added a new and more challenging idea to the care of the poor. Jesus' life serves as a model for all to follow. The four Gospels record the behavior of Jesus toward those who were disenfranchised. The message to those who will hear it is to "follow Jesus," do what Jesus did. Jesus asked his followers to love others as he loved. The reason to care about the poor is not simply the reciprocal benefit of charity or obedience to the Old Testament laws, but one's commitment to God. One cares about others, especially the poor, not because it brings benefit but because that person in need is made in the image of God: "Whatever you do for one of the least of these, you did for me" (Matthew 25:40).

The New Testament also proclaims God's concern for justice. Jesus announced his mission in his first public message in the synagogue in Nazareth. He read from the prophet Isaiah,

> The Spirit of the Lord is on me, because he has anointed me to preach good news to the poor. He has sent me to proclaim freedom for the prisoners and recovery of sight for the blind, to release the oppressed, to proclaim the year of the Lord's favor. (Luke 4:18-19)

His ministry was characterized by attention to the weak and helpless and oppressed. The early church adopted the same standard of care so that "there was no poverty among them, because people who owned land or houses sold them and brought the money to the apostles to give to others in need" (Acts 4:34). The apostle James warned the church about unequal distribution of material resources (James 5: 1-6) and about prejudicial treatment based on one's social class (James 2: 1-17).

The Bible supports the value of work and the accompanying idea that one's ability to create wealth is a gift. Adam and Eve worked in the Garden even before their fall into sin. The story of Job shows that wealth can be transitory and is subject to God's control. Jesus himself worked as a carpenter. The apostle Paul admonishes believers to "settle down and get to work and earn your own living," and "whoever does not work should not eat" (II Thessalonians 3: 10-12).

Social Welfare History in Western Cultures

Biblical principles about human relationships and God's will for humans have had a profound impact on social welfare history in the Western hemisphere. The earliest records of church life reveal radical efforts to be sure that material and spiritual needs were met. The book of Acts states that material resources were shared in the community so that none were needy. The early church stressed the need to provide help to the poor even if some that were helped were not deserving of it. The church was a "haven of vital mutual aid within the pagan environment" (Troeltsch, 1960, 134).

The charity of the early church was formulated in small Christian communities that had little or no influence on the state in the early years under Roman rule. Christianity began with many, but not all, members from the poorer classes because most people were from these ranks (Stark, 1996). The aim was to show God's love. The church was not a political movement and thus not necessarily directed at prompting social reform.

The human tendency of those with sufficient means to try to distinguish the deserving from the undeserving emerged regularly and in contrast to the earliest biblical teachings. Some early Christian leaders responded to this human tendency toward judgment. Chrysostom of Antioch in the fourth century was a strong advocate for charity based on the need of the giver to share. He was concerned with the heart of the giver and the need for those who had sufficient means to share with those who did not. Gregory of Nanzianus believed that a lack of care for the poor was a greater sin than giving to the undeserving poor (Keith-Lucas, 1989). The tension between the idea of charity as a need of the giver's soul and charity to simply meet the needs of the poor has existed throughout social welfare history.

As Christianity spread through the Roman Empire and beyond, it began to exert more influence on political, economic, and social policies. Thus, by the time Constantine institutionalized Christianity as the "state" religion, biblical ideas of justice and charity held some political power. By the Middle Ages, the church and state were enmeshed with the church taking the lead role in the care of the poor as well as many other matters of political or economic interest. Over time the church's initial interest in showing God's care for the poor was overshadowed by interest in maintaining a seat of power in the political arena. After the Middle Ages, the church's power diminished. The Renaissance, the Industrial Revolution, the Enlightenment, and the Modern Era all had the effect of shifting political and economic power from the church to more secular entities. The locus of control for social welfare shifted as well.

Who Is Responsible for the Social Welfare?

A major theme through history has addressed the question of who is responsible for the poor. As Christianity developed and became more institutionalized, the social welfare system also developed. The church provided social services –not always with compassion or justice- but nevertheless motivated by biblical imperatives. It amassed an enormous amount of property after Constantine's rule and through the Middle Ages, some of which was to be used for the benefit of the poor. The bishop of each diocese was the patron for the poor (Troeltsch, 1960). Hospitals, hospices and sanctuary were typical services provided by the church for those who did not get aid through the feudal system (Keith-Lucas, 1989). Tithing was a prominent aspect of life in the church. Usually one-third of the tithe was designated for the care of the poor (Dolgoff & Feldstein, 2003. The giving of charity became a way to earn one's salvation.

The state was reluctant to assume responsibility for the poor early in western history. In England, The Statute of Labourers in 1349 was the first law enacted that gave government the responsibility. The value of work and a person's responsibility to provide for family dominated its formulation. The law's intent was less charitable than a means to control labor and the behaviors of poor people (Dolgoff & Feldstein, 2003). A series of Poor Laws followed the Statute of Labourers from its passage in 1349 to the mid-1800s. The shift had begun from church responsibility for the poor to government responsibility. Beginning with the Poor Laws, the state gradually accepted a role in oversight. The church and its biblical understandings, though, helped to shape the laws because the bishops sat in the House of Lords and government officials were drawn from the clergy. As government involvement increased, church acceptance of responsibility slowly abated (Popple and Leighninger, 2005). However, individual church members or clergy continued to provide leadership and personnel for the actual work of relief.

Social Control

The need for order has had great popularity during certain periods of time as a way to control the poor. Reasons and motives for helping the poor are numerous. On one extreme is the biblical imperative to love as God loved. Christian believers have Jesus as a model for how to care about the most marginalized and oppressed people. Biblical injunctions include doing justice, showing mercy, valuing every life regardless of circumstances, and personal responsibility and freedom to behave in a manner that contributes to the good of all. At the same time a reason for helping the poor developed out of a need to regulate the social and economic order, to encourage productive work and discourage dependency. The Poor Laws were, in part, designed to regulate labor and the migration of people from one community to another. Minimum wage laws and various tax laws are also a means to regulate poverty through control of the economic system (Piven and Cloward, 1993).

Reasons for helping the poor and efforts toward that end can begin with the best of intentions and after time become sidetracked. The poor can be hurt by the very efforts designed to help. Assistance given in the name of Christ but not in the spirit of Christ is perhaps capable of doing the greatest harm (Keith-Lucas, 1989; Perkins, 1993). Those who profess to help, yet are judgmental, patronizing, or cruel, do not reflect the manner of help prescribed by God. Some would argue that the emergence of state-operated "help" for the poor tended to shift the emphasis from one of charity as outlined by the model of Jesus to one of social control.

Personal Responsibility

During the period of the Protestant Reformation in the church, the culture changed from an agrarian one built on a communitarian spirit to an industrial society focused on individual rights and responsibility. Families were more isolated and less interdependent. Understanding of many biblical principles was shifting as well. Rather than the one Holy Catholic Church representing the biblical tradition and having authority to interpret biblical principles, the reform movement sanctioned individual responsibility to God for understanding and interpreting scripture and for how to live one's faith. Martin Luther, John Calvin, and the Anabaptists stressed personal salvation and church authority became less hierarchical. Anyone who had faith could relate to God and interpret the Bible. Though all Christian groups continued to give consideration to the poor, the emphasis on personal responsibility meant that the poor, too, were responsible to live holy lives. God would bless faithful believers (Keith-Lucas, 1989).

The reformers were outraged at the abuses of power perpetrated by the church. They decried the greed of the ecclesiastical establishment and sought to restore biblical concern for individual dignity and faith (Couture, 1991). The perspective on social welfare was also shifting. Biblical imperatives to show compassion and mercy had ebbed in relation to the need to urge the poor toward personal responsibility and labor. The "principle of less eligibility" established in the Poor Laws continued to ensure that those who labored would not have less material resources than those who received aid (Dolgoff & Feldstein, 2003). Rigorous scrutiny and early means tests prevented those who were considered "undeserving" from enjoying the benefits of aid. The theology of the Protestant Reformation focused on personal salvation and holiness, challenged church authority as it had been practiced by Roman Catholics, and encouraged hard work and thriftiness. The Protestant work ethic became the standard applied to poor people and to social welfare programs.

The English Poor Laws crossed the Atlantic and shaped the social welfare system in the American colonies (Trattner, 1998; Axinn and Stern, 2004). Still, the Judeo-Christian tradition provided the philosophical basis for treatment of the poor (Hugen & Scales, 2002). Biblical principles, though often misconstrued in actual practice, remained the rationale for the system that existed. The biblical belief in the value of work and the responsibility to care for one's family became the dominant philosophical basis for almost all social welfare programs. Principles that were powerfully informed by the life and work of Jesus and the early church, however, were weakened by the traditions of church and society.

Personal Regeneration and Social Change

Two religious movements of the nineteenth century had particular influence on the administration of social welfare. The first of these was revivalism. The periods of the Great Awakenings stressed personal regeneration and holiness. Those transformed by the power of God were called to service in the world. The goal for the revivalist was dynamic Christian faith that would change society as a whole. George Whitefield and George Muller established orphanages. Jonathan Edwards advocated for American Indians who were being exploited by settlers. Many leaders of the abolitionist movement were products of revivals, including Harriet Beecher Stowe, John Woolman, and Charles Finney (Cairns, 1986). Numerous social ministries emerged as a result of spiritual revivals. These included urban mission centers, abolitionist societies, the Salvation Army, the Young Men's Christian Association (YMCA), the Women's Christian Temperance Union (WCTU), and Volunteers of America (Timothy Smith, 2004; Magnuson & Magnuson, 2004 Cairns, 1986). The revivals sparked concern for the spiritual salvation of souls and also for the overall welfare of society (Cairns, 1986; Poe, 2002).

The second religious trend affecting social welfare practices in the nineteenth century was the social gospel movement (Trattner, 1998). Theological liberalism of the nineteenth century was an attempt to make the Christian tradition congruent with the prevailing scientific naturalism of the day. Theologians like Walter Rauschenbusch and Washington Gladden articulated this theology for the academy. Charles Sheldon popularized it with his novel, *In His Steps*. Interestingly, a phrase from this book, "What would Jesus do?" re-emerged in evangelical Christian circles in the last decade of the twentieth century (Poe, 2002). The social gospel focused on building the kingdom of God on earth. It adopted the popular scientific methodologies of the day and hoped for social change based on humanitarian ideals rather than regenerate hearts.

This more liberal theology called into question long-standing "fundamentals" of the faith. The nature of Scripture and the doctrines of creation and Christology were subjected to scientific analysis. Liberal theologies minimized the supernatural aspects of faith while more conservative theologies emphasized them. The divergent theologies caused the two groups to disassociate from each other in their works of service in the world. Whereas liberal theologies contributed to the rise of the profession of social work and increased governmental oversight of social welfare (Wenocur and Reisch, 2001), conservative theologies focused on church growth, evangelism and the future kingdom of God, and distanced themselves from secular attempts to reform society by good works.

Philosophies dominant in the twentieth century in the United States -- naturalism, materialism, and capitalism-- do not necessarily reflect a Christian worldview that demands care for others because they are valued creations of God. These philosophies emphasize productivity, the value of work and wealth, and order in society. The profession of social work, though, espouses values of celebrating the worth and dignity of every person regardless of their circumstances. As David Sherwood asserts, it is only fair to ask of the profession "where did these values come from and what gives them moral authority"? (Sherwood, 1997,122).

Social Casework and Social Reform

The growth of the profession of social work in the late nineteenth century illustrates another recurring dilemma. Can poverty be eliminated by helping one person at a time – the social casework method? Or is poverty best fought by social reform as reflected in the settlement house movement? Through history, both approaches have been used by church and state. The early church functioned as a community in which no one had need (Acts 4:32-34). The Great Awakenings of the nineteenth century resulted in organized efforts to change aspects of the social order such as abolishing slavery. At other times, the focus was on one individual poor person at a time. For many Christians, poverty is simply a spiritual matter healed by spiritual regeneration. As people are converted, society itself will be transformed. This thinking especially dominates some forms of evangelicalism. For other Christians, poverty is a reflection of an unjust society that needs reform. Conversion of individual souls is not the focus for these Christians, but rather social action.

The state also has approached aid to the poor by addressing individual needs for change as well as changing social structures. Income transfer programs are directed at individual poor people who deserve aid to enable them to rise above poverty level. Programs such as Head Start, though, reflect a broader institutional effort to change the nature of the poor community to allow more equal opportunity in the market place. The Personal Responsibility and Work Opportunity Reconciliation Act (PRWORA) of 1996 captured both of these methods to some extent, though the emphasis is clearly individual reform. In this Act, assistance is time-limited with expectations that the poor will enter the labor market quickly. Individuals can lose benefits if they do not comply with certain lifestyle rules. For example, a mother under age eighteen must live at her parents' home or in another adult-supervised setting and attend school. Welfare mothers must identify the fathers of their children and convicted drug felons need not apply. To encourage steady employment, states can use funds for employment supports like childcare. Tax laws and minimum wage laws are examples of addressing the economic system in order to reduce poverty. The Earned Income Tax Credit is an example of a policy that "helps the poor, rewards work, strengthens the family, and discourages welfare" (Sider, 2007, 103).

The Welfare State

The early twentieth century was a period of growth and prosperity for the nation, which was still relatively young. As the free market economy matured, the United States clearly represented the land of opportunity. Immigrants flooded the borders. Natural resources abounded for the consumption of the relatively small population and a political system based on liberty and justice for all created an environment in which anyone supposedly could succeed. By the twentieth century the state was established as the primary caretaker for the poor and in this role often overlooked the contributions made by faith-based organizations (Vanderwoerd, 2002).

A prosperous nation or person tends to have little tolerance for those who cannot or do not succeed. Though Judeo-Christian ideology was still a strong undercurrent for most American life at this time, the increasing strength of liberalism, materialism, and capitalism deeply impacted public welfare policy (Dobelstein, 1986). The American ideals of rugged individualism and hard work suggested that the poor simply needed the influence and advice of those who had succeeded. Material relief was viewed as more handicap than aid. Many felt that material relief and ill-informed charity promoted laziness and pauperism. (Wilson, 1996)

The Depression of the 1930's presented an occasion to question views that held individuals alone responsible for their poverty. American society confronted the reality that poverty often was a consequence of the condition of the economic system rather than simply believing that poverty resulted from immoral living or unwise personal decisions. Congress responded with the Social Security Act in 1935 and other New Deal legislative acts that addressed economic needs. The Social Security Act assured aid to the elderly, the needy, the blind, and dependent children. The New Deal established responsibility for the poor firmly in the seat of government (Trattner, 1998; Levitan, Mangum, Mangum, & Sum, 2003).

While faith-based groups continued to provide much relief, the ultimate authority in American society for developing social welfare programming was given to government. What had begun to happen in the latter part of the Middle Ages and during the Industrial Revolution with the Poor Laws was complete. Certainly the philosophical basis for society paying attention to the poor still had some connection with the Judeo-Christian tradition of charity, but in reality the principle of stabilizing the economy and maintaining social order guided policy making. Government had decided that poverty would always be an issue and that it was the role of government to give oversight (Levitan, Mangum, Mangum, & Sum, 2003).

Government policies and programs established rigorous means tests to determine a person's eligibility for aid. The presumption persisted that many recipients of aid were out to defraud the generosity of others. The "principle of less eligibility" remained. Aid provided subsistence support but nothing more. Processes for accessing aid were often designed to protect the system rather than serve the needs of the poor. Social welfare had changed quite dramatically from that demonstrated by early Christian believers of the first few centuries after Christ.

Welfare policies since World War II have tended to sway back and forth in levels of generosity. During the Johnson era, the War on Poverty had the lofty vision of eradicating poverty. While its goals were hardly attained, there is some evidence that this era established a safety net for most of the poor (Trattner, 1998). At least most could be assured of having food and basic medical care. In this period, solving the problem of poverty involved adjusting social and economic systems and providing services to support families.

The Reagan/Bush years of the 1980's emphasized different priorities. Poverty was still a problem, but the goal was to eradicate dependency. Programs and services were designed to relieve the federal government of responsibility for the poor and to turn welfare recipients into full participants in the regular market economy. When Clinton became President the goal was to "end welfare as we know it." Welfare reform legislation passed in 1996 with the Personal Responsibility and Work Opportunity Reconciliation Act (PRWORA). This act essentially ended the federal guarantee of help for poor families with dependent children and signaled massive change in the structure and scale of the American social welfare system (Mink, 1999; Dolgoff & Feldstein , 2003; Boyer, 2006; Ozawa & Yoon, 2005). It shifted the administration of relief from the federal government to states in block grants. The act was predicated on the belief that poor relief could be better managed closer to home. The 1996 welfare reform legislation also assumed that the free market system was a level playing field where the poor could be motivated toward self-sufficiency (Wilson, 1996).

The Importance of Social, Political, and Economic Context

By the 1990s, the years of the Depression that caused the nation to realize the need for a federalized system of public welfare had faded out of memory. Many people believed that the welfare system created in the 1930's spawned a different and dangerous set of values from the American ideals of work, independence, and family. Much in the United States had changed since the earliest European settlements. The economic system was mature and now dominated worldwide markets. Society had evolved from an agrarian one to an industrial one to a technological and global one. Furthermore, the nation that had begun with decidedly Judeo-Christian values had become more and more pluralistic and postmodern. These changes in culture influenced the treatment of the poor and the programs and policies formulated to address their needs. The evangelical Christian focus on personal salvation and holiness reinforced the American belief system that each person must be independent and self-sufficient. Conservative political and economic analysts, such as Charles Murray and Lawrence Mead, ascribed the ills of poverty to the "negative effects of welfare" (Wilson, 1996, 164).

The devolution of welfare policy administration from the federal to the state level that occurred in 1996 with PRWORA demonstrates on another level the power of context to influence how people experience the system. Constituent characteristics, such as race, ethnicity and economic well-being, and available resources that vary by state are factors that impact policies and programs of aid. Different approaches by the different states since 1996 reflect a wide range of values and priorities that drive social welfare policy. The combination of variables related to context create distinct and unique policies and services (Fellowes & Rowe, 2004).

The twentieth century had ushered in welfare states, both in the United States and in Europe. A difference in the social welfare systems is found in the fundamentally different premises of American and European thought and the very different political and economic contexts. The two contexts illustrated by the United States and Europe after World War II demonstrate the power of the political, economic, and social context in shaping social welfare policies. After World War II, Europe was devastated. The entire society needed to be rebuilt. The United States, in contrast, had not experienced as much loss during the war. The Depression that preceded the war had ended and American values of independence and productivity dominated. American welfare has tended to focus on particular groups, such as the aged, blind, disabled, or orphaned. The "doctrine of less eligibility" prevails and the valuing of rugged individualism dominates. The European system places more emphasis on a communitarian belief system. Consequently, social welfare in Europe tends to be more generous and more inclusive. Social benefits related to health care, housing, child care, employment, and income support tend to be applicable to the entire population rather than limited benefits targeted to particular groups as in the United States (Wilson, 1996; Pedersen, 2006).

Faith-Based Initiatives

Those with biblical faith have always been concerned for the poor, but with the rise of the modern welfare states in the United States and Europe, the church has not prioritized a corporate responsibility for social welfare policies and programs. Charitable Choice provisions in the welfare reform legislation of 1996 created possibilities for partnerships between church and state that had essentially been closed since the New Deal of the 1930s. (Sider, 2007; Sherwood, 1998; Hodge, 1998 Vanderwoerd, 2002; Sherman, 2003). In January 2001, President Bush established the White House Office of Faith-Based and Community Initiatives (OFBCI). President Obama changed the name to the Office of Faith-based and Neighborhood Partnerships in 2009. The assignment for this office has been to strengthen the collaboration of government with faith-based and community organizations providing social services. This office appeals to the Judeo-Christian tradition of compassion and care for the poor and to the economic and political view that the poor are often best helped by non-governmental services. The question arises of who is responsible to care for the poor and how is help best given, and whether the state or faith-based initiatives should be the driving force behind social welfare policy (Belcher, Fandetti, & Cole, 2004).

Global Context

While economic prosperity and tax cuts, education reform, and faith-based initiatives were Bush's emphases upon taking the oath of office in January 2001, the terrorist events of September 11, 2001, radically changed the political and economic landscape. Global realities and needs took center-stage and displaced concern for domestic social welfare policy. Attention on the war in Iraq and Afghanistan, extreme poverty in much of the world, and the continuing ravages of AIDS and other diseases has diverted much public attention away from the "compassionate conservatism" directed at domestic policy that carried Bush into office. With Obama's election in 2008, the American public seemed to be seeking greater balance between concern for safety from terrorism and engagement with world problems and concern for the social and economic well-being of its own citizens in need. The contentious struggle to pass health care reform legislation in 2009, the economic downturn beginning in 2007, angry rhetoric about illegal immigration, the continuing global fight against terrorism, and the inefficiency in response to natural and human disasters such as the earthquake in Haiti, the flooding in Pakistan, and the oil spill in the Gulf of Mexico all signify the challenges in finding just solutions to problems that affect the United States and extend globally.

Christians who heed the call to follow Jesus should be very concerned about global social welfare and how the actions of the United States impact the rest of the world. For the richest and most powerful nation on earth to be knowledgeable about devastating poverty and disease and war in some nations and continue to live in its ease evokes the prophetic voice of the Old Testament: "Away with your hymns of praise! They are only noise to my ears. I will not listen to your music, no matter how lovely it is. Instead I want to see a mighty flood of justice, a river of righteous living that will never run dry" (Amos 5:23). "I despise the pride and false glory of Israel, and I hate their beautiful homes. I will give this city and everything in it to their enemies" (Amos 6:8).

Biblical faith calls Christians to practice good citizenship by being engaged in the public discourse about social welfare policies and programs and the impact of all policies on the poor in the world. The reality for the twenty-first century is a global economy. It is this political and economic context that will shape U.S. policy in the years ahead. Today, social welfare policies are inevitably linked to the global marketplace. Minimum wage laws, immigration laws, labor and trade laws will all influence how the poor are treated in the United States as well as around the world. The relationship of faith-based organizations and their provision of social services with the government system of social services will also continue to be a dominant theme.

Conclusion

The biblical narrative primarily challenges the non-poor to create conditions for the poor that are just and caring. God does not allow the prosperous to simply wallow in their comfort. In so doing, they become oppressors. Rather, God wants people to have open hands and hearts to the poor, to overflow with generosity and concern. The responsibility is given to family, friends, and community to offer "a liberal sufficiency so that their needs are met" (Sider, 2007, 70).

Details of time and place vary dramatically. Social, political, religious, and economic systems create contexts that warrant a variety of methods and approaches to dealing with poverty and influence understanding of the poor. The Bible says that we will have the poor with us always (Deuteronomy 15:11; Matthew 26:11). The biblical imperative to care for the poor and the weak in a manner that empowers them and values their worth and dignity as persons has not changed. What distinguishes followers of Christ is a fundamental commitment to continually work to support the most vulnerable members of society for all are God's children and made in God's image. Whether it is organizing a soup kitchen or challenging tax policies, the call of God for Christians is to bring good news to the poor. This is the mission for social workers as well.

References

Axinn, J. & Stern, M. (2004). *Social welfare: A history of the American response to need* (6th ed.). Boston: Allyn and Bacon.

Belcher, J. R., Fandetti, D. & Cole, D. (2004). Is Christian religious conservatism compatible with the liberal social welfare state? *Social Work, 49 (2),* 269-276.

Boyer, K. (2006). Reform and resistance: A consideration of space, scale, and strategy in legal challenges to welfare reform. *Antipode 38 (1),* 22-40.

Cairns, E. E. (1986). *An endless line of splendor: Revivals and their leaders from the Great Awakening to the present.* Wheaton, IL: Tyndale House.

Couture, P. D. (1991). *Blessed are the poor? Women's poverty, family policy, and practical theology.* Nashville, TN: Abingdon Press.

Dobelstein, A. W. (1986). *Politics, economics, and public welfare.* Englewood Cliffs, NJ: Prentice-Hall, Inc.

Dolgoff, R. & Feldstein, D. (2003). *Understanding social welfare (6th ed.).* Boston, MA: Allyn & Bacon.

Fellowes, M. C. & Rowe, G. (2004). Politics and the new American welfare states. *American Journal of Political Science, 48 (2),* 362-373.

Hodge, D. R. (1998). Welfare reform and religious providers: An examination of the new paradigm. *Social Work and Christianity 25 (1),* 24-48.

Hugen, B. & Scales, T. L. (Eds.). (2008). *Christianity and social work: Readings on the integration of Christian faith and social work practice, 3rd Edition.* Botsford, CT: North American Association of Christians in Social Work.

Keith-Lucas, A. (1989). *The poor you have with you always: Concepts of aid to the poor in the western world from biblical times to the present.* St. Davids, PA: North American Association of Christians in Social Work.

Levitan, S. A., Mangum, G.L., Mangum, S. L., & Sum, A. M. (2003). *Programs in aid of the poor* (7th ed.). Baltimore: Johns Hopkins University Press.

Magnuson, N. & Magnuson, B (2004). *Salvation in the slums: Evangelical social work, 1865-1920.* Eugene, OR: Wipf & Stock Publishers.

Mink, G. (Ed.). (1999). *Whose welfare?* Ithaca, NY: Cornell University Press.

Morris, R. (1986). *Rethinking social welfare: Why care for the stranger?* New York: Longman.

Ozawa, M. N. & Yoon, H. (2005). "Leavers" from TANF and AFDC: How do they fare economically? *Social Work 50 (3),* 239-249.

Pedersen, S. (2006). *Family, dependence, and the origins of the welfare state: Britain and France, 1914-1945.* New York: Cambridge University Press.

Perkins, J. (1993). *Beyond charity: The call to Christian community development.* Grand Rapids, MI: Baker Books.

Piven, F. F. & Cloward, R.A. (1993). *Regulating the poor: The functions of public welfare.* New York: Random House.

Poe, M. A. (2002). Christian worldview and social work. In D. S. Dockery & G. A. Thornbury (Eds.), *Shaping a Christian worldview: The foundations of Christian higher education* (pp. 317-334). Nashville, TN: Broadman & Holman.

Popple, P. R. & Leighninger, L. (2005). *Social work, social welfare, and American society.* (6th ed). Boston: Allyn and Bacon.

Sherman, A. L. (2003). Faith in communities: A solid investment. *Society, 40 (2),* 19-26.

Sherwood, D. A. (1997). The relationship between beliefs and values in social work practice: Worldviews make a difference, *Social Work and Christianity 24(2),* 115-135.

Sherwood, D. A. (1998). Charitable choice: Opportunities and challenge for Christians in social work. *Social Work and Christianity 25(1)* 1-23.

Sider, R. J. (2007). *Just generosity: A new vision for overcoming poverty in America.* Grand Rapids, MI: Baker Books.

Smith, T. L. (2004). *Revivalism and social reform: American Protestantism on the eve of the Civil War.* Gloucester, MA: Peter Smith Publishing.

Stark, R. (1996). *The rise of Christianity: A sociologist reconsiders history.* Princeton, NJ: Princeton University Press.

Trattner, W. I. (1998). *From Poor Law to welfare state: A history of social welfare in America.* New York: The Free Press.

Troeltsch, E. (1960). *The social teaching of the Christian churches.* Chicago: University of Chicago Press.

Vanderwoerd, J. R. (Spring, 2002). Is the newer deal a better deal? Government funding of faith-based social services. *Christian Scholar's Review 31(3)*, 301-318.

Wenocur, S. & Reisch, M. (2001). *From charity to enterprise: The development of American social work in a market economy.* Urbana, IL: University of Illinois Press.

Wilson, W. J. (1996). *When work disappears: The world of the new urban poor.* New York: Alfred A. Knopf.

CHAPTER 2

"TO GIVE CHRIST TO THE NEIGHBORHOOD": A CORRECTIVE LOOK AT THE SETTLEMENT MOVEMENT AND EARLY CHRISTIAN SOCIAL WORKERS

T. Laine Scales and Michael S. Kelly

The history of Christianity and social work is long-standing, dense, complicated, contested, and ever-evolving, all the way up to the present day. This article will certainly not settle all the myriad debates about the proper role of Christian belief in social work practice, nor will it attempt to comprehensively survey this nearly 130-year old history of Christianity and social work in the United States. Rather, by focusing on the early history of social work in the United States in two cities (Louisville and Chicago) we hope to show just how long-standing and complicated the relationship between Christian missionary work and social work practice has been, from the outset of social work's early attempts to identify its own professional identity.

In addition to discussing the efforts to address the needs of the poor in Louisville and Chicago, these diverse approaches to Christian and secular social work practice show how hard it was in those early years to draw strong distinctions between Christian and secular social workers in what they did, why they did it, and how they explained their work to others. Indeed these distinctions, while not unimportant to Charity Organization Society and settlement house workers in the late 19th century to be sure, have only become more sharply drawn in the last century, as our profession writes its own history into a reality that may not resemble much of what actually was happening in those early years.

We start this article with two brief overviews of the Charity Organization Society (COS) movement and settlement house (SH) movement; then move into a discussion of two Christian settlement houses: a Protestant example in Louisville, Kentucky, and a Catholic example in Chicago. Finally, we consider what these histories (largely unwritten or marginalized in social work scholarship and textbooks) tell us about the role(s) of Christians in social work practice.

Overview of Early U.S. Social Welfare History 1870-1920

Most introductory social work courses address some facet of our profession's early history, usually by discussing two early movements that largely predate what we consider now to be "professional" social work practice: the Charity Organization Society (COS) movement and the settlement house (SH) movement. Our recent content analysis of seven commonly-used introductory social work textbooks found that without exception, these two movements were addressed separately and often used to draw distinctions between the two different ways that early social workers were involved in helping the poor and changing society.

Indicative of the need for the kind of corrective emphasis we undertake in this article, none of the textbooks characterized the Christian roots of social work history in its actual complexity, preferring to identify COS workers as religiously-motivated and SH workers as secular change agents. While the focus of this article will be on settlement houses, a brief overview of the two movements will provide an important context for our claim that the story of our development as a profession is more complex than what is typically reported.

The Charity Organization Movement

The charity organization movement that emerged in the United States in the late nineteenth century was inspired by a similar movement in Great Britain, in reaction to a perceived proliferation of charities that practiced almsgiving without investigating the circumstances of recipients. The movement's followers sought changes in the way charities responded to need based on three key assumptions: that urban poverty was caused by the moral deficiencies of the poor, that poverty could only be eliminated by the correction of these deficiencies in individuals, and that various charity organizations would need to cooperate to bring about this change (Ginzberg, 1990).

The COS movement flourished in the United States. In fact, by the 1890s, over a hundred American cities had charity organization societies. Journals like *Lend-a-Hand* (Boston) and *Charities Review* (New York) were created to promote ideas and annual meetings of the National Conference of Charities and Corrections (one of the ancestors of today's National Association of Social Workers) provided opportunities for leaders to discuss common concerns (Boyer, 1978). Fearing misuse of resources, Charity Organization Societies typically did not give money to the poor; rather they coordinated various charitable resources and kept records of those who had received charity in order to prevent "duplicity and duplication" by "having the wealthy keep an eye on the poor" (Ginzberg, 1990, pp. 196-97).

Privileged women from the middle and upper classes (precursors of professional social workers) volunteered to establish relationships as well as investigate the circumstances of families in need. They employed the technique of "friendly visiting" which stemmed from their conviction that individuals in poverty could be uplifted through association with middle and upper class volunteers. Friendly visitors were primarily Protestant women and their emphasis on the moral uplift of individuals was reinforced in Protestant churches by regarding the value of work to the soul and a focus on individual rather than communal relationship to God (Ginzberg, 1990).

As the movement grew, an insufficient number of volunteers led COS agencies to employ "agents," trained staff members who were the predecessors of professional social workers. Leaders like Mary Richmond of the Boston COS and Edward T. Devine of the New York COS led the movement to train workers, which led to the professionalization of social work in the early twentieth century. In 1898, Devine established and directed the New York School of Philanthropy, the first formal training for workers, which eventually became Columbia School of Social Work. The case method, later used by the social work profession, is rooted in charity organization philosophies which were taught by Devine and his colleagues and focused on the individual, change through relationship, and investigation (Connaway & Gentry, 1988).

Charity Organizations and Christianity

Many leaders in the COS movement were Christians and some were clergy. In spite of their commitment to Christianity, leaders cautioned against mixing evangelism with charity. Stephen Humphreys Gurteen, a clergyman and COS leader, warned workers in his *Handbook of Charity Organization* (1882), not to use their position for "proselytism or spiritual instruction." Edward T. Devine, leader of the New York City Charity Organization Society was willing to include church-related organizations in charity work although he insisted that "friendly visiting should be done strictly for the sake of the family rather than as a means of winning converts, however desirable that also may be" (Devine, 1901, p. 99).

The Settlement House Movement

Social work introductory textbooks often oversimplify descriptions of COS and SH movements as completely separate and opposing movements. In reality, Christian workers were involved in both the COS and SH movements, often at the same time, and leaders were not as opposed to one another's philosophies as is often described in social work textbooks. In fact, some leaders, like Devine, carried out both COS and SH activities.

While supporters of the charity organization movement emphasized changing individuals, the settlement movement stressed societal reform and attempted to help those in need by changing institutions. Like the COS movement, the SH movement spread to the United States from England in the late 1800s in the midst of immigration, industrialization, and urbanization. Leaders of the movement like Stanton Coit, Robert Woods, and Jane Addams created settlements after visits to London's first and most important settlement, Toynbee Hall, located in East London. Toynbee and some of the first American settlements relied on collaboration with local universities. Students lived among the poor while professors visited to offer lectures and stimulating discussions. Although the movement in England was largely masculine, settlement leadership in the United States included both men and women. In 1889, a group of women, many of them graduates of Smith College, founded the College Settlement Association in New York City. In that same year, Jane Addams and Ellen Starr opened Hull House in a poverty-stricken area of Chicago.

Like charity organizations, settlement houses were established in urban areas, and particularly immigrant neighborhoods. The primary purpose of a settlement was to establish communication and relationships between the well-to-do and the working class. At the forefront of the SH philosophy was a democratic ideal or, as Jane Addams expressed it, settlements were based "on the theory that the dependence of classes on each other is reciprocal" (Davis, 1984, p. 19). Settlements focused their energies not exclusively on reforming individuals but on addressing urban problems. Residents researched economic and social conditions that informed social action to improve the neighborhood. In fact, settlements carried out the first systematic attempts to study immigrant communities, using their insights to initiate reforms in the area of child labor, sanitation, and women's working conditions. Education and recreation were important activities of the settlement, including college extension courses, English language classes, vocational training, demonstrations of domestic skills, kindergartens, and playgrounds, all designed to improve the lives of neighbors (Davis, 1984).

Settlements vs. Missions: How Different Were They, Really?

One of the first notions imparted in most social work introductory courses is that the COS movement focused on changing individuals (and maybe saving their souls too) and refused to engage with the larger macro-forces in society that might have made these individuals poor in the first place. While some of the COS literature bears this out, there is often a leap to assuming that all religiously-motivated mission-based work with the poor at this time was rooted in this view of the poor's problems. Likewise, SH workers are identified so strongly with the secular focus of Addams and Starr at Hull House, that it becomes hard to believe that many SH workers were themselves motivated by a desire to serve the poor based on a religious calling (Davis, 1984). This dichotomy, while helpful in identifying macro- and micro-practice distinctions that persist to this day (Specht & Courtney, 1993; Pryce, Kelly, Reiland and Wilk, 2010), is ultimately too limiting in characterizing what was happening in social work, Christianity, and urban America at this time in our history.

If we take, for example, one city, New York City, and examine the landscape of settlements around the first decade of the twentieth century, we see the religious influence on SH at its earliest point in the U. S. There were approximately 82 settlement houses in New York, with several maintaining a religious focus. For example, East Side House was headed by Clarence Gordon, who wrote *The Relation of the Church to the Settlement*. He argued, "Humanitarians, socialists, philanthropists, may do settlement work and do it well.... but only on the foundation of Christ... and His example, and grace to inspire and direct, can the settlement realize its highest possibilities." (Gordon quoted in Davis, Spearheads for Reform p 14).

In order to exemplify how settlement houses may embody Christian values, we now offer short case sketches of two settlements to illuminate the complex relationship between Christians in social work and SHs at this formative time in our profession's history. We will describe two important sites of social work innovation—Louisville, Kentucky, a river city with large immigrant populations, including Catholic, Protestant, and Jewish immigrants, and Chicago, Illinois, home to a largely Catholic immigrant neighborhood.

Louisville, Kentucky: the Baptist Training School Settlement

By the early twentieth century, Louisville was home to several settlement houses, including Neighborhood House, established in 1896, and the Baptist Settlement House. The Baptist house, later named Good Will Center, was opened in 1912 and will be the focus of our case study (Scales, 2000). It was established by a school opened in 1907 for Southern Baptist women studying social work and missions: The Woman's Missionary Training School for Christian Workers. The school's purpose was to train Baptist women as missionaries to serve overseas or in the United States, as well as social workers and Sunday School workers. Students studied missionary methods, social work, fine arts, and domestic sciences, while also completing theological studies at the all-male Southern Baptist Theological Seminary a few blocks away (Scales, 2000). In the last quarter of the twentieth century, the school would narrow its focus to social work and in 1984 emerge as the Carver School of Church Social Work, the first school of social work located in a seminary to be accredited by Council on Social Work Education. The school survived 12 years before being closed in 1997 in the midst of conflicts among Southern Baptists. (Garland, 1999).

From the school's beginning, the first principal, Maude McLure, had a vision for reaching out to Louisville's immigrant and poor populations. In 1912, she set aside a summer to study in New York City with the famous Edward Devine in the New York School of Philanthropy (now the School of Social Work at Columbia University) and to live in a New York settlement house. Maude McLure brought back to Louisville a basic understanding of the settlement movement and ideas about activities and services that such an establishment might provide.

The settlement house she established in Louisville combined the typical methods of a settlement house, but did not emphasize the call for societal reform that undergirded many settlements. Instead, it became a site for students to practice a variety of missionary methods, including evangelism so important to Southern Baptist practices. The students and faculty of the Woman's Missionary Union Training School (WMUTS) worked to evangelize the neighborhood and, like Hull House and other settlements, to socialize Louisville immigrants into American life. Undergirded by a Protestant ethic emphasizing hard work, and a Southern Baptist emphasis on salvation of the individual, women of Louisville's Training School worked to change society, but also aimed to reform the individual. The phrase used by WMUTS faculty to describe their program of social welfare was "personal service," a term reflecting the focus on individual persons.

The Personal Service program preceded professional social work, and served as the Baptist Woman's Missionary Union's (WMU) response to social need. The program was launched by WMU in 1909, just three years before the Baptist

Settlement was established in Louisville and called on women to invest in "the Christian up-building of their own communities, acknowledging a spiritual duty to the poor, neglected, and outcast of their own neighborhood" (Allen, 1987, p. 215). Personal Service included an evangelistic dimension and had "the gospel as its motive and conversion as its aim" (Allen, 1987, p. 216).

The Louisville women joined others in the settlement movement to "rebuild the diseased social climate" but, in contrast to Jane Addams and others, they focused on reforming individuals while drawing on settlement house methods. WMU women were warned against placing "the ministry to the body before or apart from the ministry to the soul" (Allen, 1987, p. 215). In these ways, they viewed the neighbors as whole persons with spiritual as well as physical and social needs.

The emphasis of WMU on dual purposes of conversion of the individual and societal uplift was in line with the thinking of most Southern Baptists of the early twentieth century. However, a few Southern Baptists embraced the Social Gospel movement, clearly operating in the activities in and around Hull House in Chicago. The Social Gospel movement promoted the general improvement of society through church action. The minority of Southern Baptist leaders who believed that societal reform goals were proper religious concerns envisioned social improvement as a method of advancing the kingdom of God on earth (Sumners, 1975).

These leaders, both men and women, became involved in social reform groups such as the Southern Sociological Congress. Created in 1912, the Southern Sociological Congress brought together Southern leaders in education, social work, religion, and government. Its social program called for prison reform, the abolition of child labor, compulsory education, and solving of the race problem. In the 1913 Congress meeting, Walter Rauschenbusch, the best-known theologian of the Social Gospel movement, and a Baptist, urged Southern leaders to involve churches in reform efforts. A few Southern Baptist women leaders, including Maude McLure, founder of the Baptist Settlement in Louisville, attended congress meetings and may have been influenced by the drive to balance secular social reform efforts with decidedly evangelical aims (Allen, 1987). As we will see, this particular Southern Baptist theological stance contrasted with the Catholic theology of Madonna House in Chicago.

Although WMU did not embrace the aims of progressive social reform, leaders used the methods developed by reformers, social scientists, and settlement house workers in striving for evangelistic goals. Agencies in which WMUTS students did field work were typically missionary in purpose. Organizations such as the Hope Rescue Mission and the Salvation Army provided students with experience in personal evangelism to people in poverty.

While local agencies provided some opportunities for field work, Training School faculty and the school's board of managers wanted the school to have an agency of its own. Therefore, after her summer of study in New York, McLure created the Baptist Training School Settlement in 1912. Its purpose was two-fold: to provide service to the community through the settlement house, while training students in missionary and social work methods (McLure, 1913). It is interesting to note that the Training School chose the term settlement to describe the new enterprise, thus aligning itself with the SH movement. However, the evangelical purposes of the new venture also echoed the purposes of the charity organization movement—reform of the individual.

For these reasons, we chose the Baptist Settlement to exemplify how problematic the dichotomized descriptions of the SH and CO movements in current social work textbooks can be. These narrow descriptions deny the reality of organizations like the Baptist Settlement that combined the two philosophies of SH and COS along with a dose of their own theological understandings. The Baptist Settlement emerged as a hybrid, using the methods of the settlement movement to reach objectives that were commonly held by charity organization supporters. In 1913 McLure described the aims of the Baptist Settlement:

1. To reach the little children that their tiny feet may be started in the upward path.
2. To inspire the older boys and girls with ideals that shall help them to improve their environment and shall give them strength against the awful temptations that sweep over them.
3. To interest the young people in sane and wholesome pleasures that their energies may be rightly directed
4. To help the women to be better home makers, more careful wives and mothers, better Christians
5. To give Christ to the neighborhood.

To attain such ends, the settlement house, even without resident workers, remained open every day of the week and several nights.

McLure (1913, p. 2) wrote that the settlement was "opened in the belief that, with Christianity as a foundation, a settlement may be a feeder to the church and a mighty force in the coming of the Kingdom."

The Training School: A Settlement or a Mission

Southern Baptist women were not the only workers to form a settlement with clear missionary aims. Other groups, including Methodist women's missionary societies, were inspired by religious motives to create similar neighborhood centers, making it difficult to distinguish between a religious settlement and a mission. This is also clear from the activity going on at various religious settlements around the famed Hull House, including Madonna Center a few blocks away.

Allen Davis notes that the majority of settlement workers in the nation were religious persons. In 1905, a poll of 339 settlement workers showed that eighty-eight percent were active church members and nearly all stated that religion had been a major influence on their lives (McClure, 1913). Therefore, the discussion about the relation of the settlement work to religion was kept alive in the settlement literature. (Davis, 1984). In the early 1920s, Mary Simkovitch argued from the Christian perspective that a settlement cannot be a mission because its purpose is not to pass on a particular conviction to others, as missions do, but to work out its own common conviction: a faith in democracy (Simkovitch, 1950). In a discussion entitled "Problems of Religion," Arthur Holden (1922) advised that settlements did not need to talk about religion or attempt to teach it. He argued that by simply living a life in service to others, the settlement worker embodied Christian principles.

Graham Taylor (1950), Congregationalist minister and founder of a Chicago settlement, noted that while religious individuals may be involved in settlements, the church and the settlement have two very different purposes. Taylor believed that a church must press the tenets of its faith, and if it does not, it ceases to be a church of that faith. A settlement, on the other hand, may not embrace any cult or creed lest it forfeit its place as being a common ground for all.

But what about a settlement that attempted to be both a spiritual home and a source of social and political support? Did these settlements "count" as actual settlement houses in this new era of secular social settlement house activity, or were they somehow assigned a different and possibly lower status? It's clear from the historical record that nearly 120 years later, social work history has emphasized the secular quality of SH activism over any spiritual and religious activity and has perhaps set up an over-determined dichotomy between a SH like Hull House and the religious missionary work going on in Louisville and Chicago. Embedded in Taylor's idea that settlements should be "common ground for all" is an assumption that this is the only way to effectively reach and serve the disadvantaged. While it is certainly arguable that religious organizations could proselytize or even coerce people while providing social services and support, it is unclear that this was going on in Louisville or Chicago in our case examples. Rather, it appears that in both cities the religious social workers had assumed an ethical commitment to their clients that resembled in many ways the efforts being adopted by Addams and her colleagues, to be sure emphasizing spiritual uplift but also civic engagement and social progress (Davis, 1984; Dobschuetz, 2004).

Still, some important differences in theology and behavior can be noted in looking at the Madonna Center in Chicago. In contrast to the work going on in Louisville and other SH related to Protestant denominations, Catholic SH workers in Chicago perceived the population they served as fellow believers who simply needed the same Catholic sacraments and services that they were already enjoying in their parish community. This theological/service distinction was crucial in understanding the diverse SH activity going on in the area around Hull House. It is also helpful in explaining why Jane Addams' team was able to coexist so peacefully with the Catholic SH workers around her: the heavily Catholic area was in no need of evangelizing to find more Catholic souls, and Addams herself was clear that part of Hull House's mission was to avoid any proselytizing of their neighbors (Addams, 1912). If anything, as we shall see, the Madonna Center was founded to minister to and protect the Catholic traditions of the Hull House area immigrant population, in part as a reaction to the Hull House presence (Skok, 2004).

The Catholics of Chicago's Nineteenth Ward: Setting a Context for Madonna 1889-1898

In 1889, Jane Addams and Ellen Gates Starr opened the social settlement Hull House on Halsted Street in the midst of one of Chicago's most dense and diverse neighborhoods. Their neighborhood, the nineteenth ward located on Chicago's near west side, was home to a wide array of recently-arrived European immigrants, including Poles, Italians, Russians, Jews from Eastern Europe, Germans, and Irish. Most, though not all, of these new immigrants were Catholic (Skerret 2001). Many of these immigrants arrived poor and found their American urban circumstances to be marked by severe economic and health hardships (Linn, 1935). The social settlement Hull House went on to earn worldwide attention for its efforts with the poor of the Hull House neighborhood. Jane Addams, in her tireless advocacy for immigrant rights, social justice, and labor, established herself as one of the preeminent social activists of her time. She was also an accomplished writer and used her skills as an essayist to argue for the plight of the poor in Chicago. In 1931, the cumulative efforts of Addams' life work were recognized by the Nobel organization, and she won the Nobel Peace Prize (Elshtain, 2002).

By 1898, the top five ethnic groups noted in Addams' 19th Ward by the Chicago school census were:

Irish	13, 065	(27%)
German	6,721	(14%)
American (Native-born citizens)	6, 184	(13%)
Italian	5,784	(12.5%)
Russian (including Russian Jews)	4,980	10.5%)
Other (Bohemian, English, Canadian, African-American, Greek, etc.)	11,400	(23%)

(Chicago Tribune, 1898)

With the exception of most of the Germans, the Americans, and some of the Irish, the majority of the 19th Ward were recent immigrants and most did not speak English (Chicago Tribune, 1898; Linn, 1935). This attracted Addams and her colleagues, as they were eager to use their Italian (Starr and Addams were both fluent in Italian from all their trips abroad) and they also wanted to focus their energies on helping these new Americans adapt to American urban life (Brown, 2004).

By 1890, the parish community of Holy Family near Hull House numbered 20,000 parishioners, leading James Sanders to call it "the single great Irish workingmans' parish" (quoted in Meagher, 1986). The parish hosted numerous social and cultural events, and provided social services and education through numerous Catholic schools and settlement houses like the Madonna Center, housed nearby at the Guardian Angel Mission on Forquer Street (Lord, 1914). The economic, cultural, and political power of Irish Catholicism only increased with the arrival of new Catholic immigrants from Italy, Germany, and other parts of Europe. Irish Catholics, who, because of immigration patterns and facility with English were the dominant clerical class in Chicago, saw an opportunity to reach out to fellow Catholics and share their Irish Catholic culture with these new Americans. As Dobschuetz (2004) writes about the sisters and laywomen of the Madonna Center (a Catholic Settlement House) in the 19th Ward:

> Chicago Catholics, however, saw the world differently from Addams and the Hull-House community. The settlement, for Addams, was a social experiment that did not foreground the religious dimension.... Catholic settlements sought to sustain a Catholic identity and affiliation that was more than a response to the social, physical, and educational needs of the poor. Catholic settlements would be a location for the exercise of a vigorous lay spirituality (Dobschuetz, 2004).

As we shall see, this strand of lay-Catholic social justice ministry formed one of several competing ideas about what it meant to be American in Chicago in the late 19th century.

Madonna Center Settlement House 1898-1962: A Competing (and Complementary) Vision Blocks Away from Hull House

In 1898, Agnes Ward Amberg was attending a church retreat at the Academy of the Sacred Heart on Taylor Street, in the 19th Ward of Chicago, roughly half a mile away from Hull House (Skok, 2001; Amberg, 1976). A prominent German-Irish Catholic social activist, Amberg heard the Jesuit priest J. R. Rosswinkle exhort her and the other well-heeled Catholics at the retreat that to assure their own salvation in heaven, wealthy Catholics had to do more than pray and take care of their own families; they must recognize that "prayer must result in spiritually productive action" (Amberg, 1976, p. 40). After that day, in collaboration with her husband (who supplied financial backing) a new lay apostolate was born to minister to the poor Italian Catholic immigrants living among the more populous (and prosperous) Irish Catholics in the 19th ward. Fellow Jesuit Daniel Lord recounts the scene as Father Rosswinkle spoke:

> If these ladies could be interested in the poor neglected strangers, of whose existence they hardly knew, if they could bring into the lives of these poor Italians something of the spirit of Catholicity that made peaceful their own lives; if they could teach the immigrants home-making, health-protection, true Americanism, a great stride would have been taken toward the solution of a mighty social problem. It was worth a trial. He (Rosswinkle) spoke to them, and they responded generously... That was fifteen years ago. A small group of these ladies, diffident, uncertain of themselves and of their strange protegees [sic], entered the heart of the Italian district and

gathered the first class of forty dirty, unkempt little youngsters for Catechism. To-day, the Guardian Angels' Mission [717 W. Forquer Street], with its flourishing clubs and Sodalities and catechism classes, counts two thousand Italian children as its members... (Lord, 1914, 285-86).

The success of the mission in offering Catholic education and other social services had an immediate impact on the Chicago Catholic hierarchy; just as they had done 40 years earlier with Holy Family, a church was constructed by 1899 (Holy Guardian Angel Church) to become the first church in the community ministering to Italian Catholic immigrants.

Jane Addams's Hull House and Its Response to a Neighboring Catholic Settlement

As we have argued, social work textbooks have ignored settlements like the Madonna Center and emphasized secular SHs such as Hull House. With these two SHs located within a half mile of one another, we might wonder what interactions these two SHs may have had with one another. For her part, Amberg thought that Madonna Center and Hull House coexisted peacefully. Amberg and her mother both reported knowing Addams and her colleagues well, and that they had a friendly sense of spirit and competition with Hull House: "All of us had looked upon Hull House as a challenge, but we never experienced anything but kindness and cooperation from Jane Addams (Amberg, 1976, p.83)."

This distinction between the secular thrust of Hull House activities and religious sites like Guardian Angels/Madonna Center could be tracked not just in what they did with their time, but with what they built. While Hull House wanted to build a "Cathedral of Humanity," (Addams, 1912, p. 35) clearly Amberg and her colleagues were interested in building actual churches and bringing a heightened sense of Catholic identity to their immigrant clients.

It appears that many of the initial residents and lay leaders of the Guardian Angels Mission (later renamed the Madonna Center) were, like Addams, women of privilege. The first head resident of the Mission certainly was: she was Mary Agnes Amberg, the young adult daughter of the Ambergs (Amberg, 1976). Amberg lived and worked at the Mission most of her adult life, living there with her friend Catherine Jordan from 1913-1962 (Skok, 2004). Again, unlike the Training School Settlement in Louisville, most of the activities conducted at Guardian Angels were led by (mostly female) teachers who lived at the mission and/or who attended the parish in the community. Additionally, it's clear from the writings and works of Amberg that the Catholic social justice teachings embedded in Pope Leo's 1891 Encyclical *RerumNovarum* resonated through the work that she and her colleagues did:

The ideas of *Rerum Novarum* were appropriated by Catholic laywomen as a basis for expanded activity through the creation of lay apostolates. The 1891 papal encyclical made the ideal of "stewardship" or consecrated benevolence a part of the League's focus and contributed to the desire on the part of middle-class Catholic women to express their faith and maintain loyalty to the church through their ministering to the poor (Dobschuetz, 2004, para. 9).

Amberg writes repeatedly in her autobiography about the urgency of physical, spiritual, and citizenship needs of the immigrants she served. Indeed, it can be said that her efforts to "Americanize" her immigrant neighbors had as much to do with establishing Catholics as a legitimate group in American life as it did about helping them survive their rough new surroundings. Again and again in her autobiography, she strikes a chord of solidarity with the Italian-American Catholic immigrants she is serving, viewing them as needing social and religious support to avoid unwittingly selling out their "Roman Catholic birthright for a mess of proselytizers and humanists' pottage" (Amberg, 1976, p. 39). She writes of the many established and prosperous Chicagoans (Catholic and non-Catholic alike) that came to serve at the mission:

> In another way the influx of such assistants from all walks of life… and many from the higher strata of the city's social and business life was a blessing for the mission. Mother often said that these people helped Father Dunne [the clergyman who helped lead the mission] impress upon our Italian Americans that Roman Catholics were as American as any of the social workers in the Protestant or secular social settlements hard by the mission (Amberg, 1976, p. 54)

Clearly it was not enough for Madonna Center to minister to the needs of Italian immigrants through Catechism and building a church where they could worship; the offering of citizenship courses, athletic teams, and scouting programs was all part of a concerted effort to help Madonna Center clients become more fully American while still retaining their Catholic identity in a place that a local Catholic writer characterized as one of "the parts of Chicago that are not Chicago" (Prindiville, 1903, p. 452). In this way, Madonna Center was similar to the Baptist Settlement and many secular settings. Americanization was an important objective.

Why isn't Madonna House more Recognized as a Pioneer Settlement House?

The Irish-American priest and sociologist Andrew Greeley has devoted a large part of his career to documenting the gradual assimilation of the Irish and other immigrant Catholic groups into American life. He writes about the late 19th century battles between reformers like Addams and Irish politicians like the corrupt Irish politician John Powers:

> From the Irish point of view, reform was merely an attempt on the part of native-born Protestants to take what they had lost to the Irish in a fair fight. Laments of reformers like Jane Addams in Chi-

cago merely amused the Irish. The native-born reformers were at least as corrupt as the Irish and, in addition, they were hypocrites. All they were interested in were jobs for their own people, which meant taking back the jobs which the Irish had won in the polling place (Greeley, 1981, p. 110).

The Irish of the 19th Ward and the reformers of Hull House had a relationship that cannot be described fully, as it remains largely undocumented. However, we do have some facts. We know that over 13,000 Irish lived within the boundaries of the neighborhood that Jane Addams and her ambitious group of social reformers documented in 1895, but thanks to Addams and her colleagues, we know little about what the Irish population of the 19th Ward needed from Hull House at the time. As Skerrett (2001) has pointed out, it's entirely possible that we don't know much about how Hull House viewed their Irish neighbors because Addams decided that the Irish didn't "need" them (Skerrett, 2001). And while far from a prosperous neighborhood, it appears that at least for the Irish of the 19th Ward, life wasn't constantly marked by the same poverty and oppression that they had fled from in Ireland in the 1840s. (Skerrett, 2001).

The same could not be said for the Italian immigrants around Hull House, most of whom had recently immigrated, and many of whom suffered from extreme poverty and in the words of Amberg:

> Here was a harvest [Italians in Chicago] that cried aloud for some practical Christians. But except for some devoted clerics and lay people, few cared to listen (Amberg, 1976, p. 29)

Interestingly, Amberg's writing is not complimentary of all Catholic lay and clergy leadership in their efforts to build parishes and minister to immigrant Catholics, and levies a strong critique that Catholic hierarchy missed a crucial opportunity to become more involved in Catholic SH work. Just as Addams did in criticizing the corrupt ward bosses in Chicago, Amberg writes about how social settlements were needed for Italian immigrants to fend off the undue influence of the "padrone" who would exploit Italian immigrants. She says that:

> the social settlement could have been a valuable adjunct of Catholic immigrant Communities everywhere in America had there been fewer social intransigents among our clergy and laity and more pastors like Fathers Rosswinkle and Ponziglione [Clergy who led the first Madonna Center efforts] (Amberg, 1976, p. 45).

In some important ways, Addams may have struck a largely unspoken and unofficial "deal" with Amberg and the other Catholic lay leaders of SH and missions in the Hull House community: she would "minister" to the perceived social needs of the same poor Italians, Irish, and Germans they served, while those groups could also attend to the spiritual and material needs of this population. While there is no written record of their working together (or even meeting), it's clear that these two incredible women brought much-needed assistance to

their community, and lived less than a mile from each other for most of their
adult lives.

Reclaiming the History of Christians in Social Work

In all of the major textbooks used in Social Work Policy courses, history like
what we have recounted here is completely absent. This raises some important
questions: 1) why is early Christian social work history so marginalized? and 2)
why does there appear to be so much effort by writers of social work textbooks to
draw sharp distinctions between COS mission social work and the secular social
work of Jane Addams, even though serious SH scholars acknowledge the religious
motivations of many SH workers (Davis, 1984)? Unpacking these questions helps
us identify some implications for Christian social workers today.

As indicated by the historical case studies in this chapter, the early history
of social work is deeply rooted in religious belief and social action. The very
real and important tension created by the potential of social work being used to
convert or proselytize has also always been with us. Rather than exploring (and
to some extent, embracing) these tensions and celebrating our historical roots
in Christian social work, the whole topic has been usually confined to the COS
movement and then quickly shuffled off to the margins. This is neither historically accurate or particularly helpful for our present day, as social work students
continue to report being motivated by religious calling in serving their clients
(Canda & Furman, 2009; Graff, 2007) and as of 2011, there are approximately
675 MSW and BSW programs in the U. S., and many of them are housed in
religiously-affiliated colleges and universities. This history is an important part
of social work's overall history and it needs to be reclaimed.

Secondly, the distinctions that have often been sharply drawn between the
secular focus of proto-social workers like Addams and COS workers has often
been overstated and discussed without the historical context we've attempted to
provide here. While Addams herself eschewed religious teaching at Hull House,
she was herself religious (Knight, 2005) and cared deeply about integrating the
cultural traditions of the people she served into the larger American mosaic
(Elshtain, 2002). And while the Baptist workers at their Settlement House were
openly religious, they modeled their work after early secular SHs in New York in
terms of their activities and programs. While it will always be important to note
the excesses and potential ethical violations of Christian social workers working
with vulnerable clients, it's important to also note that the Italian Catholic immigrants at Madonna Center wanted services from "professionals" who brought
a religious lens to their work together.

The tension between secular and Christian social workers working together
has never been completely resolved, even to this day. When social work authors
and teachers set up sharp distinctions that were neither historically accurate nor
very important to the clients they served, it is counterproductive to the need
for Christian social workers and secular social workers to continue struggling
through the many challenges they may experience in their work together. One

thing is clear from this corrective look at early social work history: without Christian social workers and their efforts to "give Christ to the neighborhood," it is hard to imagine our "professional" identity being as strong as it is today. ❖

REFERENCES

Addams, J. (1912). *Twenty years at Hull House.* New York, NY: Macmillan Press.

Allen, C. (1987). *A century to celebrate: History of Woman's Missionary Union.* Birmingham: Woman's Missionary Union.

Amberg, M. A. (1976). *Madonna Center: Pioneer Catholic social settlement.* Chicago, IL: Loyola University Chicago Press.

Boyer, P. (1978). *Urban masses and moral order in America, 1820-1920.* Cambridge, MA: Harvard University Press.

Brown, V. B. (2004). The education of Jane Addams. Philadelphia, PA: University of Pennsylvania Press.

Canda, E. R. & Furman, L. D. (2010). *Spiritual diversity in social work practice: The heart of helping. (2nd Ed.)* New York, NY: Oxford University Press.

Connaway, R. & Gentry, M. (1988). *Social work practice.* Englewood Cliffs, NJ: Prentice Hall.

Davis, A. F. (1984). *Spearheads for reform: The social settlements and the Progressive Movement 1890-1914.* Rutgers, NJ: Rutgers University Press.

Devine, E. (1901). *The practice of charity.* New York, NY: Lentilhon and Company.

Dobschuetz, B. (2004). Madonna Center: Catholic settlement in the shadow of Hull House. Retrieved on January 15, 2011, from www.uic.edu/jaddams/hull/urbanexp/contents.htm

Elshtain, J. (2002). *Jane Addams and the dream of American democracy: A life.* New York, NY: Basic Books.

Garland, D. (1999). When professional ethics and religious politics conflict: A case study. *Social Work and Christianity. 26,* 60-76.

Ginzberg, L. (1990). *Women and the work of benevolence: Morality, politics, and class in the nineteenth century United States.* New Haven, CT: Yale University Press.

Graff, D. L. (2007). A study of baccalaureate social work students' beliefs about the inclusion of religious and spiritual content in social work. *Journal of Social Work Education, 43* (2), 243-256.

Greeley, A. (1981). *The Irish Americans: The rise to money and power.* New York, NY: Harper & Row.

Gurteen, S. H. (1882). Buffalo, NY: The Courier Company.

Holden, A. C. (1922). *The settlement idea: A vision of social justice.* New York, NY: MacMillan.

Knight, L. W. (2005). *Citizen: Jane Addams and the struggle for democracy.* Chicago, IL: University of Chicago Press.

Linn, J. W. (1935). *Jane Addams: A biography.* New York, NY: Appleton-Century Publishing.

Lord, D. A., S. J., (1914). A Catholic social center. *Queen's Work, 1* (6), 285-90.

Meagher, T. J. (Ed.) (1986). *From Paddy to Studs: Irish-American communities in the turn of the century area, 1880 to 1920.* New York, NY: Greenwood Press.

McLure, M. (1913). *A glimpse of settlement work.* Baltimore: Woman's Missionary Union.

Mulkerins, T. (1923). *Holy Family Parish Chicago: Priests and people.* Chicago, IL: Universal Press.

Prindiville K. (1903, July). Italy in Chicago. *Catholic World 77*, 452-61.

Pryce, J., Kelly, M. S., Reiland, M., & Wilk, E. (2010). Does social work "prefer" the poor? Results from a content analysis of MSW program syllabi. *Social Work & Christianity, 37*(4), 407-423.

Richmond, M. (1969). *Friendly visiting among the poor; A handbook for charity workers.* Montclaire, NJ: Patterson Smith. (Original work published 1899).

Scales, T. L. (2000). *All that fits a woman: Training southern Baptist women for charity and mission, 1907-1926.* Macon, GA: Mercer University Press.

Simkovitch, M. (1950). The settlement and religion. In L. M. Pacey (Ed.). *Readings in the development of settlement work* (pp. 136-142). New York: Association Press.

Skerret, E. (2001). The Irish of Chicago's Hull-House neighborhood. *Chicago History, 30*(1), 22-63.

Skok, D. A. (2004). *Madonna Center.* Retrieved on March 3, 2011, from http://www.encyclopedia.chicagohistory.org/pages/775.html

Skok, D. A. (2001). Mary Agnes Amberg in *Women Building Chicago 1790-1990: A Biographical Dictionary*, Rima Lunin Schultz and Adele Hast (Eds.), Bloomington & Indianapolis, IN: Indiana University Press.

Specht, H. & Courtney, M. (1993). *Unfaithful angels: How social work has abandoned its mission.* New York, NY: Free Press.

Sumners, B. F. (1975). *The social attitudes of Southern Baptists toward certain issues, 1910-1920.* Master's thesis, University of Texas at Arlington.

Taylor, G. (1950). The settlement's distinctive future. In L. M. Pacey (Ed.). *Readings in the development of settlement work* (p. 196). New York, NY: Association Press.

What is the nineteenth ward? (1898, February 13). *Chicago Tribune*, p. 25.

Note

This chapter was first published in *Social Work and Christianity, 38*(3), 356-376 .

CHAPTER 3

THE BLACK CHURCH AS A PRISM FOR EXPLORING CHRISTIAN SOCIAL WELFARE AND SOCIAL WORK

Timothy Johnson

The Black church's practice of Christian charity over the last 142 years and its current orientation to living out the Christian discipline of "holistic grace and hospitality" serve as a microcosmic case example of social welfare and systematic helping that undergirds the profession of social work. This aspect of the Black church has a clearly documented history that has coexisted contemporaneously with legitimately sanctioned social welfare programs in our society.

The foundation of modern social welfare originated with the poor laws of England. It is here that the unique patina associated with social welfare in the United States had its beginning. Social welfare was both a punitive response to need as well as a parsimonious provision for those in need. It was so organized lest the needy become comfortable and lose the will to work. This framework stands as one of the twin poles of social welfare as practiced in America. Jansson (2005) captures the issue here when he refers to United States as the "Reluctant Welfare State."

The second pole that stands as a paradox to the first is the idea of Christian Charity. Lieby (1987), in his material on social welfare, referring to reformers in the late 19th century indicates that:

> "...they believed the Biblical account of creation and human nature and destiny. They believed that a divine revelation defined right and wrong and pointed the way to Heaven or Hell. Charity, or love, was, in this view, the greatest commandment, and its practice manifested the spirit of God. To obey this command was a responsibility of individuals and of communities (p. 87).

Commonly understood and accepted is the fact that social welfare responses to need were rationalized according to a religious world and life view, albeit diffuse and variable. This thinking is gathered up into the categorization of the "Judeo-Christian" roots of social welfare. Certainly the idea of "Charity" within its Biblical definition was a precursor to the social welfare enterprise of our time. Charity as an obligatory Christian practice is given its fullest development in Paul's letter to the Corinthian church. In essence, charity is a state of unconditional regard and response. The text makes clear that charity or love is constant, tolerant, hopeful, and enduring (1 Corinthians 13). This stands in stark contrast to the reluctance and mistrust that came to characterize social welfare as we know it.

The modern social welfare system represents a secondary system of resources, safety nets, and failsafe mechanisms to ameliorate needs of persons and thus maintains the stability of our society within a broadly acceptable range. By contrast, primary systems are those closest to client systems. These are comprised of their families, neighbors, friends, the church, and other organizations anchoring them to their communities. When persons cross over into secondary systems of social welfare, it is an indication that the client's primary systems are compromised, inaccessible, overwhelmed, or inoperable. From a sociological perspective, secondary welfare system structures are "artificial contrivances" of primary system entities. Yet in a mass society such as ours, where persons are often disconnected from primary systems, such responses are essential. In a social context where isolation and communal breakdown seem to be norms, the secondary social welfare system is often related to as a primary system.

The Black church is a case example of social welfare within the primary relational context of African Americans. The Black church was forged as a surreptitious institution existing behind the bastions of chattel slavery. As human property, enslaved persons had little to no autonomy in matters of life, limb, and religion. After the Emancipation Proclamation ended enslavement and the Civil War was over, reconstruction found the Black church alive, religiously functional and growing exponentially. The Black church at the threshold of freedom was the only institution that 4 million plus African Americans could claim as its own. Lincoln (1974) states:

> The Black Church, then, is in some sense a "universal Church,"
> claiming and representing all Blacks out of a long tradition that
> looks back to the time when there was only the Black Church to
> bear witness to "who" or "what" a man was as he stood at the bar
> of his community (p.116).

The community of post-enslavement Black Christians was suffering from what we would now call post-traumatic stress. The truncated lives that characterized this institution, and the pernicious social constraints that prevented slaves' needs from being meet, moved the Black church toward becoming a 19th century parallel of the early Christian church.

> All who believed were together and had all things in common;
> they would sell their possessions and goods and distribute the
> proceeds to all, as any had need. Day by day, as they spent much
> time together in the temple, they broke bread at home and ate their
> food with glad and generous hearts, praising God and having the
> goodwill of all the people (Acts 2: 41-47)..

While there was little to sell, the example certainly applies in regard to church's ethos of sharing from meager subsistence resources. The social texture of the church was that of a common concern for all members of the community, and the centrality of the Black church as the institution that anchored the lives of Black folk.

Garland (1992) indicates that "the Church and its ministries provided the seedbed for the development of the social work profession (p.1)." In every sense the Black church was the seed bed for social uplift and social welfare responses to needs of the Black community. However, if reluctance is the patina with which social welfare in America has been overlaid as a normative attribute, it has had ominous implications for African Americans. Second class citizenship, lack of political power, and the invisibility of Black people have typically placed them outside the orb of the social welfare system, or at best, allowed African Americans to be mere marginal beneficiaries of the system of services and resources. Such has historically been the situation up to present time.

An Era of Buffering Social Welfare Reluctance: Profound Hospitality and Social Uplift

One of the critiques of the Black church within conservative religious circles regards its tendency to be a multipurpose social organization as well as a place for worship. It is, in fact, true that the average Black church is a multi-focal institution. The explanation lies in an historical analysis of the social environment from the enslavement period up to the present.

In its early years, the social environment of the black church was characterized by "graciousness. " Graciousness in this context means the grace of God issuing into the practice of hospitality. Hospitality in this context comes closest to the shared root of the word "hospital" which is more than mere welcoming rather connotes "care" "cure" or palliative ministrations. Over time the auspice of hospitality served to build communal cohesion and evolved into a sustained effort of "social uplift." To achieve the goals of social uplift, the Black church gave attention to the creation and mobilization of resources and empowerment of its members, leading to social change and community building.

Profound Hospitality

The ending of slavery left over four million freedmen to their own devices. This was a wounded group of people, not without skills, but certainly without opportunity, and needing social, spiritual and psychological healing. It fell to the Black church as the Black community's single and pervasive institution to be a healing presence. The church embraced a form of "profound hospitality" that laid the foundation for all that was to follow.

The practical application of profound hospitality was demonstrated at the end of slavery when tens of thousands of freedmen wandered throughout the south looking for family members who had been lost to them by being sold away. The search to find family continued for decades after enslavement. The grace of profound hospitality that supported the nomadic searching of African

Americans after the Civil War also had the impact of keeping very loose the boundaries around black families. Displaced persons and orphans were easily taken into black families and claimed as their own. This remarkable strategy of creating foster families was not so much a strategy of the mind, but of the heart and the psyche. It was understood that, for purposes of survival, persons needed connection and a communal location. Black family life was the gate through which fictive kin, once entering, were entitled to all the privilege of citizenship in the Black church and the Black community.

The institutionalization of foster families created another important alternative social welfare mechanism. Black families and the church became the network for providing accommodations when travel was necessary, given the largely "whites only" policy in accommodations throughout the United States. It was primarily through the church that Black persons who needed to travel cobbled together accommodations with other Black families through their churches. Friends of friends became very important if one needed to move around the country. This situation existed until well past the mid-20th century, when the civil rights movement achieved non-discrimination and parity in accommodations.

The Black church as a gracious institution stood as a protective buffer for the Black community, out of which profound hospitality was practiced. Thus it involved itself in the everyday life needs of its people. Frazier (1974) states that:

> The role of religion and the Negro church in more elementary forms of economic cooperation among Negroes may be seen more clearly in the rural mutual aid societies that sprang up among freedmen after Emancipation. They were formed among landless Negroes who were thrown upon their own resources. These societies were organized to meet the crises of life –sickness and death: consequently, they were known as "sickness and burial" societies…[T]hese benevolent societies grew out of the Negro church and were inspired by the spirit of Christian Charity (p.42).

In the final analysis, profound hospitality meant that no one was a stranger in the Black community. Given that the Black church and community were one and the same, this primary social welfare mechanism was as pervasive as the Black church but remained largely hidden from public view because of the reluctant nature of social welfare.

Social Uplift

Because of the social and economic deprivation suffered by African Americans in enslavement, leaders of the race were anxious for social uplift and economic parity for their people. In the latter portion of the 19th century, the world was in flux as never before. Technology leading to industrialization and urbanization became social forces of explosive proportions. The result was mass relocation of large sectors of the Black population to urban centers of New York, Philadelphia, Chicago, Pittsburgh and an array of smaller urban units. The draw was the promise of better lives based on a money exchange economy. It was also the auspicious historical moment in which the great progressive movements began, with their goals for elevating the common life of the masses in terms of health, welfare, education and refinement.

"Social Uplift" is the Victorian term used to convey the need to raise the quality of life for the American public to higher standards. The object of social uplift was to prepare the masses for the new institutions coming into existence and the more sophisticated perspectives needed for viability in the social environment. The progressive movement was an equation of social, spiritual, and environmental forces. These were comprised of higher educational opportunity for women, scientific advances, industrialization, the great awakening, and the moral exigencies Christians believed were incumbent upon them. The goal of this movement toward modernity was the establishment of a benchmark to which citizens should be lifted. Inherent to this benchmark was that persons become humanized by the refining aspects of education, that they embrace social interactions that bespoke quality of character, and that they live out the moral dimensions of Christian principles. African Americans during this time were faced with abject need given the failure of resource systems in the social environment that would normally serve them. In this fomenting social context the Black community and the Black church felt all the more the urgency of social uplift.

Because of this sense of urgency regarding social uplift, the Black church prioritized its goals for meeting needs. They immediately gave particular attention to legitimizing slave marriages, which were based on the casual practice of "jumping the broom." One of the first tasks of organized churches in the South was to see that all couples joined in marriage by this practice, be remarried according to the tenets of the church and local law. The following quote from the January 3, 1871, minutes of the Green Street Baptist Church of Louisville, KY, is insightful:

> On the motion and second the church voted to take up the subject respecting those members of the church not married by license, carried in the affirmative. Then the clerk read the resolution passed by the church on the third of October which resolution proclaims that all members of the church that was[sic] not married in 30 days from date shall be excluded from the church (Jones, circa 1979 p. 56,,).

Another area of concern was any breach of public decorum that reflected on the race, such as vulgar language, gossiping and arguing; such matters were brought up before the church (Jones, p. 75).

However, the Black church and the Black community were not merely focused on the lives of their people, but they were also concerned about the social environment. Booker T. Washington, the president of Tuskegee Institute, was a dominant Black voice articulating the needs of African Americans. His strategy for social welfare was to push the Black community toward agricultural and industrial education as well as property ownership. The other dominant voice during the same period was W.E.B. Dubois, whose vision and organizing efforts promoted classical educational opportunity for the intelligentsia of African American Communities. The Black church served as the institution that not only provided an audience for these men, but disseminated their ideas.

As was the case with white women of the reform period who newly found their voices, Black women used leadership of the Church as their base of operation, as attested to by the following quote:

> The Baptist women's preoccupation with respectability reflected a bourgeois vision that vacillated between an attack on the failure of America to live up to its liberal ideals of equality and justice and an attack on the values and lifestyle of those blacks who transgressed white middle-class propriety (Higginbotham, 1993, p.215).

It is significant that Baptist women had a sense of the necessity to pay attention both to the social environment and to the people for whom they wished to achieve social uplift. This view is consistent with today's social work emphasis on the person in the environment.

The importance of education as the route to social uplift has been previously stated. But for African Americans, education represented much more. It was the premier credential of personhood in a society within which males had been designated legally as three-fifths of a person. Not only was the ability to read an ontological issue for African Americans, given that the penalty for learning to read while in slavery was death, but it was a spiritual issue. Freedmen coming out of slavery had a voracious desire to read, so that they could read the Bible for themselves. Often independently, or in collaboration with northern white missionaries, the Black churches created strategies for educating their people. The Sunday school was the principal setting in which this took place. Public education was eventually available for African Americans during this period, but the educational process was compromised because it was controlled by white power structures. Thus, educational resources were constrained, and inferior even though mandated by law. Whatever public education was available was usually provided in a church that served as both schoolhouse and worship center.

The Black church as a Christian social welfare institution made education one of its priorities. The fertility of the educational efforts of the Black church is demonstrated in the 1928 *Survey of Negro Colleges and Universities* (Klein,1929): There are over 50 schools listed in the survey that were operated by various African American religious denominations. To be noted is that the history of these schools demonstrates an evolving process from primary and secondary schools, to the establishment of college departments. The report is a documentation of the educational uplift of African Americans at the behest of the efforts of the Black church.

In response to the reluctance of social welfare during the late 19th century, the Black church gave its attention to the wellbeing of the African American community by focusing on the interstices of its social and religious life. Although there were outstanding efforts during this period to make resource systems in the social environment more appropriate to the needs of African Americans, the Black Church was primarily a church turned inward. The Social Welfare focus of the Black church in this period was to exercise care in welcoming strangers, not knowing when those entertained might be the angels of God (Hebrews 13:2). This inward concern was a combination of healing, nurture, and palliative care because of the social and sometime physical unds dealt to the African American community on a daily basis. Wimberly (1989) speaks to the development of the Black Church during this period:

> [African Americans] were systematically excluded from normal access to participation in the community that would lead to the fulfillment of his potential as a total person. The consequence of all of this is the fact that many of the political, social, educational, recreational, economic, and social needs of the Black person had to be fulfilled within the Black church, his only institution. This was also true for the medical and mental health needs of the Black person. Often it was the Black Church that took care of the needs of the neglected sick and mentally ill...In fact it was through the efforts of the Black Church that hospitals were established in the Black Community (p. 412).

Elias C. Morris, in his 1899 presidential address to the National Baptist Convention, captures both the results and the dynamism of the profound graciousness of the period as an antithesis to the reluctance of social welfare.

> Hence, I conclude that one of the marvels of the century will be that although it opened and looked for sixty-three years on a race of slaves, it closes with that same happy, free people, having built more churches and school houses, in proportion to their numbers, than any people dwelling beneath the sun...A little less than sixteen months from now that tireless steed, Time will come forth and announce the birth of the twentieth century...What is the duty of Negro Baptists: The answer comes back that as the nineteenth century opened upon us as slaves and closed upon us as freemen, so may the Gospel, borne on the tongues of the liberated, set at liberty during the twentieth century, the millions bound in heathen darkness (Sennet, 1985 p.283).

The Church as a Primary Care Social Welfare Agency by Default

The period of the "great migrations" between the first and second world wars and into the 1970's saw African Americans on the move from south to north. From 1870-1970, 7 million black people are reported to have moved from south to north (Lincoln, Mamiya, 1990, p. 121; Wilkerson, 2010) The great depression and boll weevil infestation limited even further the subsistence resources of the Black community. If this was the push from the south, the pull from the north was the possibility of economic stability because of northern industries. As hundreds of thousands moved to northern urban sectors, particularly between the two world wars, the problems already existing in these areas were further exacerbated. In northern cities segregation,[1]redlining and [2]restrictive covenants limited where African Americans could live. The populations of these areas increased rapidly, but the available housing remained static. While there were jobs available, employment opportunities were usually in the [3]secondary job market which was characterized by instability, lack of benefits, and undesirable residual employment rejected by whites. Access to skilled jobs was unavailable because of union practices of nepotism that maintained a "whites only" policy (Baron, 1969, pp. 146-147.)

Given the compelling challenges of urban life for African Americans, the Black church willingly wrapped itself around the needs of its community. This culture of helping was part of the definitive fiber of the Black church. What was new in this era was the unparalleled growth of northern churches. As these northern churches began to grow exponentially, many in large urban areas became mega churches before there was such a term. The northern church in its social welfare role became a figurative Ellis Island for the newly arrived southern immigrants. The social welfare activities of urban Black churches included residential location services, job referral services through word of mouth or posting of opportunities, care for those who needed nursing services, after school activities, and childcare services for working parents.

Qualifying for the Black Church's social service programs was on the basis of being a member of the Black community. Services were universal in nature and readily accessed. Distinctions were not made on the basis of longevity of membership or residence in the community. The only criterion was that help was needed.

Because the Black church itself was a primary system in terms of its functions and its potency in shaping spiritual and social perspectives, there was within it an ethos of family empathy because of shared deprivation. This created within the church a pervasive tacit understanding of the needs of brothers and sister in the church and a willingness to respond.

Fulop and Raboteau (1997), writing about Rev. J.C. Austin and Pilgrim Baptist Church of Chicago during this period, reference the church's anniversary program.

> The church itself was organized into approximately one hundred auxiliary units, to assure that every member of the congregation had a "home" in Pilgrim's vast community. Austin was particularly effective in organizing groups of church women, who among their other roles, functioned as social workers, "missionary women whose job it was to go out…into these tenements and hovels these folks were living in and teach them hygiene and how to care for their babies and make sure they had food." With the aid of five assistant ministers and a deacon board of fifty-eight, Austin turned

Pilgrim into a seven-day-a-week center for welfare, education, health care, job training and placement, youth activity, culture, and religion (p.318).

Abyssinia Baptist Church in Harlem New York functioned also as a social welfare institution and social service center:

In each city there were a few leading churches and preachers who took a prophetic stance in attempting to meet the great needs of migrants by using their church's resources to provide help with food, shelter, clothing, and employment. In the 1920's Rev. Adam Clayton Powell, Sr., opened one of the first soup kitchens for the hungry migrants…In 1939 his son, Rev. Adam Clayton Powell, Jr., involved the church in welfare work, seeking employment, and supported black workers in their strikes and attempts to unionize (Lincoln & Mamiya,1990, p.121).

Pilgrim and Abyssinia Baptist churches serve as normative examples of the way in which the organizational and social welfare structure of large urban Black churches was elaborated during the years of the depression.

It is also noteworthy that the exigencies of life for many African Americans were difficult during this period. Brokenness and mental dysfunction were not uncommon. The Black church's tradition of profound hospitality meant that there was a great deal of tolerance for those who were dysfunctional and whose life styles may have been out of sync with accepted Christian practices. Gilkes (1980) writes about the Black church's effectiveness for mitigating individual and collective mental dysfunction of its members as an alternative to the established social welfare mechanism that was inaccessible to African Americans.

The Pastors of churches north and south, on whose shoulders rested the spiritual, social, and physical wellbeing of their membership, served as the human linchpins for the various welfare roles in the church. Because ministers of this time were usually the most educated people in the congregation, they became paternal figures who protected their members' interests. Theirs was a kind of shuttle diplomacy in which it was the Black minister's responsibility to collaborate with the white power structure, assist members with legal matters, and attempt to keep the stress of population increase from destabilizing the larger community. In this role Black ministers worked toward peaceful coexistence.

An undisputed and often autocratic leader of the local church, the pastor controlled the church's resources and often meted them out himself, or through the organizational structure in the church designed to do so. The Black minister's power during this period, coupled with his expertise and the resources that he controlled, made him a figure of God-like proportions within the Black church. In the author's childhood church during the 1950's and 60's, some of the members of the church were able to become homeowners because the pastor of our church had an arrangement with a realtor that assured the availability of mortgages. In other instances, the pastor would co-sign for loans and other financial help for his members.

This period in the history of the Black church's social welfare and social services roles drew to a close with the coming of the civil rights era. The period just described was one in which the focus was on creating an organizational structure that would support the social service delivery system for the Black community. In its Christian practice during the period of the great migrations, the Black church took seriously the biblical praxiological principle of the Apostle Paul of "being all things to all people that some might be won." (1 Corinthians 9:22). There was not a sustained focus on the reluctant welfare nature of the social environment during this period. However, the Black Church's social welfare activities during the civil rights era came to include community organizing and empowerment of African Americans. The explosive dynamism of the Black church against the reluctant social welfare system was to create a direct and sustained focus on the very foundations of social welfare in America.

Forcing Open the Gates to Social Welfare Equity

Following World War II, the homeostasis of white privilege supported by Black oppression began to unravel. The war itself had exposed African Americans to the possibilities of racial parity in other countries. President Truman had integrated the Armed Forces in 1948. The G.I. bill offered educational and housing opportunities along with increased aspirations. The war became a watershed of change in social relationships. These served as social antecedents that began to bring African American citizens into direct conflict with existing social structures, ultimately leading to the civil rights movement of the 1950's and 60's.

By this time, the Black church had achieved not only organizational complexity and solidity within, but its relationship with the Black community was such that one could not be defined without the other. Another important development during this time was the evolution of a second Black institution of great influence, namely, the Black ministers' conferences and Episcopal districts which served to draw Black clergy together into well organized, prestigious, and powerful fellowship groupings. These supra organizations served as a kind of social dynamo to concentrate and magnify the power of the Black church. In this context the fertile soil of unified protest was cultivated. And it was within this same organizational context that Black leaders began to focus outward on the inequities of the American social welfare system.

An excerpted statement by the National Committee of Negro Churchmen, July 31, 1966, captures the changing focus of the Black church from its own organizational concerns to the problems of the social environment:

> ...we must build upon that which we already present to some
> extent in the Negro Church, in Negro fraternities and sororities,
> in our professional associations, and in the opportunities afforded
> to Negroes who make decisions in some of the *have.* "*Black power*"
> *is* integrated organizations in our society...The future of America
> will belong to neither white nor black unless all Americans work

together at the task of rebuilding our cities. We must organize not only among ourselves but with other groups in order that we can, together, gain power sufficient to change this nation's sense of what is important and what must be done now...To accomplish this task we cannot expend our energies in spastic or ill-tempered explosions without meaningful goals. We must move from the politics of philanthropy to the politics of metropolitan development for equal opportunity (Sernett, 1985, p. 471).

The Black Church during this time became the catalyst both for raising social consciousness and fueling social protest. The major goals were the acquisition of power in the electorate through voters' rights and the integration of accommodations. In a word, this was a campaign for equality of opportunity. What was at stake for the Black church was the social welfare of Black Americans in its broadest dimensions.

One of the most notable institutions that was created within the vortex of civil rights deprivation was the SCLS – The Southern Christian Leadership Conference, begun in Montgomery Alabama. The precipitating event was the arrest of Rosa Parks for refusing to give her seat up on the bus to a white man. The SCLC's first president was Rev. Dr. Martin Luther King, Jr.

In the northern cities, exclusion from the primary job market was part of the economic backdrop of African Americans from the time of emancipation. A creative strategy called "Selective Patronage" came out of the ministers' conference in Philadelphia in the 1950's. There was recognition on the part of the clergy that the buying power of the Black community and the leverage from using it was a powerful force. Selective patronage targeted particular companies such as Tasty Baking Company, Pepsi Cola, and some of the oil companies. The ministers agreed to encourage members of their churches not to buy from these target companies. Unity of the Black ministers in the conferences and their influence in the Black community helped the strategy succeed. Because of the economic impact of lost retail sales, company after company came to the bargaining table. The goal was simple: employment opportunities for the Black community. This highly successful community organizing tactic led eventually to the organization of the Opportunities Industrialization Centers (OIC), which became international in scope. OIC's purpose was to provide the skill sets that the Black community needed in order to be qualified for the new opportunities opening up to them (Lincoln & Mamiya, 1990, p. 263).

The Black churches' organizing efforts led to success in many of its social welfare aspirations to a more open society for African Americans, especially in the areas of economic and educational opportunity and residential mobility. But left in the wake of this successful social welfare agenda were those on the economic and social bottom rungs. As the neighborhoods surrounding urban Black churches became depopulated, these isolated inner city areas, were plagued with deteriorating housing, family disintegration, escalation of drug use and related crimes, unemployment related to a faltering economy, and continuing political invisibility. The problems of inner cities became the new community organizing targets for the Black church. In the late 20th century, the Black churches brought their expertise to bear in providing profound hospitality, mobilizing and multiplying scarce resources, political and community organizing, and organizational pervasiveness and preeminence. What was newly added to this mix was a professionally trained clergy.

Social Change as Professional Practice

The training of African American Clergy up to the civil rights movement was largely an apprenticeship model where learning took place primarily within the church, with some supportive ancillary educational experiences. With the opening of new educational opportunities and a college/seminary - educated clergy as the norm, the skill sets of clergy were vastly expanded over what they had been. Their educational backgrounds gave this new cadre of men and women perspectives on the Black church in tandem with the social environment, and skills in social service strategies for ameliorating some of the pressing social problems confronting the Black community. Along with a transformed clergy, the congregations of large urban churches were changing. Entering the cusp of the 21st century, the Black church is now amply populated with at least two to three generations of college-educated professionals. These professionals in residence have shifted the social welfare dynamics of the Church away from a residual-based, crisis-oriented social welfare institution where those in need often served others in need. Black churches in varying degrees have become fully functioning social service agencies in which professionals and volunteers in the congregation create non-profit corporations and social service programs to resource the needs of the Black community as well as their own.

Billingsley (1999) in his documentation of the Black Church and Social Reform, gives an extensive inventory of the social service ministries of an array of large urban Black churches across the country. The economic and social services programs are folded into the church structure so as to deal with the social and economic needs of persons. The list includes: housing development, rehabilitation of abandoned and deteriorating housing, housing corporations, programs for providing small business loans, nursing homes, medical clinics, conferences on social problems of African Americans, computer literacy, social services, shopping centers, mini markets, neighborhood revitalization programs, education and training programs, and credit unions (pp.144-169).

Implications for Social Work

Embedded within the social welfare history of the Black Church are its efforts to vanquish various types of durable and pervasive oppression which are unfortunate staples of the American social environment. Sustained social work community collaboration with black congregations has the potential for providing a strong social bulwark against oppression. Given that the Black church is resource rich in terms of people, property, expertise and linkages to the African

American community, it can greatly expand the scope and influence of social work agencies. What is possible here is a *quid pro quo* exchange in which social work agencies might be empowered to better serve African American Communities and African American communities in turn might be further empowered by receiving services and resources.

Conclusion

The exploration of the social welfare role of the Black church points to five important truisms that are of critical importance in the American social and economic landscape. 1) The Black church's role as social fiduciary over a huge area of social capital still remains untapped and mostly invisible to the larger society but if tapped, validated and energized, can only enhance the common good; 2) The role of the Black church as a social welfare institution, if calculated in terms of its economic value and savings to the established social welfare system, would amount to an incalculable sum of money. This kind of accounting ought to be acknowledged as an explicit and necessary economic value of the Black church as a social welfare institution. 3) The Black church's social welfare efforts have evolved over its history from ad hoc social welfare by default to sophisticated social welfare strategies and social services that bring together public and private resources focused on need. The experience of the Black church as a social welfare institution means that it has all the attributes for being an effective force in Faith Based Initiatives. 4) The Black church itself is fulfilling a role identified by Warren (2001), that of renewing American politics by furthering the rebuilding of its foundation in the values and institutions that sustain community. Warren laments the "missing" middle in American political life. The Black church in its welfare role with over a century of cultivating volunteerism, and now professionalism in service giving is actively involved in rebuilding community and filling in the missing middle. What remains to be done is for those in power, and for those who control resources and shape social reality, to pull back the curtains of invisibility and showcase the Black Church as an effective model for social welfare and social services in the 21st century.

References

Baron, Harold. (1969). The web of urban racism. In Knowles. L.L.& Prewitt, K., *Institutional racism in America.* Upper Saddle River, NJ: Prentice Hall.

Billingsley, A. (1999). Mighty like a river: *The Black church and social reform.* New York, NY: Oxford University Press.

Frazier, E. F. (1974). *The Negro church in America.* New York, NY: Schocken Books.

Fulop, T. E. & Raboteau, A. J. (1997). *The Black church in the African American experience.* Durham, NC: Duke University Press.

Garland, D. S. R. (1992). *Church social work: Helping the whole person in the context of the church.* PA: North American Association of Christians in Social Work

Gilkes, C. T. (1980). The Black church as a therapeutic community: Suggested areas for research into Black religious practice. *The Journal of the Interdenominational Theological Center,* 8 (Fall 1980).

Higginbotham, E. B. (1993). *Righteous discontent: The women's movement in the Black Baptist church, 1880-1920.* Cambridge, MA: Harvard University Press.

Jansson, B. (2005). *The reluctant welfare state: American social welfare policies –Past, present, and future.* Belmont, CA: Thomson, Brooks/Cole.

Jones, H. W. (circa 1979). *First hundred years + 35: History of Greene Street Baptist Church, Louisville, KY.* Unpublished manuscript.

Klein, A. (1929) *Survey of Negro Colleges and Universities.* Department of Interior Bureau of Education. Bulletin , 1928, No 7.

Lieby, J. (1987). History of social welfare. In *The encyclopedia of social work* (Vol. 1, p. 755). Silver Spring, MD: National Association of Social Workers.

Lincoln, E.C. (1974). *The Black Church since Frazier.* New York, NY, Schocken Books.

Lincoln, E. C. & Mamiya, L. H. (1990). *The Black church in the African American experience.* Durham, NC: Duke University Press.

Sernett, M. C. (1985). *Afro-American religious history: A documentary witness.* Durham, NC: Duke University Press.

Warren, M. R. (2001). *Dry bones rattling: Community building to revitalize American democracy.* Princeton, NJ: Princeton University Press.

Wilkerson, I. (2010). *The epic story of America's great migration.* New York NY: Random House.

Wimberly, E.P. (1989). Pastoral counseling and the Black perspective. In Gayraud, S. (Ed.), *African American religious studies: An interdisciplinary anthology.* Durham, NC: Duke University Press.

Notes

1 "Redlining" was a practice used by banks to exclude Black communities from securing mortgages. Black neighborhoods would be circled in red markings as areas for which mortgages would not be provided.

2 "Restrictive covenants" were secret agreements struck on the parts of white neighborhood associations that real estate would not be rented or sold to African Americans

3 The distinction between secondary and primary job markets is a concept coming out of the Book "Institutional Racism in America." In an addemdum by Jonathan Baron, he makes the distinction between these two job markets. The primary job market, an exclusionary one, was overwhelmingly white. It provided stable employment, with benefits and upward mobility. The secondary job market, was overwhelmingly "minority" and was characterized by low wages, instability, seasonal work, and dead end jobs.

CHAPTER 4

"ACCEPTING A TRUST SO RESPONSIBLE": CHRISTIANS CARING FOR CHILDREN AT BUCKNER ORPHAN'S HOME, DALLAS, TEXAS, 1879-1909

T. Laine Scales

On a winter day in 1908, a thirty seven year old mother, Mrs. Beatrice Dixon, traveled with her four children from Letto, Texas to the Buckner Orphan's Home in Dallas. She carried her 2-year-old son, little Jimmy, along with three daughters, 10-year-old Flora, 8-year-old Nellie, and six-year-old Grace. She would be traveling back to Letto without her family. She intended to leave her children in the care of the Buckner Home "on account of abandonment" of her 37-year-old husband, Thomas Dixon, a "railroad man" from Texas. Filling out the simple admission form, Beatrice reported that all of her children were in good health and of legitimate birth, that both parents were of good moral character, and that the family had a relationship with a Baptist church. Beatrice abdicated her parental rights by signing a fixed statement presented to her by the Buckner Home. She agreed to

> ...transfer to the Buckner Orphan's Home all authority and control over (child) during (her) minority, agreeing not to interfere in any way whatever. This I do of my own accord and preference, feeling grateful to the Institution for accepting a trust so responsible" (Buckner Admissions Form, 1908; Buckner Registry, n.d. p. 321).

At a later time, perhaps when she had secured the financial means to care for one child, she returned for her "baby," presumably Jimmy, her 2-year-old son. She signed another form, indicating that she was reclaiming possession of the child (Buckner Transfer Blank; n.d.). The Dixon children would be absorbed along with over 600 other children into the daily routine of the Buckner Home (Bullock, 1993).

Though many children, like the Dixon's, had one or two living parents, some children, like the Warrens, came from families in which both parents were deceased. Just before Christmas in 1907, 17-year-old Mary Warren made her way from Allison, Oklahoma, bringing her sister and five brothers (ages 6 to 15) to the Buckner Home, six months after the death of their mother. The children's mother had died at age 42 of "inflammation of the bowel." Mrs. Warren had been a widow for five years, since her husband, a farmer from Mississippi, died of pneumonia. The father had sustained no church relations, but was reported to have good moral character. Mrs. Warren and all but the youngest children were reported to be affiliated with the Baptist church. Her dying request was that the younger children be left in the care of their eldest sister, Mary. This was an awesome responsibility for a young girl.

Mary's five younger brothers were admitted to the Buckner Home, but her 15-year-old sister, Suzie, was not admitted due to a physical disability. Presumably, Reverend R. C. Buckner would help Suzie find an institution considered more suitable for "incurables and permanent cripples." Five months later, perhaps after attempting to make a living on her own, Mary traveled back to the Buckner Home to gain admission for herself, writing on her application form, "I beg a home." Her request was approved and she joined her brothers as a resident (Buckner Admission Form, 1908).

The Dixon children, the Warren children, and many other orphans and "half-orphans" came to the Buckner Orphan's Home during a time when orphanages were seen as the solution for helping poor children (Smith, E. P. (1995). In the eighteenth and nineteenth centuries, parents who were deceased or in poverty often left a child in the care of an institution, which was operated from private and charitable funds donated by church members, primarily Baptists (Bullock, 1993). However, the turn of the twentieth century and the rise of professional social work brought a change in philosophies and practices of child care, favoring private homes, rather than institutions as the proper setting to raise a child in poverty.

These two important changes, the professionalization of social work and the turn toward what would become our modern-day foster care system, led social workers to dismiss and even attempt to dismantle the important work of religiously-motivated workers providing care for homeless and orphaned children. The story of the Buckner Orphan's Home illustrates how institutions might have become a casualty of social work's professionalization. However, Buckner stayed true to its mission while making important adjustments and grew to be one of the largest and most well-respected orphanages of the nineteenth and early twentieth centuries.

The enormous contribution of the Buckner agency continues into the 21st century as the agency itself responds to our society's recognition of what we now call "faith based agencies." The Buckner agency of today hires professional social workers in key positions as the religiously motivated volunteer of yesterday has more opportunities to become the well-educated and licensed social worker of today. Christian social workers must keep these stories alive as we battle the tendency within the social work profession to ignore or demean the important work of church-related agencies like the Buckner Home.

For the Comfort and Education of Orphan Children

Robert Cooke Buckner, founder of the orphanage, was born in 1833 in Tennessee and moved as a young boy with his family to Kentucky. There he became a Baptist preacher and married Vienna Long. In 1859, after a serious illness he moved to the dry, healthy climate of Northeast Texas. Over the next two decades, Buckner established himself in Paris, Texas as a well-known pastor, leader in the Southern Baptist denomination, and owner and editor of *The Texas Baptist*, a denominational newspaper circulated to about 4,000 subscribers in the state. During these years Buckner, Vienna, and their children moved to Dallas, which provided a more practical setting for publishing and mailing his newspapers (Bullock, 1993, pp. 32-9).

In 1876, shortly after moving to Dallas, Buckner began articulating in *The Texas Baptist* his ideas for a plan to establish an orphanage. He hoped to form a convention of Baptist deacons from around the state to oversee and support financially the enterprise. In the October 26 issue of 1876, he wrote: "What should the Baptists of Texas do for the comfort and education of orphan children? Let us have an orphan's asylum" (Buckner, cited in Bullock, 1993, p. 41). The Deacons Convention was organized July 18, 1877 and selected fifteen representatives from across Texas to serve as an Executive Board. R. C. Buckner was appointed General Superintendent and was charged with raising funds, promoting the cause, and managing correspondence. Two years later, on April 9, 1879, the first charter was filed in the Department of State in Austin. The Executive Board had named the institution "Buckner Orphans' Home" and appointed Buckner as the General Manager. The home was to receive "any and all dependent white orphan children without regard to section or sectarian bounds." The bylaws also permitted that in some instances, "half-orphans", or children with one parent living might also be accepted (Buckner Orphan's Home, 1879).

Humble Beginnings

Buckner took the money that had been raised, adding his own large contribution, and rented a temporary home in Dallas for the children until a more permanent home in the country could be secured. The Buckner Home opened December 2, 1879 in a three-room cottage on two acres of land. It housed three children, John and Alice Cruse from McKinney and John Jones from Ellis County. Deacon L. H. Tilman and his wife served as the first superintendent and matron (Bullock, 1993; Cranfill & Walker, 1915). By September 1880, Buckner had secured an offer from J. T. Pinson for forty-four acres eight miles east of Dallas. Though the land was worth $1,216, Pinson sold it to Buckner for $500 cash, donating the remainder. A two-story dormitory was completed and in April of 1881, eight children, along with a new superintendent and matron, T. J. and Sara Reese, moved into the new home (Deacons Convention Minutes, 1881).

Children attended school for a half-day at the orphanage and were assigned chores on the farm and in the home for the remainder of the day. On Sundays, all children were required to attend church services in which Buckner presided as pastor (Bullock, 1993). Through the daily activities at school, church and work, the Buckner Home ensured that children were developing in "mind, morals, and industry" (Cranfill & Walker, 1915, p. 260).

By 1883, the Buckner Home was caring for fifty children. Baptists continued to send support, often in the form of food and dry goods such as sugar, coffee, tea, and dried fruits. Clothing and shoes were also donated, as well as cash (Cranfill & Walker, 1915). The gifts of Baptists allowed for the provision of a new school-and-chapel building, completed in June of 1883 (Bullock, 1993). The completion of such a building reflected Buckner's priorities of intellectual, moral, and religious instruction for children. Such instruction was considered imperative by Southern Baptist supporters. Buckner noted the children's progress in his latest newspaper, *The Good Samaritan*, a monthly publication addressing social issues with the motto "Good Will, Good Words, Good Works." When enough money was raised to build it, the new school-and-chapel building occupied the center of the campus, reminding children, staff, and visitors of the central place of formal schooling and religious training for orphaned children (Bullock, 1993).

The Buckner Orphan's Home School

In 1883, when the new school and chapel building opened, *The Good Samaritan* reported that "for the first time [the children] are now under a teacher, in regular school." Buckner urged supporters to send more contributions, as earnings from the children's farm labor decreased, while expenditures for school clothing and books increased. Children from the near-by community of Reinhardt were also invited to attend the Buckner school, a precious gift in the days before every community had a state-supported school (Bullock, 1993). Buckner placed a great deal of importance on education, noting:

> No public school or charitable institution should be satisfied with less than the very best of teachers: and certainly, where an individual or society is entrusted with the education of those who have no parents to look after their welfare, the greatest of care should be exercised to put them under the most skillful and approved teachers, not only competent to teach, but kind and faithful to control (Buckner, 1883, p. 6).

The teacher in charge in 1884 was described by a visitor to the Buckner Home as "a sweet Christian young lady." Miss Carrie Smith, a reporter from Dallas, had high praise for her:

> A faithful and competent teacher has clearly proved herself, judging from the practical demonstrations of her pupils. She seems to know how to make the children love and obey her, at the same time take an interest in their books (V.C.H., 1884, p. 68).

The teacher lived in the institution as a member of the Buckner Home family. She found opportunities for teaching the children outside of the classroom. She described to readers of *The Good Samaritan* the musical interests of a young boy, Oscar.

> Music has a most wonderful effect on him... He will sit around the house all day until he hears the organ... often, when I sit down to the instrument and begin running my fingers over the keys, he is instantly by my side, moving to and fro with the sound of the music, drinking it all in as if he were perfectly charmed (Sister Carrie, 1884, p. 28).

The Buckner Home relied on donations from interested Baptists to provide school supplies and advertised for what was needed in *The Buckner Orphan's Home Magazine,* printed by the children as part of their vocational training. The magazine listed specific items for donors to send such as tablets, slates, pencils, pens, wall maps, charts and other school furnishings (*Magazine,* 1896). Soon a complete library was established with newspapers and other periodicals donated by publishers (Bullock, 1993).

As the Buckner Home grew, the school made slow improvements. By 1908, a larger school and chapel building had been built "of reinforced monolithic concrete and brick." to accommodate the 550 children in school and kindergarten (Buckner Orphan's Home, *Annual Report,* 1888-1918). The school only offered elementary grades at this time and utilized six classrooms, with half the students meeting four hours in the morning, and the other half meeting in the afternoon session. Children did chores or played, according to their age and abilities, when they were not in school (*Annual Report,* 1906-7).

The school employed a principal and "five excellent graduated teachers" to serve in its nine-month program. The salaries and other school expenses were paid for by the State of Texas and run from the public free school fund (*Annual Report,* 1908-09, 1909-10). Buckner Home paid the salary of the kindergarten teacher, and provided a furnished teachers' cottage for the state employees. In addition to the traditional "three R's," the curriculum was designed to teach skills such as stenography, typewriting, and music, both vocal and instrumental. Since these courses fell outside of the standard curriculum paid for by the State, Buckner Home paid the teacher's salaries for these courses and instruments were donated (Bullock, 1991).

Religious Education

For R. C. Buckner, the clearest path to building a moral character was through Christian teachings. He often emphasized that the orphanage was open to children from all religions or no religion and he stated that the Buckner Home never forced children to make religious commitments. However, religious teachings were woven into the fabric of every day living, and attendance in Sunday School and church was an expected part of the Buckner Home routine (Bullock, 1993).

Three short years after opening, The Home established its own church, with Buckner as its pastor. In its earliest years, the Home transported the children in wagons, three hours round trip, to attend the Live Oak Baptist Church. On July 15, 1883, the Home Baptist Church was organized, allowing for stability and convenience of providing formal religious education at the Buckner Home site. On opening day, the church baptized five persons, presumably children (Bullock, 1993). Like all Southern Baptist churches, the Home Church became part of a local association of churches, the Elm Fork Association. Operating in a similar manner to other small churches of the region, preaching services were held once each month on Saturday and Sunday, with prayer meeting and Sunday school meeting weekly. By 1903, preaching services were held each Sunday (Bullock, 1993; Cranfill & Walker, 1915).

From the earliest days of the Buckner Home, visitors commented upon the strong religious flavor of the daily routine. No child ate a meal without first thanking the Lord for the food. Each morning, family worship "was conducted in a serious and impressive manner by Papa Reese...every effort is made to instruct the children in the fear of the Lord," reported a visitor (C.P.S., 1884, p. 43). Occasionally, Baptist leaders would visit the Buckner Home and provide additional sermons or religious teachings. They would also assure Southern Baptist donors that the children were being provided with a proper religious education. This description of the visit in 1885 by V. G. Cunningham, a traveling Sunday school worker, reveals the flavor of such lessons:

> These dear children have the benefit of Sunday school training, and of what—would it to God it were otherwise—many children with fathers and mothers are not blessed, that is, family worship. It did my soul good to tell the precious lambs about the tender Shepherd, and in solemn prayer to commend them to Him who hath said: "When my father and mother forsake me then the Lord will take me up." Whoever hears their childish voices sing, "I have a father—a mother—in the promised land," will have abundant use for his handkerchief (*The Texas Baptist*, 1885, p. 64).

Although a thorough religious training was provided, Buckner adamantly declared that the children were not coerced to make religious confessions: "No constraint, rewards, penalties, favoritism, or improper means of any kind are resorted to influence their faith or practice in religious matters" (*Annual Report*, 1888, p. 4). Buckner was aware of the vulnerability of children to the pressures of some revivalists and traveling evangelists who used emotional appeals to win converts. He was opposed to such practices and did not allow protracted revivals in the home. Nevertheless, the number of Home Church memberships continued to grow.

In the Southern Baptist denomination, church membership was attained by making a profession of faith in Jesus Christ and the commitment was symbolized by baptism. During his Reunion Sermon of 1903, Buckner described how the daily life of the Buckner Home led to many baptisms:

> The other day more than 40 of these [children] were baptized, within three weeks more than 60. They came to me at different times and places and told of their conversion. No revival meeting, no evangelist,

nothing but songs, Sunday school and a sermon each Sunday morning. No death bed stories, no appeal to sympathy, only heart repentance for sin, simple faith in Christ and a desire to walk in the truth (Buckner as cited in Cranfill & Walker, 1915, p. 308).

While Buckner insisted that coercion was never used in religious matters, it is clear that making a confession of faith leading to baptism was the norm for children in his institution. On August 30, 1914, he baptized 87 children within 35 minutes (Cranfill and Walker, 1915).

In 1908 a new chapel and school building was built to accommodate the growing church. In that year the Home cared for more than 650 orphans, almost 300 of whom were Buckner Home Church members The Sunday School averaged 380 for the year. In 1910 the Sunday School attendance averaged 500 with a total church membership of 412 (Bullock, 1991, p. 75).

Sunday was a busy day for Reverend Buckner and for the children. After an early breakfast, they all assembled in the chapel for a Family Talk, in which "orderly conduct of the past week is mentioned and commended" by Reverend Buckner. Sunday School was taught in age-graded classes, followed by preaching services with all assembled. After lunch, Bible study was taught in smaller groups, followed by an evening service for all, which included a sermon and sometimes, baptism of many children (Cranfill & Walker, 1915).

Lessons in Morality

In addition to formal religious training on Sundays, lessons of morality were woven into the everyday life of children at the Buckner Home. At meal times, children might have been scolded for wrongdoing, or they might have been given a little rhyme about right living. Buckner biographer Karen Bullock (1991) notes his "manner with the children was a mixture of solemnity and laughter" (p. 124). As the children described: "Father Buckner makes talks from the music stand, sometimes he makes some of us feel bad because we are bad. Sometimes he makes us feel glad. Sometimes he makes funny rhymes just to tickle us" (Buckner Orphan's Home, 1907, p. 11).

Buckner often used stories of disobedient children to provide moral instruction. On one occasion he instructed his audience:

I remember one of our dear boys, sitting years ago on the gravel walk near the well, with dejected look and fallen countenance. He had no words at command. He had gone into the path of disobedience to his matron, and tried to cover it with a falsehood. But I approached him kindly, persuaded him that truth was better than falsehood and he soon told me all, looking me in the eye and feeling better and stronger. It was his last falsehood so far as I have learned. He is now a man, a Christian man, and has a Christian wife…. he is successful in business…has self-respect and self confidence, and does not think of failure (Buckner as quoted in Cranfill & Walker, 1915, p. 303).

One little girl demonstrated that she was learning lessons of morality when she wrote the following report of Father Buckner's visit to the children at the Baptist Orphanage at Thomasville, North Carolina:

> He told us that some of his boys and girls were not always good, and had to be punished. He said one little boy was sent to look for a cow and climbed up a tree. Then he asked the boys if they would go cow-hunting up a tree. And we had a laugh. But there was a sad ending to his story. The little fellow lost his hold and fell to the ground, breaking both his arms, which was caused by disobedience (Cranfill & Walker, 1915, p. 159).

Rules and Regulations

Reverend Buckner had strict rules for teenagers, particularly concerning courtship. Orphans dated one another and sometimes married. Young men and women also dated teenagers from the nearby community of Reinhardt, or from Dallas, but young people had to follow strict decorum required by Father Buckner. He explained to supporters that young women were more properly supervised in the orphanage than if they were living with a private family: "Custom in many private families where orphans are placed, permits them to go buggy-riding or walking in single couples; from this institution never! Nor is it permitted by other institutions that are properly conducted." Instead, young women received gentleman callers in the parlors of the institution, just like in a middle class home (*Annual Report*, 1907-08, pp. 23-4).

Father Buckner assumed the role of vigilant patriarch for the young women at the Home. In 1912 he wrote this curt letter to a potential suitor from Dallas:

> Dear Sir,
>
> > Referring to your proposition to my ward, Miss XX, to call on her tomorrow, also to bring your " pal" with a desire that another of my young lady wards be about so he can meet her, I beg to request that the visit be not made, either of yourself or your "pal". I have just talked with both the girls and have read your last two letters. If you should desire to cultivate the acquaintance of the young lady or any of the young ladies in B. O. Home, it is requisite that with proper recommendations you first seek my acquaintance and permission. (Buckner, R. C. to E. A. Sellars, July 1912).

Buckner expected that children would behave in a manner considered appropriate and that they would create among themselves a norm of obedience. One young boy who ran away requested to come back to the Home. He was asked to acknowledge in writing his wrongdoing and then to promise "to be a truthful, obedient, and honest boy, [and] to tell on any boy in the Home who may not be honest and truthful." (Buckner, R. C., to Master Paul Reed, June 26, 1899).

As was common in those days, corporal punishment was sometimes used to discipline children, though Buckner insisted it was used sparingly, "only in extreme cases, and then only in a mild and judicious way" (Buckner, 1886). In the following letter he provides moral instruction to a boy who ran away because he had been whipped by a staff member. The child asked to re-enter the Buckner Home "because I knew I did wrong and wanted to go to school and do my duty." In his response to the boy, Buckner justifies the whipping, but also shows his openness to receive any reports of abuse from the children.

> I well know that many boys need the rod sometimes, and at the Home it is often spared when it should be used. In that fit of anger you did what in cooler moments you regret. You ought always to cool off before doing such a serious thing. I forgive the past and restore to you the privileges and advantages of the Home. If you should ever believe you are seriously mistreated come to me about it and tell the whole truth whether it is hard on yourself or any body else. The past is forgiven... (Buckner, R. C. to "Eugene," Archives, BBB, 1902).

Buckner's View of Character Education

Buckner often spoke of his institution's emphasis on moral and religious development: "It is a character builder, and husbands the material... Orphan children are as good and worthy as anybody's children. They are not responsible for their sad condition" (*Annual Report*, 1909-10, n.p.). Buckner's emphasis on the teaching of good character reveals his philosophy of human development. He viewed children as innocent victims of their parents and of society. "What is prettier than a child?", he asked those listening to him preach in 1903, "What more innocent? Of such is the Kingdom of Heaven" (Buckner, 1903 as quoted in Cranfill & Walker, 1915, p. 307).

Like most evangelicals of his day, Buckner believed that philanthropic motivations to help others were not sufficient; rather Christian soul-winning was the goal. He wrote in the *Good Samaritan*: "The motives of the philanthropist are good and commendable, as he endeavors to reclaim any who are in any of the whirlpools [of sin such as alcohol, gambling, brothels, crime] or drifting in any way. But the motives of the Christian are equally so, and then they reach further, desiring poor, drifting souls to be saved in Christ...." (Buckner, 1884 as cited in Cranfill & Walker, 1915, p. 298).

Buckner's firm belief that good or bad character was learned led him to lobby for reformatories for young boys in trouble. He believed the reformatory could save the young boy and urged Dallas leaders to create a system "for proper restraint and training for these crooked young sprouts, for after awhile it would be impossible to straighten them out" (*Reformatory for boys*, 1903). Presumably, Buckner also wanted to insure that delinquent boys would not be sent to the Buckner Home to live with the orphans and teach the Buckner boys behaviors considered immoral.

Buckner believed that good or bad character could be taught, and he proudly took credit for the moral training of the children. According to Buckner, some of the children arrived at the Home having formed undesirable characters through improper learning. "Some have come who had not heard the name of God except as used in profanity. They had seen the inside of the saloon and almost every or any kind of place but the inside of school and church buildings (*Annual Report*, 1912-13, p. 11). Buckner described these children as "ignorant, untidy, immoral, and with other evidences of having been under the influences of vicious, degrading environments," but under the Buckner Home influence, they quickly "take on better ways, the use of better language and cherish higher ideals" (*Annual Report*, 1915-16, p. 12).

Former wards of the Buckner Home were held up as examples of good character in hopes that children would be inspired to emulate them. In the following letter that Buckner received from an employer, the feminine qualities of a former ward are described, and Buckner is given the credit for cultivating her good character. He published the letter under the heading "A Sample Training":

> Yes, Dr. Buckner, Miss Wagnon is a jewel, a most charming young lady, kind, industrious, and full of sunshine. Few people will ever meet her without admiring her goodness of nature and disposition. She surely reflects great credit upon your noble work in staging the habits and disposition of a Godly and queenly type (*Annual Report*, 1918, pp. 8-9).

Children were taught patriotism and devotion to the United States and many young men joined the military once they left the home. *The Annual Report* noted, "They love the flag of their country and the Banner of the Cross. Hear them sing "my Country 'Tis of Thee, Sweet Land of Liberty" and your patriotic hearts would swell with pride..." (1912-13, p. 3).

In the same way that children learned "good" character, they could also learn "bad" character, in Buckner's view. A child could be trained for immorality so that he or she may never be able to walk the proper moral path (Cranfill & Walker, 1915). Relatives and others who visited the Home were expected to set an example for the children. They were instructed not to use tobacco in any form in the presence of children and not to indulge in "ardent spirits" nor profane language. Violators would be asked to vacate the premises (*Buckner Orphan's Home Magazine*, Oct. 1896).

Labor and Industrial Training

R. C. Buckner expected children to work in the Home and learn "habits of industry." The daily routine included chores supervised by matrons or workmen:

4:00am	kitchen girls rise to prepare breakfast
5:00am	rising bell
5:30am	first bell, prepare dining room tables

6:00am	breakfast; "at the ringing of this last bell the boys and girls form into lines in their respective corridors, the smallest in the lead, and march in single file to organ music, and fill nine tables."
7:00am	various household chores
8:30am	half to school, half to chores
11:30am	prepare for dinner
12 noon	Dinner
1:30pm	second half day of school
4:30pm	school is dismissed
5:30pm	prepare for supper
6:00pm	supper
7:00pm	some are engaged in study, some promenading the walks, others talking or singing or swinging.
9:00pm	bedtime (Cranfill & Walker, 1915, p. 181)

The daily example was reinforced by lessons and sermons emphasizing the value of work. Buckner often repeated this reminder: "Without work it is impossible to please God" (*Annual Report*, 1910-11, p. 19). One of Buckner's sermonettes, printed in the *Baptist Standard* and perhaps preached to the children, demonstrates the value of work. Buckner quoted from Ecclesiastes: "Whatsoever thy hand findeth to do, do it with thy might." Buckner went on to emphasize the importance of all tasks "Whatsoever, whether it be great or small, hard or easy, pleasant or disagreeable" (Cranfill & Walker, 1915, pp. 287).

Lessons about the value of work were reinforced by experiences. Children at the Buckner Home performed daily chores in order to learn the value of hard work for all. In addition, the children's labor functioned to support the Home financially. In keeping with an ethic that disparages "a free hand out," the children of the Buckner Home were not receiving charity but were, through their labor, contributing something for the care they received (Bullock, 1993).

Each child attended school for a half-day and for the rest of the day all children were busy in industry. Assigned chores reflected popular notions of gendered division of labor. The boys worked in farming: plowing, planting, harvesting, and dairy operations. Girls stayed busy with the cooking, sewing, laundry and ironing. On Sundays, there was no laboring, and all children were required to attend church services (Bullock, 1993).

Though not often engaged in manual labor himself, Buckner certainly was industrious. Buckner's reputation for being a hard worker was legendary, and it was said that he could do the work of six men (Bullock, 1991). Reporting on his writing and correspondence for 1907, he notes that in addition to writing many newspaper articles, sermons, and other addresses and traveling in connection with the Home, he wrote about forty letters a day, amounting to 14,600 for the year. This work was in addition to the management and oversight of the orphanage, as well as other charitable operations he managed, such as the Cottage Homes for the Aged, the Children's Hospital, the city Annex, and the farming operation (*Annual Report*, 1906-07, p. 20).

Through his publications, Buckner assured supporters that their money was not being used to support lazy children. When Mrs. K. E. Hewett visited the Home, she assured readers that Southern Baptist dollars were being well spent: "Now to the question I have been asked: 'Are these children supported in idleness? Let me say that industry is the life of the Home; the larger ones serving alternately in the house and in school" (Hewett, 1884, p. 42). However, Buckner also stated clearly that the children's labor was not enough to support the Buckner Home. Some expenses were reduced, and the value of industry was taught, but no profits were realized. In the 1907 *Picturebook*, the young narrator notes: "Father Buckner says the shops do not really make money, but they help to make useful men out of what might be idle boys. But by handling the water and fans, lights and laundry they do save very much money as well as time" (p. 20).

In the earliest days of the Buckner Home, before a regulated nine- month school year, children sometimes had opportunities to earn their own money by laboring for neighbors. A teacher at the Buckner Home reported in 1884:

> The boys feel about three inches higher, on account of the new boots they bought with their "cotton money" i.e. what they made by picking cotton for some of the neighbors. It makes them quite proud to get some shiny dimes of their own.... (Sister Carrie, 1884, p. 28).

Buckner made it clear that the orphanage did not send children to families that would exploit their labor. He described a well-to-do family intending to exploit a boy, requiring him to do farm work "and do other things for a man who wants to send his own boy off to school, or wants cheap labor that he can control...." (Buckner Orphan's Home, 1906-07, p. 25). Buckner would not supply labor for such a family in the form of an orphan child. Nor would he send a girl to care for children and perform other housekeeping duties and "do such things as the own daughter "must not do" (Buckner Orphan's Home, 1906-07, p. 25). Buckner did not mind children working, but he did mind them being exploited and particularly in the face of other children in the family who did not have to work. This fear of favoritism was perhaps the reason he established a policy of only giving children to adoption by couples that were childless (Buckner Orphan's Home, 1906-07, p. 25). Buckner was aware that some adoptive parents were motivated to take children in to provide needed labor. In his publications, he warned prospective parents that his orphanage was "not a labor bureau.... It trains for independent citizenship in the best government on earth. It is meant that young men and women shall go out as farmers, teachers, mechanics, preachers and into the various industries and professions" (*Annual Report,* 1909-10, p. 22).

The Buckner Home was not considered transitional or temporary placement for orphan children; rather it was rare that children were adopted. Buckner said:

> During thirty years of experience in orphan work, and close ob-

servation, I have formed, and been thoroughly confirmed in the opinion that at least nineteen of every twenty who seek to get possession of an orphan child, or children, are actuated by selfish motives; that not one in a hundred mean it simply for the good of the child... Those without children of their own seldom know how to treat a child; adopting or indenturing one from an orphanage, they are likely to spoil it by overindulgence, or to break its spirit by being too exacting and severe... Then they want to be rid of the child and it is left without home; and some such drift into shame and ruin.... (*Annual Report*, 1906-7, pp. 25-6).

Twentieth Century Changes

Two important trends intersected in the late nineteenth and early twentieth centuries to bring changes to the Buckner Home. On the national scene, as the new profession of social work emerged, professionals with social work education and credentials would differentiate themselves from clergy or volunteers, at times devaluing the contributions of those who had served faithfully. At the same time, the nation's child welfare advisors, led by social workers, expressed preference to place orphaned children in family homes, rather than in institutions like the Buckner Home.

The Rise of Professional Social Work

By the late nineteenth century, social workers began searching for a way to explain their own contributions and to gain respect from other professionals and the public. In the early twentieth century this became a preoccupation, especially after 1915 when the landmark speech of Abraham Flexner entitled "Is Social Work a Profession?" caused a flurry of activity to professionalize (Bledstein, 1976; Lubove, 1972). The rise of new schools of social work, beginning with the New York School of Philanthropy, provided credentials to create a sharp separation between educated professionals and the proto-social workers who had served faithfully in agencies. (Klein, 1968).

While professionalization brought important gains to social work, some losses were sustained. For example, social work historian David Austin argued that social work's obsession with one speech, Flexner's speech in 1915, prevented social workers from creating their own criteria for becoming a profession. While attempting to fulfill Flexner's recommendation, based on his experience with medicine, rather than social work, the new profession became distracted from its own work (Austin, 1983).

Another loss to social work came when the new professionals embraced scientism and a more efficient and rational approach (Lubove, 1972; Kunzel (1988) argues that the move toward scientism was launched to gain prestige for the profession by identifying with the more "masculine" professions such as medicine. Whatever the mixture of motives, it is clear that by the twentieth century the new social work profession had launched on to the values of "efficiency, objectivity, and expertise. (Kunzel, p. 25).

While the Flexner speech and the trend toward scientism are often noted in social work histories an additional story that is seldom told, but is one of the most important for Christian social worker to understand recounts the devaluing of church-related volunteers, board members, and paid workers. Diana Garland describes this decline in her book, *Church Agencies: Caring for Children and Families in Crisis:*

> Social workers, anxious to guard their claim to professional knowledge and skill, questioned the ability of laypeople to set policies. That required professional expertise. They hoarded information about their work and their clients, excluding board members from meaningful roles in what had been their institutions (1994 pp. 77-78).

Garland points out that the professionalization of social work certainly made services more effective and more efficient for some clients. But what was "lost in the shift," she argues, was the personal relationship between religiously motivated workers and their clients (Garland, 1994 pp. 77-78).

The Rise of Modern Foster Care

In addition to the trend toward professionalization, the nation's decision to abandon institutional care as a viable option for dependent children shaped the future of the Buckner Home. On January 25, 1909, at the White House Conference on Dependent Children, a notable change in the methods of caring for dependent children would transform child welfare strategies for the rest of the twentieth century. Soon thereafter, Congress passed The Children's Bureau Bill to advance the emerging movement advocating the placement of orphaned children in families rather than in institutions (Lundberg, 1947). The Bill passed without the votes of the Texas senators. They had been persuaded by their familiarity with the advantages of the Buckner Home, as well as by the arguments of R. C. Buckner and other Texas supporters, to vote against the bill (Cranfill and Walker, 1915).

As the modern foster care system emerged, institutions like the Buckner Orphan's Home were dismissed by members of the emerging social work profession as outmoded, cold, and sterile. At the 1909 Conference on the Care of Dependent Children, called by Theodore Roosevelt, the consensus of child welfare workers, which included the new professional social workers, was expressed in these words: "Home life is the highest and finest product of civilization. Children should not be deprived of it except for urgent and compelling reasons. Surely poverty alone should not disrupt the home." Leaders in child welfare proposed that widows and women who had been deserted "should be given such aid as may be necessary to enable them to maintain suitable homes for rearing their children.... Children from unfit homes and children who have no homes, who must be cared for by charitable agencies, should, so far as practicable, be cared for in families" (Proceedings, 1909).

This shift in philosophy brought about important benefits for children. It created a foster care system, as well as supplemental income or "welfare" for poor mothers, first known as Mother's Pensions in 1911 and, in 1935, known as Aid to Families with Dependent Children. These changes contributed to the professionalization of social workers in child welfare, a positive step indeed. However, the contributions of faith-based agencies like the Buckner Home were not recognized by the new profession of social work as the important contributors they were (Garland, 1994; Keith-Lucas, 1962).

By the end of the first decade of the twentieth century, national changes in the child welfare scene set in motion by the Children's Bureau set the course for a new system of foster care and adoption. In addition, the emerging profession of social work claimed child welfare and "home finding" as its turf. This shift was symbolized when the social workers, preparing the list for the 1909 conference, omitted most of the leaders of church-related institutions. Buckner and other leaders of church-related institutions had for years attended the National Convention of Charities and Corrections along with Jane Addams, Mary Richmond, and others that today's social workers claim as founders of the profession. However, when he did not receive an invitation to the table, Buckner and other leaders of institutions caring for children recognized what was about to happen (Cranfill and Walker, 1915).

Forging ahead

So what happened to institutions like the Buckner Home? In spite of the new bill, institutional care did not disappear immediately and, particularly church-related institutions would house children through the first half of the twentieth century (Garland 1994). However, the new system of foster care and adoption, growing alongside the emerging profession of social work, was firmly set in motion by the bill.

It would be over 30 years before the number of children in orphanages began to decline nationally (Jones, 1989). By the 1930s, there were more foster homes than ever. However, due to the Great Depression, which displaced many children, both foster families and orphanages were needed to care for more children who were staying longer in care (Jones 1989). The new Social Security Act of 1935 placed the care of foster children and poverty-stricken children living with their parents in the hands of governmental agencies. The government provided very little institutional care in orphanages, leaving that task to church agencies.

According to Alan Keith-Lucas, social worker, Christian, and pioneer in training workers in church institutions, the divisions were made along the lines of church vs. government. Child welfare professionals supported or attacked a system of care, not based on its intrinsic strengths and limitations, but rather because they were pro-church or anti-church. (Keith-Lucas, 1962).

Although the Children's Bureau Bill aimed to put professionally trained social workers in the new child welfare system, by the turn of the twenty-first century, state agencies employed fewer and fewer social workers on the front lines. Scarce resources and high turn-over led to the employment of case workers and child welfare workers without social work degrees or licensure.

Church-related institutions like Buckner continued caring for children, but their purposes shifted over time to providing residential treatment for troubled children and facilitating adoption and foster care for non-residential children (Garland, 1994). By the end of the twentieth century, critics of the modern foster care system called for a revival of orphanages, arguing that institutions would address some of the flaws of foster care including expense, abuses, and too few homes ready for placement ("Minnesota Brings," 1998; "Social Workers Condemn," 1994); While orphanages have not reappeared on the American scene, a new appreciation of faith-based social welfare emerged in the twenty-first century with the creation of the White House Ofice for Faith-Based and Community Initiatives (now called the White House Office for Faith-Based and Neighborhood Partnerships) (Travers, 2009).

Today's Buckner International, thriving in Dallas, maintains the vision of its founder: addressing the church's mandate to care for our most vulnerable members of society—populations we used to call "orphans and widows." Expanding beyond Texas, the Buckner agency continues to provide a wide array of programs and services for children, families and older adults, both in the US and abroad. ("Who We Are," 2011).

Some faith-based institutions, like Buckner, have increased their hiring of professional social workers. Determined to hire MSW-level graduates with strong Christian commitments, the Buckner agency of the 21st century is addressing the divide between church agencies and professional social workers. Buckner partners with undergraduate and graduate social work programs located in Christian universities, such as Baylor University in its home state of Texas, to hire the very best professionals who combine Christian faith with a sound social work professional training ("About Us," 2011). Rather than being excluded, as R. C. Buckner was in 1909, today's Buckner social workers disseminate their knowledge and experience by presenting at social work conferences such as National Association of Social Workers, Texas Chapter, and North American Association of Christians in Social Work.

"Accepting a trust so responsible"—Reclaiming Our Stories

The Buckner Home adopted, nurtured, and reared the infant child welfare system by raising money, discovering best practices, and saving children lost or abandoned after the Civil War. When the child welfare enterprise was adopted by the U. S. Government in 1909 for oversight and regulation, the now "adolescent" system operated by social workers showed contempt for its church-related roots, as teenagers often do. The 1909 White House meeting, as well as the 1935 Social Security Act, increased government roles. But without the early care and nurturing of institutions like the Buckner Orphan's Home, the child welfare system as we know it today could not have survived its childhood years. As Mother Dixon felt gratitude in 1908 to the Buckner Home for "accepting a trust so responsible," the profession of social work must also recognize and appreciate the important work of institutions like the Buckner Home who nurtured the fledgling child welfare system.

The stories of early child welfare agencies like the Buckner Orphan's Home must be told, not only to Christian social workers, but to all social workers. Unfortunately, authors of social work text books often distill the complex and variegated story of our profession's roots into a page or two of text for students. Social work authors sometimes report a distorted version of the profession's entire history as resting on the shoulders of two venerated figures—Mary Richmond and Jane Addams—with no mention of the contributions of early church-related agencies like the Buckner Orphan's Home (Scales & Kelly, 2011). If church- affiliated agencies are mentioned at all, they may be portrayed as over-zealous or incompetent meddlers operating poorly-run agencies.

Christian scholars must continue to study, record, and publish stories of the dedicated and competent faith-based agencies and their leaders who cared for vulnerable children. Moreover, we must report and celebrate the cooperative spirit of the past that brought Reverend Buckner yearly to the National Conference of Charities and Corrections to work with and learn from other social welfare agencies. We must resist adopting our profession's tendency to emphasize divisions between professional and volunteer and social worker and clergy when recounting our profession's history. Christians in social work can lead the way by making an intentional effort to move forward in celebrating both our Christian and "secular" roots together. My hope is that the Buckner Home story has inspired you, readers exploring the history of social welfare, to seek out and publish stories of early social welfare services from your own faith traditions.

References

About us. Retrieved from Baylor University School of Social Work website, http://www. baylor.edu/social_work

Austin, D. M. (1983). The Flexner myth and the history of social work. *The Social Service Review, 57*(3).

Buckner Admissions Form (Feb 13, 1908), Buckner Archive. Dallas, TX.

Buckner Orphan's Home. (1879). *Charter*. Dallas: Author.

Buckner Orphan's Home. (1888- 1918). *Annual Report*. Dallas: Author.

Buckner Orphan's Home. (1896). *Magazine*. Dallas: Author.

Buckner Orphan's Home. (1907). *Picturebook*. Dallas: Author.

Buckner, R. C. (1883). *Good Samaritan, 1*(1), 6.

Buckner, R. C. (1886). *Good Samaritan, 3*(11), 1.

Buckner, R.C. (1889-1912). Correspondence. Buckner Archives, Dallas, TX.

Buckner Registry, n.d., Buckner Archive, Dallas, TX.

Buckner Transfer Blank, n.d., Buckner Archive, Dallas, TX.

Bledstein, B. (1976). *The culture of professionalism*. New York: Norton Publishing.

Bullock, K. O. (1991). *The life and contributions of Robert Cooke Buckner, progenitor of organized social Christianity among Texas Baptists, 1860-1919*, Thesis (Ph.D., Southwestern, Baptist Theological Seminary Ft. Worth, TX.

Bullock, K. O. (1993). *Homeward bound: The heart and heritage of Buckner*. Dallas: Buckner Baptist Benevolences.

C. P. S. (Feb 1884). Inside the Buckner Orphan Home. *Good Samaritan, 1*(6), 43.

Cranfill, J. B. & Walker, J. L. (1915). *R. C. Buckner's life of faith and works*. Dallas: Buckner Orphans Home.

Cunningham, V. G. (1885, April). *The Texas Baptist*, p. 64.

Deacons Convention minutes (July 22, 1881), Buckner Baptist Benevolences Archive, Dallas, TX.

Garland, D. S. R., & Child Welfare League of America. (1994). *Church agencies: Caring for children and families in crisis*. Washington, D.C.: Child Welfare League of America.

Hewett, K. E. (1884). A visit to the Buckner Orphan's Home. *Good Samaritan*. Dallas: Buckner Orphan's Home.

Jones, M. B. (1989). Crisis of the American orphanage 1931-1940. *Social Service Review*. 613-29.

Keith-Lucas, A. (1962). *The church children's home in a changing world*. Chapel Hill, NC: The University of North Carolina Press.

Klein, P. (1968). *From Philanthropy to Social Welfare*. San Francisco: Jossey Bass.

Kunzel, R. (1988). The professionalization of benevolence: Evangelicals and social workers in the Florence Crittenton Homes, 1915-1945. *Journal of Social History, 22*(1).

Lubove, R. (1972). *The professional altruist*. New York: Atheneum.

Lundberg, E. O. (1947). Unto the least of these: social services for children. New York: Appleton Century-Crofts.

Minnesota brings orphanages into the 21st century. (1998, June 14). *The Dallas Morning News*, p. 30A.

Proceedings of the Conference on the Care of Dependent Children, Jan 25-26, 1909, Washington, D.C., Government Printing Office.

Reformatory for boys, Rev RCB declares need for such a state institution is urgent. (1903, February 20). *The Dallas Morning News*.

Scales, T. L. & Kelly, M. S. (2011). To give Christ to the neighborhood: A corrective look at the Settlement Movement and early Christian social workers. *Social Work and Christianity, 38*(3), 356-376 .

Sister Carrie. (1884). Affairs at Buckner Orphan's Home. *Good Samaritan, 2*(4), 28.

Smith, E. P. (1995). Bring back the orphanages? What policymakers of today can learn from the past. *Child Welfare, 74*(1), 115-42.

Social workers condemn orphanages as old technology. (1994, Dec 15). *PR Newswire*.

Travers, K. (2009). Obama names 26-year-old director of faith-based office. Retrieved from http://abcnews.go.com/Politics/President44/story?id=6806913&page=1.

V. C. H. (1884). *Good Samaritan, 1*(9), 68.

Who we are. Retrieved from Buckner International (2011) website, http://www.buckner.org

Notes

1 This chapter was first published in *Social Work and Christianity*, 38(3), 332-355 .

2 I dedicate this article to my dear daughter April, a modern-day "Buckner girl," entrusted to us in 2005 by Buckner Baptist Benevolences (now Buckner International) and Child Protective Services of Texas. It has been the joy of my life to accept "a trust so responsible."

3 The names of children and families mentioned in the article have been changed to protect their identities.

CHAPTER 5

"GO IN PEACE AND SIN NO MORE": CHRISTIAN AFRICAN AMERICAN WOMEN AS SOCIAL WORK PIONEERS

Tanya Smith Brice

Professional social work is rooted in indigenous helping traditions; that is, helping grows out of the social and cultural contexts of each client system. As different cultures settled in the industrialized centers of the Northeast and Midwest regions of the United States, settlement houses were founded to help these mostly European immigrants become acculturated to their new life in the United States (Crocker, 1992; Kraus, 1980). These immigrants, as well as migrants from the American South, became the primary workforce in the growing industrial factories, resulting in an emerging working class, as well as increased social issues. Some of these issues included harsh working conditions, high rates of death and injury among children who worked in these factories, unsupervised children in the city streets, high crime rates, poor housing options and rampant health epidemics (Clapp, 1998; Hart, 2010; O'Connor, 2004; Stein, 1962).

Out of the need to address these social concerns, the profession of social work arose. Women formed philanthropic and charitable organizations as a part of their religious practices (Abramovitz, 1998; Ehrenreich, 1985; Simon, 1994). In 1898, the New York School of Philanthropy at Columbia University, began offering the first professional social work training program (Meier, 1954; Ravitch, 2000; Work, 1921). Unfortunately, White women and men created these organizations and training programs for Whites only (Carlton-LaNey, 1999; Lasch-Quinn, 1993). This chapter highlights the social welfare efforts of African Americans for African Americans, efforts often overlooked when social workers recount stories of our professional beginnings. Using the example of the North Carolina Industrial Home for Colored Girls in Efland, NC, the values and practices of African American social work pioneers will be illustrated.

African American helping tradition

African Americans have an indigenous helping tradition rooted in African communal traditions (Billingsley & Giovannoni, 1972; E. P. Martin & Martin, 1995). The values of the African community transcended the trans-Atlantic slave trade, the institution of chattel slavery, and the transition to life as free persons. The African community is characterized by the following values: (1) Group identity is paramount; and, (2) Spirituality is integral to understanding the world (Martin & Martin, 2003; 1985).

Group identity is an important value in African American cultures. There is an ancient African proverb that says, "I am because we are, therefore, we are because I am." This proverb speaks to the interconnectedness of the individual and the community. In the African American helping tradition, addressing community needs is a personal task.

In addition, valuing one's spirituality is an essential practice in African American communities (Billingsley, 1968; Blackwell, 1975; DuBois, 1909; McCluskey, 1997). There is an understanding that humans are spiritual, as well as physical beings. When addressing the physical and social needs of the African American community, spiritual needs are tended to as well. These two values: group identity and spirituality would become very important to African American social work pioneers.

African American women as helpers

African American women played an integral role in the development of the social work profession, particularly as it relates to the African American community. In the African tradition, women are seen as the life-bearers of the community (Brice, 2007a). Because women are the sole bearers of new life, mothers have a revered place in the African community. Social work services, developed by African American women, focused on protecting African American womanhood. These services were characterized by four principles: self-help, mutual aid, race pride, and social debt(Carlton-LaNey, 1999). Self-help is the notion that African Americans were uniquely positioned to address most adequately the needs of the African American community. Mutual aid further supports this ideology; women were committed to helping one another and relied on support from the African American community. Pride in their race motivated these pioneers to serve the least of their race, as a means of uplifting the race. Just like their White counterparts, these women pioneers were of the upper socioeconomic classes. Their motivation for developing services to the lower classes was to pay a social debt. Based on the value of interconnectedness, these social work pioneers believed that they were obligated to uplift African Americans of the lower classes.

Lifting as we climb

It is in this context that African American women, individually and through organizations, saw the need for an intentional effort to address the needs of the African American community, with particular emphasis on African American girls. The National Association of Colored Women (NACW), founded in 1896, developed in response to growing social concerns. While exemplifying the theme of social uplift through the motto, "Lifting as we climb", these women were instrumental in creating a social order through their meticulous attention to education, benevolence, and social graces (Cook, 2001; Gilmore, 1996; Hodges, 2001; Salem, 1994). Made up of African American women in 40 states, the NACW collectively developed a private social welfare system that included orphanages, old age homes, kindergartens, homes for working girls, homes for wayward girls, as well as other programs (Carlton-LaNey, 2001; Hodges, 2001; Lerner, 1974; Salem, 1994).

The work of African American clubwomen was an intentional effort to address the spiritual needs of the African American community. It has been described as a "socioreligious movement aimed at reforming society through the 'uplift' efforts of African American women" (Riggs, 2006, p. 865). Fannie Barrier Williams, a founding member of NACW, suggests that the African American clubwomen's movement was born from church work. She clarifies by explaining:

> The training which first enabled colored women to organize and successfully carry on club work was originally obtained in church work. These churches have been and still are the great preparatory schools in which the primary lessons of social order, mutual trustfulness and united effort have been taught..." (Williams, 1900, p. 383).

Mary Church Terrell, a founding member and the first president of the NACW, further describes these women as "women [who] were filled with the spirit of Christ...to save the race from immorality and vice; to put forth every effort to prevent the young from going astray" (Mary Church Terrell Papers, n.d., as quoted in Riggs, 2006, p.869).

Clubwomen across the nation formed state federations to coordinate the efforts of the national organization. Each federation was made up of individual clubs. The North Carolina Federation of Colored Women (NCFCW), founded in 1909, was instrumental in developing programs and services for African American girls (Gilmore, 1994) through the founding of the North Carolina Industrial Home for Colored Girls, also known as Efland Home for Girls. Dr. Charlotte Hawkins Brown, a prominent educator and founder of Palmer Memorial Institute, a finishing school for upper class African American students from around the nation, was the founding president of NCFCW.

In North Carolina, there was no state institution for African American girls deemed delinquent until 1943. During this time period, the term "female delinquency" meant sexual delinquency (Bloom, Owen, Rosenbaum, & Deschenes, 2003; Sedlak, 1983; Tice, 1998). Girls who were either victims of sexual violence or rumored as promiscuous, were at risk of being deemed delinquent. African American girls were particularly at risk of being labeled delinquent, as they were often viewed by Whites as being "innately promiscuous" and "erotic icons" (Brice, 2007b; D'Emilio & Freedman, 1998; Gilman, 1985; Russett, 1989; Weeks, 1986). This misperception was of particular concern for African American clubwomen. While the North Carolina's juvenile court system handled an average of 192 cases of African American girls deemed delinquent between

1919 and 1939, many of these young girls were sent to adult penitentiaries or simply returned to their communities without supervision.

The NCFCW sought to address the needs of these young girls and to save African American womanhood. After years of fundraising, coalition building, and lobbying for support from key policy makers and community members, this group of women purchased 142 acres of land, approximately two miles from Efland, North Carolina, for the purpose of building a facility to serve delinquent African American girls.

Efland Home began accepting African American girls deemed delinquent by the state in October 1925. The philosophy of Efland Home was "to save the young Negro girl who is on the verge of wasting her life". It served as a mechanism "to give her a second chance." The underlying mission of Efland Home was to "save Negro womanhood and we shall hope to surround these girls with the spirit of Jesus whose memorable words were 'Go in peace and sin no more'" (North Carolina Industrial Home for Colored Girls, 1925). The mission embodies the values of African American women's work-- group identity, as well as an important spiritual component.

The first board of trustees was made up of an influential group of seven clubwomen, who were influenced by a "distinct religious, ethical tradition" (Collier-Thomas, 2010; Riggs, 2006; McArthur, 1998). The first chairwoman of the Board of Trustees was Fannie Yarborough Bickett, wife of a former North Carolina governor, and an active member of the North Carolina Federation of Women, the White counterpart to the NCFNW. Governor and Mrs. Bickett, both lawyers, were instrumental in establishing North Carolina's juvenile court system, as well as advancing reforms in North Carolina's education system. Minnie Sumner Pearson, a former teacher and active member of the NCFNW, served as co-chair of the Board of Trustees. Her husband, Dr. William G. Pearson, a professor of Business Education at North Carolina College for Negroes, in Durham, served as special treasurer to the Board of Trustees. Lula Kelsey, of Salisbury, was a licensed embalmer who owned two businesses with her husband, Noble & Kelsey, a fire insurance company, and Kelsey & Kelsey, a funeral home. Kelsey succeeded Brown as president of the NCFNW in 1928. Maude Cotton, of Henderson, was a Presbyterian missionary, a classically trained musician, and principal of Henderson Institute, a school for African American children (Vann, 2000). Ophelia Griffin, of High Point, was a teacher at the High Point Normal High School and was married to the vice president of Ramsey Drug Company. Lillian Mebane, of Rocky Mount, was an educator. Moselle L. Gullins, director of admissions at Brown's Palmer Institute, served as corresponding secretary to the board. By 1930, the board had grown to thirteen members.

These board members appealed to the upper classes for funding by comparing the girls at Efland Home to the daughters of the elite classes. They asked potential donors a set of provocative questions: "Suppose it was your girl who had gone astray? Would you want to give her a second chance?" (North Carolina Industrial Home for Colored Girls, 1925, 1931). It was their ability to provide a different perspective of delinquency among girls, that raised North Carolina's awareness of the need for "girl saving efforts" like Efland Home. As a result, the board members were able to raise funds from the African American community, through "nickel and dime" campaigns by churches and civic groups (Martin & Martin, 1985). These financial donations were often supplemented by in-kind donations of farm animals, dishes and utensils, maintenance services, and clothes for the girls (Pearson, 1926, 1927, 1928, 1929). Despite these fundraising efforts, the needs of the home quickly outgrew their facilities. Consequently, the board of trustees began lobbying for state support in 1929, and continued over the next ten years.

North Carolina Board of Public Welfare (NCBPW) and the county juvenile courts referred African American girls under the age of 16 to Efland Home. In addition to those referral sources, Efland Home's board and local community also participated in the admission process. For instance, the NCBPW identified a potential candidate, and would make a written presentation of the candidate, identified as being delinquent, to the Home's board of trustees. The Home's admissions subcommittee would determine if the candidate was suitable for Efland Home. If she were suitable, NCBPW would petition the juvenile courts for commitment orders to Efland Home. Upon admission, the young girl was paroled to the custody of Efland Home (Benton, 1931; Brice, 2011).

Life at Efland Home

The goal of Efland Home was to "enable the young girls to prepare themselves for efficient service in obtaining a livlihood [sic]" ("Efland Home Charter," 1925). The curriculum provided the young girls with elementary school courses and industrial courses, such as farm work and food cultivation and preparation. They received 261 days of instruction annually. The academic instruction took place in the morning hours, and the industrial instruction took place in the afternoons. A number of individuals, organizations, and local Historically Black Colleges and Universities (HBCUs) were instrumental in providing consultation to Efland Home, particularly in curriculum development.

Like many early training schools, Efland Home had a working farm. The young girls were expected to participate in all aspects of growing and preparing food. For instance, in 1928, the young girls consumed 580 gallons of "fresh cow's milk", having produced 478 gallons at the Home's dairy. Of the 147 acres of land purchased for Efland Home, the young girls cultivated ten acres, producing vegetables and fruit for sustenance. The young girls also prepared and canned vegetables and fruit for future consumption.

The young girls were provided with recreation activities such as swing ball, croquet, jumping rope, basketball, as well as other games. Recreation was provided under the direct supervision of a teacher or matron and kept the young girls physically fit as well as providing some enjoyment,

Religious instruction was also a fundamental aspect of services provided at Efland Home. The young girls were required to attend church services every Sunday afternoon, to participate in morning and evening prayers, and to attend weekly prayer meetings. In a fundraising pamphlet, the clubwomen provided an additional explanation of the motivation for their work. They wrote, "In His name we are launching this effort to save Negro womanhood, and we hope to surround these girls with the spirit of Jesus whose memorable words were, 'Go in peace and sin no more'"(North Carolina Industrial Home for Colored Girls, 1925). Cultivating spirituality was viewed by these clubwomen as one strategy of protecting these young girls from further delinquency (Brice, 2011).

Efland Home was usually filled beyond capacity. Approximately 22 girls were admitted to Efland Home annually, although the intended capacity was 15 annually. The board of trustees decided that "it is better to start with a small group and make a success of the work than to take so many that criticisms will arise as to methods of treatment" ("Suggested plan for organization of Efland School for Girls," n.d.). The Home accepted girls as young as six years old, however, the majority of the young girls were between the ages of 14 and 16. These girls were often discharged to working homes, parents or relatives, or to hospitals. Girls who ran away from the home were often consequently discharged.

A staff of three to four employees ran the Home, including a matron, superintendent, teacher, and farm supervisor. Each of these staff members lived at the Home. The Board of Trustees agreed that the superintendent must meet the following qualifications:

1. A woman who has had some training in social work;
2. She should have had experience in handling girls who are problem cases;
3. She should have executive ability and be resourceful and energetic; and,
4. She should have a sense of financial values and be able to make proper and just expenditures of money ("Suggested plan for organization of Efland School for Girls", n.d.).

This requirement for social work training is extraordinary, as there were only thirteen trained African American social workers in the state of North Carolina during this time (Crow, Escott, & Hatley, 1992), and there were very few opportunities for African Americans to receive formal social work training (Carlton-LaNey, 1994). These limited opportunities were due to Jim Crow policies that restricted the daily activities and education of African Americans throughout the United States. The matron, who often served as the superintendent, supervised the daily operations. Due to budgetary constraints, the matron sometimes provided classroom instruction to the girls.

The Virginia Federation of Colored Women was founded in 1908 by Janie Porter Barrett, its first president. This group of clubwomen founded the Virginia Industrial School for Colored Girls with the same motive as their North Carolina counterparts (Peebles-Wilkins, 1995). This school provided services to African American girls labeled delinquent by the Virginia juvenile courts. The Efland Home was modeled after the Virginia school. Consequently, the matrons at Efland Home were trained at Janie Porter Barrett's Virginia Industrial School for Colored Girls, for eight weeks to several years prior to coming to the Home. This ensured fidelity to the program model provided by the Virginia school.

There were one to two teachers at any given time employed at Efland Home, nearly all of whom were certified and formally trained to teach. Efland Home teachers received training primarily from the Teachers College in Winston-Salem, the North Carolina Agricultural & Technical College in Greensboro, or from various normal schools around the state. Teachers often served as residential advisors, assisting the matron in providing daily care to the young girls.

The farm supervisor oversaw the industrial operations of the home and provided instruction in agricultural techniques. He was also usually the spouse of the Home's matron and served as a father figure to many of the young girls.

Impact of Efland Home

Through Efland Home, the women of NCFCW carried out their African American helping traditions. They were able to provide a second chance for young African American girls deemed delinquent to lead a productive and meaningful life. These young girls were given the opportunity to develop skills that would enable them to seek gainful employment, as well as to maintain a morally respectable lifestyle.

Efland Home provided a respite to the families of these troubled girls. Before Efland Home, delinquent girls were often returned to the community with no treatment or sent to the harsh penitentiary system; however, this home provided services that equipped the girls with necessary life skills. So, while many of these girls did not return to their home of origin, the acquisition of these skills provided a peace of mind to the families that their daughters, sisters, or nieces would be able to live a moral and wholesome lifestyle (Brown, 1921, 1930; North Carolina Industrial Home for Colored Girls, 1925, 1931). In a 1931 Efland Home brochure, this process was described this way: "[Knowledge with efficiency is what will aid in transforming the idle mind into a fertile field for the production of healthy, happy, clean thinking". The brochure further claimed that most of the girls paroled from the home "are able to earn a living and to become useful members of their communities" (North Carolina Industrial Home for Colored Girls, 1931).

Efland Home was seen as a necessary facility in the African American community. For clubwomen, it served as a mechanism to save the race. The young girls were provided with the opportunity to engage in a moral lifestyle, thus improving the image of the race to Whites, which was a major concern for many clubwomen. One motivation for this work was to "save true Black womanhood" (Aery, 1915; Blair, 1980; Terrell, 1900). To improve the image of these young girls in the eyes of Whites was to improve the image of the African American clubwomen. For the community, as a whole, it served as an example of the self-help principle inherent in the African American culture. The African American community made many contributions, both financially and in-kind, to Efland Home, through Sunday school collections, social clubs, sororities and fraternities, secret orders, business loans, as well as individual contributions. This support helped to ensure Efland Home's survival for over 14 years.

Efland Home had a positive impact on North Carolina's juvenile justice system. It served the state in two ways: (1) the home provided services to a neglected segment of the juvenile justice system; and, (2) it saved the state money by independently providing care to this neglected population.

By the time Efland Home was established in 1925, North Carolina had already invested in meeting the needs of delinquent boys of both races and to White girls. In 1907, Stonewall Jackson Manual Training and Industrial School was established in Concord for delinquent White boys under age 16; Samarcand Manor State Home and Industrial School for Girls was established in 1918 in Eagle Springs, for White girls under the age of 18; Morrison Training School for Delinquent Negro Boys was established in Hoffman, in 1921, for boys under age 16; and, Eastern Carolina Training School was established in Rocky Mount, in 1923, for White boys under age 18. There were no plans to establish a facility for African American girls, although the court system was inundated with cases involving this population (North Carolina Board of Public Welfare-Institutions and Corrections, 1920-1939).

The existence of Efland Home allowed the juvenile justice system to maintain a passive and distant position with regard to the treatment of delinquent African American girls. While the juvenile courts validated the necessity for such a facility, through the commitment of girls to Efland Home, there was a scant amount of financial support provided to the home. Efland Home received a state operational grant of $2000 annually, which was reduced to $1400 annually in 1933. The other four training schools in the state, although they all housed a comparable number of young girls, received much higher appropriations ranging from $20,000 to $35,000 annually at the inception of Efland Home and growing to $50,000 to $60,000 by the closing of Efland Home (Carolina Times, 1939; *Undated report written after March 15, 1939.*).

Despite consistent, organized lobbying efforts by the board of trustees, and other supporters of the Home, the state refused to provide appropriate funding (Bailey, 1931; Bost, n.d.; North Carolina Board of Public Welfare-Institutions and Corrections, 1920-1939). Efland Home was forced to close in 1939 because of inadequate financial support. It was not until 1943 that the state appropriated adequate funds for the establishment of the State Training School for Negro Girls, known as Dobbs Farm. It was because of Efland Home's reputation for successful intervention that Dobbs Farm was established and funded by the state (Carlton-LaNey, 1994b, 1994c; Carolina Times, 1939; Inman & Covington, 1981).

"Of Such is the Kingdom of Heaven"

While these women were motivated by a quest to save "true Black womanhood", they were guided by their Christian convictions. They relied on their faith, as they attempted to address the needs of delinquent girls. One clubwoman declared,

But in connection with such work, let us not neglect, let us not forget, the children, remembering that when we love and protect the little ones, we follow in the footsteps of Him, who when He wished to paint the most beautiful picture of Beulah land it is possible for the human mind to conceive, pointed to the children and said—"Of such is the kingdom of heaven" (Terrell, 1900, p. 343).

In addition to expressing their Christian convictions, the women of the NCFCW and other organizations contributed to the development of the social work profession. They understood the need for a holistic approach to address delinquency among African American girls. They built coalitions with supporters of their efforts, both inside and outside of the African American community. These women engaged in policy practice by gaining an understanding of the juvenile court and child welfare systems. With this knowledge, they were able to use those systems to provide services to delinquent girls. These women understood the role of a social worker. Despite having a limited pool of candidates, they insisted on having a professionally trained social worker to oversee the daily operations of Efland Home. Indeed, the work at Efland Home was seen by these pioneering women as kingdom work and social work as they engaged in social uplift, encouraged mutual aid, girded by racial pride, and repaid their social debts.

References

Abramovitz, M. (1998). Social work and social reform: An arena of struggle. *Social Work, 43*(6).

Aery, W. A. (1915). Helping wayward girls. *Southern Workman*, 598-604.

Bailey, A. (1931). Letter to Mrs. T. W. Bickett. Raleigh, NC Public Welfare Collection, NC Department of Archives and History. (Box 163).

Benton, J. G. (1931). Letter to Mr. R. Eugene Brown, State Board of Charities. Raleigh, NC Public Welfare Collection, NC Department of Archives and History. (Box 163).

Billingsley, A. (1968). *Black families in White America*. Englewood Cliffs, NJ: Prentice-Hall.

Billingsley, A., & Giovannoni, J. M. (1972). *Children of the storm: Black children and American child welfare*. Atlanta: Harcourt Brace Jovanovich.

Blackwell, J. (1975). *The Black community: Diversity and unity*. New York: HarperCollins Publishers.

Blair, K. J. (1980). *The clubwoman as feminist: True womanhood redefined, 1868-1914*. New York: Holmes & Meier.

Bloom, B., Owen, B., Rosenbaum, J., & Deschenes, E. P. (2003). Focusing on girls and young women: A gendered perspective on female delinquency. *Women & Criminal Justice, 14*(2/3), 117-136.

Bost, W. T. (n.d.). The need for a state training school for delinquent negro girls (from State Commissioner Mrs. W.T. Bost, 1930-1944). Raleigh, NC Public Welfare Collection, NC Department of Archives and History. (Box 163).

Brice, T. S. (2007a). War on African American girls: Overcoming adversities. In S. Logan, R. Denby, & P. Gibson (Eds.), *Mental health care in the African American community*. Binghamton, NY: Haworth Press.

Brice, T. S. (2007b). Undermining progress in progressive era North Carolina: Genuine attitudes towards delinquent African American girls. *Journal of Sociology and Social Work, 34*(1), 131-152.

Brice, T. S. (2011). Faith as a protective factor against the social misconception of Black girls: A historical perspective. *Social Work and Christianity: An International Journal, 38*(3), 315-331.

Brown, C. H. (1921). Letter to Kate Burr Johnson (Mrs. C.A. Johnson), Commissioner, NC Board of Public Welfare, Raleigh, NC: Public Welfare Collection, NC Department of Archives and History. (Box 163).

Brown, C. H. (1930). Negro woman not freed by emancipation, Mrs. Brown says (printed in the Buffalo Progressive Herald, Buffalo, NY on 3/15/1930). Raleigh, NC: Public Welfare Collection, NC Department of Archives and History. (Box 163).

Carlton-LaNey, I. (1994a). Training African-American social workers through the NUL fellowship program. *Journal of Sociology and Social Welfare, 21*(2), 43-54.

Carlton-LaNey, I. (1994b). Birdy Henrietta Haynes: A pioneer settlement house worker. *Social Service Review, 68*(2), 254-273.

Carlton-LaNey, I. (1994c). Introduction: The legacy of African-American leadership in social welfare. *Journal of Sociology and Social Welfare, 21*(1), 5-12.

Carlton-LaNey, I. (1999). African American social work pioneers' response to need. *Social Work, 44*(4), 311-322.

Carlton-LaNey, I. (2001). *African American leadership: An empowerment tradition in social welfare history.* Washington, DC: NASW Press.

Carolina Times. (1939). The Efland Home. Durham, NC.

Clapp, E. J. (1998). *Mothers of all children: women reformers and the rise of juvenile courts in progressive era America.* University Park, Pa.: The Pennsylvania State University Press.

Collier-Thomas, B. (2010). *Jesus, jobs, and justice: African American women and religion.* New York: Random House Digital, Inc.

Columbia University School of Social Work. (1921). *Studies in social work* (Vol. 1). New York: New York School of Philanthropy.

Cook, S. W. (2001). Mary Church Terrell and her mission: Giving decades of quiet service. In I. B. Carlton-LaNey (Ed.), *African American leadership: An empowerment tradition in social welfare history* (pp. 153-162). Washington, DC: National Association of Social Workers.

Crocker, R. (1992). *Social work and social order: the settlement movement in two industrial cities, 1889-1930.* Champaign, IL: University of Illinois Press.

Crow, J. J., Escott, P. D., & Hatley, F. J. (1992). *A history of African Americans in North Carolina.* Raleigh: North Carolina Division of Archives and History.

D'Emilio, J., & Freedman, E. B. (1998). *Intimate matters: A history of sexuality in America* (2nd ed.). University Of Chicago Press.

DuBois, W. E. B. (1909). Some efforts of Negroes for Social Betterment. *14th Annual conference for the study of the Negro problems.* Atlanta, GA.

Efland Home Charter. (1925). Raleigh, NC Public Welfare Collection, NC Department of Archives and History. (Box 163). c. 1925.

Ehrenreich, J. (1985). *The altruistic imagination: A history of social work and social policy in the United States.* Ithaca, NY: Cornell Univ Press.

Gilman, S. (1985). Black bodies, White bodies: Toward an iconography of female sexuality in late nineteenth-century art, medicine and literature. *Critical Inquiry, 12*(1), 204-242.

Gilmore, G. E. (1994). North Carolina Federation of Colored Women's Clubs. In D. Hines, E. Brown, & R. Terborg-Penn (Eds.), *Black women in America: A historical encyclopedia* (pp. 882-884). Bloomberg: Indiana University Press.

Gilmore, G. E. (1996). *Gender and Jim Crow: Women and politics of White Supremacy in North Carolina, 1896-1920.* Chapel Hill, NC: University of North Carolina Press.

Hart, P. S. (2010). *A Home for Every Child: The Washington Children's Home Society in the Progressive Era.* Seattle, WA: University of Washington Press.

Hodges, V. G. (2001). Historical development of African American child welfare services. In I. B. Carlton-LaNey (Ed.), *African American Leadership: An empowerment tradition in social welfare history* (pp. 203-213). Washington, DC: National Association of Social Workers.

Inman, M. J., & Covington, E. B. (1981). *Dobbs School History (unpublished report).* Dobbs School.

Kraus, H. P. (1980). *The settlement house movement in New York City, 1886-1914.* North Stratford, NH: Ayer Publishing.

Lasch-Quinn, E. (1993). *Black neighbors: race and the limits of reform in the American settlement house movement, 1890-1945.* Chapel Hill, NC: University of North Carolina Press Books.

Lerner, G. (1974). Early community work of Black club women. *Journal of Negro History, 59*(2), 158-167.

Martin, E. P., & Martin, J. M. (1995). *Social work and the Black experience.* Washington, DC: NASW Press.

Martin, E. P., & Martin, J. M. (2003). *Spirituality and the Black helping tradition in social work.* Washington, DC: NASW Press.

Martin, Joanne M., & Martin, E. P. (1985). *The helping tradition in the Black family and community.* Washington, DC: National Association of Social Workers, Inc.

McArthur, J. N. (1998). *Creating the new woman: the rise of southern women's progressive culture in Texas, 1893-1918.* Champaign, IL: University of Illinois Press.

McCluskey, A. T. (1997). We specialize in the wholly impossible: Black women school founders and their mission. *Signs, 22*(2), 403-426.

Meier, E. G. (1954). *A history of the New York school of social work.* New York: Columbia University Press.

North Carolina Board of Public Welfare-Institutions and Corrections. (1920-1939). *North Carolina Training School for Negro Girls. Box 163.* Raleigh, NC: North Carolina Division of Archives and History.

North Carolina Industrial Home for Colored Girls. (1925). Save Our Girls. *author.* Raleigh, NC Public Welfare Collection, NC Department of Archives and History. (Box 163). c. 1925.

North Carolina Industrial Home for Colored Girls. (1931). Save Our Girls. *author.* Raleigh, NC Public Welfare Collection, NC Department of Archives and History. (Box 163). c. 1931.

North Carolina Industrial Home for Colored Girls. (1939). Undated report written after March 15, 1939. Raleigh, NC Public Welfare Collection, NC Department of Archives and History. (Box 163).

O'Connor, S. (2004). *Orphan trains: the story of Charles Loring Brace and the children he saved and failed.* University of Chicago Press.

Pearson, W. G. (1926). Financial Statement of the Reform School. Public Welfare Collection, NC Department of Archives and History (Box 163).

Pearson, W. G. (1927). Efland Home Report (financial). Raleigh, NC Public Welfare Collection, NC Department of Archives and History. (Box 163). c. 1927.

Pearson, W. G. (1928). Efland Home Report (financial). Raleigh, NC: Public Welfare Collection, NC Department of Archives and History. (Box 163). c. 1928.

Pearson, W. G. (1929). Efland Home Report (financial). Raleigh, NC: Public Welfare Collection, NC Department of Archives and History. (Box 163). c. 1929.

Peebles-Wilkins, W. (1995). Janie Porter Barrett and the Virginia Industrial School for Colored Girls: community response to the needs of African American children. *Child Welfare*, 74(1), 143–61.

Ravitch, D. (2000). *The great school wars: A history of the New York City public schools.* Baltimore, MD: Johns Hopkins University Press.

Riggs, M. (2006). "Lifting as we climb": National Association of Colored Women (NACW)/National Council of Negro Women (NCNW). In R. S. Keller, R. R. Ruether, & M. Cantlon (Eds.), *Encyclopedia of women and religion in North America* (Vol. 2, pp. 864-872). Bloomington, IN: Indiana University Press.

Russett, C. E. (1989). *Sexual science: The Victorian construction of womanhood.* Cambridge, Massachusetts: Harvard University Press.

Salem, D. (1994). National Association of Colored Women. In D. Hines, E. Brown, & R. Terborg-Penn (Eds.), *Black women in America: A historical encyclopedia* (pp. 842-851). Bloomington: Indiana University Press.

Sedlak, M. W. (1983). Young Women and the City: Adolescent Deviance and the Transformation of Educational Policy, 1870-1960. *History of Education Quarterly*, 23(1), 1-28.

Simon, B. L. (1994). *The empowerment tradition in American social work: A history.* New York: Columbia University Press.

Stein, L. (1962). *The triangle fire.* Ithaca, NY: Cornell University Press.

Suggested plan for organization of Efland School for Girls. (n.d.). Raleigh, NC: Public Welfare Collection, NC Department of Archives and History. (Box 163).

Terrell, M. C. (1900). Duty of the National Association of Colored Women to the Race. *A. M. E. Church Review*, 16(3), 340-354.

Tice, K. W. (1998). *Tales of wayward girls and immoral women: Case records and the professionalization of social work.* Champaign, IL: University of Illinois Press.

Vann, A. (2000). *Vance County, North Carolina.* Mount Pleasant, SC: Arcadia Publishing.

Weeks, J. (1986). *Sexuality.* London: Routledge.

Williams, F. B. (1900). The club movement among Colored women of America. *New Negro for a New Century.* Chicago: American Publishing House.

SECTION 2

CHRISTIANS CALLED TO SOCIAL WORK: SCRIPTURAL BASIS, WORLDVIEWS AND ETHICS

CHAPTER 6

THE RELATIONSHIP BETWEEN BELIEFS AND VALUES IN SOCIAL WORK PRACTICE: WORLDVIEWS MAKE A DIFFERENCE

David A. Sherwood

In some circles (including some Christian ones) it is fashionable to say that what we believe is not all that important. What we do is what really counts. I strongly disagree. The relationship between what we think and what we do is complex and it is certainly not a simple straight line, but it is profound. Social work values, practice theories, assessments, intervention decisions, and action strategies are all shaped by our worldview assumptions and our beliefs.

I believe that a Christian worldview will provide an interpretive framework which will solidly support and inform commonly held social work values such as the inherent value of every person regardless of personal characteristics, self-determination and personally responsible freedom of choice, and responsibility for the common good, including help for the poor and oppressed. And it will challenge other values and theories such as might makes right, exploitation of the weak by the strong, and extreme moral relativism. At the same time, other worldviews, including materialism, empiricism, and postmodern subjectivism will lead to quite contrasting conclusions regarding these values.

Worldviews Help Us Interpret Reality

What is a "Worldview?"

Worldviews give faith-based answers to a set of ultimate and grounding questions. Everyone operates on the basis of some worldview or faith-based understanding of the universe and persons— examined or unexamined, implicit or explicit, simplistic or sophisticated. One way or another, we develop functional assumptions that help us to sort through and make some sort of sense out of our experience. And every person's worldview will always have a faith-based component (even belief in an exclusively material universe takes faith). This does not mean worldviews are necessarily irrational, unconcerned with "facts," or impervious to critique and change (though they unfortunately might be). It matters greatly how conscious, reflective, considered, or informed our worldviews are. The most objectivity we can achieve is to be critically aware of our worldview and how it affects our interpretations of "the facts." It is far better to be aware, intentional, and informed regarding our worldview than to naively think we are (or anyone else is) objective or neutral or to be self-righteously led by our biases which we may think are simply self-evident truth.

These worldviews affect our approach to social work practice, how we understand and help people. What is the nature of persons—biochemical machines, evolutionary products, immortal souls, all of the above? What constitutes valid knowledge—scientific empiricism only, "intuitive" discernment, spiritual guidance (if so, what kind)? What kinds of social work theories and practice methods are legitimate? What are appropriate values and goals—what is healthy, functional, optimal, the good?

Worldviews and the Hermeneutical Spiral: A Beginning Place

I like to use the concept of the *"hermeneutical spiral"* (the term is not original with me, cf. Osborne, 1991, Wood, 1998). We always come to the world, including social work practice, with our faith(worldview assumptions)—wherever we got it, however good or bad it is, and however embryonic it may be. This worldview faith strongly affects what we perceive (or even look for). But the world (God's creation, in the Christian worldview) is not a totally passive or subjective thing. So, we run the risk of coming away from any encounter with the world having our faith and our categories somewhat altered, perhaps even corrected a bit. Then we use that altered faith in our next encounter with the world.

So, for me, the starting place for integration of my beliefs and social work practice is always at the level of basic faith, worldview assumptions. What are the implications of my core beliefs? And what are the implications of the idea, theory, interpretation, or practice that I am examining? To use a currently fashionable phrase, how do they "interrogate" each other? What kind of assumptions about the nature of the world lie behind Freudian theory? Behavioral theory? The scientific method? The strengths perspective? The social work belief that all persons have intrinsic value (a radical notion not particularly supported by either modernism or postmodernism in their materialist, subjectivist versions)?

To put it another way, we all form stories that answer life's biggest questions. As I become a Christian, I connect my personal story to a much bigger story that frames my answers to these big questions. For Christians, the biblical story of God's nature and action in human history, culminating in Jesus Christ, is the "meta-narrative" that frames our personal stories and within which the meaning of our stories is rooted. Middleton and Walsh (1995, p. 11) summarize the basic worldview questions this way (with my illustrative additions):

1. **Where are we? *What is the nature of the reality in which we find ourselves?*** Is the nature of the universe meaningful or absurd? Created or accidental? Materialistic only, or also spiritual?

2. **Who are we? *What is the nature and task of human beings?*** What does it mean to be a person? What is human life? What is its source and value? Is there such a thing as freedom or responsibility?

3. **What's wrong?** *How do we understand and account for evil and brokenness?* And how do we account for our sense of morality, love, and justice? Is evil only stuff I happen not to prefer? Or are some things really good and other things really wrong? Is love only lust or well-disguised selfcenteredness? Does justice have a claim on us and what we call "ours"?

4. **What's the remedy?** *How do we find a path through our brokenness to wholeness?* What kinds of things will help? Do we need a Savior or just a positive (or cynical) attitude? Will chemicals or incarceration do the trick?

Interpreting the Facts

"Facts" have no meaning apart from an interpretive framework. "Facts" are harder to come by than we often think, but even when we have some "facts" in our possession, they have no power to tell us what they mean or what we should do.

That human beings die is a fact. That I am going to die would seem to be a reliable prediction based on what I can see. In fact, the capacity to put those observations and projections together is one of the ways we have come to describe or define human consciousness. But what do these "facts" mean and what effect should they have on my life?

One worldview might tell me that life emerged randomly in a meaningless universe and is of no particular value beyond the subjective feelings I may experience from moment to moment. Another worldview might tell me that somehow biological survival of life forms is of value and that I only have value to the extent that I contribute to that biological parade (with the corollary that survival proves fitness). Another worldview might tell me that life is a gift from a loving and just Creator and that it transcends biological existence, that death is not the end of the story. Different worldviews lend different meanings to the same "facts."

The major initial contribution of a Christian worldview to an understanding of social work values and ethical practice is not one of unique, contrasting, or conflicting values. Rather, a Christian worldview gives a coherent, solid foundation for the basic values that social workers claim and often take for granted (Holmes, 1984; Sherwood, 1993, 2000, 2007). Subsequently, a Christian worldview will shape how those basic values are understood and how they interact with one another. For example, justice will be understood in the light of God's manifest concern for the poor and oppressed, so justice can never be defined only as a procedurally "fair" protection of individual liberty and the right to acquire, hold, and transfer property (Lebacqz, 1986; Mott, 1982; Wolterstorff, 1983, 2006).

The Interaction of Feeling, Thinking, and Behavior

Persons are complex living ecological systems—to use a helpful conceptual model common in social work—systems of systems, if you will. Systems within our bodies and outside us as well interact in dynamic relationships with each other. For example, it is impossible to meaningfully separate our thinking, feeling, and behavior from each other and from the systems we experience outside ourselves, yet we quite properly think of ourselves as separate individuals.

The lines of influence run in all directions. What we believe affects what we experience, including how we define our feelings. For example, does an experience I might have of being alone, in and of itself, *make* me feel lonely, or rejected, or exhilarated by freedom, for that matter? Someone trips me, but was it accidental or intentional? I have had sex with only one woman (my wife Carol) in over sixty years of life. How does this "make" me feel? Are my feelings not also a result of what I tell myself about the meaning of my experience? But it works the other way too.

All this makes us persons harder to predict. And it certainly makes it harder to assign neat, direct, and one-way lines of causality. The biblical worldview picture is that God has granted us (at great cost) the dignity and terror of contributing to causality ourselves through our own purposes, choices, and actions. We have often used this freedom to hurt others and ourselves, but this also means that we are not mechanistically determined and that significant change is always possible.

And change can come from many directions—thinking, emotions, behavior, experience. We are especially (compared to other creatures) both gifted and cursed by our ability to think about ourselves and the world. We can form purposes and act in the direction of those purposes. Our beliefs about the nature of the world, other persons, and ourselves interact in a fundamental way with how we perceive reality, how we define our own identity, and how we act.

If this is true in our personal lives, it is equally true as we try to understand and help our clients in social work practice. And it is no less true for clients themselves. What we believe about the nature of the world, the nature of persons, and the nature of the human situation is at least as important as the sheer facts of the circumstances we experience.

Worldviews Help Construct Our Understanding of Values

Cut Flowers: Can Values Be Sustained Without Faith?

One significant manifestation of the notion that beliefs aren't all that important is the fallacy of our age which assumes that fundamental moral values can be justified and sustained apart from their ideological (ultimately theological) foundation. Take, for example, the fundamental Christian and social work belief that all human beings have intrinsic dignity and value.

Elton Trueblood, the Quaker philosopher, once described ours as a "cutflower" generation. He was suggesting that, as it is possible to cut a rose from the bush, put it in a vase, and admire its fresh loveliness and fragrance for a short while, it is possible to maintain the dignity and value of every human life while denying the existence or significance of God as the source of that value. But the cut rose is already dead, regardless of the deceptive beauty which lingers for a while. Even uncut, "The grass withers, and the flower falls, but the Word of the Lord endures forever" (I Peter 1:24-25).

Many in our generation, including many social workers, are trying to hold onto values—such as the irreducible dignity and worth of the individual—while denying the only basis on which such a value can ultimately stand. We should be glad they try to hold onto the value, but we should understand how shaky such a foundation is. A secular generation can live off its moral capital only so long before the impertinent questions (Why should we?) can no longer be ignored (Sherwood, 2007).

Doesn't Everybody "Just Know" That Persons Have Dignity and Value?

But doesn't everybody "just know" that human beings have intrinsic value? You don't have to believe in God, do you? In fact, according to some, so-called believers in God have been among the worst offenders against the value and dignity of all persons (sadly true, in some cases). After all, a lot of folks, from secular humanists to rocket scientists to New Age witches to rock stars, have declared themselves as defenders of the value of the individual. Isn't the worth of the person just natural, or at least rational and logically required? The plain answer is, "No, it's *not* just natural or rational or something everyone just knows."

I received a striking wake-up call in regard to this particular truth many years ago when I was a freshman at Indiana University. I think the story is worth telling here. I can't help dating myself—it was in the spring of 1960, the time the Civil Rights movement was clearly emerging. We were hearing of lunch room sit-ins and Freedom Riders on buses. Through an older friend of mine from my home town I wound up spending the evening at the Student Commons talking with my friend and someone he had met, a graduate student from Iran named Ali. I was quite impressed. My friend Maurice told me Ali's father was some sort of advisor to the Shah (the ruling despot at that point in Iran's history).

The conversation turned to the events happening in the South, to the ideas of racial integration, brotherhood, and social justice. Ali was frankly puzzled and amused that Maurice and I, and at least some other Americans, seemed to think civil rights were worth pursuing. But given that, he found it particularly hard to understand what he thought was the wishy-washy way the thing was being handled. "I don't know why you want to do it," he said. "But if it's so important, why don't you just do it? If I were President of the United States and I wanted integration, I would do it in a week!" "How?" we asked. "Simple. I would just put a soldier with a machine gun on every street corner and say 'Integrate.' If they didn't, I would shoot them." (Believable enough, as the history of Iran has shown)

Naive freshman that I was, I just couldn't believe he was really saying that. Surely he was putting us on. You couldn't just do that to people. At least not if you were moral! The conversation-debate- argument went on to explore what he really did believe about the innate dignity and value of the individual human life and social responsibility. You don't just kill inconvenient people, do you?

I would say things like, "Surely you believe that society has a moral responsibility to care for the widows and orphans, the elderly, the disabled, the emotionally disturbed." Incredibly (to me at the time), Ali's basic response was not to give an inch but to question *my* beliefs and values instead.

"Society has no such moral responsibility," he said. "On the contrary. You keep talking about reason and morality. I'll tell you what is immoral. The rational person would say that the truly *immoral* thing is to take resources away from the strong and productive to give to the weak and useless. Useless members of society such as the disabled and mentally retarded should be eliminated, not maintained." He would prefer that the methods be "humane," but he really did mean eliminated.

It finally sunk into my freshman mind that what we were disagreeing about was not facts or logic, but the belief systems we were using to interpret or assign meaning to the facts. Ali was a thoroughly secular man; he had left Islam behind. If I were to accept his assumptions about the nature of the universe (e.g. that there is no God, that the material universe is the extent of reality, that self-preservation is the only given motive and goal), then his logic was flawless and honest. As far as he was concerned, the only thing of importance left to discuss would be the most effective means to gain and keep power and the most expedient way to use it.

In this encounter I was shaken loose from my naive assumption that "everybody knows" the individual person has innate dignity and value. I understood more clearly that unless you believed in the Creator, the notion that all persons are equal is, indeed, *not* self-evident. The Nazi policies of eugenics and the "final solution" to the "Jewish problem" make a kind of grimly honest (almost inevitable) sense if you believe in the materialist worldview.

The "Is-Ought" Dilemma

Not long afterward I was to encounter this truth much more cogently expressed in the writings of C. S. Lewis. In *The Abolition of Man* (1947) he points out that both the religious and the secular walk by faith if they try to move from descriptive observations of fact to any sort of value statement or ethical imperative. He says "From propositions about fact alone no *practical* conclusion can ever be drawn. 'This will preserve society' [let's assume this is a factually true statement] cannot lead to 'Do this' [a moral and practical injunction] except by the mediation of 'Society ought to be preserved' [a value statement]" (p. 43). "Society ought to be preserved" is a moral imperative that no amount of facts alone can prove or disprove. Even the idea of "knowing facts" involves basic assumptions (or faith) about the nature of the universe and human beings.

The secular person (social worker?) tries to cloak faith by substituting words like natural, necessary, progressive, scientific, rational, or functional for "good," but the question always remains— For what end? And why? The answer to this question always smuggles in values from somewhere else besides the facts.

Even the resort to instincts such as self-preservation can tell us nothing about what we (or others) *ought* to do. Lewis (1947, p. 49) says:

We grasp at useless words: we call it the "basic," or "fundamental," or "primal," or "deepest" instinct. It is of no avail. Either these words conceal a value judgment passed *upon* the instinct and therefore not derivable *from* it, or else they merely record its felt intensity, the frequency of its operation, and its wide distribution. If the former, the whole attempt to base value upon instinct has been abandoned: if the latter, these observations about the quantitative aspects of a psychological event lead to no practical conclusion. It is the old dilemma. Either the premise is already concealed in an imperative or the conclusion remains merely in the indicative.

This is called the "Is-Ought" dilemma. Facts, even when attainable, never have any practical or moral implications until they are interpreted through the grid of some sort of value assumptions. "Is" does not lead to "Ought" in any way that has moral binding, obligation, or authority until its relationship to relevant values is understood. And you can't get the values directly from the "Is." We always come down to the question—what is the source and authority of the "Ought" that is claimed or implied?

The social work Code of Ethics refers to values such as the inherent value of every person, the importance of social justice, and the obligation to fight against oppression. It is a fair question to ask where those values come from and what gives them moral authority and obligation.

A Shaky Consensus: "Sexual Abuse" or "Intergenerational Sexual Experience?"

For an example of the "Is-Ought Dilemma," is child sexual abuse a fact or a myth? Or what is the nature of the abuse? Child sexual abuse is an example of an area where there may seem to be more of a consensus in values than there actually is. In any event, it illustrates how it is impossible to get values from facts alone. Some intervening concept of "the good" always has to come into play.

Fact: Some adults have sexual relations with children. But so what? What is the practical or moral significance of this fact? Is this something we should be happy or angry about? Is this good or bad? Sometimes good and sometimes bad? Should we be encouraging or discouraging the practice? Even if we could uncover facts about the consequences of the experience on children, we would still need a value framework to help us discern the meaning or practical implications of those facts. And to have moral obligation beyond our own subjective preferences or biases, this value framework must have some grounding outside ourselves. What constitutes negative consequences? And even if we could agree certain consequences were indeed negative, the question would remain as to what exactly was the cause.

In the last few years there has been a tremendous outpouring of attention to issues of child sexual abuse and its effects on adult survivors. I must say that this is long overdue and much needed. And even among completely secular social workers, psychologists, and other therapists there currently appears to be a high degree of consensus about the moral wrong of adult sexual activity with children and the enormity of its negative consequences on the child at the time and in later life. As a Christian I am encouraged, especially when I recall the self-described "radical Freudian" professor I had in my master's in social work program who described in glowingly approving terms high levels of sexual intimacy between children and each other and children and adults as "freeing and liberating" (that was the early 1970s).

However, if I look more closely at the worldview faith underlying much of the discussion of sexual abuse and its effects, the result is not quite so comforting to me as a Christian. The moral problem tends not to be defined in terms of a well-rounded biblical view of sexuality and God's creative design and purpose or an understanding of the problem of sin. Rather, it tends to be based on a more rationalistic and individualistic model of power and a model of justice that pins its faith on reason. Sexual abuse grows out of an inequity in power which a person rationally "ought not" exploit. Why not, one might ask.

But what if we take away the coercive element and get rid of the repressive "body-negative" ideas about sexual feelings? What if much or all of the negative effects of non-coercive sexual activity between adults and children is the result of the misguided and distorted social attitudes which are passed on to children and adults? Defenders of "non-exploitive" sexual activity between adults and children can (and do) argue that any negative consequences are purely a result of sex-negative social learning and attitudes. Representatives of a hypothetical group such as P.A.L. (Pedophiles Are Lovers!) would argue that what needs to be changed is not the "intergenerational sexual behavior," but the sexually repressive social values and behavior which teach children the negative responses. These values are seen as the oppressive culprits. Then, the argument might go, should we not bend our efforts to eradicating these repressive sexual values and attitudes rather than condemning potentially innocent acts of sexual pleasure? Indeed, why not, if the only problem is exploitation of power?

You should also note that this argument in favor of intergenerational sexual behavior is not exclusively scientific, objective, or based only on "facts." It has to make faith assumptions about the nature of persons, the nature of sexuality, the nature of health, and the nature of values. By the same token, my condemnation of adult sexual activity with children is based on faith assumptions about the nature of persons, sexuality, health, and values informed by my Christian worldview. It is never just "facts" alone that determine our perceptions, conclusions, and behavior.

Right now, it happens to be a "fact" that a fairly large consensus exists, even among secular social scientists and mental health professionals, that adult sexual activity with children is "bad" and that it leads quite regularly to negative consequences. Right now you could almost say this is something "everyone knows." But it would be a serious mistake to become complacent about this or to conclude that worldview beliefs and faith are not so important after all.

First, not everyone agrees. Although I invented the hypothetical group P.A.L. (Pedophiles Are Lovers), it represents real people and groups that do exist. The tip of this iceberg may be appearing in the professional literature where it is becoming more acceptable and common to see the "facts" reinterpreted. In preparing bibliography for a course on sexual issues in helping some time ago, I ran across a very interesting little shift in terminology in some of the professional literature. One article was entitled "Counterpoints: Intergenerational sexual experience or child sexual abuse" (Malz, 1989). A companion article was titled "Intergenerational sexual contact: A continuum model of participants and experiences" (Nelson, 1989). Words do make a difference.

Second, we shouldn't take too much comfort from the apparent agreement. It is sometimes built on a fragile foundation that could easily come apart. The fact that Christians find themselves in wholehearted agreement with many secular helping professionals, for example, that sexual activity between adults (usually male) and children (usually female) is exploitive and wrong may represent a temporary congruence on issues and strategy, much more so than fundamental agreement on the nature of persons and sexuality.

But back to the "Is-Ought" dilemma. The fact that some adults have sexual contact with children, by itself, tells us *nothing* about what, if anything, should be done about it. The facts can never answer those questions. The only way those questions can ever be answered is if we interpret the facts in terms of our faith, whatever that faith is. What is the nature of the world? What is the nature of persons? What is the meaning of sex? What constitutes health? What is the nature of justice? And most important—why should I care anyway?

Worldviews Help Define the Nature and Value of Persons

So—Worldviews Have Consequences

Your basic faith about the nature of the universe has consequences (and everyone, as we have seen, has some sort of faith). Faith is consequential to you personally, and the content of the faith is consequential. If it isn't *true* that Christ has been raised, my faith is worthless (I Corinthians 15:14). And if it's *true* that Christ has been raised, but I put my faith in Baal or the free market or the earth goddess (big in New England these days) or Karl Marx (not so big these days) or human reason, then *that* has consequences, to me and to others. What are we going to *trust*, bottom-line?

In I Corinthians 15, the apostle Paul said something about the importance of what we believe about the nature of the world, the *content* of our faith. He said, "Now if Christ is proclaimed as raised from the dead, how can some of you say there is no resurrection of the dead? If there is no resurrection of the dead, then Christ has not been raised; and if Christ has not been raised, then our proclamation has been in vain and your faith is also in vain … If Christ has not been raised, your faith is futile and you are still in your sins … If for this life only we have hoped in Christ, we are of all people most to be pitied" (12-14, 17, 19).

I've been a student, a professional social worker, and a teacher of social work long enough to see some major changes in "what everyone knows," in what is assumed or taken for granted. "What everyone knows" is in fact part of the underlying operational *faith* of a culture or subculture—whether it's Americans or teenagers or those who go to college or social workers — or Southern Baptists, for that matter.

When I went to college, logical positivism was king, a version of what C. S. Lewis called "naturalism," a kind of philosophical materialism. It said that the physical world is all there is. Everything is fully explainable by materialistic determinism. Only what can be physically measured or "operationalized" is real (or at least relevantly meaningful). In psychology it was epitomized in B. F. Skinner's behaviorism.

I remember as a somewhat bewildered freshman at Indiana University attending a lecture by a famous visiting philosophy professor (a logical positivist) from Cambridge University (whose name I have forgotten) entitled "The *Impossibility* of any Future Metaphysic" (his take-off on Kant's title "Prolegomena to any Future Metaphysic"). I can't say I understood it all at the time, but his main point was that modern people must permanently put away such meaningless and potentially dangerous ideas as spirituality, the supernatural, and any notion of values beyond subjective preferences. We now know, he said, that such language is meaningless (since not empirical) except, perhaps, to express our own subjective feelings.

In a graduate school course in counseling, I had an earnest young behaviorist professor who had, as a good behaviorist, trained (conditioned) himself to avoid all value statements that implied good or bad or anything beyond personal preference. When faced with a situation where someone else might be tempted to make a value statement, whether regarding spaghetti, rock and roll, or adultery, he had an ideologically correct response. He would, with a straight face, say, "I find that positively reinforcing" or, "I find that negatively reinforcing." (I don't know what his wife thought about this kind of response). Notice, he was saying "I" (who knows about you or anyone else) "find" (observe a response in myself at this moment; who knows about five minutes from now) "that" (a particular measurable stimulus) is "positively reinforcing" (it elicits this particular behavior now and might be predicted to do it again).

Above all, the idea was to be totally scientific, objective, and *value-free*. After all, values were perceived to be purely relative, personal preferences, or (worse) prejudices induced by social learning. And "everyone knew" that the only thing real was physical, measurable, and scientific. If we could only get the "facts" we would know what to do.

But this was, and is, a fundamental fallacy, the "Is-Ought" fallacy we discussed earlier. Even if facts are obtainable, they have no moral power or direction in themselves. If we say they mean something it is because we are interpreting them in the context of some values that are a part of our basic faith about the nature of the world.

Shifting Worldviews: The Emperor Has No Clothes

In the meantime we have seen some rather amazing shifts in "what everyone knows." I am old enough to have vivid memories of the 1960s and the "greening of America" when "everybody knew" that people under 30 were better than people over 30 and that human beings are so innately good all we had to do was to scrape off the social conventions and rules and then peace, love, and total sharing would rule the world. An astounding number of people truly believed that—for a short time.

In the '70s and early '80s "everybody knew" that personal autonomy and affluence are what it is all about. Power and looking out for Number One became the articles of faith, even for helping professionals like social workers. Maximum autonomy was the obvious highest good. Maturity and health were defined in terms of not needing anyone else (and not having any obligation to anyone else either). Fritz Perls "Gestalt Prayer" even got placed on romantic greeting cards:

> I do my thing, and you do your thing.
> I am not in this world to live up to your expectations.
> And you are not in this world to live up to mine.
> You are you and I am I,
> And if by chance we find each other, it's beautiful.
> If not, it can't be helped.

If you cared too much, you were labeled enmeshed, undifferentiated, or at the very least co-dependent.

And here we are in the 21st century and, at least for awhile, it looks as though values are in. *Time* magazine has had cover stories on ethics. We have had occasion to feel betrayed and outraged at the exposure of unethical behavior on the part of corporate executives, accountants, stock brokers, and especially government officials. Even more amazing, philosophy professors and social workers are not embarrassed to talk about values and even character again. "Family Values" are avowed by Republicans and Democrats. The books and articles are rolling off the presses.

But we should not be lulled into a false sense of security with this recovery of values and ethics, even if much of it sounds quite Christian to us. The philosophical paradigm has shifted to the opposite extreme, from the modern faith in the rational and empirical to the postmodern faith in the radically subjective and relative, the impossibility of getting beyond our ideological and cultural horizons. Our culture now despairs of any knowledge beyond the personal narratives we make up for ourselves out of the flotsam of our experience and fragments of disintegrating culture (Middleton & Walsh, 1995). Postmodernism says each person pieces together a personal story through which we make sense out of our lives, but there is no larger story (meta-narrative) which is really true in any meaningful sense and which can bind our personal stories together.

It is remarkable, as we have seen, how rapidly some of these assumptions can shift. The seeming consensus may be only skin-deep. More importantly, unless these values are grounded on something deeper than the currently fashionable paradigm (such as a Christian worldview), we can count on the fact that they will shift, or at least give way when they are seriously challenged. It's amazing how easy it is to see that the emperor has no clothes when a different way of looking is introduced to the scene. Remember, both enlightenment empiricism and postmodern subjectivity agree that values have no transcendent source.

What Is a "Person?"

Controversies regarding abortion and euthanasia illustrate the profound consequences of our worldview faith, especially for worldviews that deny that values have any ultimate source. Even more fundamental than the question of when life begins and ends is the question: What is a person? What constitutes being a person? What value, if any, is there in being a person? Are persons owed any particular rights, respect, or care? If so, why?

If your worldview says that persons are simply the result of matter plus time plus chance, it would seem that persons have no intrinsic value at all, no matter how they are defined.

From a purely materialist point of view, it may be interesting (to us) that the phenomena of human consciousness and agency have emerged which allow us in some measure to transcend simple biological, physical, and social determinism. These qualities might include the ability to be self-aware, to remember and to anticipate, to experience pleasure and pain, to develop caring relationships with others, to have purposes, to develop plans and take deliberate actions with consequences, and to have (at least the illusion of) choice. We may choose to define personhood as incorporating some of these characteristics. And we may even find it positively reinforcing (or not) to be persons. But then what? In this materialist worldview there are no inherent guidelines or limits regarding what we do to persons.

Do such persons have a right to life? Only to the extent it pleases us (whoever has the power) to say so. And what in the world could "right" mean in this context? But what if we do choose to say that persons have a right to life? What degree or quality of our defining characteristics do they have to have before they qualify? How self-conscious and reflective? How capable of choice and action?

It is common for people to argue today that babies aren't persons before they are born (or at least most of the time before they are born) and thus that there is no moral reason for not eliminating defective ones, or even just unwanted or inconvenient ones. And there are already those who argue that babies should not even be declared potential persons until they have lived long enough after birth to be tested and observed to determine their potential for normal growth and development, thus diminishing moral qualms about eliminating "wrongful births" (Singer, 1996). After all, what is magic about the birth process? Why not wait for a few hours, days, or weeks after birth to see if this "fetal material" is going to measure up to our standards of personhood? And at any point in life if our personhood fails to develop adequately or gets lost or seriously diminished through accident, illness, mental illness, or age, what then? Was my college acquaintance Ali right? Is it immoral to take resources from the productive and use them to support the unproductive? Do these "fetal products" or no-longer-persons need to be terminated?

A Solid Foundation

If I balk at these suggestions, it is because I have a worldview that gives a different perspective to the idea of what constitutes a person. I may agree, for example, that agency—the capacity to be self-aware, reflective, remember and anticipate, plan, choose, and responsibly act—is a central part of what it means to be a person. But I also believe that this is a gift from our creator God which in some way images God. I believe that our reflection, choice, and action have a divinely given purpose. This purpose is summarized in the ideas of finding and choosing God through grace and faith, of growing up into the image of Jesus Christ, of knowing and enjoying God forever. All of this says that persons have a special value beyond their utility to me (or anyone else) and that they are to be treated with the care and respect befitting their status as gifts from God. Even when something goes wrong.

Having a Christian worldview and knowing what the Bible says about God, the world, and the nature of persons doesn't always give us easy answers to all of our questions, however. And having faith in the resurrection of Jesus Christ doesn't guarantee that we will always be loving or just. But it does give us a foundation of stone to build our house on, a context to try to understand what we encounter that will not shift with every ideological or cultural season. I can assert the dignity and worth of every person based on a solid foundation, not just an irrational preference of my own or a culturally-induced bias that I might happen to have. What "everybody knows" is shifting sand. Even if it happens to be currently stated in the NASW Code of Ethics for social workers.

Some Basic Components of a Christian Worldview

Space does not permit me to develop a detailed discussion of the components of a Christian worldview here, but I would at least like to try to summarize in the most basic and simple terms what I perceive to be quite middle-of-the-road, historically orthodox, and biblical answers to the fundamental worldview questions I posed at the beginning (cf. Middleton & Walsh, 1995). This suggests the Christian worldview that has informed me and has been (I would hope) quite evident in what has been said. This little summary is not the end of reflection and application, but only the beginning.

1. *Where are we?* We are in a universe which was created by an eternal, omnipotent, just, loving, and gracious God. Consequently the universe has built-in meaning, purpose, direction, and values. The fundamental values of love and justice have an ultimate source in the nature of God which gives them meaning, authority, and content. The universe is both natural and supernatural.

2. *Who are we?* We are persons created "in the image God" and therefore have intrinsic meaning and value, regardless of our personal characteristics or achievements. Persons are both physical and spiritual. Persons

have been given the gift of "agency"—in a meaningful sense we have been given both freedom and responsibility. Persons created in the image of God are not just autonomous individuals but are relational-created to be in loving and just community with one another. Persons are objects of God's grace.

3. **What's wrong?** Oppression and injustice are evil, wrong, an affront to the nature and desire of God. Persons are finite and fallen—we are both limited in our capacities and distorted from our ideal purpose because of our selfishness and choice of evil. Our choice of selfishness and evil alienates us from God and from one another and sets up distortion in our perceptions, beliefs, and behavior, but we are not completely blind morally. Our self-centeredness makes us prone to seek solutions to our problems based on ourselves and our own abilities and accomplishments. We can't solve our problems by ourselves, either by denial or our own accomplishments.

4. **What's the remedy?** Stop trying to do it our way and accept the loving grace and provisions for healing that God has provided for us. God calls us to a high moral standard but knows that it is not in our reach to fulfill this standard completely. God's creative purpose is to bring good even out of evil, to redeem, heal, and grow us up—not by law but by grace. "For by grace you have been saved through faith, and this is not your own doing; it is the gift of God—not the result of works, so that no one may boast. For we are what he has made us, created in Christ Jesus for good works, which God prepared beforehand to be our way of life." (Ephesians 2:8-10)

Why Should I Care? Choosing a Christian Worldview

Moral Obligation and Faith: Materialism Undermines Moral Obligation

To abandon a theological basis of values, built into the universe by God, is ultimately to abandon the basis for any "oughts" in the sense of being morally bound other than for purely subjective or cultural reasons. Normative morality that is just descriptive and cultural ("This is what most people in our society tend to do"), subjective ("This is what I happen to prefer and do," or "It would be convenient for me if you would do this"), or utilitarian ("This is what works to achieve certain consequences") has no power of moral *obligation*.

Why should I care? On materialist or subjective grounds I "should" do this or that if I happen to feel like it or if I think it will help me get what I want. But this is using the word "should" in a far different and far more amoral sense than we ordinarily mean by it. It is a far different thing than saying I am *morally obligated or bound* to do it.

Many will argue that reason alone is enough to support moral obligation. This is the argument used by Frederic Reamer in his excellent book on social work ethics, *Ethical dilemmas in social services* (1990), based on Gewirth (*Reason and morality*, 1978). If, for example, I understand that freedom is logically required for human personal action, then this theory says I am logically obligated to support freedom for other persons as I desire it for myself. But I have never been able to buy the argument that reason alone creates any meaningful moral obligation for altruistic behavior. Why *should* I be logical, especially if being logical doesn't appear to work for my personal advantage? Any idea of moral obligation beyond the subjective and personally utilitarian seems to lead inevitably and necessarily to God in some form or to nowhere (Sherwood, 2007; Evans, 2004, 2006; Smith, 2003).

The "Method of Comparative Difficulties"

Although it is logically possible (and quite necessary if you believe in a materialist or postmodernist universe) to believe that values are only subjective preferences or cultural inventions, I have never been able to completely believe that is all our sense of values such as love and justice amounts to. There are, in all honesty, many obstacles in the way of belief in God as the transcendent source of values. But can we believe, when push comes to shove, that all values are either meaningless or totally subjective? Elton Trueblood calls this the "Method of Comparative Difficulties" (1963, p. 73; 1957, p. 13).

It may often be hard to believe in God, but I find it even harder to believe in the alternatives, especially when it comes to values. It's easy enough to say that this or that value is only subjective or culturally relative, but when we get pushed into a corner, most of us find ourselves saying (or at least *feeling*), "No, *that* (say, the Holocaust) is really wrong and it's not just my opinion." (Cf. C. S. Lewis, "Right and Wrong As a Clue to the Meaning of the Universe," *Mere Christianity*, 1948)

Dostoevski expressed the idea that if there is no God, all things are permissible.

C. S. Lewis (1947, pp. 77-78) said that "When all that says 'it is good' has been debunked, what says 'I want' remains. It cannot be exploded or 'seen through' because it never had any pretensions." Lust remains after values have been explained away. Values that withstand the explaining away process are the only ones that will do us any good. Lewis concludes *The abolition of man* (1947, p. 91):

> You cannot go on "explaining away" forever: you will find that you have explained explanation itself away. You cannot go on "seeing through" things forever. The whole point of seeing through something is to see something through it. It is good that the window should be transparent, because the street or garden beyond it is opaque. How if you saw through the garden too? It is no use trying to "see through" first principles. If you see through everything, then everything is transparent. But a wholly transparent world is an invisible world. To "see through" all things is the same as not to see.

Looking for Christian Implications

A Christian worldview is not going to give us simple answers to all of our questions. It is not as though there is a simple translation of Christian values and principles into practice implications, or that there is a unitary "Christian" version of every human activity from French cooking to volleyball to politics.

Even though we may agree on fundamental values and principles, such as love and justice, as fallen and finite human beings, the more specific we get in terms of translating love and justice into particular attempts to solve concrete problems the more we are likely to honestly and conscientiously disagree with one another in our interpretation of what the problem is or what, in fact, might actually do more good than harm in attempting to deal with it (Sherwood, 1999).

I assume, for example, that if we are Christians and we have read the Bible, we have been impressed with our obligation to work for social justice and to help the poor. But what are the causes of poverty and what can we do to help the poor that will do more good than harm? Not simple and not obvious.

May I be so bold as to say that there is *no* simple, single "Christian" answer to those questions? We are going to be working to deal with poverty (and conscientiously disagreeing about how to do it) until Jesus returns. And I will submit that there is *no* policy or program to help the poor, individually or collectively, privately or publicly that will not *advance some* of the legitimate values that we have at the *risk or cost of some* of our other legitimate values.

So, everything we do will be a compromise of sorts and will need to be adapted as much as possible to the unique situation. But what we do needs to be an imperfect solution shaped both by our Christian faith and by our professional social work values, knowledge, and skills.

A Christian perspective is not always totally unique or different in every respect from what another perspective might offer, but it always informs and critiques these perspectives. An example from social work is the NASW Code of Ethics. Even some Christian social workers may be laboring under the impression that it somehow contradicts Christian values. Far from it. Anyone who has this impression should take a closer look at the Code of Ethics. There is no principle in the Code that a Christian cannot strongly affirm. In fact, I would argue that a Christian worldview is quite compatible with the social work Code of Ethics, and in fact is the soil out of which much of the Code has sprung (Sherwood, 2000, 2002, 2007).

As we have discussed before, one of the core social work values in the Code is the inherent dignity and value of every person. Now, what in modernism or postmodernism gives such a value ground to stand on and to claim obligation over us? Not much. When push comes to shove, the inherent dignity and value of every person is pretty hard to sustain under assumptions of relativism, subjectivism, material determinism, and survival of the fittest.

At the same time that a Christian worldview upholds this core social work value, it also informs and critiques it. For example, a Christian perspective might say that individual freedom is not the only or necessarily always the highest value when legitimate values come into tension with each other in a given situation. The good of others and the community (deriving from both love and justice) has a powerful moral claim in every situation. Yet individual freedom tends to be granted privileged status in most social work ethical thinking.

So, not all social workers, Christian or otherwise, will necessarily agree on how to prioritize legitimate values when they come into conflict with one another, which they inevitably do in complex cases. One of the admirable virtues of the current Code of Ethics is its clear recognition in the preamble and throughout that legitimate values *do* come into tension with one another in actual practice situations, that professional judgment will *always* be required to prioritize them, and that conscientious and competent professionals will *not always* be in agreement.

Furthermore (given the hermeneutical spiral), it must be remembered that other perspectives may inform and critique our Christian perspectives. Many contemporary Christians seem to need to be reminded, for example, that individual peace and prosperity do not necessarily rank high in the list of biblical virtues compared to sacrifice for the common good (Sherwood, 1999).

Seeing Through a Mirror Dimly: Real Values But Only a Limited, Distorted View

So, I believe in God as the ultimate source and authenticator of values. I believe that real values exist beyond myself. And I believe these values put us under real moral obligation. To believe otherwise, it seems to me, ultimately makes values and moral obligation empty shells, subjective and utilitarian, with no real life or content. It may be true that this is all values are, but I find it very hard to believe. Belief in a value-less world, or one with only "human" (that is to say, purely subjective) values, takes more faith for me than belief in God.

But (and this is very important) this understanding of values as having ultimate truth and deriving from God is a very far cry from believing that I fully comprehend these values and the specific moral obligations they put me under in the face of a particular moral dilemma when these values come into tension with one another and priorities have to be made. Much humility is required here, an appropriate balance. At any given moment, my (or your) understanding of these values and what our moral obligations are is very limited and distorted. In fact our understandings are in many ways subjective, culturally relative, and bounded by the interpretive "language" available to us. And any particular place where I can stand to view a complex reality at best only yields a partial view of the whole. Remember the story of the blind men and the elephant ("It's like a snake," "It's like a wall," "It's like a tree").

We can see, but only dimly. God has given us light but we will only be able to see completely when we meet God face to face (I Corinthians 13:8-13). In the meantime we are on a journey. We are pilgrims, but we are not wandering alone and without guidance. We see through a mirror dimly, but there is something to see. There is a garden beyond the window.

Love never ends. But as for prophecies, they will come to an end; as for tongues, they will cease; as for knowledge, it will come to an end. For we know only in part, and we prophesy only in part; but when the complete comes, the partial will come to an end. When I was a child, I spoke like a child, I thought like a child, I reasoned like a child; when I became an adult, I put an end to childish ways. For now we see in a mirror, dimly, but then we will see face to face. Now I know only in part; then I will know fully, even as I have been fully known. And now faith, hope, love abide, these three; and the greatest of these is love. (I Corinthians 13:8-13)

Now we have received not the spirit of the world, but the Spirit that is from God, so that we may understand the gifts bestowed on us by God. And we speak of these things in words not taught by human wisdom but taught by the Spirit, interpreting spiritual things to those who are spiritual. Those who are unspiritual do not receive the gifts of God's Spirit, for they are foolishness to them, and they are not able to understand them because they are spiritually discerned. Those who are spiritual discern all things, but they are themselves subject to no one else's scrutiny. "For who has known the mind of the Lord so as to instruct him?" But we have the mind of Christ. (I Corinthians 2:12-16)

Now the Lord is the Spirit, and where the Spirit of the Lord is, there is freedom. And all of us, with unveiled faces, seeing the glory of the Lord as though reflected in a mirror, are being transformed into the same image from one degree of glory to another; for this comes from the Lord, the Spirit. (II Corinthians 3:17-18)

References

Evans, C. S. (2004). *Kierkegaard's ethic of love: Divine commands and moral obligations.* New York: Oxford University Press.

Evans, C. S. (2006). Is there a basis for loving all people? *Journal of Psychology and Theology, 34*(1), 78-90.

Gewirth, A. (1978). *Reason and morality.* Chicago: University of Chicago Press.

Holmes, A. (1984). *Ethics: Approaching moral decisions.* Downers Grove, IL: InterVarsity Press.

Lebacqz, K. (1986). *Six theories of justice: Perspectives from philosophical and theological ethics.* Minneapolis, MN: Augsburg Publishing House.

Lewis, C. S. (1947). *The abolition of man.* New York: Macmillan Publishing Company.

Lewis, C. S. (1948). *Mere Christianity.* New York: Macmillan Publishing Company.

Malz, Wendy. (1989). Counterpoints: Intergenerational sexual experience or child sexual abuse. *Journal of Sex Education and Therapy, 15,* 13-15.

Middleton, J. R., & Walsh, B. J. (1995). *Truth is stranger than it used to be: Biblical faith in a post-modern age.* Downers Grove, IL: InterVarsity Press.

Mott, S. (1982). *Biblical ethics and social change.* New York: Oxford University Press.

Nelson, J. A. (1989). Intergenerational sexual contact: A continuum model of participants and experiences. *Journal of Sex Education and Therapy, 15,* 3-12.

Osborne, G. R. (1991). *The hermeneutical spiral: A comprehensive introduction to biblical interpretation.* Downers Grove, IL: InterVarsity Press.

Reamer, F. G. (1990). *Ethical dilemmas in social service* (2nd Ed). New York: Columbia University Press.

Sherwood, D. A. (1993). Doing the right thing: Ethical practice in contemporary society. *Social Work & Christianity, 20*(2), 140-159.

Sherwood, D. A. (1999). Integrating Christian faith and social work: Reflections of a social work educator. *Social Work & Christianity, 26*(1), 1-8.

Sherwood, D. A. (2000). Pluralism, tolerance, and respect for diversity: Engaging our deepest differences within the bond of civility. *Social Work & Christianity, 27*(1), 1-7.

Sherwood, D. A. (2002). Ethical integration of faith and social work practice: Evangelism. *Social Work & Christianity, 29*(1), 1-12.

Sherwood, D. A. (2007). Moral, believing social workers: Philosophical and theological foundations of moral obligation in social work ethics. *Social Work & Christianity, 34*(2), 121-145.

Singer, P. (1996). *Rethinking life and death: The collapse of our traditional ethics.* New York: St. Martin's Press.

Smith, C. (2003). Moral, believing animals: Human personhood and culture. New York: Oxford University Press.

Trueblood, D. E. (1963). *General philosophy.* New York: Harper and Row.

Trueblood, D. E. (1957). *Philosophy of religion.* New York: Harper and Row.

Wolterstorff, N. (1983). *When justice and peace embrace.* Grand Rapids, MI: Eerdmans Publishing Company.

Wolterstorff, N. (2006). Justice, not charity: Social work through the eyes of faith. *Social Work & Christianity, 33*(2), 123-140.

Wood, W. J. (1998). *Epistemology: Becoming intellectually virtuous.* Downers Grove, IL: InterVarsity Press.

CHAPTER 7

CALLING: A SPIRITUALITY PERSPECTIVE FOR SOCIAL WORK PRACTICE

Beryl Hugen

In making a career choice, many Christian students find the social work profession a good fit with their religious faith. Or at least at first glance it appears so. For example, as part of the application process for the social work program I teach in, students are asked to explain why they have chosen social work as a major. What motivates them to enter this field of study? Some answer the question by relating past experiences with social work services or role models who were social workers, but almost all describe a moderate or fairly strong religious impulse to serve people and society.

Many specifically relate their faith to their choice of social work—stating something like this: In being loved by God, they in turn wish to share some of this love with those who are poor or hurting or are in need of help of some kind. Some of these students believe that to be a Christian in social work they must work in an agency under religious auspices, whereas others plan to work in programs that do not have a specific religious base or affiliation, but are part of the larger community of governmental social welfare responses to those in need. Despite these differences, almost all are interested in finding ways to integrate their faith and their newly chosen field of study.

But it doesn't take long in their social work studies for these students to begin to recognize the complex tensions between their religious faith, agency auspices, and the secular values of the social work profession. This discovery is not surprising; social work is, after all, a secular profession. At times, students find the profession very critical of religion, even suspicious of anyone who claims to have religious motives for helping others.

This feeling is understandable, for in the last forty to fifty years, the social work profession has simply ignored religious insights and accepted the principle of separating the sacred and secular. Religion came to be seen as having no particular insight to offer or relevance for everyday professional practice. Because of this attitude, the recent professional literature does not offer much help to students in thinking through the relationship of religious faith and professional practice. It is ironic that social work, which claims as its unique focus the "whole person" in the whole environment, has for so long neglected the religious dimension of life.

Not only do students continue to come to the profession with religious motivations, but the roots of social work are largely grounded in religious faith

(Devine, 1939). Social work originated and came of age under the inspiration of the Judeo-Christian traditions and the philanthropic and service motivation of religious people. As Leiby (1985) indicates, the Christian biblical command to love God and to love one's neighbor as oneself was directly translated into a sense of moral responsibility for social service. As the social work profession secularized in the 20th century, these earlier religious rationales and models for service were replaced by doctrines of natural rights, utilitarianism, and humanistic ideology.

Dealing with human need apart from religious motives and methods is actually a very recent development in the history of charity and philanthropy. The notion of a secular profession focused on responding to human suffering would have struck many of our professional ancestors as quite inconsistent and confusing. Many of them were religiously motivated and expressed their faith by means of social work as a vocation, a calling from God to serve their brothers and sisters who were in need. With their perception of social work as a calling, a vocation, they formalized a link between their religious faith and social work practice.

What is meant by viewing social work as a calling? Several recent articles have addressed this "old fashioned" concept of calling or vocation, sensing its power and value for current social work practice (Gustafson,1982; Reamer, 1992). However, these writers essentially have attempted to take the religious concept of calling and use it in a secular fashion. They have done so in order to provide a moral purpose for the profession—to counteract what they perceive to be the focus on self-interest inherent in the social work profession which has become increasingly professionalized, specialized and bureaucratic.

My intent in this chapter is to explain, or more accurately to reintroduce, the religious model of calling as used by Christian social workers, past and present, in linking Christian faith and professional social work practice. Both its attractiveness and shortcomings as a model will be addressed. My purpose is not only to help social workers and the profession understand or correct misunderstandings related to this model, but also help social workers better understand the broader issues related to the spirituality of social work practice, in that other religious models and spiritual traditions address many of the same integration of faith and practice questions. Also, reintroducing the model of calling will lead us to see the significance of how the perspectives and writings of our religiously motivated social work ancestors—of which there are many— can contribute to the profession's current discussions regarding spirituality and social work practice.

Religion, Faith, and Spirituality

Before discussing the model of calling, it is helpful to define what is meant by the terms spirituality, religion, belief and faith. The profession has long struggled with this definitional dilemma. The dilemma has focused on how to reintroduce religious or spiritual concerns into a profession which has expanded beyond specific sectarian settings and ideologies to now include diverse sources of knowledge, values and skills, and how to respond to the needs of a much more spiritually diverse clientele. Addressing this dilemma, Siporin (1985) and Brower (1984) advocated for an understanding of spirituality that includes a wide diversity of religious and non-religious expressions, with such an inclusive understanding of spirituality encouraging social workers to reflect upon their clients. both within and outside of particular institutional religious settings and ideologies.

From this beginning, Canda (1988a, 1988b) further developed a concept of spirituality for social work that incorporates insights from diverse religious and philosophical perspectives. He identifies three content components to spirituality—values, beliefs and practice issues—"all serving the central dynamic of a person's search for a sense of meaning and purpose, developed in the context of interdependent relationships between self, other people, the nonhuman world, and the ground of being itself" (Canda, 1988a, p. 43).

In the same vein, the work of James Fowler, known more for his model of faith development, is particularly instructive. Fowler (1981) states that to understand the "human quest for relation to transcendence," the key phenomenon to examine is not religion or belief, but faith (p. 14). According to Fowler, who draws upon the ideas of religionist Wilfred Smith, *religions* are "cumulative traditions," which represent the expressions of faith of people in the past (p. 9). Included in a cumulative tradition are such elements as "texts of scripture, oral traditions, music, creeds, theologies," and so forth. *Belief* refers to "the holding of certain ideas" or "assent to a set of propositions" (p. 13). *Faith* differs from both religion and belief. Fowler describes faith as a commitment, "an alignment of the will...in accordance with a vision of transcendent value and power, one's ultimate concern" (p. 14). One commits oneself to that which is known or acknowledged and lives loyally, with life and character being shaped by that commitment. Defined in this way, faith is believed to be a universal feature of human living, recognizably similar everywhere, and in all major religious traditions.

What does faith consist of then? Fowler describes three components of what he calls the contents of faith. The first he terms *centers of value*, the "causes, concerns, or persons that consciously or unconsciously have the greatest worth to us." These are what we worship, things that "give our lives meaning" (p. 277). The second component of faith is described as our *images of power*, "the power with which we align ourselves to sustain us in the midst of life's contingencies" (p. 277): these powers need not necessarily be supernatural or transcendent. Finally, faith is comprised of "the *master stories* that we tell ourselves and by which we interpret and respond to the events that impinge upon our lives." Essentially, our master stories reveal what we believe to be the fundamental truths, "the central premises of [our] sense of life's meaning" (p. 277).

In discussing spirituality and faith, Fowler and Canda both emphasize its pervasive, all encompassing nature in an individual's life. Faith or spirituality is not a separate dimension of life or compartmentalized specialty, but rather an orientation of the total person. Accordingly, the three components of faith—

centers of value, images of power, and master stories (Fowler, 1981)—and spirituality—values, beliefs, and practices (Canda, 1988a)—exert "structuring power" in our lives, shaping our characters and actions in the world, including our work. Faith and spirituality are defined here as the essence of religion. Faith and spirituality take on a Christian religious meaning when the centers of value, images of power, and master stories of one's faith, the central dynamic of one's search for a sense of meaning and purpose, are grounded in the creeds, texts of scripture, and theology of the Christian tradition. I will attempt to present the Christian religious concept of calling within these more inclusive frameworks of spirituality and faith.

Calling in Action

Perhaps the best way to develop an understanding of the religious concept of calling is to start with an illustration. Robert Coles, in his book *The Call to Service* (1993), tells of a six year old black girl who initiated school desegregation in the South in the early 1960s. Tessie, a first grader, each day facing an angry and threatening mob, was escorted by federal marshals to school. The mob almost always greeted her with a litany of obscenities. Tessie's maternal grandmother, Martha, was the family member who usually got Tessie up and off to school each morning.

Coles reports that one day Tessie was reluctant to go to school— claiming to feeling tired, having slipped and fallen while playing in a nearby back yard, and having a difficult time with a current substitute teacher. Tessie suggested to her grandmother that she might stay home that day. Her grandmother replied that that would be fine if Tessie truly wasn't well, but if she was more discouraged than sick, that was quite another matter. She goes on to say:

> It's no picnic, child—I know that, Tessie—going to that school. Lord Almighty, if I could just go with you, and stop there in front of that building, and call all those people to my side, and read to them from the Bible, and tell them, remind them that He's up there, Jesus, watching over all of us—it don't matter who you are and what your skin color is. But I stay here, and you go—and your momma and your daddy, they have to leave the house so early in the morning that it's only Saturdays and Sundays that they see you before the sun hits the middle of its traveling for the day. So I'm not the one to tell you that you should go, because here I am, and I'll be watching television and eating or cleaning things up while you're walking by those folks. But I'll tell you, you're doing them a great favor; you're doing them a service, a big service.
>
> You see, my child, you have to help the good Lord with His world! He puts us here—and He calls us to help Him out. You belong in that McDonogh School, and there will be a day when everyone knows that, even those poor folks—Lord, I pray for

them!—those poor, poor folks who are out there shouting their heads off at you. You're one of the Lord's people; He's put His Hand on you. He's given a call to you, a call to service—in His name! There's all those people out there on the street (pp. 3-4).

Later Coles questions Tessie whether she understood what her grandmother meant by "how you should be of service to those people out there on the street." She replied:

If you just keep your eyes on what you're supposed to be doing, then you'll get there—to where you want to go. The marshals say, 'Don't look at them; just walk with your head up high, and you're looking straight ahead.' My granny says that there's God, He's looking too, and I should remember that it's a help to Him to do this, what I'm doing; and if you serve Him, then that's important. So I keep trying (pp. 4-5).

The heart of what Tessie had learned was that for her, service meant serving, and not only on behalf of those she knew and liked or wanted to like. Service meant an alliance with the Lord Himself for the benefit of people who were obviously unfriendly. Service was not an avocation or something done to fulfill a psychological need, not even an action that would earn her any great reward. She had connected a moment in her life with a larger ideal, and in so doing had learned to regard herself as a servant, as a person called to serve. It was a rationale for a life, a pronouncement with enormous moral and emotional significance for Tessie and her grandmother. This call was nurtured by the larger black community, her pastor, family, and the biblical values of love and justice—the stories of exile and return, of suffering and redemption—the view of the powerful as suspect and the lowly as destined to sit close to God, in His Kingdom.

Coles himself recounts how ill-prepared professionally he was to understand this family and their sense of calling:

I don't believe I could have understood Tessie and her family's capacity to live as they did, do as they did for so long, against such great odds, had I not begun to hear what *they* were saying and meaning, what *they* intended others to know about their reasons and values—as opposed to the motivations and reactions and "mechanisms of defense" *I* attributed to them. Not that there wasn't much to be learned by a psychoanalytic approach. Tessie and her companions, like human beings everywhere (including those who study or treat other human beings), most certainly did demonstrate fearfulness and anxiety; she also tried to subdue those developments by not acknowledging them, for instance, or by belittling their significance. Mostly, though, she clung hard to a way of thinking in which she was *not* a victim, *not* in need of "help" but someone picked by fate to live out the Christian tradition in her life. "I'm trying to think of the way Jesus would want me to think," she told me one evening. When I asked how she thought Jesus wanted her to think, she replied, "I guess of others, and not myself, I'm here to help the others" (p. 26).

Calling: The Meaning of Work

For some Christians, like Tessie and her grandmother, connecting one's work to the divine intentions for human life gives another dimension to the meaning and purpose of one's work and life. Certainly adequate pay, financial stability, social status and a sense of personal fulfillment remain significant criteria in choosing a career, but they are not the central motivation. The central motivation is the means by which one's Christian religious tradition has tied one's work and faith together, this concept of vocation, or calling.

Martin Luther originally formulated the notion of vocation or calling largely in reaction to the prevailing attitude toward work in medieval society. Medieval thinkers devalued work. They believed that in and of itself, work had little or no spiritual significance. They held, like the Greeks earlier, to the idea that the highest form of life, the form in which humans can realize their noblest potential, is the contemplative life of the mind. By thinking, we liken ourselves to God. Work was thus a hindrance to an individual's relation to God, which could be cultivated only in the leisure of contemplation. Because peasant serfs did most of the work in medieval society, and because the earthly character of their occupations prevented them from participating directly in the religious life, they received grace through the church by means of the sacraments.

Not only the life of productive work, but also the practical or active life, consisting of doing good to one's neighbor, was viewed by many medievals as an impediment to the true goals of the religious life. The activity given precedence was always the contemplative life. An early church father, St. Augustine (1950) wrote: "the obligations of charity make us undertake virtuous activity, but if no one lays this burden upon us, we should give ourselves over in leisure to study and contemplation" (p. 19). The need for the active or charitable life was temporary, whereas contemplation of God was eternal.

Luther's concept of vocation or calling fits neatly within the compass of this thought since he draws a basic theological distinction between the kingdom of heaven and the kingdom of earth. To the kingdom of heaven belongs our relationship to God, which is to be based on faith; to the kingdom of earth belongs our relationship to our neighbor, which is to be based on love. A vocation, properly speaking, is the call to love my neighbor that comes to me through the duties attached to my social place or *station* within the earthly kingdom. A station in this life may be a matter of paid employment, but it need not be. Luther's idea of station is wide enough to include being a wife or a husband, a mother or a father, a judge or politician, as well as a baker, truck driver, farmer or social worker. Thus, the call to love one's neighbor goes out to all in general. All of these callings represent specific and concrete ways of serving my neighbor, as I am commanded to do by God Himself.

What do we accomplish when we discharge the duties of our stations in life, when we heed the call of God to serve our neighbor in our daily tasks? Luther believed the order of stations in the kingdom of earth has been instituted by God Himself as His way of seeing to it that the needs of humanity are met on a day-by-day basis. Through the human pursuit of vocations across the array of earthly stations, the hungry are fed, the naked are clothed, the sick are healed, the ignorant are enlightened, and the weak are protected. That is, by working we actually participate in God's providence for the human race. Through our work, people are brought under His providential care. Far from being of little or no account, work is charged with religious significance. As we pray each morning for our daily bread, people are already busy at work in the bakeries.

Luther conceived of work as a way of serving others. He never recommended it as either the road to self-fulfillment or a tool for self-aggrandizement. We, of course, find it natural to assess the attractiveness of a particular job on the basis of what it can do for us. But Luther saw quite clearly that work will always involve a degree of self-sacrifice for the sake of others, just as Christ sacrificed himself for the sake of others.

During the time of Luther, and for many centuries preceding him, people thought of human society to be stable, static, and as incapable of change, as the order of nature itself. Shortly after Luther's time, however, European civilization underwent a dramatic transformation under the combined influence of a rapidly expanding market economy, accelerated urbanization, technological innovation, and vast political reorganization. In the face of these astounding changes on all fronts of social life, people soon saw that the structure of human society is itself in part a product of human activity, changeable and affected by sin. Once people recognized this fact, it became clear, in turn, that to the degree human activity is motivated by sinful desires and worldly ambitions, the society thus produced is also likely to be structurally unsound and in need of reform. For example, an economy based upon greed and a government based on the arbitrary use of power stand in just as much need of repentance as the individuals who are a part of them. For this reason, other reformers insisted that not only the human heart, but also human society must be reformed in accordance with the Word of God. The emergent vision of the Christian life at the dawn of modern social work practice, then, required not only that people obey God in their callings, but that the callings themselves be aligned with the will of God.

Calling Within Social Work

Although historically there have been many models of spirituality in social work, the calling model perhaps has been the most prominent, or at least the most extensively referred to in the social work literature. In fact, in the very early years, it was the dominant model. This dominance is certainly related to the fact that Protestantism was the dominant religious form at the time. Many early social workers in their writings refer to the relationship of their spirituality and social work within this calling model. Their response is not surprising, since many of them grew up in devoted religious families, many had theological training, and still others were very active as lay people in their churches. All found in their spiritual experiences something which gave impetus, meaning, and value to their work of service.

The following examples illustrate the prominence of the calling model and how it has been articulated and practiced by a variety of different leaders within the profession.

Edward Devine, a leader in the Charity Organization Society and the first director of one of the first schools of social work, records in his book *When Social Work Was Young* (1939) the early experiences in social work education and summarizes these experiences as follows:

> The real start towards the professional education of social workers as such was made in 1898, when the Society launched its summer school of philanthropy with thirty students enrolled.
> For several years this summer school gathered from all parts of the country a substantial number of promising candidates, and a brilliant corps of instructors, who for one day, or sometimes for an entire week, expounded and discussed the fundamentals of the slowly emerging profession. Jane Addams, Mary Richmond, Zilpha Smith, Mrs. Glendower Evans, Graham Taylor, Jeffrey Brackett, John M. Glenn, Mary Willcox Brown, before and also after she became Mrs. John M. Glenn, James B. Reynolds, Mary Simkhovitch—a full roster of the lecturers in the school would be like a list of the notables in the National Conference of Social Work. Certainly no religious gathering could have a deeper consecration to that ideal of learning how to do justly, and to love mercy, and to walk humbly, which Micah described as being all that is required of us (pp. 125-6).

He ends the book by stating that in his opinion the spirit of social work finds its power, value, and purpose from the biblical Sermon on the Mount.

Richard Cabot (1927) addressed the model of calling more specifically in an article entitled "The Inter-Relation of Social Work and the Spiritual Life." He writes:

> religion is the consciousness of a world purpose to which we are allied...when I speak of the purpose being a personality, I speak of the person of God of whom we are children... I think it makes absolutely all the difference in social work to know this fact of our alliance with forces greater than ourselves. If a person wants to find himself and be somebody he has got to find his particular place in the universal plan. In social work, we are trying to help people find themselves, find their places and enjoy them. The chief end of man is to glorify God and to enjoy Him forever (p. 212).

Cabot also articulated several spiritual powers applicable to social work practice that come to those who hold this faith: courage, humility and the ability to stand by people. He goes on to explain that the goal of social work is to:

> ...maintain and to improve the channels of understanding both within each person and between persons, and through these channels to favor the entrance of God's powers for the benefit of the individuals.... Unblocking channels is what social workers do. The sort of unblocking that I have in mind is that between capital and labor, between races, or between the members of a family who think they hate each other.... Spiritual diagnosis, I suppose, means nothing more than the glimpse of the central purpose of the person, unique and related to the total parts of the world. Spiritual treatment, I suppose, is the attempt to open channels, the channels I have been speaking of, so as to favor the working of the world purpose. In this way social workers participate in the providence of God (pp. 215-16).

Perhaps the most prominent example of the power and dominance of the calling model is illustrated in Owen R. Lovejoy's presidential address to the National Conference of Social Work in 1920, entitled "The Faith of a Social Worker." In the speech he attempts to draw upon the foundations of faith of the members in order to aid in their approach to discussions during the Conference and to help create a real basis for unity. He begins by first disclaiming any intention of committing the Conference to any specific creed of social service. His desire, rather, is to discover "some of the those underlying principles which bind people together."

He states that all social workers have a philosophy of life, a faith, a "basic enthusiasm," and those who act on this faith can choose to:

> regard this as a sacred ministry and claim their commission as the ancient prophet claimed his when he said: "The Lord hath anointed me to preach good tidings to the meek, to bind up the broken hearted, to proclaim liberty to the captives, the opening of prison to them that are bound, to give a garland for ashes, the oil of joy for mourning, the garment of praise for the spirit of heaviness." Certainly this is not a slight task to which we are called, but the expression of a joyful faith carried with cheerfulness to those in the world most in need of it...a field of service based on the conviction that men are warranted in working for something corresponding to a divine order "on earth as it is in heaven (p. 209).

He warns those "who look upon the visible institutions connected with their religion as the essential embodiment of faith," recognizing such a sectarian position frequently leads to imposing one's own values on others and proselytizing—similar issues we face today. He ends the address stating that the secret of their usefulness as social workers is found in the following litany.

God is a Father,
Man is a brother,
Life is a mission and not a career;
Dominion is service,
Its scepter is gladness,
The least is the greatest,
Saving is dying,
Giving is living,
Life is eternal and love is its crown (p. 211).

It is difficult to imagine an address on such a topic being given today. Such was the significance of spirituality and the calling model in the social work profession at that time.

The calling model's chief apologist, however, was Ernest Johnson, a prolific writer and interpreter of Protestant religion and the social work profession. His writings detail the principles which he hoped would govern efforts to bring Protestantism to bear through the social work profession in meeting human needs. Recognizing that Protestantism had a majority position and influence in the culture, he strongly advocated, with some exceptions, for a pattern of social work based on the calling model. The result was to minimize the operation and control of agencies and social welfare enterprises by churches or religious groups and maximize Protestant participation in non-sectarian agencies.

Later in life he recognized that Protestantism, particularly when its pre-eminent position was beginning to wane, would never obtain complete cultural dominance or create an approximation to the ideal of a Christian society—the Corpus Christianum. The result, he lamented, would be only a partial trans-formation of the culture—and regrettably, a partial accommodation on the part of Protestantism to the culture. But despite this limitation, he still believed the Protestant pattern or model of influencing social work enterprises and social movements "indirectly" (through the means of one's calling or vocation) was essentially sound. Johnson (1946) states:

It [the calling model] affords the most effective channel through which our churches, in the midst of a religiously heterogeneous population, can bring to bear their testimony through community endeavor and make their impact on a secular culture. This means, however, a recovery of the sense of lay Christian vocation, which has been so largely lost. The major Protestant contribution to social work can be made, I believe, through the consciously Christian activities of persons engaged in non-sectarian enterprises and movements. In the existing situation in America a revival of a sec-tarian, possessive attitude toward social work would be definitely reactionary....

In a word, then, we need to devise our social strategy in the light of our Protestant history, with its emphasis on freedom, and in the light of our cultural situation, which puts a premium on vocational work as Christian testimony. We can make our best contribution without seeking to enhance Protestant prestige, seeking rather to influence contemporary life and to meet human need through the activities of those whose lives have been kindled at our altars and nourished in our fellowship (pp. 2-4).

As Johnson relates, the calling model has not always functioned as intended. Already in 1893, one leader of the new social work profession, responding to the widening gap between religion and the emerging influence of scientific models in social work, characterized social work as "a revolutionary turning of thought in our society from a religious service to God to a secular service to humanity" (Huntington, 1893). Along this line of thought, Protestant theologian Reinhold Niebuhr (1932) grappled with the practical consequences of the calling model for social work. With three-fourths of social workers then functioning under secular auspices, many had become "inclined to disregard religion." This development he regarded as a significant loss for social work—"destroying or remaining oblivious to powerful resources and losing the insights religion provided in keeping wholesome attitudes toward individuals" and "preserving the sanity and health in the social worker's own outlook upon life" (p. 9). He believed social workers needed, therefore, a renewed sense of vocation or calling. In addition, this loss of calling partially contributes to what church historian Martin Marty (1980) later referred to as "godless social service," or the migration (privatization) of faith or spirituality from social work.

Conclusion

Because of our distance from the thoughts and assumptions of our predecessors in social work and perhaps from the language of spirituality itself, efforts regarding such historical reflections as these may seem awkward and archaic. The goal is not, however, to recreate the past, but rather to identify the models of spirituality that guided our social work ancestors and then to find ways to translate and apply the spirit of these models to our present situation.

This model of calling offers significant insight into current discussions relating spirituality and professional social work practice. Within this calling model, religious faith is not the private possession of an individual, but is grounded in tradition and divine revelation, permeating the whole of life, connecting public and private spheres, and linking the individual with the community. The model also places professional techniques and methods in the context of larger goals and values that give life meaning and purpose for both clients and practitioners.

Historically, religiously motivated persons and groups found their faith propelling them into actions of concern for others, especially the poor and the vulnerable in society. These social workers have affirmed in a variety of ways their shared belief that the faith dimension of life leads to a transcendence of individualism, and to a commitment to others—to social work practice motivated by a calling to a life of service.

The model presented is helpful to social workers from the Christian faith tradition, but also to others who seek to acquire a better understanding of the meaning and effects of spirituality in their own and their clients' lives. A social worker's own cultivation of spirituality is a crucial preparation for the competent application of knowledge and skills in practice. The model is particularly helpful in taking into account the distinctive values, sources of power and master stories of one particular religious and cultural tradition, Christianity—represented by many persons like Tessie and her grandmother whom social workers daily encounter in practice, as well as by many social workers themselves.

Although the model does not resolve the tensions and conflicts which exist between the Christian spiritual tradition and the current largely secular profession, it does provide a beginning framework for integrating Christian spirituality and social work at both the personal and professional levels. The profession's roots are significantly tied to this particular model of spiritual/professional integration, and many social workers as well as clients continue to define their lives, personally and professionally, in the context of this Christian-based spiritual call to service. The Christian values of love, justice, and kindness; its stories related to the poor, the vulnerable, and those of liberation from oppression; and its emphasis on self-sacrifice, are the "passion of the old time social workers" that many find attractive and wish to bring back—albeit in a form more adaptable to a more diverse clientele and changed environment (Constable, 1983; Gustafson, 1982; Reamer, 1992; Siporin, 1982, 1985; Specht & Courtney, 1994).

References

Augustine, St. (1950). *City of God.* XIX, 19, New York: Modern Library.

Brower, I. (1984). *The 4th ear of the spiritual-sensitive social worker.* Ph.D. diss., Union for Experimenting Colleges and Universities.

Cabot, R. C. (1927). The inter-relation of social work and the spiritual life. *The Family,* 8(7), 211-217.

Canda, E. R. (1988a). Conceptualizing spirituality for social work: Insights from diverse perspectives. *Social Thought,* Winter, 30-46.

Canda, E. R. (1988b). Spirituality, religious diversity and social work practice. *Social Casework,* April, 238-247.

Coles, R. (1993). *The call of service.* New York: Houghton Mifflin Company.

Constable, R. (1983). Religion, values and social work practice. *Social Thought,* 9, 29-41.

Devine, E. T. (1939). *When social work was young.* New York: Macmillan Company.

Fowler, J. W. (1981). *Stages of faith.* San Francisco: Harper and Row.

Gustafson, J. M. (1982). Professions as "callings." *Social Service Review,* December, 105-515.

Huntington, J. (1893). Philanthropy and morality. In Addams, J. (Ed.), *Philanthropy and social progress,* New York: Crowell.

Johnson, E. F. (1946). The pattern and philosophy of protestant social work. *Church Conference of Social Work,* Buffalo, New York.

Leiby, J. (1985). Moral foundations of social welfare and social work: A historical view. *Social Work,* 30(4), 323-330.

Lovejoy, O. R. (1920). The faith of a social worker. *The Survey*, May, 208-211.

Marty, M. E. (1980). Social service: Godly and godless. *Social Service Review*, 54, 463-481.

Niebuhr, R. (1932). *The contribution of religion to social work*. New York: Columbia University Press.

Reamer, F. G. (1992). Social work and the public good: Calling or career? In Reid, N. P. & P. R. Popple (Eds.), *The moral purposes of social work*, (11-33), Chicago: Nelson-Hall.

Specht, H. & Courtney, M. (1994). *Unfaithful angels*. New York: The Free Press.

Siporin, M. (1982). Moral philosophy in social work today. *Social Service Review*, December, 516-538.

Siporin, M. (1985). Current social work perspectives on clinical practice. *Clinical Social Work Journal*, 13, 198-217.

CHAPTER 8

SOCIAL WORK FOR SOCIAL JUSTICE: STRENGTHENING PRACTICE WITH THE POOR THROUGH CATHOLIC SOCIAL TEACHING

Julia Pryce

This chapter focuses on the ways by which Catholic social teaching (CST), specifically the CST value of the "preferential option for the poor," is present in social work education and practice. That this should require mention in a book devoted to Christian social work practice reflects the central argument advanced in this chapter. That is, despite clear calls to both social work education and Catholic social workers to put the needs of the poor in the foreground, the mission of social work practice seems to be partially characterized by viewing poverty as another aspect of "diversity" that, while respected, is not a career focus of social work students or of the programs training them. In this chapter, a brief discussion of the "preferential option for the poor" and its relationship to larger Christian teachings will lead to an analysis of how CST is reflected in the social work Code of Ethics (COE), social work practice, and social work education. Finally, specific examples of ways to better integrate CST into social work practice and education will challenge social workers of all faiths to re-examine their own commitments to practice the preferential option for the poor.

Case Example #1: A Catholic Hospital Adrift?
Helen was a BSW student doing her field placement in the inpatient unit of a Catholic hospital. She loved the work and felt that her calling to be a hospital social worker was validated by the feeling of relief she saw in her patients as she helped them with discharge planning. However, she recently had been troubled by some changes she witnessed at the hospital. Along with her supervisor, she attended a meeting at the hospital where the Chief Operating Officer (COO) discussed the need for the hospital to market their services to potential patients from the newly-gentrifying neighborhood around the hospital. These new neighbors were affluent and represented a stark contrast to the low-income, largely immigrant population that this Catholic hospital served over its 100 year history. During the meeting, the COO invited staff to join in the strategic planning process to "chart this new course" for the hospital. Following the meeting, Helen asked for an overview of the economic pressures facing the hospital at this time and reviewed the particulars with another

staff member. While at Mass in the hospital chapel later that day, Helen found herself wondering about the hospital's new direction and whether she should inquire about her supervisor's intentions in advocating that the hospital preserve its mission and prioritize serving the poor. "Isn't that the role of a Catholic hospital? Isn't that its purpose?" she wondered to herself. Subsequently, Helen considered how to advocate for ways by which the hospital could preserve its mission while responding to the current financial pressures it was facing.

Perspectives on Change from the frameworks of Christianity and Social Work

Helen's experience might resonate with many social workers, whether Christian or not. They may share Helen's concern that the agency or site where they work is failing its patient population. This tension may be particularly strong within students like Helen, given her Catholic beliefs and the tradition of Catholic Social Teaching (CST) that informs her concerns. From the perspective of CST, the hospital's "new course" is not just about trying to make a profit; rather, it is about the hospital potentially abandoning a central aspect of its Catholic mission--the preferential option for the poor. As an approach, CST informs social work's core mission and is the basis for considering the intersection of CST and social work ethics.

The profession of social work has historically grappled with the ways by which change can occur at the individual and societal levels. Conversations between some of the mothers of the profession are well known for the struggle to identify the most appropriate way to address issues of justice among marginalized populations (Addams, 1911; 1990; Reynolds, 1934; 1951; Richmond, 1922). In more recent years, scholars have continued to consider the merit of addressing issues of social justice within social work curricula (Brenden, 2007; Longres & Scanlon, 2001; Finn & Jacobson, 2003; Abramovitz, 1998). Debates continue regarding the definition and nature of social justice (Hawkins, Fook, & Ryan, 2001; McPherson, Terry, & Walsh, 2010) and the contextual and political influences that contribute to its relevance at any given time.

In the midst of this struggle, the stated value placed by the profession on social justice via its Code of Ethics (COE) remains clear (NASW, 2008). The term "social justice" is referenced multiple times in the COE and is listed as one of the core ethical principles of the document (NASW, 2008). Further, social justice is referenced via a myriad of mission statements, both within secular and religious social work programs. Primary professional conferences, such as the Council on Social Work Education Annual Program Meeting, continue to reference "justice" in their core themes (CSWE 2009).

Alongside the profession of social work, many Christian theologians and leaders have continuously prioritized the role of justice as core to their belief system, although the conceptualization has shifted over time. According to St. Augustine, for example, the source of justice comes from within. In other words, justice is the connection between an internal faith and external action

(Deane, 1963). Martin Luther, on the other hand, often conceived of justice in the context of education (Luther, Pelikan, Poellot, Hansen, Oswald, Grimm, Lehmann, & Hillerbrand, 1955). The social gospel movement, which preceded Vatican II, represents a Protestant Christian intellectual movement that was most prominent in the early 20th century. This movement was based on the idea that justice was critical to facilitating the second coming of Christ. That is, without the amelioration of social ills in the context of social justice, the second coming of Christ will not occur. Although the peak of this movement occurred in the mid-20th century, the principles of this movement continue to inspire more recent Protestant movements. These serve as just a few of many examples of the ways by which the founders of the Christian, and particularly Catholic, traditions have conceptualized social justice as central to the faith.

Catholic Social Teaching

Catholic Social Teaching (CST) is based on church doctrine and Catholic social movements that have been incorporated into church teaching since the late 19th century (http://www.osjspm.org/social_teaching_documents.aspx, 2008). While all aspects of CST are considered important for Catholics, most scholars and theologians agree that in the approach to social justice, the issue of the Catholic preferential option for the poor represents a central tenet and has been a more prominent focus of Pope John Paul II and Pope Benedict (Pope John Paul II, 1995; Twomey, 2005).

In concept, the preferential option for the poor was initially discussed over a century ago, in the 1891 papal encyclical, "*Rerum Novarum*: On the condition of workers", by Pope Leo XIII (Pope Leo XIII, 1891). Through this seminal work, *Rerum Novarum* addressed for the first time barriers that separated the church from the common worker. This encyclical's comprehensive treatment of such social issues set it apart from its counterparts. The concept was again prominently articulated as part of the liberation theologies of Latin America and was formalized in the Latin American Bishops Conferences in Medellin, Columbia in 1968 and Puebla, Mexico in 1979 (Twomey, 2005).

In its application, this option for the poor served to organize peasants in Latin America into more self reliant "Christian-based communities," which began to create solidarity among participants. In the United States, however, consideration of the preferential option did not formally begin until the late 1970s and has vacillated in its doctrinal centrality since then. The approach within the United States differed some from that of the liberation theology movement, focusing more on responsibility to the larger community rather than specifically to that of the poor (U.S. Catholic Bishops, 1986). In other words, while the church is supposed to show a special solicitude for the poor, it should not ignore those who are not poor. This reflects the continuing debate in the laity and institutional church worldwide regarding the role the church should play in advocating for the poor in political and economic terms (Cooney, Medaille, & Harrington, 2002; Twomey, 2005).

When applying preferential option for the poor to real-life situations, roles can become muddled when the people working with the poor view themselves as saviors rather than as partners and fellow travelers. "Bill," the social worker in our next case example, explores this tension when working with Catholic Charities to deliver mentoring programs to youth living in under-resourced neighborhoods.

Case Example #2: Mentoring At-Risk Youth: Saving or Solidarity?

Bill has recently graduated with his Masters of Social Work from a Catholic university. He is a recent convert to Catholicism, and was raised Lutheran. He was hired by Catholic Charities to provide training and supervision to three mentoring programs for at-risk, minority youth in suburban and rural areas in his region. At his first meeting with mentoring coordinators of each site, the discussion quickly turned to the shared sense of the staff that many of the recently recruited mentors are not following the goals of vocational mentoring in the program. One of the mentor coordinators said, "It's like the mentors pity these kids and view them as needing a rescue from their families…one mentor told me last year that she returns home from her mentoring sessions so sad because she wishes she could adopt her mentee to give her a better life." Another coordinator, acknowledging that her program serves youth who live in high-poverty, high-crime neighborhoods, shared that she is struggling to find ways to get her mentors involved in the community and in the lives of their mentees' families. "It's like they just want to come to our building, do their mentoring, and get out of there as fast as they can." Bill observed that all three of the mentoring programs used the parish house of the local Catholic parish as their meeting space. He made a note to himself to talk to the parish priest and his staff about how they might partner to create some community-focused events to encourage the mentoring programs to become better integrated into the surrounding communities. Additionally, he told the group that he intended to address the mentors' approach through a revamped training program. The modified program would emphasize the importance of building healthy connections with their mentees by focusing on mentees' strengths and dignity, rather than focusing only on their problems and perceived dysfunctions of their families.

Social Justice and the Practice of Social Work

As illustrated by the case example above, Bill is a Catholic social worker operating from the CST value of attending to the needs and strengths of the poor. Through this value base, he is actively seeking to make CST come alive in his social work practice by engaging the community and prioritizing its needs rather than allowing it to remain marginalized and misunderstood. However, while Bill should be applauded for these efforts, it is also critical to explore the origins of these values. It is not clear that Bill learned about the importance of CST as part of his MSW program at a Catholic school. As we will see in this next section, the infusion of CST in social work education is hardly a given, even when it involves teaching and learning about the poor.

The mission statements of Catholic schools of social work consistently reflect a desire to incorporate the values of faith and social justice into their curricula (Brenden, 2007). Similarly, scholars often promote the role of spirituality in professional education (Ai, 2002). The relationship between social work and religion is well documented through analysis of the literature (Graham & Shier, 2009), which specifically reinforces the importance of religion and spirituality in assessing the "person-in-environment" perspective of professional social work.

However, the integration of religion and spirituality into professional education has continued to be a struggle (Barker, 2007), as the role of spirituality in formal education remains in tension with more traditional approaches to learning (Cohlic, 2006). Further complicating this struggle is the lack of guidance provided in the curriculum for social work students about integrating professional social work with faith and spirituality (Northcut, 2005, Praglin, 2004). Additional challenges come from others who suggest that preparing students as social workers should not include an explicit focus on faith as part of the human experience (Sheridan, 1994).

In the context of these tensions, I developed, in collaboration with colleagues, a content analysis used to understand what is being taught in Catholic schools of social work (Pryce, Kelly, Reiland, & Wilk, 2011). In so doing, my aim was to understand how students are being prepared to grapple with concepts proposed by CST, particularly the "preferential option for the poor", as social work professionals. Through this analysis, course syllabi of foundation level MSW courses were collected from 11 of the 12 accredited Catholic schools of social work. In total, 38 (N=38) syllabi were included in the analysis. After developing a coding manual together and employing several additional methods to ensure rigor and trustworthiness (Pryce et al., 2011), the research team coded these syllabi with particular attention to the ways by which course content descriptions, assignments, and themes addressed poverty.

Findings from the analysis suggest that concepts such as "diversity", "strengths", and "social justice" are emphasized far more than explicit attention to poverty in the four introductory-level core courses standard to first-year curricula within accredited Catholic MSW programs. Not surprisingly, policy courses attend to economic and structural issues more often than their clinical and practice-focused counterparts, particularly in terms of the kinds of assignments offered to students. Unfortunately, the analysis suggests that students are not receiving the kind of formal guidance and support in addressing issues of poverty in their courses, even in Catholic MSW programs. Instead, findings suggest that at this point, much responsibility is left to students themselves to systematically and critically engage issues of poverty within their education and practice (Pryce et al., 2011).

In this final case example, a group of MSW students at a Catholic institution extend the ideas of social justice and the preferential option for the poor into the vital current national debate about income inequality and its impact on American institutions.

Case Example #3: A Student Social Work Group Responds to the Occupy Wall Street Movement

As co-leaders of their MSW Student Organization, Tammy and Carla were concerned that their student colleagues were focusing their career aspirations too narrowly. In a meeting with other students, they cited a recent exit survey of students as a point of discussion. According to the survey, though many recent MSW graduates from their Christian program found work in government and not-for-profit social service agencies, students' greatest aspirations were to become private practice therapists. As the meeting progressed, the group argued about whether it would be prudent to offer a critique of their fellow students' career goals as part of their student organization.

In an effort to raise student awareness of the larger issues facing society, the group eventually agreed to hold a series of workshops explicitly addressing the issues raised by the Occupy Wall Street movement regarding the acceleration of income inequality in the United States. The workshops aimed to challenge students to examine policy-practice solutions that social workers can integrate into their future work to better address individual and structural issues related to income inequality and poverty. They decided to reach out to the national Catholic Charities Campaign to Reduce Poverty to seek technical assistance and speakers for the workshop series.

Implications for Social Work Practice

The work of students like Tammy and Carla need not be exceptional for future social work students if the profession (and religiously-affiliated schools of social work in particular) takes the initiative to return social work back to some of its first principles. For social work practice and education, I propose the following recommendations to students, faculty, and practitioners to strengthen social work programs and empower students in the efforts to increase attention to the needs of the poor.

> 1. *Students can attend to poverty explicitly and systematically in their education and choice of social work career path.* Although students bring hope and openness to the educational experience as aspiring social workers, students may not personally come from a lived experience of poverty. This is not meant as a criticism of new social work students as much as a reflection on the reality that Specht & Courtney (1994) identified over 15 years ago: many incoming social work students aspire to work as therapists, and intend to focus on mental health concerns most explicitly, often with clients possessing similar backgrounds to themselves (Perry, 2009). It is critical for social work students to challenge themselves and their peers (as Clara and Tammy did, above) to reflect on their identity as social workers within the historic context of the profession. This attention to the role of economic status seems to be of particular salience at this point in American life, as our country faces severe economic credit and housing crises, as reflected in the

burgeoning Occupy Wall Street movement. One way to engage in this reflection is to initiate action as a student body on behalf of social justice, particularly among the poor. Social work students can lead peers at their college or university to address justice issues. In a study of student writing (McPherson, Perry, & Walsh, 2010), the concept of action emerged as key to student understanding of social justice, despite the fact (according to the content analysis featured in this chapter) that the social work curricula do not seem to engage in this action-oriented framework. One's role and identity as a student may allow social work students the support needed to leverage some of these values in service of the community and profession.

2. *Students might exercise caution in "opting out" of addressing issues of poverty in assignments.* Although the chance to customize an assignment based on personal interests and comfort level is appealing and commonly offered, this approach, particularly within initial social work course work and practice, will likely significantly limit a student's experience with issues of poverty, both in the classroom and in the field. In other words, students can challenge themselves to incorporate issues of poverty into papers and group assignments. In so doing, social work students will gain experience and comfort in effectively addressing these complex issues (as Bill and Helen do in the case vignette above). Issues of poverty and social justice inevitably will be a component of students' future work (Davis & Wainwright, 2005).

3. *Both students and faculty must avoid the diversity trap in dealing with social justice issues related to poverty and the preferential option for the poor.* Based on the content analysis presented above, it is clear that all MSW programs examined are supportive of student interest in social justice on behalf of their clients. The problem, however, is that sometimes social justice is discussed under the concept of "diversity", which may mask the structural and economic issues most powerful in addressing issues of poverty. While attending to issues of diversity (e.g., gender, sexual orientation, race, religious identity) thoughtfully and competently in our practice is critical to the ethics of our profession, we may lose sight of the needs of the poor, who arguably suffer the most serious long-term negative life outcomes (e.g., health, life expectancy, educational attainment, exposure to violence), regardless of their race, sexual orientation, or religious affiliation (Iceland, 2006).

4. *All social workers, students, faculty, and practitioners must consider our commitment to the poor as critical to the future of the profession.* In extending findings from these MSW programs into the larger practice domain, it is important to consider the ways by which the absence of focus on issues of poverty may influence the profession of social work across domains. At the professional level, our ongoing distancing from the needs of the poor place both the profession and the larger society

at risk. If social workers fail to address the needs of the poor, a few questions will linger: can social work claim to be a profession that advocates effectively for the vulnerable when so little of our time is spent preparing new social workers to work effectively with clients in poverty? Without such an emphasis, what ultimately will distinguish social work from other helping professions that tend to offer psycho-therapy as the main intervention to address clients' problems?

Broader implications

The complex issues highlighted in these various case vignettes outline some of the important challenges facing the profession of social work. Addressing these issues is imperative for our profession to provide effective service to those in economic need. Poverty continues to be the dominant social crisis in our society, and our current economic circumstances suggest it is of heightened concern. Recent data from the Census Bureau suggest that the number of Americans living below the poverty line reached its highest level since the inception of the Bureau in 1959. Along the same lines, median household income levels in 2010 fell to levels similar to those of 1997 (Tavernise, 2011). These data suggest a lack of growth within the middle class, and an even direr situation for the poor in the United States than previously understood.

In sum, students, educators, and practitioners must consider creative ways to support one another in working with clients impacted by poverty. This support is critical within all social work contexts, including those religiously-affiliated programs that may explicitly identify the unique importance of the poor. Such support can include facilitating collaboration, both at the student and professional levels, between more senior and junior social workers. Social work departments, including faculty and field staff, can work together to identify ways to enhance attention to issues of poverty in and outside the classroom. At a curricular level, improvements to syllabi can be complemented with explicit attention within field education to support students in learning about and con-tending with issues of poverty among their clients. Further, given the impact of federal and state budget cuts on systems of care, it is critical that social work educators engage students in formal exposure to advocacy (Kilbane, Pryce, & Hong, in press) as a means of addressing client needs within very serious fiscal constraints.

Beyond these suggested changes, it is worth considering ways that reli-giously-affiliated social work programs can engage issues of poverty explicitly around conversations regarding faith. For many social workers, a faith-based orientation toward working with the poor may prove more compelling than a secular approach. Each faith tradition has stated values regarding the impor-tance of addressing the needs of the poor (Swatos & Kivisto, 1998). Through these traditions, social work students and practitioners may find inspiration or provocation to engage in work on behalf of the poor beyond what they may encounter in a secular framework.

References

Abramovitz, M. (1998). Social work and social reform: An arena of struggle. *Social Work* 43(6), 512-526.

Addams, J. (1911/1990). *Twenty years at Hull-House, with autobiographical notes, by Jane Addams; with illustrations by Norah Hamilton.* New York, NY: The Macmillan Company.

Ai, A. (2002). Integrating spirituality into professional education: A challenging but feasible task. *Journal of Teaching in Social Work, 22*(1-2), 103-130.

Barker, S. (2007). The integration of spirituality and religion content in social work education: Where we've been, where we're going. *Social Work and Christianity, 34*(2), 146-166.

Brenden, M. A. (2007). Social work for social justice: Strengthening social work practice through the integration of Catholic social teaching. *Social Work & Christianity, 34*(4), 471-497.

Cohlic, D. (2006). Spirituality in social work pedagogy: A Canadian perspective. *Journal of Teaching in Social Work, 26*(3-4), 197-217.

Cooney, A., Harrington, P., & Medaille, J. C. (2002). Catholic social teaching. Third Way Publications.

Council on Social Work Education, (2009). Annual Program Meeting, Final Program, Retrieved February 7, 2012, from http://www.cswe.org/Meetings/APMArchives/2009APM.aspx

Davis, A. & Wainwright, S. (2005). Combating poverty and social exclusion: Implications for social work education. *Social Work Education. 24*(3), 259-273.

Deane, H. A. (1963). *The political and social ideas of St. Augustine.* New York: Columbia University Press.

Finn, J. L., & Jacobson, M. (2003). Just practice: Steps toward a new social work paradigm. *Journal of Social Work Education, 39*(1), 57-78.

Graham, J.R., & Shier, M. (2009). Religion and social work: An analysis of faith traditions, themes, and global north/south authorship. *Journal of Religion and Spirituality in Social Work, 28*(1-2), 215-233.

Hawkins, L., Fook, J., & Ryan, M. (2001). Social workers' use of language of social justice. *British Journal of Social Work, 31*(1), 1-13.

Hong, P. Y. & Hodge, D.R. (2009). Understanding social justice in social work: A content analysis of course syllabi. *Families in Society: The Journal of Contemporary Social Services, 90*(2), 212-219.

Iceland, J. (2006). *Poverty in America: A handbook.* (2nd Ed.) Berkeley, CA: University of California Press.

Kilbane, T., Pryce, J., & Hong, P. (in press). Advocacy Week: A Model to Prepare Clinical Social Workers for Lobby Day. *Journal of Social Work Education.*

Longres, J. F., & Scanlon, E. (2001). Social justice and the research curriculum. *Journal of Social Work Education, 37*(3), 447-463.

Luther, M., Pelikan, J., Poellot, D. E., Hansen, W. A., Oswald, H. C., Grimm, H. J., Lehmann, H. T., Hillerbrand, H. J. (1955). *Luther's works.* Saint Louis, MO: Concordia Publishing House.

McPherson, M., Terry, P., & Walsh, F. (2010). Investigating social justice understanding through student writing samples: an emergent theme analysis approach. *The International Journal of the Scholarship of Teaching and Learning, 6*(1), 1-24.

National Association of Social Workers. (2008). NASW code of ethics. Retrieved January 25, 2007, from http://www.socialworkers.org/pubs/code/code.asp.

Northcut, T. (2005). The role of religion and spirituality in clinical social work: Creating a space for integration in MSW/MDiv joint programs. *Journal of Religion and Spirituality*, 24(1-2), 45-54.

Perry, R. (2009). Factors influencing M.S.W. students' interest in clinical practice. *Journal of Teaching in Social Work*, 29(1), 1540-7349.

Pope John Paul II. (1995). Evangelium vitae. Retrieved January 20, 2009, from http://www.vatican.va/edocs/ENG0141/_INDEX.HTM.

Pope Leo XIII (1891). Rerum Novarum: On the condition of workers. Retrieved September 19, 2011, from http://faculty.cua.edu/pennington/law111/papalsocialencyclicals.htm.

Praglin, L. (2004). Spirituality, religion, and social work: An effort towards interdisciplinary conversation. *Journal of Religion and Spirituality*, 23(4), 67-84.

Pryce, J., Kelly, M., Reiland, M., & Wilk, E. (2011). Do Catholic Social Work Programs "Prefer" the Poor? Results from a Content Analysis of MSW Program Syllabi. *Social Work & Christianity*.

Reynolds, B. C. (1934). *Between client and community: A study in responsibility in social case work*. Northampton, MA: Smith College School for Social Work.

Reynolds, B. C. (1951). *Social work and social living: Explorations in philosophy and practice*. New York, NY: Citadel Press.

Richmond, M. E. (1922). *What is social case work? An introductory description*. New York, NY: Russell Sage Foundation.

Sheridan, M. J. (1994). Inclusion of Content on Religion and Spirituality in the Social Work Curriculum: A Study of Faculty Views. *Journal of Social Work Education*, 30(3), 363-76.

Specht, H., & Courtney, M. (1994). *Unfaithful angels: How social work has abandoned its mission*. New York: Free Press.

Swatos, W. H., & Kivisto, P. (1998). *Encyclopedia of religion and society*. Walnut Creek, CA: AltaMira Press.

Tavernise, S. (2011, September 13). Soaring poverty casts spotlight on 'lost decade'. *The New York Times*. Retrieved from http://www.nytimes.com/2011/09/14/us/14census.html?_r=1

Twomey, G. S. (2005). *The "preferential option for the poor" in Catholic social thought from John XXIII to John Paul II*. Lewiston, NY: Mellen Press.

U.S. Catholic Bishops. (1986). Pastoral letter on Catholic social teaching and the U.S. economy. Retrieved January 20, 2009, from http://www.osjspm.org/economic_justice_for_all.aspx.

Wayne, J.; Bogo, M. & Raskin, M. (2006). The need for radical change in field education. *Journal of Social Work Education* 42(1). 161-169.

CHAPTER 9

JOURNEYS TOWARD INTEGRATING FAITH AND PRACTICE: STUDENTS, PRACTITIONERS, AND FACULTY SHARE THEIR STORIES

T. Laine Scales, Helen Harris, Dennis Myers, and Jon Singletary

Perhaps you remember family vacations that included road trips across the country; trips that started with the unfolding of a map on the dining room table or an internet search for driving directions. You found your current location and your destination. Then you began the exploration of various routes to get there. The journey really started before you opened the map or booted up the computer. It very likely started as you considered your destination and the purpose of your trip. Once you knew where you were going, your focus could move to the "how to" of getting there.

In this chapter we share several stories of one of the most challenging journeys for Christians in social work: the journey toward integration of faith and social work practice. The student perspectives include both their responses while students and their reflections five years later with practice experience in public, private and congregational settings. We are a group of four social work faculty members at a Christian university, Baylor University in Waco, Texas. We spend a lot of time pondering this journey toward integration. We think about Christianity and social work very personally, in relation to ourselves and our callings; we talk about this often with other faculty members on retreats or in meetings. Most importantly, we explore this topic with students in advising, in classrooms, in conducting research with our students, and in continued professional relationships with our graduates. We are intentional in our exploration of this topic because we are deeply affected by our own responses to the question, Where am I on the journey toward integrating Christian faith and social work practice?

Our purpose in writing this chapter is three-fold. First, we want to share with you the stories from Christian students at our university who have been on this journey toward becoming a social worker and from those same students as graduates implementing and refining their own discoveries around the integration of faith and practice. Second, as we present their stories, we comment on the various themes emerging from their reflections as they share stories of seeking God's plan, dealing with obstacles, and seeking companionship for the journey. At times, we will repeat their reflections as we illustrate the variety of themes we gleaned from their narratives. Finally, we invite you to join with other

Christian travelers as we figure out together various ways to integrate Christian faith and social work practice.

We are addressing our comments primarily to student readers, though we realize that faculty members, social work practitioners, and others may read this chapter. Our hope is to introduce students and others to the stories of our Baylor students and graduates as they reflect on their own journeys. We expect that, for our readers, these conversations about calling have been and will continue to be a central part of the dialogue concerning Christians in social work: a dialogue involving other students, advisors, supervisors, teachers, families, and friends. One last caution: this chapter is not based solely on our data analysis and is not presented as research findings. We report those findings in other publications (Singletary, Harris, Myers, & Scales, 2006). Instead, this is a personal sharing of selected quotes from students and faculty that we hope will serve as information and inspiration as you consider your calling and your pilgrimage. We invite you to travel with us.

The Road Trip of a Lifetime

For the Christian student, the most compelling question, Where am I going? has been answered ultimately: I am going to God, to eternity with my Creator, to Heaven. But if life is truly a journey leading us to our Home, it seems very important to consider how we get there. It is frequently easier for Christian students to talk freely about their eternal destination while struggling significantly with the direction of their life journeys. Which of the many career paths available, for example, shall I take? What is it I am to do with this life I have been given? We look at the life map of possible destinations and consider our options while many voices, from parents to mentors to detractors, offer a variety of pathways. Shall I travel major highways with large loops that let me travel quickly and efficiently, but that guide me around the inner cities where the bustle of life and pain of others is almost palpable? Shall I travel the back roads of life where the pace is slower and the interactions more measured and deliberate? Will my travels take me through many small adventures or will this journey center on one or two defining highways?

For Christian social workers, there is a real sense that we serve a Navigator who has charted our path, who created us with particular gifts and talents to accomplish the purposes of God's creation. But getting the message and instructions of the Navigator that are specific to our journey is often the challenge. Has God called me to a specific work? And if so, how will I hear the call and know the path? We find ourselves asking, What are the roads or pathways that will get me to the work and then through the work to which God is calling mee?

Students called to social work hear the Navigator's voice in a variety of ways. Becoming a social worker is a process, a journey that may begin from any place at any time. Some social workers can trace the beginning of their travels to childhood: parents who modeled for them the giving of self in service of others and encouraged the journey of helping. For some, the journey toward social work began later in life, after several apparently false starts down roads that were blocked or just seemed to be the wrong direction. Eventually the Navigator provided directional clarity in the midst of disorientation and aimless pursuits. In some cases, graduates found directional clarity as part of the journey. One graduate summed it up this way: "I just keep finding open doors, opportunities leading me to the next step. I simply wait, do the best job I can while waiting for the next step in His plan to emerge."

For Christian social workers, the paths toward life as a Christian and as a professional social worker are traveled simultaneously, leading Christian social work students to explore questions such as these: How does my journey as a Christian intersect with, complement, replicate, or diverge from travel along my journey toward professional social work? One graduate made this observation: "Social work provides me one avenue to fulfill my calling. It allows me to get paid, but more importantly, it allows me to step into other people's lives and help them through tough situations in life. It allows me to walk a journey with others." Students also wonder: Will I be confronted with the choice between two roads, one representing my faith journey and the other representing my professional journey? As graduates, many discovered that the integration of their own faith experience and their practice experience can take place in both secular and non-sectarian settings. Of the follow-up respondents, their experience in public and private agencies was essentially equal. Three of the eight had experience in both public and private agencies over the five year period since graduation.

The question for students is often this: Is there truth in the statement that social work and Christianity really are quite compatible with one another? Is it possible that we have been called by the Navigator to forge a new road that brings our path across the most vulnerable, the most wounded, those lost needing a guide to get back to the road? While graduates worked with both Christian colleagues and colleagues who were not believers and in both public and private settings, they reported that their faith experience was consistently positive in their social work practice. One respondent said it this way:

"I honestly believe that God has brought me down the path I have been on professionally this far, and I have no doubts that He has a future plan for me as well."

That statement rang true with graduates working in both traditional social work agencies and in the church. "I have found I fit best when my mission is expanded beyond that of the church to the many people on the fringes of society who lack even the basic community that most churches offer." This is possible because "I did learn how to walk away at the end of the day and feel confident that God is in control. Because of this skill I anticipate being a social worker for years and decades to come."

Why Social Work Education?

Our students' stories remind us that all journeys must begin somewhere, even though the map has not been secured or the destination is not in view.

Some students are very comfortable with wandering. Some are taking a leisurely journey that may be spontaneous and filled with last-minute decisions about destinations and activities, a bit like buying a month-long rail pass and traveling around Europe. In some instances, students may enter social work to check it out, wander around, and decide along the way what is interesting. In contrast, other students are on a carefully defined path to a very specific destination. They have a particular vocational goal in mind and their social work education is a point on their map. One student described where she hopes to be in ten years:

> I want to have started a non-profit [agency] for doing job training for women. For impoverished women-- that's what I would like to be doing in ten years. To get there, I think in two years I am going to be working at an agency doing very micro work.... I really need to have that perspective. [1]

One can imagine this student viewing social work classes as particular points on a map that will lead to the ten-year goal.

In some cases, students found their way to social work after developing a commitment to a particular population. For example, one young woman found that she was gifted in working with children so she planned to pursue teaching in a school setting. In conversation with her own teachers she began to broaden her view of careers in which she might work with kids. Soon she was imagining social work as an option. In her own words:

> I just easily attached to kids; they easily attached to me. And I was just a real good people person. People said it all the time,... [With social work] I would have more job options... and if I'm a school teacher, then that's what I do with kids, I just teach them, but with social work I could do a whole bunch of different things and I liked that.

Another student began social work in order to work with children and adolescents, but through experience in internships and classes, opened her mind to consider work with additional populations:

> I always thought... I was going to work with children. And it's switched a lot. ... our society's changing as well, so Alzheimer's and caregivers are going to be big needs our population is going to have...I definitely could see myself in that kind of field...I have lots of options....

In another case, the student's ultimate goal was ministry, but this student intentionally sought a social work education to gain particular skills and information. Encountering two other travelers with social work competencies motivated this student to walk with them:

> I want to connect to people and really help them work through these issues that they've got. I thought that I could do that in seminary, and I think that you can, but when I got in there - that's

where the catch was - when I started asking questions about wife beatings and children getting hit - those things. And when the only two people in the room that knew were social work students, that was what really did it for me. This is some information that I have always wanted to know. How do I get this information? And social work has that information with it.

While this student wanted to pursue social work to gain particular knowledge or skills, another student wanted to journey alongside social workers because she appreciated the value base of the profession:

The first draw that was in my mind was that I thought that social workers worked with the poor, that was the initial lead in. But also, helping the oppressed and the poor in justice issues from a biblical basis and seeing that as a value of the social work profession…So social work values are definitely places that attracted me as a means of vocation or a job where I live out the values.

Where Am I Going?

In contrast to students who had a clear picture about why they chose social work education, other students were wandering, with or without a compass. One student was simply lost in the journey and stated bluntly "I have no direction on my future at this point." Another traveler expressed outwardly a feeling of confidence that she would find the way as she goes, but at the same time, admits an "uneasy feeling" as well.

To me, at this point, there's still just—it's all very unclear. I'm pushing around things right now, but I'm learning that there are so many options out there and that I have to just kind of give it time to know things will develop, and I'll find it as I go. So I'm doing my education to help give me some more options and some more places, but I can't see down the line right now. And it's kind of an uneasy feeling, not knowing which direction or any of the options that are available—in either direction.

This inability to see around the corner is both the joy and the challenge of traveling free and easy, wherever the wind may take us. We may know that good things can happen along the way and that the path will be there when we need it. But, the uneasiness described above leads to a natural question for students; will we really like what we find along the way? And, perhaps a more troubling question, when we arrive at our destination, will the satisfaction we find be worth the time and effort we have invested?

Sometimes it is easier to see where we are on the path by looking behind us, at where we have been. This student reflects on the calling to social work as a process; looking back, she can see that there were signposts of confirmation points on her journey.

I don't think it was one instance, like one minute, all of a sudden, I was like, I'm called to social work. I think it was a process... the constant affirmation. I believe when people are walking with God, and in His word every day, and are really seeking Him, then He'll lead you in a certain direction, and so as I've been seeking Him throughout college, my college experience and life, I've felt confirmed over and over again to continue in the path of social work. And more so every day, even today, more so than yesterday.

Once graduates entered professional social work, they gained wisdom from looking back to " younger years" and seeing the patterns of God's plan at work. Experience, along with trial and error, often helped students discern the best fit.

In my younger years I identified my calling to be in a faith-based environment. At other times I felt it to be as an academic. Over time I have learned that the pursuits which fit me best are those in which I am able to work with a variety of people and help them at times of crisis. While faith-based organizations offer me this opportunity, I have found I fit best when my mission is expanded beyond that of the church to the many people on the fringes of society who lack even the basic community that most churches offer.

After starting professional and family life, one graduate could take a long view of her calling that began when she was a child and encompasses values she is passing on to her own children:

The feeling of helping others has been with me from a very young age, I have distinctive memories as early as 3rd grade. The urge to help others has never really waned. It has taken different shapes. As I was going through school, it is what helped shaped my professional choices, as well as extracurriculars. Now that I am in my profession and my roles of wife and mother are put above my profession, the idea of helping others looks a little different. I value what it means to help others and I work to teach my children the importance of helping others.

Am I on the Right Road?

One of the lessons we learned from the students and alumni we interviewed was that entering and staying on the path to a vocation in social work can be an uncertain and complicated task. Their experiences made us more aware of the unexpected turns, intersections, and detours that accompany most who travel this way. These honest, onsite reports of the terrain will alert you to the possibility that you may encounter obstacles in the pathway--you or others in your life may question the direction you are going, the accuracy of your map, and the worth of your destination. You will discover that others have traveled the path that you are now on or that you are thinking of entering. They have much to say about the challenges you face and about how God keeps them on the path and helps them make sense of the journey.

Some students told us that, in the beginning, they didn't want to be on the path toward a career in social work. It seems that God's plan for their life's journey was very different from the life map envisioned by the student. This reflection illustrates how God's plans may not be our plans:

> I remember a point where I sat there and I said, 'I don't want to go this direction.' I remember praying and saying, 'God, you got something confused here. You got the wrong plan for the wrong girl.' There was a point where I really remember just about screaming my head off going, 'God; you're just off, here! I don't understand why you're doing this!'

Another student described the experience of misinterpreting God's plan:

> I think, for me, I misinterpret God, definitely because I am a selfish person and have my own agenda and my own plans that aren't necessarily in conjunction with His, so I do get a little confused and can't see the line--but I definitely know that from my experience, He's used other people and you know, initially by just planting a seed in my heart, or maybe a desire or maybe just a little interest.

It seems that once these students reluctantly entered the path of God's plan for their Christian vocation, confirmation that they were in the right place reassured the travelers. Students reported confirmation from a number of sources.

This student described the sense of peace that confirmed the chosen path:

> I think it's completely natural for me to be in social work. And if I try to pursue other things, it really doesn't give me that sense of peace, it gives me more of a sense of like I don't belong there. That's really the role that social work plays and that's how I feel as far as my calling, when I know that when I'm doing something that God doesn't want me to do, I don't have that peace. And when God wants me to do something and that's where I should be, and that's where I am, I have that sense of peace and I'm fine with it even if it makes me uncomfortable, but I feel just natural to be there.

Confirmation came for graduates when they had opportunities to try different jobs. One graduate suspected in her student years that she wanted to work with children and families and had this confirmed when she tried a different job for awhile:

> I believe that I was created to work with youth, and I am unable to imagine myself doing anything else (long-term). I worked a part-time position with a non-medical in home care provider organization (working with the elderly and handicapped)...and although I still enjoyed helping and serving a different group of people.....

my passion for my job just wasn't the same as I have when I am serving children and families.

Graduates had new opportunities to try their skills and get affirmation of their callings from colleagues and clients. "I often get the comment that I'm a good listener or that they [clients] feel a radiant energy from me that is different," says one graduate. " I have always had this sense of calling but my calling has come to be more prominent as I began to do clinical work."

Encountering Obstacles

It became clear to us that unanticipated obstacles are part of the journey, whether you are just entering the path or you are five years down the road. At the beginning, students reported obstacles to their desire to enter the path toward faithful social work practice such as family members who questioned their vocational choices and the public perception of social work. In a few cases, obstacles created temporary loss of destination, which eventually led students to find the professional path God intended for them. Five years later, graduates view the obstacles as more related to their work setting and relationships with colleagues.

Family concerns

Confusion or concern may be the response of parents and family members to students who choose social work as a career. Family members may want to understand the motivation and reasoning that underlie this sometimes controversial decision. These two quotes from students reflect the concerns that some family members may have about the choice of social work as a career:

> No matter what I do, there is [from my parents] this, ok what is your reasoning behind this? I think that is a real big key thing, is to see where my motivation is coming from, and seeing, what makes me do this, to make sure I am doing it for the right reasons. Also, I think, part of it is for bragging rights, so that when people ask them, they can say, well, she's doing it because she wants to dah, dah, dah. I get a kick out of that—that that's one of the things that they do.

Another student described a negative reaction to the career path from family:

> Oh, well, they definitely have not influenced me to be called to—I mean, they are—my grandparents still are in denial that I am a social work major. I mean, no one in my family wanted me to be a social work major. So, they really have not done anything to encourage me to do that. But I think they just really wanted me to do business. But, I don't know.

Public perception of social work

Professional prestige and societal recognition may affect career choice. This was not an often mentioned concern in these interviews but there were at least several references to this potential obstacle. One student described a narrow perception of social work when initially considering the profession, asking "Aren't they just CPS [Child Protective Services] workers?" That was my whole idea of social work. Another student suggested that, "Social work, I guess widely speaking, isn't that glamorous of a profession." He described the questions of others:

> ...is social work a real profession?... people look down on social workers. They don't think that that's a real thing. In court, they don't listen to their testimony, they don't think it's real, but that's just how it was with Jesus.

Obstacles as a path to new directions

Obstacles can detour the traveler in a direction that actually leads to God's intention for the social work student. Consider this observation:

> I wish I could say I was that trusting and that easy to influence on it, but one of the characteristics I have, and it usually has a negative connotation to it, but for me it's a good thing, is being stubborn. I am someone who's not very easy to move and be manipulated and I just don't, I tend to want to stay in the same spot because it's kind of, I don't like to move into the unknown very easily and so for me, it seems like it's one instance after another and I keep getting hit from different directions until I'm finally going, ok maybe this, maybe I'm being told something here. That includes some of the people that I know. I'm wanting to go on this path and I keep getting stumbling blocks that are really actually people who are kind of going, you might want to consider doing this, you're fitted for this.

Five years later

At least eight graduates currently practice in social work related arenas, seeking to integrate their faith and practice. When we asked them again about obstacles to the integration of faith and practice after five years of practice, their narratives did not repeat the themes of their student days: the influence of family and societal values on vocational choice. Instead, they focused on the influence of their agency's context on faithful practice. In three cases, the graduates did not report any current obstacles, but found their work facilitated faith integration For example, one graduate working in a public agency responded: "I have struggled with more ethical integration of state and federal law and social work practice than with the integration of my faith. I feel fortunate enough that my faith actually enhances my practice, and in my opinion, makes me a stronger practitioner, employee, and supervisor." Another graduate, agreeing that faith could be integrated effectively, attributed this outcome to effective educational preparation:

> In this context I feel that the social worker's ability to address issues of faith in their practice is based largely on the background and

training they received prior to their employment there. Because my background included an emphasis on understanding spirituality as a component of any holistic social work, I am comfortable when my clients discuss the impact of their faith in their lives and I feel confident in my ability to address their faith in ways that does not direct or influence their belief, but better helps them understand how their faith impacts their lives.

Graduates who did report obstacles to the integration of faith and practice focused on their work settings. The graduates offered insight into how their agency's public, private, and/or non-profit status, as well as religious affiliation, shaped their attempts at faith integration. In these contexts, they also highlighted the roles (sometimes supportive and sometimes unsupportive) of colleagues within and outside the organization. By sharing their stories, the graduates revealed interesting and unanticipated ways that agency context and collegial relations can be both facilitators for and obstacles to faithful practice.

Agency context as a facilitator or obstacle

The graduates agreed that practice within a publically funded agency created obstacles to the integration of faith and practice. One reflection captured this observation: "I have currently worked in a public agency for nearly a year. In this context, faith conversation has been isolated institutionally, not only from clients but among employees as well." Another graduate raised a unique client-social worker boundary issue related to practice in a public agency—" I have multiple clients and/or their families who attend my church. Since I do not work at a faith-based agency, trying to figure out boundaries [related to faith-talk] has been somewhat of a challenge."

Is spite of these obstacles, the graduates in public sector organizations offered unexpected perspectives on faith life in these contexts. Even though the agency is publically funded, the religious beliefs of the employees and administration may open the organization to accept the role of faith. Consider this observation: "While the agency itself was non-faith based, many of the employees and administrators came from Christian faith backgrounds. This made it easy to address faith in the work environment." Meanwhile, one graduate who has worked in both a public and a private faith-based agency observed that the prohibitions of a public setting actually facilitated her own personal faith and practice development:

> I think my faith and the way I integrate faith and practice has become stronger NOT working at a faith-based agency, because I have had to struggle with how to do it and work at it, when it was so easy at the private faith-based agency.

In contrast to public agencies, private, non-profit organizations with a religious affiliation can be a venue for deepening the faith and professional practice conversation. Graduates working in these settings often identified "freedom" and "openness" as primary factors. One graduate who is an educator in a Christian college expressed it this way:

Each time I am asked about the integration of my faith in practice by others, I recognize the freedom I have in my work environment to share my faith and allow it to inform my teaching. These conversations allow me the opportunity to further reflect upon the impact I am able to have in and outside the classroom by integrating faith principles in the ways I interact with students and colleagues.

Another graduate echoed this theme: "...being in settings in which the faith beliefs are a good enough fit has allowed me to integrate faith into practice more openly, whereas that would very likely not be the case in a public agency or college setting."

While some contexts facilitated integration, other settings may also present obstacles. One possibility is that clients are not allowed freedom to embrace their unique beliefs. A graduate working in a non –faith- based setting observed the importance of making additional efforts to ensure clients did not feel pressured to embrace a particular faith.

Taken together, the graduates provided clear evidence that organizational identity may be an important factor in faith and practice integration. Their narratives also reveal the complexity and unpredictability of this relationship; in other words, public agencies may facilitate integration of faith in surprising ways, while religiously affiliated contexts may unpredictably deter integration.

Christian colleagues as supporters and obstacles

Collegial relations of the graduates join organizational status as central themes in the reflections on faith and practice integration. This statement simply and powerfully expresses the observation made by most of the graduates: "It is beneficial to have someone else in the profession who has the same faith background as I do to talk with."

In religiously affiliated agencies, supportive colleagues may be more available and the opportunities for shared involvement in faith practices richer: "When I worked at the faith-based agency I felt more support and more connection with some of my co-workers as we had weekly bible study and prayer time." When the setting does not provide this kind of faith-related sharing, graduates sought support outside of the agency:

Most of my friends/colleagues outside of work are not social workers, however, we talk often about working to change society, but more specifically through the lens mentioned above—Kingdom of God on earth in the here and now. They encourage, inspire, and motivate me to continue striving and though they do not have the social work frame of reference or language, I am able to bridge that gap a bit in our conversations and in work we might do together on the side. With my colleagues, we talk about the integration of faith and practice in the work...

Sometimes Christian colleagues at work present obstacles to graduates who are committed to faithful practice. When Christian colleagues violate ethical principles of self-determination or proselytize in ways that can be viewed as manipulative, the graduates viewed this as an obstacle, though one that could be overcome. Consider this observation:

> Surprisingly, there is one specific co-worker of mine who is prob-
> ably the most outspoken person of faith in our entire agency. I've
> found this to be a hindrance to our relationship….Unfortunately,
> I always tend to find the highest number of obstacles among very
> conservative Christians, whether co-workers or clients. I rarely
> find it difficult to manage though. It's just a part of life.

Whether or not agency context and work relationships present obstacles or opportunities, graduates affirm the central place of faith in their practice. All of these social work graduates are seeking a path that leads them to ethically live into their vocation and their faith. Their stories provide maps for travelers that aspire to the same destination. The pathway can be clearly marked with signs of confirmation and direction. We also have seen that, along the way, social work students and graduates who embrace Christian faith encounter unanticipated obstacles that disorient and even cause them to lose their way. Amazingly, the God who called them to the journey is also able to set their feet on the life-long path of service and Christian vocation. And, fortunately, Christian social workers do not ever have to travel alone.

Fellow Travelers

Social workers know perhaps better than most that no one successfully journeys alone in this life. As you learn how to walk alongside the people you serve, you also may begin to wonder, "Who will travel with me? Family, faculty, supervisors, student colleagues, God?" You may experience the presence of God calling in many ways; some direct and some indirect, but a part of God's calling is found in the voices of those who go with you on the journey.

Students in our program discussed their understanding of God's call through the influence of other people. We heard about direct and indirect influence of family members, co-workers, social workers, faculty, or others who helped students understand social work as an option for responding to God's call. Interpersonal relationships helped students discern God's call to the profession of social work and to know that there was someone on the journey with them. Here we highlight some of these relationships on the journey.

Who will guide my journey? God.
In trusting God's presence in our midst, we heard students describe the meaning of this for their journeys. One student said that "God's hand was there and, just kept guiding me through." Another student offers, "The calling for me is just following what God wants me to do and where God is leading me to." And also, "With me, I feel like God really, strongly directed me towards this."

Who will go with me? Family and friends.

The most common travelers alongside students were their family and friends. Sometimes these loved ones question the turns we make on the journey. Sometimes, they aren't sure how to support us along the way. Looking back on years of family strife, a student reflected on her family's role in her journey saying, "I don't know if my family necessarily, in a positive way, influenced my decision for social work." Yet, other students had different experiences as families ventured forth with them: "I knew that by choosing a profession where I would be helping people," said one student, "I would be understood by my family and they would support that decision because that's what I wanted to do." Another student also voiced the encouragement of family traveling with them, "I think that there is an experience where your family, they are helping me through a lot of this. That's one thing I feel very blessed with, is that they have been very supportive."

Who will go with me? Social workers such as faculty, classmates, and field supervisors.

Social work education offers opportunities for significant relationships that are influential in helping you make your way down the road into professional social work practice. Students spend a great deal of time with classmates, faculty, and field supervisors, who are a part of their journeys of discernment. They often recognize right away the importance of these relationships.

One new student described one of her attractions to the program: "I knew the faculty was very friendly and very interested in their students succeeding." Students commented on the relationships faculty intentionally developed with students on this journey. "I think it's pretty much invaluable,' said one student, "At least if it's set up properly, because you can draw on the experience of your professors, who have years of experience in the field, as well as the experience of the people who are even writing the textbooks." Professors are described as mentors in students' lives as they walk alongside them, "they really push to a high standard, but they're also there to, not hold your hand, but support you, encourage you, and I just got a really strong sense of community and support."

Faculty understood the importance of engaging with students. After a weekend of discussions about our own vocational journeys, faculty in our program wrote about the role they envisioned for themselves in walking alongside students: "My assessment is that sharing about our journeys and aspirations enabled us to see and appreciate the complexity and richness of the fabric of our collective relationship," offers one professor. Another adds her reflections, "My renewed awareness of my own calling and what has contributed to living it out has made me more aware of the potential significance of every interaction I have with students. I find myself asking my advisees and other students more open-ended questions about their purpose and urging them to see their inner promptings and long-held dreams."

As students, you also have supervisors guiding you while you learn, preparing you for the road ahead: "I talk to my supervisor constantly about what is going on with this client," said one person we interviewed. She lets me do the work, but she is there for advice and consultation. This is uncharted territory for me, but I am learning so much." Students express appreciation for the learning that comes in supervision. One offers, "It was tremendously helpful to me that my supervisor went out on an assessment with me. I was able to discuss advanced practice with her and it was really good to have her feedback from the assessment." And another echoes the support on the journey of learning: "In the middle of the crises of moving the clients I was on the phone with my supervisor. I wasn't sure what to do, and she talked me through it. But she also let me do it on my own, for which I am now thankful. It was a great experience."

The graduates surveyed for this research bring a slightly different perspective to this discussion. They reflected on what it is like to have or not have colleagues who share their faith while providing social work services together. In some cases graduates found that "my colleagues are working in the same profession because of their philosophy/faith but come from different faith backgrounds." Often, graduates found that working with colleagues who share their faith experience is a comfort and encouragement. "When I worked at the faith-based agency, I felt more support and more connection with some of my co-workers as we had weekly bible study and prayer time." In some cases, graduates identified a particular colleague whose support was invaluable: "The discussions that I have with this colleague reaffirm my purpose and the work that I do." Still others recognized the challenge of faith and practice to some of their colleagues: "Further, while the general social work education I received was second to none, the emphasis on preparing me to address areas of faith in my practice has provided me with an additional tool I feel many of my colleagues lack." One graduate summed up both the struggle and the blessing of working with colleagues who do not share her faith:

> When I worked at the faith-based agency I felt more support and more connection with some of my co-workers as we had weekly bible study and prayer time. At the agency I am at now, there is not the same level of support, I have had to seek support from other sources [friends, family].

Who will go with me? Clients

In social work education, you will have opportunities to reflect upon and then practice traveling with your clients, whether you are in generalist practice, direct practice, or practice with larger systems, you will be asking how to accompany your clients and how they will accompany you on this journey. One graduate from the study reflected on the impact of relationship with clients in this way: "I believe that *social work* is a verb that means working with people.... all types of people, and I find that I am happiest when I am able to work directly with others, and I am able to build ongoing and consistent relationships with my clients in a way that I don't think I would have in any other area." This graduate found that her faith was strengthened and encouraged by the work with her clients. Another graduate affirmed the importance of her work with clients this way: "I'm not just pushing paper around, I'm helping build forever families, keeping children safe, and enjoying every minute of my work."

Our students may be aware of where they have stumbled along the way, but they are not sure that the people they serve understand the challenges of their journeys, "sometimes, it's harder to meet people's needs because sometimes you have to convince them they have needs, or they don't realize they have needs." What this suggests is that students are learning the reciprocal nature of walking alongside others. They walk with clients in hopes of making a difference in their journeys. One student said, "If you can intervene and somehow help them realize that they are worth something and they have true potential, I feel like it changes so many things." After a similar experience with a client, another student said, "That made me feel good because I didn't force anything on him, I just lived right and tried to treat him like I treat anybody else."

As students on the journey into the profession walk with clients, they want to help them, but we know they also learn to "have the clients be the expert of their experience," as one student put it. In this, the clients also walk with students. They help students move further down the journey. Graduates found this to be important and reciprocal as well:

> Because my background included an emphasis on understanding spirituality as a component of any holistic social work, I am comfortable when my clients discuss the impact of their faith in their lives and I feel confident in my ability to address their faith in ways that does not direct or influence their belief, but better helps them understand how their faith impacts their lives.

One of the more cogent student responses pointed out through poetry the deep connection students and graduates may experience to their own faith journey and the impact it has on their work with clients. This is a verification of the scriptural admonition that we are able to use the comfort provided to us in order to comfort and minister to and work with others. Here are selected stanzas of her poem to illustrate how environment, opportunity, and God's calling come together for this faithful social worker.

What is to Become of Her?[2]

I see a little girl who is sitting quietly all alone
Watching the clock and waiting for the rest of her family to get home
Her mother is a single parent working hard to care for three
Her father is always in jail so his face she never sees

She is growing up in the projects which is also known as the 'hood'
And the acts of people surrounding her rarely measure up to good
She is no stranger to violence because it is witnessed almost everyday
People often fight and at times are killed simply for looking at someone
    the wrong way...

She has multiple skills to do and be all that she wants and more
But she doesn't know if she'll make it because it's life or death just walk-
ing to the store
So what is to become of this little girl who sits alone each day?
With peer pressure and temptation constantly being thrown her way

How can we help this little girl to remain on a path that's right?
And convince her that in due time she'll get to see the finer things in life
In my opinion, in order to help her, we must first believe
That no matter the environment around her she still has a chance to
succeed

Some of you may doubt her chances of being all that she could be
But I know that her success is possible because this little girl is me
It seems as if the odds were against me but I have been the exception to
every rule
And my ability to stand here today is why I've worked so hard at School

Everyday throughout my internship I have been able to see
Students who have less and others who have more but in many ways they
are just like me
Only somewhere along the line some of them have learned to believe
That the way you start life is how you will finish so there's no point in
trying to achieve

So what became of this little girl? Some of you still may not know
Well in spite of all the things around me I found ways to learn and grow
I did so by building relationships with adults who kept me on track
So working in schools and connecting with kids is simply my way of
giving back

Integration of Christian Faith and Social Work Practice

Now we have come to the heart of what we learned from our interviews.
If you are reading this book you probably have some interest in exploring the
integration of Christian faith and social work. Maybe you are faculty members,
like us, who have thought about this for years. Maybe you are a student, who
is exploring various aspects of what it means to travel this road. Social work
students and graduates who embrace Christian faith seek a path leading to places
where they can integrate professional values and ethics with their religious beliefs. The journey down this path usually creates a unique set of opportunities,
challenges and blessings.

Opportunities
For some students, Christian faith adds an extra measure of compassion to
their work. This student articulated how faith integration may allow the worker
to understand the client more completely:

My faith shapes who I am—kind of like my thought processes....
as I'm in social work, I'm learning to evaluate situations and just
know who I am and what my beliefs are, but then to see that person
for who they are and to work with them in where they're at. So, I
think how I approach situations may be different. I may be a little
more compassionate than somebody else would be.

Another student explored a similar theme, acknowledging that her own
Christian values are a lens through which she sees the world, but this lens does
not prevent her from valuing the different perspectives of her clients.

I'm at peace, I guess, as far as, I'm able to discuss with clients about
their own views and their own wants and desires for whom—for
who they are. Without imposing my own values. Because I realize
that my values are, maybe, different from theirs. But that doesn't
mean that I cannot help that person.

Perhaps most significantly, a number of students reported the important
interplay between their faith and their professional identity and practice. This
student described this as "accountability":

Another great blessing I have had is that it [social work] has made
me,—it has held me accountable to my faith. But it has made me
more genuine in my faith. It has really made me examine what it
means to be a Christian—what it means to minister. The word
ministry to me just means doing good social work......The profession has held me more accountable to my faith, and my faith has
held me more accountable to my profession.

Even several years into their professional journey, we hear similar responses
to the opportunities graduates have to integrate faith and practice, but this time
with more experience guiding them. We heard opportunities for integration in
relation to working with individual clients.

Because my background included an emphasis on understanding
spirituality as a component of any holistic social work, I am comfortable when my clients discuss the impact of their faith in their
lives and I feel confident in my ability to address their faith in ways
that does not direct or influence their belief, but better helps them
understand how their faith impacts their lives.

From our graduates, with just a few years of practice experience, we can
hear their faithful responses that keep them taking advantage of opportunities
on the journey: "I just keep finding open doors, opportunities leading me to
the next step. I simply wait, do the best job I can do while waiting for the next
step in His plan to emerge."

Challenges and Dilemmas

For some of the students and graduates we interviewed, the potential dissonance between faith and practice created significant, but not overwhelming concerns along the way. For one student this blend was a "dangerous" idea:

> I think that calling and social work sometimes can be dangerous words to associate together for the social work profession because you don't want to minimize the professionalism of social work. And by classifying social work as a ministry, is very dangerous. I think that it does take out the element of professionalism that's there. But at the same time—and I am still, I am definitely in the learning process of this—you need to know how to effectively balance faith and practice, because you are never going to be just a social worker....I am going to be going somewhere as a Christian, with the title social worker. And I think that's a wonderful and such an amazing blessing to have that opportunity, but it can be very dangerous because you are representing two amazing things. ... And I think that's why so many people are so afraid of having faith in practice, and those two words together are like an oxymoron to so many people. I think it's sad, but I think there is a delicate balance there.

Other interviewees, preparing for ministry roles, echoed the potential dissonance between the role of social worker and the role of minister.

> I like the fact that in social work, you know—there are certain things you can do that you can't seem to do in ministry. And there's the other catch where there are certain things you can't do in social work that you can in ministry. For example, with a pastor, they can openly go in and say, this is what I believe and all of this. In social work, it's not really—that's kind of frowned upon.

Students admitted that learning to do this integration was a process; one that sometimes involved some "hard knocks." One student, who described the process of integration as "a little confusing," told us about a learning experience.

> For the most part, it's just a hard issue. You take it case by case. I had a hard experience this past semester in my agency where I did an intake and I asked my client if she ever prayed and it helped our conversation and I didn't regret doing it but my supervisor and I had to talk a long time about why that would have been a bad idea and it was hard. In the end I really saw where he was coming from. I just want to know what is best for the client. I just want to be led by the Holy Spirit and not necessarily by the [NASW] Code of Ethics. It's just really hard for me, but I am learning a lot and I am open to learning a lot more.

Some students reported that trying to reconcile the values of the social work profession with Christian values presented a major obstacle for them. One felt frustrated, stating "I don't know that I have been able to integrate it [faith and social work] to the point that I feel that it works; I feel really torn." Another student described in more detail:

> I think that there are major conflicts with how I was raised and the element of faith in my life. And that was something I struggled with a lot in undergrad is kind of taking on my parents' values and the things that I learned in the church, you know things that I was supposed to do and how I was supposed to act, and my expectations on life, and what I needed to do I felt like conflicted greatly with social work, and that troubled me.

As our graduates report back, having gained several years of practice wisdom, we see them celebrate the challenges of making sense out of the integration:

> Since graduation I have worked at a faith-based agency for a year and now a public agency for almost five years. When I worked at the faith-based agency I felt more support and more connection with some of my co-workers as we had weekly bible study and prayer time. At the agency where I am now, there is not the same level of support. I have had to seek support from friends and family. At the same time I think my faith and the way I integrate faith and practice has become stronger not working at a faith-based agency, because I have had to struggle with how to do it and work at it, when it was so easy at the private faith-based agency.

From others, we hear how experiences with colleagues and clients continue to serve as challenges for what the integration of faith in their practice means for them.

> I encountered obstacles both from colleagues and from clients. I have worked with colleagues who felt clients should share their world view, values, and faith background prior to receiving the full level of help and support available. To these colleagues I provided dialogue and insight into the importance of individual self-determination and the uniqueness of the individual. From clients I have encountered many who desired me to tell them what to believe and to lead them as a spiritual leader would. In these contexts I help the individuals identify more appropriate sources to which they can turn and to help them find some of their answers within themselves and their community.

As graduates look back at us and their time in school, they reflect on what it meant to first learn about faith and practice from our faculty, recognizing that part of the challenge of integration is the diversity of thought on the matter.

> I know that when I was a student I saw the honesty of faculty saying, 'we don't have this entirely figured out as to what it is supposed

to look like 100% of the time, and part of that is because we don't all necessarily see it the same way,' and that made it okay to say to oneself that I may not have this figured out for myself entirely either.

There is some diversity of thought on how we as faculty approach topics of faith and practice. There is even more in the world of social work practice. Our alumni express the challenge of what it means to incorporate this kind of diversity into their own integration.

I have had friends and colleagues from a diverse variety of backgrounds. The conversations I believe are most meaningful are when I am confronted by someone from a different faith background. Often colleagues from various backgrounds have misunderstandings regarding my faith and religion, while my knowledge of their background is incomplete as well. I believe that such conversations enable both of us to gain a better understanding of one another's faith backgrounds and apply that understanding to clients from those backgrounds and provide better and more informed social work services.

These are the dilemmas that social workers describe on their journey toward embracing the authentic integration of social work and Christian faith. While the struggles are significant and formative, there are also encounters with blessings that mark the journey.

Blessings

In spite of encountering challenges, the students we interviewed reported a wide array of blessings that they perceive as being associated with the blending of Christian faith and professional identity. At a deeply personal level, students indicated that their intentional efforts at integration resulted in "the feeling of inner harmony", "freedom and flexibility", and helping "me realize more of who I am and making me understand... what I want to do." Sometimes the reward is a feeling of comfort and joy as reflected in this statement: "I prayed about it, and I feel great about it."

One frequently mentioned outcome of the intentional integration of faith and practice was that faith was strengthened in the process. For example, "my social work education has shaped my faith and has made me— it's kind of really helped me be a better Christian." These words echoed this same conclusion—"it [social work] has made me more genuine in my faith." This kind of integration may also have the power to change important assumptions. One student described herself as "a Christian wearing the hat of a social worker," with training that " is going to be shaping how I speak to people, even though it [professional education] may not have changed everything how I feel, but it has changed how I think."

As students graduate and begin their professional journeys, the identification of blessings continues. One graduate articulated the way that faith and practice work together this way, "For me at least, I think it is fairly second nature to integrate faith and practice because I see a lot of overlap in the values of the social work profession and the Christian tradition."

Furthermore, they are able to be a blessing to others as their faith is expressed in practice, "As a part of my faith I believe that I can do all things through Christ, and I know that I am simply an instrument in his plan. So in my practice I do all that I can to use my gifts and talents as a way to bless those that I am working with and providing services for."

The process of blending faith and practice seemed to have beneficial consequences for interactions with clients. Consider this observation—"I think that's my biggest thing that I've enjoyed ...it's what pulled me into it is being able to identify a need and to be aware of needs more than probably the average person is." One student counted among her blessings: "I have gotten to work with people who I never would have ever talked to or met..." While there may be dilemmas and challenges related to an intentional quest to integrate Christian faith and social work practice, you may also find blessings and opportunities to discover and claim along the way.

Don't Travel Alone

Whatever you encounter, please know that you do not have to travel alone. Christians have expressed this idea in the worship hymn "The Servant Song":

> *We are trav'lers on a journey,*
> *Fellow Pilgrims on the road*
> *We are here to help each other*
> *Walk the mile and bear the load.*

Engaging the dilemmas and claiming the blessings becomes more possible if you will allow others to travel alongside of you. Perhaps you may find mentors who are willing to walk with you and share the benefit of their own experiences on this journey. Find a Christian social worker or faculty member who cares about you and the integration of faith and practice. Form meaningful and trusting relationships with other social work students who are motivated by their Christian faith. Consider joining the North American Association of Christians in Social Work (NACSW) and take advantage of the opportunity to collaborate with a community of Christians in social work and to discover resources that are available to help you as you celebrate and struggle with the integration of faith and practice.

As graduates spent time in the field, they learned the value of this lesson in new and meaningful ways. One graduate shares the experience of a small group for support:

> I have found that in a group of women that I meet with weekly to have Bible study, we find ourselves talking about our faith and our work. There is another social worker in the group as well and we are able to talk about how our own faith impacts how we do

social work, and how we view the situations are clients are in. It is beneficial to have someone else in the profession who has the same faith background as I do to talk with.

Another shares the value of conversations with other peers:

Most of my friends/colleagues outside of work are not social work-ers, however, we talk often about working to change society, but more specifically through the lens mentioned above - Kingdom of God on earth in the here and now. They encourage, inspire, and motivate me to continue striving and though they do not have the social work frame of reference or language, I am able to bridge that gap a bit in our conversations and in work we might do together on the side.

With a few years of practice, the experience of not traveling alone shows it has the power to sustain and inspire. Traveling companions make a meaning-ful difference in helping us understand where we are going and they help us appreciate the journey itself.

It Really Is All About the Journey

The scriptures are replete with journey metaphors that help us understand that our relationship with God and our response to God's call is about the day to day living out of our faith rather than rushing headlong toward a destina-tion. Moses, called to deliver the people, died after a life of leadership with the discovery that his ministry was about the journey, not about the destination. Saul was out looking for donkeys when Samuel found him and communicated God's call for leadership. David was tending sheep when God called him to lead an army and eventually a nation. Jesus' ministry occurred from village to village as he traveled, preached, healed, and loved. He called to his disciples (who were not sure where he would take them), "Come follow me." He invited them to participate with him in ministry rather than to arrive at a particular destination.

We know from the life and ministry of Jesus that the journey is not always easy or without challenges. The words of our students, both during their time in the program and after graduation, confirmed that in spite of challenges, they found strength to continue, by faith, as followers of Jesus, to travel with Him as He equips us and leads us to the hungry, the poor, the broken in body and spirit, the dying, the rejected and lonely, the least of these. Let us journey on together, bound by the call to be fellow travelers with the One who taught us best about the ministry of presence.

We end our chapter with a prayer offered up for social workers by our dean, Dr. Diana Garland, long-time NACSW member and former president. It is our intercession on behalf of you who are joining us on the journey.

We are grateful, Lord God, that when you call us on this journey,
You don't call us to walk it alone.
We thank you for one another to share the journey,
To comfort and encourage one another.
Hold us together, Lord; hold our hands and steady us on the way.
Show us just the next steps to take—
We don't need to see all the way, for we trust the destination to you.
Give us courage to go, step by step, with one another and with you.

Notes

1 This and all other quotes are from interviews conducted in 2004-2005 with Baylor University students and in 2010-11 with Baylor alumni. To protect their anonymity, names will not be cited.

2 To preserve interviewee anonymity we will not cite the author's name here.

CHAPTER 10

FAIRNESS IS NOT ENOUGH: SOCIAL JUSTICE AS RESTORATION OF RIGHT RELATIONSHIPS

Mary Anne Poe

Social justice is a foundational concept for both social work practice and Christian faith. This chapter identifies various historical definitions and approaches to thinking about social justice and explores the challenges that arise for Christians in social work who wish to integrate their biblical faith with current understandings of social justice. Justice as a legal term connoting fairness, especially in the distribution of and access to resources, has been the dominant conceptual framework through history. This chapter presents a conceptual framework that goes beyond justice as fairness to describe justice as an ideal that reflects the human longing for wholeness and harmony in social relationships. Christian faith provides a standard for measuring this state of justice in relationships.

When my two daughters were young, I heard the refrain regularly, "But that's not fair!" Usually, this exclamation occurred over some rather trivial distribution of goods or punishments, like cookies or "time out." Their innate sense of justice had been violated and thus the appeal to fairness. Distribution of resources, retribution for wrongs, and concern for fairness have dominated the discussion about social justice through the ages. These approaches to social justice have directed attention away from the most fundamental meaning of justice—the restoration of right relationships.

Though the human reaction to perceived injustice often defaults to an appeal to fairness, as my daughters' reactions suggest, fairness is simply not adequate to satisfy the human spirit and longing for justice. Additionally, strategies for determining fairness are multiple and complex, including random selection, greatest merit, or first-come, first-serve. Both the processes for promoting and attaining justice and the final outcome are occasions for discontent in the human spirit.

Social justice is an ideal that has captured the imagination of people from the beginning of recorded history. Philosophers, theologians, and political leaders from every historic era have grappled with this most elusive virtue. Justice is one of the most sought after notions, with most every society invoking it as a worthy goal. John Rawls' classic work, *A Theory of Justice*, claims that it is the "first virtue of social institutions, as truth is of systems of thought" (Rawls, 1971, p. 3). The concept is deeply rooted in cultural and religious traditions and beliefs. Because people exist within culture, their understanding of justice is shaped by their cultural context. American revolutionaries had a quite different perspective on the justice of their times than either the American Indians or the British loyalists. This relativity of perspectives does not mean the ideal does not exist. Theologian Miroslav Volf (1996, p, 199) explains that we have to distinguish between the idea of justice and justice itself. Evidence of the efforts to make this distinction pervades the history of law, economics, and politics.

The Christian faith is deeply rooted in the idea of justice. The Old and New Testaments relate both conceptual themes about justice and narratives that describe its application in practice. Scholars have debated whether the two testaments describe different concepts of justice and its application or whether the Bible as a whole has one continuous theme of justice. Understanding the language of justice and the various meanings and applications of the Scriptures has been a major occupation through Christian history (Dunn & Suggate, 1993 McGrath, 1986; Solomon & Murphy, 1990).

In the twentieth century, the profession of social work claimed the promotion of justice as a core value in its code of ethics (NASW, 1996). To some extent, the profession emerged out of the mission of the church in the context of theological debates about the language and meaning of justice (Poe, 2002b). Defining social justice has been elusive for the profession of social work just as it has been for the Christian faith and for philosophers (Pelton, 2001; Scanlon & Longres, 2001). Banerjee (2005) conducted a literature review that revealed very little agreement among social workers about the meaning of social justice and how to achieve it.

This paper identifies through a broad overview various historical definitions and approaches to thinking about justice and gives consideration to some of the linguistic and philosophical difficulties. Since social justice represents a foundational construct for both social work practice and Christian faith, I will explore both challenges and points of congruence that arise for Christians in social work practice who wish to integrate their biblical faith with current understandings of social justice. Justice as a legal term connoting distribution of resources or fairness in court proceedings has been the dominant conceptual framework for thinking about justice in both historic Christianity and the profession of social work. This paper presents a conceptual framework that goes beyond justice as fairness to justice as an ideal that reflects the human longing for wholeness and harmony in human relationships.

Historic Understandings of Justice

Definitions of social justice abound, as do descriptions of various types of social justice. The most common idea of justice is distributive in nature. Distributive justice is concerned with how resources, material goods, influence, and power are shared among people. Sometimes this is summed up by the classic phrase, *suum cuique*, "to each what is due" (Hollenbach, 1977, p. 207). Retributive justice is concerned with punishing wrongdoers, commonly represented by the idea of "an eye for an eye." The American criminal justice system is largely based on retributive justice. In recent years, the criminal justice system has experimented with restorative justice, a form of justice that goes beyond punishing wrongdoers and strives to reconcile criminals and victims (Burford & Adams, 2004; Colson, 2001; Wilson, 2000). Commutative justice refers to a balanced and fair system for agreements or contracts, such as wage laws.

Historically, justice was seen as supreme among all the virtues. It was one of the four cardinal virtues. Socrates posed the question "What is justice?" to Plato in *The Republic* and launched the centuries-long philosophical discourse that has shaped much of western philosophy (Solomon & Murphy, p. 13). Cicero asserted two principles that defined justice. The first was to "do no harm, unless provoked by wrong." The second was to contribute to the common good or overall social welfare (as cited in Langan, 1977, p. 157).

For the ancient Greeks, justice was linked to human well-being, but it accepted class differences and inequality. Plato's conception of justice was one of harmony in the community, but within the community of one's natural status or class. Aristotle followed Plato's lead. He did not believe that people were equal. For him, justice was the single virtue that was directed at "the other" but justice did not require a redistribution of resources in order to arrive at a more fair distribution with the other. Rather, justice entailed accepting one's position in life in the hierarchical scheme established by one's birth (McGrath, 1986; Reisch, 2002).

The Greek philosophers reflect an enduring tension between the retributive principles of just deserts or vengeance that characterize some ideas of justice with the civic virtues of harmony and peace. The ideal of justice that Plato describes as a virtue has to be worked out in the practicalities of life. How do we achieve a just society?

In ancient religious and political practices, both in the East and the West, the appeal for justice is to a divine or singularly authoritative being, such as an emperor. Both the Bible and the Koran appeal to divine authority. The idea of "an eye for an eye" is balanced with appeals to divine and human mercy (Solomon & Murphy, 1990) and suggests the limitations of retribution, an "eye" and no more than an "eye." In ancient China and in Greece, Confucius and Plato assert the authority of the state in settling issues of justice (Solomon & Murphy, 1990). This early acknowledgement of the need for a standard bearer in identifying and upholding justice is a critical point for contemporary discussion of justice.

In *The Republic*, Plato asserts that "the just man and the just city will be no different but alike as regards the very form of justice." The way to identify or define justice is "when each one of us within whom each part is fulfilling its own task will himself be just and do his own work" (as cited in Solomon & Murphy, 1990, 36). The question of whose justice and what standard establishes justice endures to contemporary times. One modern effort to offer a global standard for basic human rights and justice is the United Nations' 1948 *Universal Declaration of Human Rights*. The use of this document, though, requires interpretation about whether in fact justice exists in a given society and begs the question about what privileges this document more than others to define human rights.

The idea of justice in the West bore the imprint of the ancient philosophers' questions about the nature of existence coupled with the theology of the church. Discussion about justice tended to be focused on civil order. In *Summa Theologica*, Aquinas joined the Christian faith and the metaphysics of the philosophers, especially Aristotle, to articulate a theology that dominated the life and thought of the Church until the eighteenth century. Regarding justice, Aquinas emphasized distributive principles.

By the eighteenth century, Thomas Hobbes, John Locke, and Jean-Jacques Rousseau had given shape with various new twists to the idea of justice as a social contract (Solomon & Murphy, 1990). John Stuart Mill advocated utilitarianism as a means to arbitrate the social contract in the nineteenth century and, in doing so, further undermined the idea that justice is an ideal inherent in nature (Solomon & Murphy, 1990). The social contract idea has pervaded the discussion about justice until modern times and is reflected in documents such as the Declaration of Independence and the Universal Declaration of Human Rights.

In the twentieth century, John Rawls' *A Theory of Justice* became the central and dominant voice about the meaning of justice (Banerjee, 2005; Solomon & Murphy, 1990). His theory is a version of the social contract but added the idea of social responsibility to those who are disadvantaged. By this time the idea of justice as an ideal or virtue, or as something more than mere distribution or retribution, had virtually disappeared from the conversation about justice. Justice was linked with the social contract and with the idea of fairness, whether in distribution of resources or in response to wrongdoing. The ancient Hebrew belief in an ideal state of harmony, peace, equality, virtue, and right relationships called justice had been set into a legal and rationalistic framework of contractual law. The essence or character of justice had given way to the practicalities of how to do it.

Biblical Backgrounds

The ancient Hebrew concept of justice appears in the earliest biblical records. The idea of justice is a central theme throughout the Old Testament as it gives an account of the history of the revelation of God's justice. In the Hebrew Bible, two words are translated justice: *sedaqah* and *mishpat*. These two terms are often used in combination for emphasis. *Sedaqah* is about God's plan to build community, to establish right relationships. Some older meanings connect the idea to victory and to the right ordering of affairs (McGrath, 1986). It is not used in the Old Testament in a legal sense to refer to punishment. *Mishpat* is commonly a legal term or claim on an individual. (Mott, 1982; Ripley, 2001).

Emil Brunner noted that the modern age restricted the original meaning of justice and its immense scope and reduced it to mean "giving to each what is due" (as cited in Lebacqz, p. 114). Mott (2000) claims that justice in the Hebrew mind was closer in meaning to "love" than to the distributive meaning of the modern age. Ripley (2001) asserts that the "root of God's justice, no matter how exacting, is always in the context of God's desire for a loving relationship."

McGrath (1986) analyzes the etymology for the Hebrew word *sedaqah* and asserts the fundamental meaning connects the idea to covenantal relationships and in that context to "conformity to a norm." The basic idea of *sedaqah* had meaning for the ancient Hebrews in the law court where the standard for the court was the covenant law with God, the Torah. Thus, being just was being in conformity to the covenant with God (Wright, 2006). It was bound to the idea of wholeness and harmony in relationships.

The New Testament treatment of justice continues the Hebrew focus on right relationships. *Dikaiosune* is the Greek word in the New Testament generally translated "justice" or "righteousness." According to Vine (1966, p. 298), it is the "character or quality of being right or just" or whatever has been appointed by God as right. It designates a relationship rather than an inherent personal quality (Williams, 1980). The word reflects the Hebraic concept of covenant, the establishment of a loving, faithful, and true relationship. A covenant is a binding commitment, with reciprocal benefits and responsibilities. The biblical sense of justice is one of hope and promise, salvation and victory, so that people will thrive in social relationships (Ripley, 2001). Wolterstorff (1983) connects justice with *shalom*. *Shalom* is the "human being dwelling at peace in all his or her relationships" (p. 70). Justice is fundamental to *shalom*.

The grand narrative of the Bible relates the story of justice. God created people who fractured their relationship with the Creator in an act of rebellion. The rebellion resulted in broken relationships, not only with God, but also in the family and throughout society. Human history provides the evidence of pervasive brokenness and records human efforts to create systems, structures, and laws that reach toward the establishment of justice, or a restoration of right relationships. The incarnation of Jesus, his death and resurrection, and redemption for believers provides a way to restore justice in all relationships.

Christian justice is not dependent on context or culture or individuals. It is founded on the very nature and character of God. The two great commandments, "to love God with all your heart, soul, strength, and mind, and to love your neighbor as yourself" express this nature in a succinct fashion (Kunst, 1983, p. 111).

The Essence of Justice

When conflicts arose between my two daughters and their sense of justice was violated, I sometimes had them sit at a table together and take turns saying kind things to the other. They despised this discipline at the time, but the eventual result was usually laughter, their recognition of the many positive traits of the other, and a realization that good relationships were valuable. They had wanted me to be fair and punish the one who had wronged the other, but trying to arrive at "fairness" seemed to exacerbate the problem.

I could rarely assess who was at fault because I often had not directly observed the contested interaction. I also could not judge them equally responsible because they were not equal. Oliver Wendell Holmes once observed that "there is no greater inequality than the equal treatment of unequals" (as cited in Rosado, 1995). One child was three years older, thus bigger, stronger, and more verbally adept. How could I determine fairness between the two?

I found trying to assess fairness frustrating and it did not produce the outcome that I actually desired. I wanted my daughters to grow old together, be lifelong friends, and enjoy genuine harmony and peace. What I wanted was a peaceful and loving relationship to develop between them and within the household. I wanted the *shalom* of the Bible.

A value such as social justice only has meaning for a culture if everyone has a similar understanding of what that value is. For example, love is a value esteemed in American society, but love means many different things to people. For one person, love is self-sacrifice. For another, it is a romantic liaison. Love may mean "never having to say you are sorry" or it may be "do unto others as you would have them do unto you." Americans have not settled on a standard definition for love. Regardless of the number of definitions for love, the value is fundamentally social in nature. Justice, like love, is also fundamentally social in nature, and, like love, how it is understood depends on one's perspective.

Justice is dependent on the connections between and among persons. Justice is often associated with love or contrasted with charity or mercy (Sider, 1999). Augustine defined justice in terms of love in his essay, *De Moribus ecclesiae catholicae* (as cited in Langan, 1977, p. 173). Volf (1996, p. 223) asserts, "If you want justice without injustice, you must want love." Cassidy (1989, p. 442) suggests that justice is about "putting love into structures." If love establishes right relationships, then just structures serve to ensure the desired outcome; justice defines the laws or means that result in loving relationships. The apostle John captures this connection, especially in relation to distributive justice, "But whoever has the world's goods, and beholds his brother in need and closes his heart against him, how does the love of God abide in him?" (I John 3:17, NASB).

It is much easier to identify justice by what it is not than by what it is. Injustice is easily recognized when it happens to us or to "our group." We are much less adept at identifying injustice when it happens to groups of others outside our familiar social categories. Only when we are well connected with others can we recognize when they are experiencing a sense of injustice. Thus, assessing justice requires a level of intimacy in relationships that acknowledges the experienced reality of others. We "enlarge our thinking" by listening to others, especially those with whom we differ, and allowing them to help us see from their perspective (Volf, 1996, p. 213).

Dorothy Day, a Christian activist in the Catholic Workers' Movement, voiced concern for justice in the 1930s. She said, "We need always to be thinking and writing about [poverty], for if we are not among its victims, its reality fades from us. We must talk about poverty because people insulated by their own comfort lose sight of it" (as cited in Kauffman, 2003). Dr. Martin Luther King, Jr. in his *Letter from a Birmingham Jail* extended the responsibility to know the experience of others far beyond the immediate family or neighborhood relationships. He said, "Injustice anywhere is a threat to justice everywhere" (King, 1963, p.

77). Concern for social justice requires knowledge and understanding beyond one's own small circle of friends, extending to the world.

The Social Work Profession and Social Justice

The social work profession has its own history and claim on the concept of social justice. *The Social Work Dictionary* defines justice as "an ideal condition in which all members of a society have the same basic rights, protection, opportunities, obligations, and social benefits," (Barker, 2003, p. 404). This definition suggests a distributive principle in which resources and opportunities are spread about the entire population in a fair manner. Rawls' work has shaped the contemporary landscape for the profession of social work as well as for the larger society (Banerjee, 2005; Rawls, 1971). His development of the idea of the social contract rests on a definition of justice as relational, but based on fair distribution. He is also concerned that the least advantaged are helped in any process of redistribution. Other contemporary social work voices emphasize various dimensions of the concept of justice. Young (1990) argues for a relational type of social justice that includes more than simply a just distribution of goods, but also insists upon fair representation, participation, and influence in decision-making. Others have linked social justice with structures that lead to oppression and thus connected social justice to diversity and multiculturalism (Finn & Jacobsen, 2003; Reisch, 2002). In a more recent and radical step, Reichert (2001, 2003) believes that the lack of a clear definition for social justice begs for a shift in social work thought to that of a "rights-based perspective" utilizing the *Universal Declaration of Human Rights* as a guide or standard.

The social work profession mandates that social workers challenge injustice. It is one of the six core values and ethical principles of the profession as written in the *Code of Ethics* of the National Association of Social Workers (NASW). The Council on Social Work Education (CSWE, 2003) mandates in its *Educational Policy and Accreditation Standards* that curriculum includes social justice content "grounded in an understanding of distributive justice, human and civil rights, and the global interconnections of oppression." Though social justice is not defined explicitly by the CSWE in this document, it does assert that social work practice should entail "strategies to promote social and economic justice" and "advocacy for nondiscriminatory social and economic systems."

Wakefield (1988a) views social justice as the primary mission of social work and insists upon fairness and access to resources. Reid and Popple (1992) argue for a moral foundation to social work, an objective rule that supplies a standard for measuring what is right. They do not offer a source or basis for their moral foundation or describe the standard apart from the ethical assertions of the profession. Even though no clear agreement exists regarding the components of justice or appropriate strategies for achieving justice, the profession's conversation continues. Questions about whose rights trump the others' and how goods should be distributed seem to change with the winds of culture and political realities. Countless others in social work have written about social justice with the usual emphasis on distribution of resources and access to them (Gil, 1998; Pelton, 2001; Scanlon & Longres, 2001).

Standards of Justice

Defining justice in social terms suggests the possibility that "right" or just relationships can happen, that a standard for right relationships exists. The challenge begins with describing what right relationships are like and is fulfilled with achieving them. Metaphors and symbols serve an important function as societies strive to achieve the ideal. Perhaps the most common symbol for justice is a scale. This symbol confines justice to the idea of distribution. It was used for measurements of goods until recent times. The scale as a metaphor illustrates the push and pull of often opposing voices striving for justice. It demonstrates the power of perspective and social location. In the construction industry a plumb line serves as a symbol of what is just. A wall is straight, or just, if the plumb line measures it as straight. The plumb line functions because of the law of gravity that establishes a universal standard of perpendicularity to the ground. Modern computers can "justify" margins either to the left or the right or the middle of a page. Accountants "justify" or reconcile the debits and credits for a business, bringing the account into balance. The ancient mythological image of Justitia, an angelic, blindfolded woman with a sword in one hand and scales in the other, represents an ideal justice that holds no special interest, is blind to the objects of justice and thus can render justice fairly and truly. All of these metaphors for justice rely on the idea that a standard exists by which justice can be assessed. The standard varies from a natural law such as gravity, to a balance between two existing products such as debits and credits.

From ancient time to the present, a system of measurements ensured a common and reliable standard for measurements of tangible materials. This system is gaining precision. In ancient times, the measurement of a foot, or twelve inches, was roughly equivalent to the length of a man's foot. In the present time, scientists can measure distance to sub-atomic precision in nanometers or to galactic proportions in light years. If justice is by its nature relational, it must be evaluated in relation to something, or someone, that is consistent across time and space. When measuring social relationships, the standard has to be a social relationship. Societies have produced social standards for justice, all of which have been declared obsolete or have changed over time. The emperor or king may have set the standard in some cases. When one king died, his standard of justice died with him. The new king had a different set of standards. In other cultures, laws and rules arose, but laws and rules change. Some cultures created and lived by mythologies or religious beliefs about gods who ruled the world. Whatever happened was at the will of the gods. People accepted the "justice" of the gods.

The incarnation of God in Jesus Christ poses an entirely different kind of standard. C.S. Lewis sums up his view of all the fundamental myths that have dominated human literature and culture in a 1931 letter to his friend Arthur Greeves: "Now the story of Christ is simply a true myth: a myth working on us in the same way as the others, but with this tremendous difference—that *it really happened*" (Hooper, 2004, p. 977). Christian faith offers an unequivocal and unchanging standard of justice—God in the person of Jesus Christ. If Jesus, the incarnation of God on earth, serves as the standard, then the acquisition of justice is dependent on a right relationship to this person.

Justice is not ever going to be satisfied by a set of rights or laws or moral principles or anything less than that encompassed in the story of relationship. Other approaches to justice lack a standard that is consistent over time and space by which to evaluate what is just. Jesus Christ is an historical figure. He lived, died, and was resurrected in history. He sets a standard for just relationships unparalleled in any other mythological or philosophical system. Christians, then, accept Jesus himself as the model and standard for justice. He was the bearer of a new possibility of human, social, and therefore political relationships (Scott, 1980; Yoder, 1972). How believers behave in social relationships is "just" based only on its likeness to the way that Jesus would have behaved. Jesus states it this way in Matthew 25: "to the extent that you did it to one of these brothers of Mine, even the least of them, you did it to me" (Mt. 25:40, New American Standard Bible).

Two Streams of Christian Tradition

The Christian tradition is rooted in the grand narrative of the Bible, but Christian tradition is not pure. It represents coalescence of multiple cultures and times interpreting the Scriptures and the traditions in various ways. Volf (1996) argues that the church should not, even if it could, attempt to develop one "coherent tradition." Rather, the church should be interested in "affirming basic Christian commitments in culturally situated ways" (pp. 210-211).

The historic Christian tradition has produced two dominant streams of thought about social justice; one emphasizes the common good or institutional well-being, and the other the rights and responsibilities of the individual. Both offer a pathway toward a just and caring society, though with different means to the end. Many variations of these two themes have emerged through the years depending on the political, economic, and social context for the church.

The Catholic Church has a long tradition of Christian social teaching and represents an emphasis on the institutional community of faith and the common good. This tradition is marked by three fundamental values or premises: 1) All people are created in the image and likeness of God and thus have value and dignity; 2) God created people to live in community together; we are social creatures and need each other, and 3) Each person has a right to share in the abundance of nature, though this right is accompanied by responsibilities (Lebacqz, 1986).

For many centuries the Catholic Church dominated the western Christian landscape. The vision for justice was set in a worldview that understood individual rights, for each person was uniquely made by God, but the emphasis was on the social nature of our condition. It is for the welfare of individuals that society, and especially Christians, should be concerned for the common good. The emphasis in Catholic social teaching on the common good serves as a harness to runaway individualism. It keeps in check the human tendency toward seeking one's own interests at the expense of others. In the nineteenth and twentieth centuries, Catholic teaching understood Hebrew Scriptures to suggest that God gave preferential treatment to the poor and so should the church. The Bishop's Letter of 1971 asserts that the "justice of a community is measured by its treatment of the powerless in society" (as cited in Lebacqz, 1986, p. 72).

The second stream of Christian teaching emerged significantly during the years of the Protestant Reformation. As Martin Luther challenged the bureaucracy and practices of the Catholic Church, he ushered into Christian teaching what became a more privatized and personalized religious life. "Faith alone" became the theme of Protestant thought and eternal salvation the goal, not by works, but by faith. The phrase in Romans 1:17 (NASB), "the righteousness (*dikaiosune*) of God is revealed from faith to faith," served as a basis for Luther's stand that human effort could not achieve what the work of God could in the heart of a person (Ripley, 2001).

Each person had the ability and responsibility to stand before God with his eternal destiny in the balance. The kingdom of God and his justice (*dikaiosune*) described a future kingdom. Justice in this present age was beyond reach. According to some, the influence of the church to shape civil society decreased and interest in social justice declined as a result of the Protestant Reformation (Dulles, 1977; Emerson & Smith, 2000; Haughey, 1977; Lebacqz, 1986; Roach, 1977). However, other influences such as the breakdown of the feudal system with its social contract and the rise of urbanization and industrialization also had significant impact on how church and state both viewed social welfare.

How society approaches social justice depends somewhat on the starting place for discussion. The two streams of Christian thought represented by Catholic thought and Protestant thought are not as simple as described above. They are much more complex based on the particularities of the historical context and the multitude of voices that have articulated differing positions along the continuum. Catholic tradition certainly has not always emphasized the common good, nor has Protestant tradition neglected the pursuit of the common good. What began with Constantine as an attempt to Christianize the western world and serve the general social welfare devolved into a pursuit of political power and status among the clergy and systems of indulgences and penances that strapped the common folk. These two streams can serve, though, as a picture of the dichotomy, or tension, which exists between an emphasis on the common good and that of individual rights and responsibilities.

Linguistic Challenges

The ancient Greeks had two words commonly translated as justice. They are *isotes*, which means equality, and *dikaiosune* which is translated as righteousness (Solomon & Murphy, 1990). The selection of words used in translation suggests nuances of meaning, and over time translations can alter the original intent of the user. Though *isotes* means equality, the ancient Greeks hardly espoused an egalitarian society. On the other hand, *dikaiosune,* when translated as righteousness, suggests a connection with the idea of personal and civic virtues that were so important to the ancient Greek philosophers. Language translation reflects the persistent difficulty in capturing the meaning of justice through history and across cultures and also within cultures.

The translation of the Bible has played an important, though subtle, role in how Christians have thought about justice. New Testament translations have a particularly powerful impact on current understanding.

The Latin Vulgate, used in the early life of the church, translated the Greek word *dikaiosune* into the word *justitio* (McGrath, 1986). Early English translations, such as the King James Version, translated the Latin Vulgate's *justitio* as "justice." After the powerful influence of the Reformation, and more translations developed, the New Testament rendering of *dikaiosune* often became "righteousness." With the Protestant emphasis on personal faith and individual rights and responsibilities, righteousness began to be connected commonly with personal regeneration and likeness to Christ. The connotation of social justice, that is right relationships between and among people, was subsumed by the drive toward personal morality and piety.

Interestingly, modern English translations seldom translate *dikaiosune* as justice. However, *dikaiosune* is the central theme in Jesus' Sermon on the Mount in the Gospel of Matthew. It is used at every juncture to signify the mission of Jesus to usher in the kingdom of God. For his inaugural sermon in the synagogue at the beginning of his public ministry, Jesus draws on the prophet Isaiah's rendering of the future kingdom, "The spirit of the Lord is upon me, because he anointed me to preach the Gospel to the poor. He has sent me to proclaim release to the captives, and recovery of sight to the blind, to set free those who are downtrodden, to proclaim the favorable year of the Lord" (Luke 4: 18-19, NASB). This seems to indicate that Jesus saw his own mission in "justice" terms as Isaiah had foretold. The coming kingdom was to establish "justice to the nations" (Isaiah 42:1, NASB). In fact, Jesus is announcing that he is justice incarnated (Haughey, 1977).

When *dikaiosune* is translated as righteousness, as it is in most modern English translations, it is commonly understood as doing what is right or holy and faithful to the promises of God as an individual. A pardon from sin "interiorizes the meaning too much and fails to account adequately for the dimension of practical social justice" (Scott, 1980, p. 85). This translation fails to evoke the "powerful social transformation" that the word suggests in the original language. Reconciled and restored relationships identify the central motif in all justice issues (Bader-Saye, 2003). Luther's reformation, though probably not intended by Luther himself, taught that God expects believers to be just, or righteous by their faith alone, an interior state of being. Belief in Jesus will ensure that people will have God's righteousness, but it can be a highly individualized and compartmentalized faith that has little relevance to social relationships and the larger social order (Ripley, 2001). Personal conversion and piety with a view toward the afterlife become paramount rather than the present social order.

In contemporary society, the word "justice" inevitably draws one's attention to the legal aspects of the word. Distribution of resources, fairness in law, crime, and its consequences, and the system that executes "justice" over wrongs are the images that emerge. Justice and judgment are inextricably linked. The affirmation that "God is just" suggests that God is the great judge who will bring punishment and condemnation for wrongdoers.

The original linguistic intentions of *sedaqah* and *dikaiosune* that reflect a positive image of restoration of covenant relationships have been lost. The connection of justice with love and mercy has disappeared. Mercy and justice serve as contrasting approaches to wrongs committed rather than as a picture of restoration of wholeness.

Church and State

Since Constantine, the church in the West had assumed major responsibility for addressing social problems such as poverty, illness, and abuse. Understanding of the new life in Christ and biblical mandates, as well as tradition, suggested that the church was responsible for alleviating pain and suffering and providing for the needy. The poor and needy were offered help as an act of worship of God, not because they had a "right" to it. The church and synagogue were the standard bearers for social services (Leiby, 1985). The early church teachings, including the *Didache, The Shepherd of Hermas,* as well as teachings of Polycarp, Clement, Cyprian, and many others, asserted the rights of the poor and the responsibility of the rich. They exhibited a radical sense of community across economic strata (Walsh & Langan, 1977). The poor were seen as entitled to care because they are made in the image of God.

These teachings persisted through the history of the church, though the implementation of justice was certainly not always in accord with this ideal (Poe, 2002b). As Protestantism developed and the church and state became less bound together in the eighteenth and nineteenth centuries, the nature of care for the needy changed; understanding of social justice shifted as well. Which social institution, the church or the state, was the keeper of social justice? Increasingly, the state alone became the arbiter of social justice. The rule of law articulated the standard for social justice and the means for executing it.

The profession of social work emerged largely from the impetus of the faith community and its adherents (Poe, 2002a). The motivation toward promoting social welfare was one's faith and the societal belief that God was concerned for all. In the early twentieth century as the social work profession was developing credibility, practice models, leadership, and relevance, its relationship with the faith community began to change. In the twentieth century, the social work profession bought into state jurisdiction of social welfare while evangelical and mainline churches largely relinquished it. The Catholic Church persisted with a strong emphasis on social justice in such efforts as the Catholic Workers' Movement, but it had lost a considerable amount of political power. Under the influence of the

Enlightenment, mainline Protestant churches reacted to an evangelical emphasis on personal regeneration and bought into a rationalistic and empirical emphasis during the nineteenth and twentieth centuries (Poe, 2002a). The state became accepted as the arbiter of social welfare and all issues of justice.

With the church as the entity giving meaning and direction for social justice, the standard for justice and indeed for all social relationships was Jesus. The aim was the kingdom of God. When the state became the defining institution for implementing social welfare services, the standard became the rule of law and human rights. The goal of social welfare shifted to following welfare policies, "regulating the poor," or controlling protest against injustice rather than eliminating injustice (Burford & Adams, 2004; Leiby, 1985; Piven & Cloward, 1971).

The modern evangelical church has largely missed its opportunities to promote justice during seasons of great social upheaval. Two examples may illustrate the impact that the privatization of faith and righteousness may have had on the role of the church as champion of social justice.

In the United States, the Civil Rights movement of the 1960s had little support from White, evangelical churches. The battle was fought primarily in the public and political arenas and the courts. The Catholic Church and more liberal, mainline Protestant churches had more representation, but, generally, the fight for social justice was dependent on the legal and political systems of the state. The Black church with its limited power embraced the idea of systemic change and provided leadership to advocate for it. It understood that the arbiter of justice was the state but they appealed to the witness of the church. King's *Letter from a Birmingham Jail* (1963) illustrates his dismay at the inability of White clergymen to connect social justice and Christian living. The White evangelical voice was not engaged as an advocate for social justice.

Likewise, in the 1970s and 1980s, evangelical leaders were not concerned with apartheid in South Africa. The "talk was of justification, personal, wonderful justification by faith, but never of justice" (Cassidy, 1989, p. 73). Individual church leaders, such as Archbishop Desmond Tutu, were advocates for biblical justice. The South African ship of state, though, hearkened for many long years to a rule of law that was undergirded by an entrenched but flawed theological system that privatized faith and left social justice out of the equation. Both of these social movements reflect the power of the state to shape social welfare policy. The voice of the church was mediated by individuals through governmental structures, leaving the true witness of the institutional church for social justice to be compromised.

Contemporary Challenges

A challenge exists for both the social work profession and biblical Christianity when defining and promoting social justice. For the profession, the challenge is to identify what standard can be used to evaluate the attainment of justice. Reichert's suggestion to move the profession away from the concept of social justice to one of human rights does not solve this problem (Reichert,

2001, 2003). In fact, to abandon a foundational value of the profession due to its elusiveness seems irresponsible. The profession has to grapple with its roots in the Judeo-Christian tradition that provided a philosophical and ethical basis for the values that shaped its development (Sherwood, 1996). It surely cannot be satisfied if each person has their portion and their rights, but relationships between and among people are still fractured and strained.

The *NASW Code of Ethics* asserts in another of its six core ethical principles that social workers are to recognize the central importance of human relationships. The *Universal Declaration of Human Rights*, while extremely valuable as a guide toward distributive justice, does not give guidance to restore broken relationships and establish *shalom*. And though it is used as a standard, measuring alignment with the standard is elusive. How much education or health care does one have a right to claim? While grounded in the belief that being human merits certain rights and deems one worthy of value, it simply aims at freedom from harm and a minimal fairness in material distribution and access to resources. It does not in fact offer a universal standard for determining when the claims of justice have been met. The profession separates social justice and human relationships into two separate core values. These two values are inextricably linked and undergirded as well by the NASW core value of the worth and dignity of the each person.

Christians do have a universal and objective standard for measuring justice, though Christians themselves do not have the capability of fully attaining or even assessing alignment with the standard with precision. This poses a challenge.

Another challenge is to restore the balanced, biblical understanding of justice that includes both the individual and the social dimension of the concept. Personal faith has to be accompanied by an engagement in the social dimensions of righteousness as reflected through orthodox Christian belief and tradition. Not doing justice is not an option for Christian discipleship. Consider the multiple appeals of the prophets to "do justice" (Micah 6:8, NASB); to "establish justice" (Amos 5:15, NASB); to "preserve justice" (Isaiah 56:1, NASB). The justice of the Bible is not simply fairness. It includes an "embrace of the other" (Volf, 1996, p. 221). What matters is the relationship. This is ultimately what defines justice for a Christian believer. Martin Luther King, Jr. said that social advance in history does not "roll on the wheels of inevitability. Every step towards the goal of justice requires…tireless exertions" (as cited in Cassidy, 1989, p. 463).

The exertions promoting social justice suggest personal responsibility and engagement in the social order. The triumph of early Christianity was its radical sense of community, that everyone would be brought into the fellowship and cared for (Walsh & Langum, 1977). Christians are called to faith and works that lead to a restoration of right relationships, whether an individual's relationship with a neighbor, the relationship of one tribe to another, or one nation to another. Fairness simply does not satisfy the demands of justice.

Societies have constructed elaborate systems of laws and rules, and in the process have settled for fairness as the ultimate expression of justice. The distributive principle of justice has dominated the thinking. The Christian concept of justice, based on biblical principles, involves much more than fairness in the distribution of resources. It is fundamentally a restoration of relational harmony.

Jesus serves as a model for demonstrating justice by the manner in which he related to different people and different societal institutions. He did not treat everyone the same, as though some law or guidebook instructed him. Rather, Jesus demonstrated the capacity to make nuanced judgments, informed by laws but not restricted by the merely human standards or customs of the day. Jesus touched the untouchables, breaking the rules but offering a possibility of restored relationships to a community. He challenged the religious leaders, again violating the customs of the day, but in so doing, offered to the community a chance for *shalom.* Jesus crossed ethnic and gender barriers that produced oppressive environments in efforts to demonstrate what a just and caring world might require. Ultimately, Jesus' death and resurrection give hope to the Christian faithful and a vision for a community of wholeness.

Christian social workers must struggle along with the profession regarding how justice plays out in the world. Christians should be concerned about the distribution of resources and power and access to these resources. They should be concerned about legal systems and human rights. Christians should also strive to understand the biblical concept of social justice, grounded in the very nature of God, and the implications for a just society that is guided by Christian faith. As Christians in social work, the ultimate goal for practice entails a much deeper and richer reality for the nature of human relationships than fairness. The movement in criminal justice settings toward restorative justice is one example of the yearning for this approach.

The prophet Micah proclaims for all time the requirements of God for his people, "to do justice, to love kindness, and to walk humbly with your God" (Micah 6:8, NASB). In the poetic literary tradition of the Hebrew language, this is not three requirements, but one. Doing justice, loving kindness, and walking with humility are rhyming thoughts in Hebrew. They are all part of a unified endeavor that brings wholeness to relationships in the community.

Thus the radical call of God for justice is more than just an even distribution of goods or a fair retribution for wrongs. It is concerned with the quality and nature of the relationships between and among people. This is what I wanted my daughters to experience together in their simple experiences of injustice and this is what I desire for Christians who give their lives to promoting social justice in their social work practice.

References

Aquinas, T. (1981). *Summa Theologica.* Westminster, MD: Christian Classics,.

Bader-Saye, S. (2003). Violence, reconciliation, and the justice of God [Electronic version]. *Crosscurrents, 52*(4), 536-542.

Banerjee, M. (2005). Social work, Rawlsian social justice, and social development [Electronic version]. *Social Development Issues 27*(1), 6-24.

Barker, R. (2003). *The Social Work Dictionary* (5ᵗʰ ed.). Washington D. C.:NASW Press.

Burford, G. & Adams, P. (2004). Restorative justice, responsive regulation and social work. *Journal of Sociology and Social Welfare, 31*(1), 7-26.

Cassidy, M. (1989). *The passing summer: A South African's response to White fear, Black anger, and the politics of love.* London: Hodder & Stoughton.

Colson, C. (2001). *Justice that restores.* Wheaton, IL: Tyndale House Publishers, Inc.

Council on Social Work Education. (2003). *Handbook of accreditation standards and procedures, (5ᵗʰ ed.).* Alexandria, VA: CSWE.

Dulles, A. (1977). The meaning of faith considered in relationship to justice. In J. C. Haughey, (Ed.). *The faith that does justice: Examining the Christian sources for social change.* New York: Paulist Press.

Dunn, J. D. G & Suggate, A. M. (1993). *The justice of God: A fresh look at the old doctrine of justification by faith.* Grand Rapids, MI: Wm. B. Eerdman's Publishing Co.

Emerson, M. O. & Smith, C. S. (2000). *Divided by faith: Evangelical religion and the problem of race in America.* Oxford: Oxford University Press.

Finn, J. & Jacobsen, M. (2003). *Just practice: A social justice approach to social work.* Peosta, IL: Eddie Bowers Publishing Co.

Gil, David G. *Confronting Injustice and Oppression: Concepts and Strategies for Social Workers.* New York: Columbia UP, 1998. Print.

Haughey, J. C. (Ed.). (1977). *The faith that does justice: Examining the Christian sources for social change.* New York: Paulist Press.

Hollenbach, D. (1977). Modern Catholic teachings concerning justice. In Haughey, J. C. (Ed.) *The faith that does justice: Examining the Christian sources for social change.* New York: Paulist Press.

Hooper, W. (Ed.). (2004). *The collected letters of C. S. Lewis, volume 1.* NY: Harper San-Francisco.

Kauffman, R. A. (2003). Justice. *Christianity Today, 37*(3), 70.

King, M. L. Jr. (1963). *Why we can't wait.* New York: The New American Library-Mentor Books.

Kunst, T. J. W. (1983). The kingdom of God and social justice [Electronic version]. *Bibliotheca sacra 140 (April-June),* 108-116.

Langan, J. P. (1977). What Jerusalem says to Athens. In Haughey, J. C. (Ed.) *The faith that does justice: Examining the Christian sources for social change.* New York: Paulist Press.

Lebacqz, K. (1986). *Six theories of justice: Perspectives from philosophical and theological ethics.* Minneapolis, MN: Augsburg Publishing House.

Leiby, J. (1985). Moral foundations of social welfare and social work: A historical view. *Social Work, 30*(4), 323-330.

McGrath, A. (1986). *Justitia Dei: A history of the Christian doctrine of justification.* Cambridge: Cambridge University Press.

Mott, S. C. (2000). Foundations of the welfare responsibility of the government. In S. W. Carlson-Thies & J. W. Skillen (Eds.). *Welfare in America: Christian perspectives on a policy in crisis.* Grand Rapids, MI: Wm. B. Eerdman's Publishing Co.

Mott, S. C. (1982). *Biblical ethics and social change.* New York: Oxford University Press.

National Association of Social Workers. (1996). *NASW code of ethics.* Washington D. C: NASW Press.

Pelton, L. H. (2001). Social justice and social work [Electronic version]. *Journal of Social Work Education. 37*(3) 433-439.

Piven, F. F & Cloward, R. A. (1971). *Regulating the poor: The functions of public welfare.* New York: Vintage Books.

Poe, M. A. (2002a). Christian worldview and social work. In D. S. Dockery & G. A. Thornbury (Eds.). *Shaping a Christian worldview: The foundations of Christian higher education*. Nashville, TN: Broadman & Holman Publishers. Pp. 317-334.

Poe, M. A. (2002b). Good news for the poor: Christian influences on social welfare. In B. Hugen & T. L. Scales (Eds.). *Christianity and social work: Readings on the integration of Christian faith and social work practice* (2nd ed.). Botsford, CT: NACSW.

Rawls, J. (1971). *A theory of justice*. Cambridge, MA: Harvard University Press.

Reichert, E. (2003). *Social work and human rights*. New York: Columbia University Press.

Reichert, E. (2001). Move from social justice to human rights provides new perspective. *Journal of Professional Development, 4*(1), 5-11.

Reid, P. & Popple, P. (1992). *The moral purposes of social work*. Chicago, IL: Nelson-Hall Press.

Reisch, M. (2002). Defining social justice in a socially unjust world [Electronic version]. *Families in Society, 83*(4), 343-354.

Ripley, J. I. (2001). Covenantal concepts of justice and righteousness, and Catholic-Protestant reconciliation: Theological implications and explorations [Electronic version]. *Journal of Ecumenical Studies, 38*(1) 95-109.

Roach, R. R. (1977). Tridentine justification and justice. In J. C. Haughey, (Ed.). *The faith that does justice: Examining the Christian sources for social change*. New York: Paulist Press.

Rosado, C. (1995). God's affirmative justice, *Christianity Today, 39*(13) 34-35.

Scanlon, E. & Longres, J. F. (2001). Social work and social justice: A reply to Leroy Pelton [Electronic version]. *Journal of Social Work Education, 37*(3) 441-444.

Scott, Waldron (1980). *Bring forth justice*. Grand Rapids, MI: Wm. B. Eerdman's Publishing Co.

Sherwood, D. (1996). Asking the impertinent question: Why should I care? *Social Work and Christianity, 23*(2) 79-85.

Sider, R. (1999). *Just generosity: A new vision for overcoming poverty in America*. Grand Rapids, MI: Baker Book House.

Solomon, R. C. & Murphy, M. C (1990). *What is justice? Classic and contemporary readings*. New York: Oxford University Press.

United Nations. (1948). *Universal Declaration of Human Rights*. Retrieved June 13, 2006 fromhttp://www.unhchr.ch/udhr/lang/eng.htm.

Vine, W. E. (1966). *An expository dictionary of New Testament words with their precise meanings for English readers*. Old Tappan, NJ; Fleming H. Revell Co.

Volf, Miroslav (1996). *Exclusion and embrace*. Nashville, TN: Abingdon Press.

Wakefield, J. C. (1988a). Psychotherapy, distributive justice, and social work. Part 1: Distributive justice as a conceptual framework for social work [Electronic version]. *Social Service Review, 62*(2), 187-210.

Walsh, W. J. & Langan, J. P. (1977). Patristic social consciousness: The church and the poor. In J. C. Haughey (Ed.). *The faith that does justice: Examining the Christian sources for social change*. New York: Paulist Press.

Williams, S. K. (1980). The 'righteousness of God" in Romans [Electronic version]. *Journal of Biblical Literature, 99*(2), 241-291.

Wilson, J. (2000). Crying for justice: When victims in grief meet offenders in shame, profound new healing takes place. HOPE, 3-8.

Wolterstorff, N (1983). *Until justice and peace embrace*. Grand Rapids, MI: Wm. B. Eerdman's Publishing Co.

Wright, N. T. (2006, May 1). Righteousness. *New Dictionary of Christian Theology*. Retrieved on 5/1/2006 from http://www.ntwrightpage.com/right_NDCT_Righteousness.htm

Yoder, J. H. (1972). *The politics of Jesus*. Grand Rapids, MI: Wm. B. Eerdman's Publishing Co.

Young, I. M. (1990). *Justice and the politics of difference*. Princeton, NJ: Princeton University Press.

CHAPTER 11

DOING THE RIGHT THING:
A CHRISTIAN PERSPECTIVE ON ETHICAL
DECISION-MAKING FOR CHRISTIANS IN
SOCIAL WORK PRACTICE

David A. Sherwood

You are on the staff of a Christian Counseling Center and in the course of a week you encounter the following clients:

1. A minister who became sexually involved with a teen-age girl at a previous church several years ago. His current church is not aware of this. He says he has "dealt with his problem."
2. A Christian woman whose husband is physically abusive and who has threatened worse to her and their young child if she tells anyone or leaves him. She comes to your office with cuts and bruises, afraid to go home and afraid not to go home. She doesn't know what she should do or can do.
3. A single mother who is severely depressed and who is not taking adequate care of her two young children, both under the age of four. She denies that her personal problems are affecting her ability to take care of her children.

The list could easily go on. Helping professionals, Christian or otherwise, are daily confronted with issues that are immensely complex and which call forth judgments and actions that confound any attempts to neatly separate "clinical knowledge and skill," our preferred professional roles and boundaries, and, fundamentally, our world-view, faith, moral judgment, and character. Much as we would like to keep it simple, real life is messy and all of a piece. All kinds of things interconnect and interact. How would you respond to clients like the ones I just mentioned?

Christian social workers need to know who they are and what resources they have to do the right thing as children of God—personally, socially, and professionally. What are our resources and limits in choosing and acting ethically as Christians who are placed in helping relationships with others? I will try to review briefly a Christian perspective on:

- When we have a moral problem.
- Conditions under which we choose and act.

- Faith and the hermeneutical spiral (understanding God's will).
- How the Bible teaches us regarding values and ethics.
- The Principle/Practice Pyramid.
- A decision-making model which integrates the deontological (ought) dimensions with the teleological (purpose and consequences) dimensions of a problem.
- The fundamental role of a character formed through the discipleship and the guidance of the Holy Spirit.

We cannot devise or forcibly wrench out of the scriptures a set of rules which will simply tell us what to do if we will only be willing to obey. It appears that God has something else in mind for us as He grows us up into the image of Christ. Ultimately, "doing the right thing" results from our making judgments which grow out of our character as we are "changed into his likeness from one degree of glory to another; for this comes from the Lord who is the Spirit" (II Corinthians 3:18).

When Do We Have a Moral Problem?

When do we have a moral "problem?" I would argue that value issues are so pervasive in life that there is virtually no question we face that does not have moral dimensions at some level. Even the choice regarding what brand of coffee to use (or whether to use coffee at all) is not a completely value-neutral question. However, for practical purposes I think it is helpful to realize that moral "problems" tend to be characterized by the following conditions:

1. **More than one value is at stake and they are in some degree of conflict.**
   This is more common than we would like to think. It need not be a conflict between good and bad. It is more usually differing goods or differing bads. A maxim that I drill into my students is "You can't maximize all values simultaneously." Which is to say life continually confronts us with choices, and to choose one thing *always* means to give up or have less of something else. And that something else may be a very good thing, so serious choices are usually very costly ones. A familiar, lighthearted version of this is the adage "You can't have your cake and eat it too." This is one of life's truisms which is very easy to forget or tempting to ignore, but which is at the heart of all value and moral problems. No conflict, no problem.
2. **There is uncertainty about what values are, in fact, involved or what they mean.**
   For example, what are all the relevant values involved in a decision regarding abortion? And what, exactly, is meant by choice, right to life, a person? Where do these values come from? What is their basis? How do they put us under obligation?
3. **There is uncertainty about what the actual facts are.**

What is the true situation? What are the relevant facts? Are they known? Can they be known? How well can they be known under the circumstances?

4. **There is uncertainty about the actual consequences of alternative possible choices and courses of action.**

Often we say that choices and actions should be guided by results. While it is true that their morality is at least in part influenced by their intended and actual consequences, Christians believe that God has built certain "oughts" like justice and love into the creation and that results always have to be measured by some standard or "good" which is beyond the naked results themselves. It is also crucial to remember that consequences can never be fully known at the time of decision and action. The best we can ever do at the time is to *predict*. We are obligated to make the best predictions we can, but we must be humbled by the limitations of our ability to anticipate actual results. However, unintended consequences turn out to be every bit as real and often more important than intended ones, especially if we haven't done our homework.

Under What Conditions Do We Have to Choose and Act?

Given this understanding of a moral "problem," it seems to me that real-life value choices and moral decisions are always made under these conditions:

1. **We have a problem.**

An actual value conflict is present or at least perceived. For example, we want to tell the truth and respect our dying parent's personal rights and dignity by telling him the prognosis but we don't want to upset him, perhaps hasten his death, or create possible complications for ourselves and the hospital staff.

2. **We always have significant limitations in our facts, knowledge, understanding, and ability to predict the consequences of our actions.**

What causes teen-age, unmarried pregnancy? What policies would lead to a decrease in teen-age pregnancy? What other unintended consequences might the policies have? Correct information and knowledge are very hard (often impossible) to come by. As Christians we know that human beings are both finite (limited) and fallen (liable to distortion from selfishness and other forms of sin). The more we can do to overcome or reduce these limitations the better off we'll be. But the beginning of wisdom is to recognize our weakness and dependence.

3. **Ready or not, we have to decide and do *something*, at least for the time being, even if the decision is to ignore the problem.**

Life won't permit us to stay on the fence until we thoroughly understand all the value issues, have all the relevant data, conduct a perfectly complete analysis, and develop a completely Christ-like character.

So, we have to learn how to make the best choices we can under the circumstances. ("You can't maximize all values simultaneously" but you have to give it your best shot!)

4. **Whatever decision we make and action we take will be fundamentally influenced by our assumptions, world-view, faith—*whatever* that is.**

   "Facts," even when attainable, don't sustain moral judgments by themselves. They must be interpreted in the light of at least one faith-based value judgment. Where do my notions of good and bad, healthy and sick, functional and dysfunctional come from? Never from the "facts" alone (Lewis, 1947, 1943).

5. **We would like to have definitive, non-ambiguous, prescriptive direction so that we can be completely certain of the rightness of our choice, but we never can.**

   Not from Scripture, not from the law, not from our mother. We want to *know* without a doubt that we are right. This has always been part of the allure of legalism, unquestioning submission to authorities of various stripes, and simplistic reduction of complex situations. The only way (to seem) to be saved by the law is to chop it down to our own puny size.

6. **We may not have legalistic, prescriptive formulas, but we *do* have guidance and help.**

   Doing the right thing is not just a subjective, relativistic venture. God knows the kind of help we really need to grow up in Christ and God has provided it. We need to be open to the kind of guidance God actually gives instead of demanding the kind of guidance we think would be best. What God has actually given is Himself in Jesus Christ, the story of love, justice, grace, and redemption given witness in Scripture, the Holy Spirit, and the community of the church, historically, universally, and locally.

7. **Ultimately, doing the right thing is a matter of identity and character.**

   In the last analysis, our morality (or lack of it) depends much more on *who* we are (or are becoming) than what we know or the procedures we use. We must become persons who have taken on the mind and character of Christ as new creations. And it turns out that this is precisely what the Bible says God is up to—growing us up into the image of Christ, from one degree of glory to another. The "problem" of making and living out these moral decisions turns out to be part of the plot, part of God's strategy, suited to our nature as we were created. Instead of fighting and resenting the hardness of moral choice and action, maybe we should *embrace* it as part of God's dynamic for our growth.

Faith and the Hermeneutical Spiral

Walking By Faith Is Not Optional

Christian or not, consciously or not, intentionally or not, we all inevitably approach understanding the world and ourselves on the basis of assumptions or presuppositions about the nature of things. Walking by faith is not optional. All human beings do it. We do have some choice (and responsibility) for what we continue to put our faith in, however. That's where choice comes in.

Is love real or a rationalization? Does might make right? Do persons possess inherent dignity and value? Are persons capable of meaningful choice and responsibility? Are human beings so innately good that guilt and sin are meaningless or destructive terms? Is human life ultimately meaningless and absurd? Is the physical universe (and ourselves) a product of mindless chance? Is there a God (or are *we* God)? These are a few of the really important questions in life and there is no place to stand to try to answer them that does not include some sort of faith.

Interpreting the Facts

Like it or not, the world, life, and scripture are not simply experienced or known directly. Things are *always* interpreted on the basis of assumptions and beliefs we have about the nature of the world that are part of our faith position. Knowingly or not, we are continually engaged in hermeneutics, interpretation on the basis of principles.

My interpretation of the meaning of scripture, for example, is strongly affected by whether or not I believe the Bible is a strictly human product or divinely inspired. It is further affected by whether or not I assume the Bible was intended to and can, in fact, function as a legal codebook providing specific prescriptive answers to all questions. My beliefs about these things are never simply derived from the data of the scripture only, but they should never be independent of that data either. In fact, a good hermeneutical principle for understanding scripture is that our interpretations *must* do justice to the actual data of scripture (Osborne, 1991; Swartley, 1983).

The same is true regarding our understanding or interpretation of the "facts" of our experience. The same event will be seen and interpreted differently by persons who bring different assumptions and expectations to it.

On the day of Pentecost, the Bible records that the disciples "were filled with the Holy Spirit and began to speak in other tongues as the Spirit enabled them" (Acts 2:4). Some in the crowd didn't know anything about the Holy Spirit, but were amazed by the fact that they heard their own native languages. "Are not all of these men who are speaking Galileans? Then how is it that each of us hears them in his native tongue" (Acts 2:7-8). Some, however, heard the speech as drunken nonsense and said, "They have had too much wine" (Acts 2:13). Different interpretive, hermeneutical frameworks were in place, guiding the understanding of the "facts."

As a child, I occasionally experienced corporal punishment in the form of spankings from my mother (on one memorable occasion administered with a willow switch). The fact that I was on rare occasions spanked is data. But what did those spankings "mean" to me? Did I experience abuse? Was I experiencing loving limits in a way that I could understand? The experience had to be interpreted within the framework of the rest of my experiences and beliefs (however formed) about myself, my mother, and the rest of the world. And those "facts" continue to be interpreted or re-interpreted today in my memory. In this case, I never doubted her love for me or (at least often) her justice.

The Hermeneutical Spiral

We come by our personal faith position in a variety of ways—adopted without question from our families, friends, and culture; deliberately and critically chosen; refined through experience; fallen into by chance or default. Or, more likely, it comes through some combination of all of these and more. However it happens, it is not a static, finished thing. Our interpretation and understanding of life proceeds in a kind of reciprocal hermeneutical spiral. Our faith position helps order and integrate (or filter and distort) the complex overload of reality that we confront. But at the same time reality has the capacity to challenge and at least partially modify or correct our assumptions and perceptions (Osborne, 1991; Sherwood 1989).

Once the great 18th century English dictionary-maker, writer, conversationalist, and sometime philosopher Samuel Johnson was asked by his biographer Boswell how he refuted Bishop Berkeley's philosophical theory of idealism (which asserted that the physical world has no real existence). Johnson replied, "I refute it *thus*." He thereupon vigorously kicked a large rock, causing himself considerable pain but gaining more than enough evidence (for himself, at least) to cast doubt on the sufficiency of idealist theory as a total explanation of reality.

This is a hermeneutical spiral. You come to interpret the world around you through the framework of your faith, wherever you got it, however good or bad it is, and however embryonic it may be. It strongly affects what you perceive (or even look for). But the world is not a totally passive or subjective thing. So you run the risk of coming away from the encounter with your faith somewhat altered, perhaps even corrected a bit, or perhaps more distorted. Then you use that altered faith in your next encounter (Osborne, 1991; Pinnock, 1984; Sire, 1980). Unfortunately, there is no guarantee that the alterations are corrections. But, *if* the Bible is true, and *if* we have eyes that want to see and ears that want to hear, we can have confidence that we are bumping along in the right general direction, guided by the Holy Spirit.

How Does the Bible Teach Us?

The Heresy of Legalism

For Christians, the desire for unambiguous direction has most often led to the theological error of legalism, and then, on the rebound, to relativism. Legalism takes many forms but essentially uses the legitimate zeal for faithfulness to justify an attempt to extract from the Bible or the traditions of the elders a system of rules to cover all contingencies and then to make our relationship to God depend on our understanding and living up to those rules (Sherwood, 1989).

It is theological error because it forces the Bible to be something that it is not—an exhaustive theological and moral codebook yielding prescriptive answers to all questions. It distorts the real nature and meaning of God's self-revelation in the incarnation of Jesus Christ, the Holy Spirit, the Scriptures, and even nature. Taken to its extreme, it effectively denies the gospel of justification by faith in Jesus Christ and substitutes a form of works righteousness. It can take the good news of redeeming, reconciling love and distort it into a source of separation, rejection, and condemnation.

The paradigm case in the New Testament involved some of the Pharisees. Jesus had some very strong words for them. When the Pharisees condemned the disciples for breaking the Sabbath by gathering grain to eat, Jesus cited the example of David feeding his men with the temple bread, also a violation of the law, and told them, in effect, that they were missing the point of the law. "The Sabbath was made for man, not man for the Sabbath" (Mark 2:23-28). In the parable of the Pharisee and the tax collector Jesus warned about those who "trusted in themselves that they were righteous and despised others" (Luke. 18:9-14). He talked of those who strain out gnats and swallow camels, careful to tithe down to every herb in their gardens but neglecting the "weightier matters of the law, justice and mercy and faith" (Mt. 23:23-24). When a group of Pharisees condemned the disciples because they didn't wash their hands according to the Pharisees' understanding of the requirements of purification, saying, "Why do your disciples transgress the tradition of the elders?" Jesus answered, "And why do you transgress the commandment of God for the sake of your tradition? . . . For the sake of your tradition you have made void the word of God. Hear and understand: not what goes into the mouth defiles a man, but what comes out of the mouth" (Matthew 15:1-11).

The Heresy of Subjective Relativism

If the Bible isn't a comprehensive lawbook out of which we can infallibly derive concrete, prescriptive directions for every dilemma, what good is it? Aren't we then left to be blown about by every wind of doctrine, led about by the spirit (or spirits) of the age we live in, guided only by our subjective, selfish desires? This is a good example of a false dichotomy, as though these were the only two alternatives. Either the Bible is a codebook or we land in total relativism. Yet this is the conclusion often drawn, which quite falsely restricts the terms of the discussion. Once we cut loose from the deceptively certain rules of legalism it is very easy to become the disillusioned cynic—"I was tricked once, but I'm not going to be made a fool again." If the Bible can't give me all the answers directly then it's all just a matter of human opinion. So the false dilemma is stated.

The Orthodoxy of Incarnation—What if God Had a Different Idea?

Such conclusions assume that, to be of any practical use, God's revelation of His will can only be of a certain kind, an assumption we are more likely to take *to* the Bible than to learn *from* it. It assumes that divine guidance must be exhaustively propositional, that what we need to be good Christians and to guide our moral lives is either specific rules for every occasion or at least principles from which specific rules can rationally be derived. What if such an assumption is wrong? What if it is not in keeping with the nature of God, the nature of human beings, the nature of the Bible, or the nature of the Christian life?

What if the nature of Christian values and ethics cannot be adequately embodied or communicated in a book of rules, however complex and detailed? What if it can only be embodied in a life that is fully conformed to the will of God and communicated through the story of that life and its results?

What if God had to become a man, live a life of love and justice, be put to death innocently on the behalf of others, and raise triumphant over death to establish the kingdom of God? What if the Bible were book about that? A true story of how to become a real person?

The point I am trying to make is that if we go to the Bible for guidance on its *own* terms, not deciding in advance the nature that guidance has to take, what we find is neither legalism nor relativism but precisely the kind of guidance that suits the kind of reality God actually made, the kind of creatures we actually are, the kind of God with whom we have to do.

We learn that ethical practice has more to do with our identity, our growth in character and virtue, than it does with airtight rules and that the Bible is just the kind of book to help us do this. It may not be as tidy as we would like. It may not be as easy as we would like to always tell the good guys from the bad guys. We may not always be able to act with the certain knowledge that we are doing just the right (or wrong) thing. But we will have the opportunity to get closer and closer to the truth of God, to grow up into the image of Christ. Growth is not always comfortable. But the Bible tells us who we are, whose we are, and where we're going.

God is Bigger Than Our Categories but the Bible is a Faithful Witness

The reality of God and biblical truth shatters our categories. At least, none of them, taken alone, can do the God of the Bible justice. Taken together, our categories have the potential to balance and correct each other. Human language can only carry so much divine freight in any particular car.

We are *all* susceptible to distorted use of Scripture. We need the recognition that we (*all* of us) always take preconditions to our Bible study that may seriously distort its message to us. In fact, we often have several *conflicting* desires and preconditions at work simultaneously. For example, we have the hunger for the security of clear-cut prescriptive answers ("Just tell me if divorce is always wrong or if I have a scriptural right to remarry") *and* a desire to be autonomous, to suit ourselves rather than submit to anyone or anything ("I don't want to hurt anyone, but my needs have to be met").

So, how do I think the Bible teaches us about morality? How does it guide us in making moral judgments in our professional lives? Struggling to rise above my own preconditions and to take the Bible on its own terms, to see how the Bible teaches and what the Bible teaches, I think I am beginning to learn a few things.

God's Project: Growing Us up into the Image of Christ

It seems to me that God is trying to reveal His nature and help us to develop His character. And it seems that the only way He could do that is in *personal* terms, creating persons with the dignity of choice, developing a relationship with a nation of them, becoming one of us Himself, revealing His love, grace, and forgiveness through a self-sacrificial act of redemption, and embarking on a process of growing persons up into His own image. The process requires us to be more than robots, even obedient ones. It requires us to make principled judgments based on virtuous character, to exercise wisdom based on the character of Christ. Neither legalism nor relativism produces this.

According to the Bible, growing us up to have the mind and character of Christ is an intrinsic part of God's redemptive project. We are not simply forgiven our sins that grace may abound but we are being rehabilitated, sanctified— being made saints, if you will. The theme is clear, as the following passages illustrate.

In Romans 6:1-2, 4 Paul says that, far from continuing in sin that grace may abound, we die to sin in Christ, are buried with him in baptism, and are raised that we too may live a new life. Romans 12:2 says that we do not conform to the pattern of this world but are to be transformed by the renewing of our minds which makes us able to test and approve what God's will is. II Corinthians 3:17-18 says that where the Spirit of the Lord is, there is freedom and that we are being transformed into His likeness with ever-increasing glory. Ephesians 4:7, 12-13 says that each one of us has been given grace from Christ to prepare us for service so that the body of Christ might be built up until we all reach unity in the faith and knowledge of the Son of God and become mature, attaining to the whole measure of the fullness of Christ. I John 3:1-3 marvels at the greatness of the love of the Father that we should be called children of God and goes on to affirm that, although what we shall be has not yet been made known, we do know that when Christ appears we shall be like him. In Philippians 2, Paul says that, being united with Christ, Christians should have the same servant attitude as Christ, looking out for the interests of others as well as ourselves. Then he makes this remarkable conjunction—"Continue to work out your own salvation with fear and trembling, for it is God who works in you to will and to act according to his good purpose."

And in I Corinthians 2 Paul says that we speak a message of wisdom among the mature, God's wisdom from the beginning, not the wisdom of this age, revealed to us by His Spirit. He explains that we have received the Spirit who is from God that we might understand what God has freely given us. He concludes, "Those who are unspiritual do not receive the gifts of God's Spirit for they are foolishness to them, and they are unable to understand them because they are spiritually discerned … But we have the mind of Christ."

A Key: Judgments Based on Wisdom Growing Out of the Character of Christ

It would seem that the key to integrating Christian values into professional practice (as in all of life) is making complex judgments based on wisdom growing out of the mind and character of God, incarnated in Jesus Christ.

In our personal and professional lives we face many complex situations and decisions, large and small. Real-life moral dilemmas confront us with having to make choices between (prioritize) values that are equally real (though not necessarily equally important—remember Jesus' comments on keeping the Sabbath versus helping a human being). Whatever we do, we cannot fully or equally maximize each value in the situation. (If the father embraces the prodigal son and gives him a party, there will be some who will see him as rewarding irresponsibility.) Whatever we do, we have to make our choices on the basis of limited understanding of both the issues involved and the consequences of our actions. Moreover, our decision is complicated by our fallen nature and selfish desires.

In situations like this, the answer is not legalism (religious or scientific) or relativism. The *mind* of Christ helps us to figure out *what* to do and the *character* of Christ helps us to have the capacity (i.e., character or virtue) to actually *do* it. It seems to me that in the very process of struggling through these difficult situations we are dealing with a principle of growth that God has deliberately built into the nature of things. The people of God are continually required to make decisions based on principles embodied in our very identity—the character of who we are, whose we are, and where we are going.

These virtues are not just abstract ones but rather they are incarnated in the history and *character* of Jesus Christ. Love and justice are the fundamental principles but we learn what they mean because Jesus embodies them. (Yes, keep the Sabbath but don't let that keep you from helping someone.)

How should a Christian social worker respond when a client says she wants an abortion? How should parents respond when an unmarried daughter tells them she is pregnant? How should a church respond to a stranger's request for financial aid? Should I be for or against our Middle Eastern policy? Should my wife Carol and I invite my mother to come and live with us? How much money can I spend on myself? It appears I have some complex judgments to make in order to live a life of love and justice.

So, one of God's primary dynamics of growth seems to be to place us in complex situations which require decisions based on judgment. These decisions require our knowledge of the character of Christ to make and they require that we be disciplined disciples at least beginning to take on the character of Christ ourselves to carry them out. It seems to me there is a deliberate plot here, daring and risky, but the only one that works, which fits the world as God made it.

Can the Preacher Have a Boat?

Permit me a personal example to illustrate the point. I remember a lively debate in the cafeteria as an undergraduate in a Christian college over whether or not a preacher (i.e. completely dedicated Christian) could have a boat. The issue, of course, was stewardship, our relationship and responsibility toward material wealth, our neighbors, and ourselves. How should faithful Christians spend money?

Being mostly lower middle class, we all easily agreed that a yacht was definitely an immoral use of money and that a rowboat or canoe was probably o.k. But could it have a motor? How big? Could it possibly be an inboard motor? How many people could it carry? It was enough to cross a rabbi's eyes. Since we believed the Bible to contain a prescriptive answer to every question, we tried hard to formulate a scriptural answer. But we found no direct commands, approved apostolic examples, or necessary inferences that would nail it down.

What we found was much more challenging—things like:

- The earth is the Lord's and the fullness thereof (Psalm 24:1).
- Give as you have been prospered (I Corinthians 16:2).
- What do you have that you did not receive (II Corinthians 4:7)?
- Remember the fatherless and widows (Jas. 1:27).
- Don't lay up treasures on earth (Mt. 6:19-20).
- Follow Jesus in looking out for the interests of others, not just your own (Phil. 2:1-5).

Plenty of guidelines for exercising love and justice, lots of examples of Christ and the disciples in action—in other words, no selfish relativism. But no ironclad formulas for what to spend or where—in other words, no legalism.

Instead, every time I turn around I am faced again with new financial choices, fresh opportunities to decide all over again what stewardship means—plenty of chances to grossly rationalize, distort, and abuse the gospel, to be sure. But also plenty of opportunities to get it right this time, or at least better. To grow up into the image of Christ.

Gaining the Mind and Character of Christ

So, only persons of character or virtue can make the kind of judgments and take the actions required of us. To do the right thing we need to be the right kinds of persons, embodying the mind and character of Christ (MacIntyre, 1984; Hauerwas, 1981).

The most direct route to moral practice is through realizing our identity as Christ-Ones. In Galatians 2:20 Paul said, "I have been crucified with Christ and I no longer live, but Christ lives in me. The life I live in the body, I live by faith in the Son of God, who loved me and gave himself for me" and in Galatians 5:13-14 he said "You were called to freedom, brothers and sisters; only do not use your freedom as an opportunity for self-indulgence, but through love become slaves to one another. For the whole law is summed up in a single commandment, 'You shall love your neighbor as yourself.'"

The mind and character of Christ is formed in us by the Holy Spirit as we submit to God's general revelation in creation (Romans 1-2), written revelation in Scripture (II Tim. 3:15-17), and, ultimately, incarnated revelation in Jesus Christ (John 1:1-18; Col. 1:15-20). We can only give appropriate meaning to the principles of love and justice by knowing the God of the Bible, the Jesus of incarnation, and the Holy Spirit of understanding and power. This happens best (perhaps only) in the give and take of two living communities—Christian families and the church, the body of Christ.

What we have when this happens is not an encyclopedic list of rules that gives us unambiguous answers to every practical or moral issue we may ever encounter. Neither are we left in an uncharted swamp of selfish relativity. And, it should be noted well, we are not given a substitute for the clear thinking and investigation necessary to provide the data. The Bible and Christ Himself are no substitute for reading, writing, and arithmetic (or practice wisdom, theory, and empirical research)—getting the best information we can and thinking honestly and clearly about it.

Instead, what we have then is the enhanced capacity to make and carry out complex judgments that is more in harmony with God's love and justice than we could make otherwise (Hauerwas & Willimon, 1989; Adams, 1987). We are still limited. We still know in part and "see but a poor reflection as in a mirror" (I Corinthians 13:12).

We may be disappointed that the Bible or Christ Himself doesn't give us the kind of advice, shortcuts, or easy black-and-white answers we would like, but what they give us is much better—the truth. Do you want to live a good life? Do you want to integrate your Christian values and your professional helping practice? Do you want to do what is right? The only way, ultimately, is to know God through being a disciple of Christ. This doesn't mean that only Christians can have good moral character—God's common grace is accessible to all. But it really is *true* that Jesus is the way, the truth, and the life (John 14:6). God is the one who gives *content* to the idea of "good." The mind of Christ is really quite remarkable, filling up and stretching to the limit our humanity with God.

> Lord, help us to know
> **who** we are,
> **whose** we are, and
> **where** we are going.

Applying Values in Practice: The Principle/Practice Pyramid

As I think about the relationship between basic faith (worldview assumptions and beliefs), core values or principles that grow out of our faith, the rules that we derive in order to guide our application of those principles to various areas of life, and the application of those values and rules to specific day-to-day ethical and practical decisions we must make, it helps me to use the image of

a "Principle/ Practice Pyramid." The shape of the pyramid gives a rough suggestion of the level of agreement and certainty we may have as we go from the
abstract to the concrete. You can turn the pyramid whichever way works best
for your imagination—sitting on its base or balanced on its top. I put it on its
base (Sherwood, 2002).

Fundamental Worldview and Faith-Based Assumptions

The base or widest part of the pyramid represents our fundamental worldview and faith-based assumptions about the nature of the world, human beings,
values, and God. All persons, not just "religious" people or Christians, have no
choice but to make some sort of faith-based assumptions about the nature of
the world and the meaning of life. These are the basic beliefs that help us to
interpret our experience of life. This is part of the "hermeneutical spiral" we
spoke of earlier. It is on this level that Christians are likely to have the broadest
agreement (There is a God, God is creator, God has given human beings unique
value, values derive from God).

Core Values or Principles

On top of and growing out of the faith-based foundation sits our core
values or principles. What is "good"? What are our fundamental moral obligations? As a Christian I understand these to be the "exceptionless absolutes" of
love and justice (Holmes, 1984). God is love. God is just. There is no situation
where these values do not apply. And we must look to God to learn what love
and justice mean. The social work analogy would be the core values expressed
in the Code of Ethics: service, social justice, dignity and worth of the person,
importance of human relationships, integrity, and competence (NASW, 1999).

Moral or Ethical Rules

On top of and growing out of the "principle" layer are the moral rules that
guide the application of the principles to various domains of life. These are the
"deontological" parameters that suggest what we ought to do. Biblical examples
would be the Ten Commandments, the Sermon on the Mount, and other Biblical
teachings that help us to understand what love and justice require in various
spheres of life. Tell the truth. Keep promises. Don't steal. In the Social Work
Code of Ethics, these would be the specific standards relating to responsibilities
to clients, colleagues, practice settings, as professionals, the profession itself, and
the broader society. Each of these categories in the Code has a set of fairly specific
and prescriptive rules. Don't have sexual relationships with clients. Maintain
confidentiality. Avoid conflicts of interest. These rules are very important in
giving us guidance, but they can never provide us with absolute prescriptions
for what we should always do on the case level (Sherwood, 1999, Reamer, 1990).

Cases Involving Ethical Dilemmas

At the top of the pyramid sit the specific cases involving ethical dilemmas in which we are required to use the principles and rules to make professional judgments in the messiness of real life and practice. It is at this very concrete level that we will find ourselves in the most likelihood of conscientious disagreement with each other, even when we start with the same values, principles, and rules. The short answer for why this is true is found in what we have discussed before. It is that we are fallen (subject to the distortions of our selfishness, fear, and pride) and finite (limited in what we can know and predict). And even more challenging, our principles and rules start coming into conflict with each other on this level. We must maintain confidentiality; we have a duty to warn. Our ability to know relevant facts and to predict the consequences of various courses of action is severely limited, yet some choice must be made and some action taken, now.

An Ethical Decision-Making Model

Given this understanding of the human situation, how God is working with us to grow us up into the image of Christ and the proper role that the Bible plays in giving us guidance, I would like to briefly introduce an ethical decision-making model for Christian helping professionals. It is a simple "problem-solving" model that assumes and is no substitute for developing the mind and character of Christ. It is simple only in concept, not in application. And it is what we need to do in all of our lives, not just in our work with clients.

Deontological and Consequentialist/Utilitarian Parameters

Ethical judgments and actions can generally be thought of as being based on two kinds of criteria or parameters—deontological and consequentialist/utilitarian. These are philosophical terms for describing two types of measuring sticks of whether or not something is good or bad in a moral sense and either ought or ought not to be done.

Deontological Parameters—The "Oughts"

Deontological parameters or criteria refer to moral obligation or duty. What are the moral imperatives or rules that relate to the situation? What are the "oughts?" For the Christian, it can be summed up by asking "What is the will of God in this situation?" Understanding the deontological parameters of an ethical dilemma we face is extremely important. But it is not as simple as it may first appear. Some think that ethics can be determined by deontological parameters only or that deontological parameters operate without consideration to consequences in any way. For example, the commandment "Thou shalt not lie" is taken to be an absolute, exceptionless rule that is to be obeyed in all circumstances and at all times, regardless of the consequences. By this principle, when Corrie Ten Boom was asked by the Nazis if she knew of any Jews, she should have led them to her family's hiding place.

Trying to answer all moral questions by attempting to invoke a particular deontological principle in isolation, even if the principle is biblical, may wind up leading us into actions which are contrary to God's will. That is the legalistic fallacy that we discussed before. Normally we have an ethical dilemma because we are in a situation in which more than one deontological principle applies and they are in conflict to some degree. Do we keep the Sabbath or do we heal? The Ten Commandments or the Sermon on the Mount, for example, contain deontological principles that are vitally important to helping us understand the mind of Christ and doing the will of God. But they cannot be handled mechanistically or legalistically or we will become Pharisees indeed. Does "turning the other cheek" require us to never resist evil in any way?

Most Christians properly understand that God's will is fully embodied only in God's character of love and justice, which was incarnated in the person of Jesus Christ. Love and justice are the only "exceptionless absolutes" in a deontological sense. The moral rules and principles of scripture provide important guidelines to help us to understand what love and justice act like in various circumstances, but they cannot stand alone as absolutes nor can they be forced into a legal system which eliminates the need for us to make judgments.

Consequentialist/Utilitarian Parameters—The "Results"

For God and for us, moral reality is always embodied. Part of what this means, then, is that the deontological "oughts" can never be completely separated from the consequentialist/utilitarian parameters. The consequentialist/utilitarian parameters refer to the results. Christian ethical decisions and actions always have to try to take into account their consequences. What happens as a result of this action or that, and what end is served?

Many people (quite falsely) believe that moral judgments or actions can be judged exclusively on the basis of their results. Did it have a "good" or desired result? Then it was a good act. Many believe that if we value the end we implicitly accept the means to that end, no matter what they might be (say, terrorism to oppose unjust tyranny). This is just as much a fallacy as the single-minded deontological judgment. Pure utilitarianism is impossible since there must be some deontological basis for deciding what is a "good" result, and this can never be derived from the raw facts of a situation. And "goods" and "evils" must be prioritized and balanced against one another in means as well as the ends.

It is a fact that some adults engage in sexual activity with children. But so what? What is the moral and practical meaning of that fact? Is it something we should encourage or prevent? Without some standard of "good" or "health" it is impossible to give a coherent answer.

Another major limitation of consequentialist/utilitarian criteria in making moral judgments is that at best they can never be more than guesses or *predictions* based on what we *think* the results might be, never on the actual consequences themselves. If I encourage my client to separate from her abusive husband, I may think that he will not hurt her or the children, but I cannot be sure.

So, ethical and practical *judgments* are always required. They aren't simple. And they always involve identifying, prioritizing, and acting on *both* deontological and consequentialist/utilitarian parameters of a situation (Sherwood, 1986).

The Model: Judgment Formed By Character and Guided By Principle

1. Identify and explore the problem:
What issues/values (usually plural) are at stake? What are the desired ends? What are the alternative possible means? What are the other possible unintended consequences?

2. Identify the deontological parameters:
What moral imperatives are there? What is the will of God, the mind of Christ? What are the principles at stake, especially in regard to love and justice? Are there any rules or rule-governed exceptions, biblical injunctions, commands, or codes of ethics which apply?

3. Identify the consequentialist/utilitarian parameters:
What (as nearly as can be determined or predicted) are the likely intended and unintended consequences? What are the costs and benefits? How are they distributed (who benefits, who pays)? What must be given up in each particular possible course of action? What values will be slighted or maximized?

4. Integrate and rank the deontological and consequentialist/utilitarian parameters:
What best approximates (maximizes) the exceptionless absolutes of love and justice?

5. Make a judgment guided by character and act:
After gathering and analyzing the biblical, professional and other data, pray for wisdom and the guidance of the Holy Spirit.

Make a judgment and act growing out of your character as informed by the character of Christ.

Refusing choice and action is choice and action, so you must do the best you can at the time, even if, in retrospect it turns out you were "sinning bravely."

6. Evaluate:
Grow through your experience. Rejoice or repent, go on or change.

Character Formed through Discipleship and the Guidance of the Holy Spirit

Ultimately, ethical Christian practice depends on one thing—developing the mind and character of Christ. It depends on our growing up into the image of Christ. This begins in the new birth as we become new creations in Christ. We are filled with the Holy Spirit and called to a life of discipleship in which we bring every thought and action in captivity to Christ (II Corinthians 10:5). We present our bodies "as a living sacrifice," not conformed to this world, but "transformed by the renewal of your mind" (Rom. 12:1-2). We hunger and thirst after righteousness. We seek to know God's will through scripture, the guidance of the Holy Spirit, and the community of the church. We identify with Jesus and the saints of God down through the ages. We daily choose to follow Christ as best we know and can. We repent and confess to our Lord when we fall. We thankfully receive his grace. We choose and act again.

Certainly piety is not a substitute for the discipline of professional training, careful research, and thoughtful analysis. Rather, the use of all of these is simply a complimentary part of our stewardship and discipleship. The most solid possible assurance that we will do the right thing in our personal lives and in our professional practice is our discipleship, growing to have more and more of the character of Jesus Christ, as we make judgments more in harmony with God's character and Spirit.

We become a "letter from Christ ... Written not with ink but with the Spirit of the living God, not on tablets of stone but on tablets of human hearts, . . . ministers of a new covenant, not in a written code but in the Spirit; for the written code kills, but the Spirit gives life ...Now the Lord is the Spirit, and where the Spirit of the Lord is, there is freedom. And we all, with unveiled face, beholding the glory of the Lord, are being changed into his likeness from one degree of glory to another; for this comes from the Lord who is the Spirit" (II Corinthians 3:3, 6, 17-18).

Note

A version of this chapter was previously published in *Social Work and Christianity*, 20(2), 1993.

References

Adams, R. M. (1987). *The virtue of faith*. New York: Oxford University Press.

Hauerwas, S. (1981). *A community of character: Toward a constructive Christian social ethic*. Notre Dame: University of Notre Dame Press.

Hauerwas, Stanley and Willimon, William H. (1989). *Resident aliens: Life in the Christian colony*. Nashville: Abingdon Press.

Holmes, A. (1984). *Ethics: Approaching moral decisions*. Downers Grove, IL: InterVarsity Press.

Lewis, C. S. (1947). *The abolition of man*. New York: Macmillan.

Lewis, C. S. (1943). *Mere Christianity*. New York: Macmillan.

MacIntyre, A. (1984). *After virtue: A study in moral theory*. 2nd Ed. University of Notre Dame Press.

NASW. (1999). *Code of ethics*. Washington, DC: National Association of Social Workers.

Osborne, G. R. (1991). *The hermeneutical spiral: A comprehensive introduction to biblical interpretation*. Downers Grove, IL: InterVarsity Press.

Pinnock, C. (1984). *The scripture principle*. New York: Harper and Row.

Reamer, F. (1990). *Ethical dilemmas in social service*. 2nd Ed. New York: Columbia University Press.

Sire, J. W. (1980). *Scripture twisting*. Downers Grove, IL: InterVarsity Press.

Sherwood, D. A. (Spring-Fall 1981). Add to your faith virtue: The integration of Christian values and social work practice. *Social Work & Christianity, 8*, 41-54.

Sherwood, D. A. (Spring 1989). How should we use the bible in ethical decision-making? Guidance without legalism or relativism. *Social Work & Christianity, 16*, 29-42

Sherwood, D. A. (Fall 1986). Notes toward applying Christian ethics to practice: Growing up into the image of Christ. *Social Work & Christianity, 13*, 82-93.

Sherwood, D. A. (1999). Integrating Christian faith and social work: Reflections of a social work educator. *Social Work & Christianity, 26*(1), 1-8.

Sherwood, David A. (2002). Ethical integration of faith and social work practice: Evangelism. *Social Work & Christianity, 29*(1), 1-12.

Smedes, Lewis. (1983). *Mere morality*. Grand Rapids: Eerdmans.

Swartley, Willard M. (1983). *Slavery, sabbath, war, and women: Case issues in biblical interpretation*. Scottsdale, PA: Herald Press.

Resources

Evans, C. S. (2004). *Kierkegaard's ethic of love: Divine commands and moral obligations*. New York: Oxford University Press.

Evans, C. S. (2006). Is there a basis for loving all people? *Journal of Psychology and Theology, 34*(1), 78-90.

Keith-Lucas, A. (1994). *Giving and taking help*. Botsford, CT: North American Association of Christians in Social Work.

Keith-Lucas, A. (1985). *So you want to be a social worker: A primer for the Christian student*. Botsford, CT: North American Association of Christians in Social Work.

Mott, S. C. (1982). *Biblical ethics and social change*. New York: Oxford University Press.

O'Donovan, O. (1986). *Resurrection and the moral order: An outline for evangelical ethics*. Grand Rapids: Eerdmans.

Sherwood, D. A. (2000). Pluralism, tolerance, and respect for diversity: Engaging our deepest differences within the bond of civility. *Social Work & Christianity, 27*(1), 1-7.

Sherwood, D. A. (2007). Moral, believing social workers: Philosophical and theological foundations of moral obligation in social work ethics. *Social Work & Christianity, 34*(2), 121-145.

Smith, C. (2003). Moral, believing animals: Human personhood and culture. New York: Oxford University Press.

Verhay, A. (1984). *The great reversal: Ethics and the new testament*. Grand Rapids: Eerdmans.

Wolterstorff, N. (2006). Justice, not charity: Social work through the eyes of faith. *Social Work & Christianity, 33*(2), 123-140.

SECTION 3

HUMAN BEHAVIOR AND SPIRITUAL DEVELOPMENT IN A DIVERSE WORLD

CHAPTER 12

SPIRITUAL DEVELOPMENT

Hope Haslam Straughan

Within the social work profession, there is a growing movement that affirms that spirituality and religious beliefs are integral to the nature of the person and have a vital influence on human behavior (Hugen, 1998). Canda (1988) identifies spirituality as a basic aspect of human experience, both within and outside the context of religious institutions. If a social worker is going to approach a person in a holistic manner, he or she must be willing to consider each person as a wondrous compilation of bio-psycho-social-spiritual elements. In this way, workers will have an extremely broad base from which to approach the strength and resiliency in the people with whom they interact. Spiritual development, a component of this broad understanding of a person, seems to occur both in a measurable, outward, predictable manner, as well as in a less tangible, personal journey. These complex and intertwined spiritual growth markers will be explored within this chapter, primarily from a Christian point of view.

Smith (1997-1998) claims that Christians are 'meaning makers,' taking "the raw material of lived experience – the gladness and the sorrows – and trying to seek the deeper meaning, see the larger picture, understand the levels and layers of life in all its fullness and intensity. We live, and then in faith we try to discover meaning" (p. 2). Faiver, Ingersoll, O'Brien, and McNally (2001) note:

> Spirituality may be described as a deep sense of wholeness, connectedness, and openness to the infinite . . . We believe spirituality is an innate human quality. Not only is it our vital life force, but at the same time it is also our experience of the vital life force. Although this life force is deeply part of us, it also transcends us. It is what connects us to other people, nature and the source of life. The experience of spirituality is greater than ourselves. (p.2)

Spiritual deepening, or development then, is about becoming more consciously aware – being attentive, present in the moment, and paying attention to life as we seek meaning. Gaining understanding of this broad, yet unique set of guiding beliefs and thought frameworks is central to working with children, adolescents, and adults of any age. By "incorporating spirituality and religion when addressing a client's needs, the social worker broadens the client's resources and support base and is given an opportunity to collaborate with the client's spiritual and/or religious leaders" (Furman, Zahl, Benson, & Canda, 2007, p. 252).

On a global scale, the United Nations Convention on the Rights of the Child (UNCRC) (1991) indicates that spiritual development is a factor in children's lives (Scott, 2003). The UNCRC accepts spiritual development as a category of human development and health worthy of rights protection. Article 27 recognizes "the right of every child to a standard of living adequate for the child's physical, mental, spiritual, moral and social development" (p. 14). Article 17 identifies the right of "access to information and material from a diversity of national and international sources, especially those aimed at the promotion of his or her social, spiritual and moral well-being and physical and mental health" (p. 8). Article 32 claims children have the right "to be protected from economic exploitation" (p. 16) or any development, including spiritual development. Spirituality is seen in these articles as a "distinct aspect of human experience that is not contained by categories of moral or mental or social development" (Scott, p. 118).

The Council on Social Work Education (2000) added the concept of spirituality to the required list of content areas to be addressed within the curriculum of accredited schools of social work in 2000. There are many important ways in which to incorporate this information in the overall social work curriculum. For instance, the role of religious institutions in society can be investigated, while considering the impact of their presence, and the potential natural support networks such entities might lend for some persons. In addition, techniques utilized by social workers that value a variety of possible religious experiences or spiritual beliefs might be explored in a practice course (Cascio, 1998; & Russel, 2006). One aspect of the growing self-awareness of social work students might be focused on their personal faith or spiritual experiences, including awareness of their own beliefs, and the impact of these on the people and their environments with which students will interact. Finally, one might argue that spiritual development content must be included in a course in which community is considered, as many religious traditions feature a strong cultural and communal identity and experience.

Incorporating spirituality within the Human Behavior and Social Environment life span content is a foundational attempt to honor holistic personal development. One can consider the development of an individual's spirituality from gestation through the years of life to death, while considering the socioeconomic, political, racial, ethnic, and greater societal influences impacting a person's faith journey. This approach is based on a clear assumption that an individual's spiritual capacity and awareness is not stagnant, but indeed develops, changes, and potentially increases. This type of thinking immediately causes us to consider whether spiritual information is best presented utilizing a traditional stage-based theoretical approach, or if the concepts lend themselves to a more fluid consideration in which particular themes are revisited throughout life. James Fowler (1981) and others have drawn from a deep psychological understanding of human development and crafted models of spiritual development containing multiple stages of faith, which hold true to many of the assumptions of the traditional stage-models. Joan Borysenko (1998) and others have proposed more fluid approaches to spiritual development and have recognized that spiritual themes may be re-occurring throughout the life span. This concept is consistent with the spiral approach to growth and development. These ideas, often building upon the familiar concepts of the stage-based developmental patterns, will be presented in a later portion of this chapter.

Social workers commonly work within community-serving agencies, while seeking to help people who often have few choices about the conditions under which essential human needs are met. In this role, we must ensure that every protection is given the client and that his or her helplessness is not exploited (Spencer, 1961). "Certainly, in the light of the high value the social work profession has always placed upon the client's right to solve his [or her] own problems in the way that seems right to him [or her], it is assumed that any considerations of the social worker's role in the area of religion would be set in this context" (pp. 519-520).

In order to accomplish this, a level of spiritual competency must be developed. This competency is based upon the workers' own awareness of his/her spirituality and belief systems, an acknowledgement of the spiritual nature of all persons, an open stance when hearing the stories of clients, and paying attention to the language used and the meaning the client attributes to spiritual components of their lives (Guadalupe, 2005). In addition, spiritual competency demands a level of growing knowledge and understanding of the spiritual experiences of diverse populations.

Definitions

The roots of social work contain many religious and spiritually based components, lending motivation, direction, foundation, and location for social service provision. When approaching the issue of spiritual development and the impact of this on an individual, family, group, community or organization, it is crucial to define the terms that create the backbone for this important discussion. Sue Spencer (1961) was one of the first to attempt to define religion and spirituality from the perspective of a social worker. She identified three major hurdles experienced by those desiring to discuss spirituality and social work. "The first of these is the wide variety of religious beliefs held by individuals and by organized church bodies" (p. 519). The second hurdle is the difficulty of looking at the issue of religion and spirituality in an objective, yet comfortable and sympathetic way, as any discussion of religion is likely to be colored by considerable feeling and emotion that often stem from one's early experiences with organized religion. The third difficulty is found in our cultural bias, which celebrates the freedom to express religious impulses and to meet religious needs as persons see fit. This hurdle thereby cautions persons against infringing upon the right of spiritual or religious freedom of others.

"From the rain dances of Native Americans to the celebratory dances of Hasidic Jews, from the whirling dervishes of Islam to the meditating monks of Zen Buddhism, from the ecstatic worship services of charismatic churches to the solemn, silent meetings of the Quakers, spirituality takes on many expressions"

(Elkins, 1999, p. 45). Given the hurdles identified by Spencer, and the rich descriptions of spiritual expression listed by Elkins, it is crucial that when discussing spirituality and social work practice, we define terms consistently and clarify what is meant by spirituality. Edward Canda (1988), a social work educator who has made significant contributions to conversations about spirituality and practice, has provided a definition that will serve as the cornerstone for this chapter and be continually integrated with our discussion of spiritual development. Canda suggests an understanding of spirituality that encompasses human activities of moral decision-making, searching for a sense of meaning and purpose in life, and striving for mutually fulfilling relationships among individuals, society, and ultimate reality (however that is conceptualized by the client). "In that these aspects of human activity are common to all people, they are necessarily relevant to all areas of social work practice" (p. 238). Canda further delineates this spiritual component, by stating that the "professional helping relationship must be a genuine expression of the social worker's spiritual commitment to compassion and social justice – an 'I' who empathically relates with a 'Thou'" (p. 245). Hodge (2003) describes the development of a persons' spiritual orientation as it engenders a distinctive worldview, a spiritual worldview. Though Canda does not limit his approach to a particular religious tradition, such as Christianity, the focus of this chapter is that of Christian faith and a Christian understanding of God as the foundation for a person's spiritual worldview.

Approaches to Thinking about Spiritual Development

Schriver (2004) utilizes a very helpful delineation of traditional and alternative paradigms as a way to structure thinking about people and their environments. The traditional paradigm, characterized in this chapter as those theories based on stage-based, predictable, ladder-oriented development, has sometimes led to a belief in only one route to only one answer rather than many routes to many answers. These theories have offered very important concepts that are often utilized and expanded within broader or alternative ways of thinking about development. "Alternative ways of viewing the world such as interpretive, consensual, non-Eurocentric, and feminist perspectives can add much to what we know and what we need to know to *do* social work" (p. xix). Building on these assumptions, the remainder of the chapter will be organized in such a way as to demarcate particular spiritual development approaches. These approaches will be divided between those which seem to follow traditional paradigms, and those which lend themselves to alternative processes of understanding the spiritual journey of people, all the while acknowledging the crucial and unique role of their environments.

Traditional Ways of Thinking about Spiritual Development

Many researchers have found that a stage-based model of development, whether psychosocial, cognitive, spiritual, or moral, is descriptive and informative when considering the normal development of human beings. The work of two such researchers, Erik Erikson and Lawrence Kohlberg, will be considered in this chapter in relation to James Fowler's proposed stages of spiritual development. Erik Erikson (1950) proposed a theory of psychosocial development comprising eight stages. These established eight stages were later expanded to include a ninth stage by his wife, Joan, after Erikson's death (Erikson, 1997). In reviewing their life's research and writings, as well as experiencing life into her 90's, she found cause to expand to a ninth stage which encompasses the realities of persons living into their eighth and ninth decade into very old age. The key component in Erikson's work is the development of the sense of self by going through a series of crises. He proposes that the society within which one lives makes certain psychic demands at each stage of development, and that the individual must adjust to the stresses and conflicts involved in these crises in order to move to the next stage of development. Lawrence Kohlberg (1969) proposed a series of six stages through which people progress as they develop their moral framework. A summary of the stages presented by Erikson, Kohlberg, and Fowler can be seen in Table 1.

According to stage theorists, the growth in authentic self-transcendence that results from the individual's taking responsibility for him or herself, "moves from infant, impulse-dominated self-centeredness to a conformist identity with one's social group and finally to post-conventional self-determination and integration of internal and external reality" (Helminiak, 1987, p. 77). Helminiak proposes James Fowler's work as *the* stages of spiritual development, "at least within middle-class American and equivalent cultures" (p. 84). A summary of James Fowler's (1981) stages of faith development across the lifespan will be utilized as a point of reference for a discussion of spirituality as it relates to Erikson's and Kohlberg's research. Following Fowler's stages, the five stages of faith developed by Rabbi Terry Bookman will be discussed for additional insights on adult spiritual development (2005).

James Fowler: Stages of Faith

Perhaps the most recognized contributor to the stage-theory approach to considering spiritual development is James Fowler (1981). A theologian and religious psychologist, Fowler set off a new wave of thinking about faith-based on the work of such renowned developmental psychologists as Erik Erikson, Jean Piaget and Lawrence Kohlberg. "He claimed that faith, like life itself, goes through distinct stages as a person matures" (Kropf, 1991, p. 12). Jung (1933) and Fowler (1981) view spirituality as a person's "soul or essence which contains a potential needing to be fulfilled through a developmental process," providing the energy for this life-long process beginning at birth, of "actualizing and realizing one's potential" (Carroll, 2001, p. 14). Fowler's (1981) concept of 'faith' is based on a sense of meaning and purpose in life, as well as the belief in an ultimate reality, and is closely linked to the concepts Canda (1988) presents in his definition of spirituality. Fowler considers the interface of the religious/spiritual dimension with other psychosocial aspects of the person (Joseph,

1988). Marra (2000) describes this phenomenon as developing sequentially. As in other stage-based developmental theories, it is possible to accelerate growth, or impede it, but steps cannot be skipped.

Fowler (1981) discerns six stages in faith development. A pre-stage called Undifferentiated Faith is reflective of the infant up to about one and a half years of age, and is unavailable to empirical research (see Table 1). The faith of early infancy is characterized by the mutuality between infant and nurturers (Helminiak, 1987). "The emergent strength of faith in this stage is the bond of basic trust and the relational experience of mutuality with the one(s) providing primary love and care" (Fowler, p. 121). Looking at Table 1, we can see obvious similarities in the descriptions of Erikson's Stage-1 of psychosocial development, Basic Trust versus Basic Mistrust, and Fowler's pre-stage. Both researchers identify the most important task during the first 18 months of life as the development of trust due to the infants' needs being met by nurturers. Erikson discusses religion and notes that children may not need a religious upbringing. But, says Erikson (1950), they do need a sense of basic trust, a feeling not only that their fundamental bodily needs will be met and that their parents love them and will take care of them, but also that they have not been abandoned to the empty haphazardness of existence. The trust of the infant in the parents finds its parallel - and takes its mature form - in the parents' trust in God (Brandt, 1991).

Fowler (1986a) states that "faith begins in relationship. Faith implies trust in-reliance upon another; a counting upon or dependence upon another" (p. 16). If one is to accept the basis for Erikson's stage progression, crisis completion, it raises a basic question related to spiritual development. At this early point in one's life, what impact would a child's inability to successfully reach basic trust or mutuality have on his or her spiritual development? Canda (1988) and Guadalupe (2005), also define spiritual development partially as striving for mutually fulfilling relationships among individuals, society, and ultimate reality.

The transition to Stage-1, according to Fowler, begins when children are three to seven and are beginning to use symbols in speech and ritual play (1981). This occurs with the convergence of thought and language. Stage-1 Faith, called Intuitive-Projective Faith, involves a child thinking of God only in literal terms. This fact coupled with Kohlberg's (1969) suggestion that the moral development of children at this age is motivated by avoidance of punishment, can lead to behavior based on fear. Stage-2 Faith, Mythic-Literal Faith, is normative for children from the age of six to twelve, but as with all the subsequent stages of faith, they may remain in that stage throughout life. Robert Coles (1990) asked a class of fifth graders to respond to the following question: "Tell me, as best you can, who you are" (p. 308). One boy wrote that "I was put here by God, and I hope to stay until He says OK, enough, come back" (p. 312). A Puerto Rican girl who usually did not say much responded with "Well, how *does* He decide? How can He possibly keep track of everyone? I asked our priest, and he said all kids want to know, and you just have to have faith, and if you don't, then you're in trouble, and besides, you'll never know, because that's God's secret. . . But I still can't see how God can keep His eyes on everyone, and my uncle says it's all a lot of nonsense" (p. 312). This child fully embraces the idea of God keeping track of so many persons, informed by the stories, beliefs and words of their families, faith communities, and spiritual leaders.

Some adolescents begin to evolve into Stage-3 Faith, Synthetic-Conventional Faith, and tend to see God as personal and relational, in a more spiritual sense than before, assigning great value to religious symbols (Fowler, 1981). Teens in this stage of faith may find great attachment to a cross necklace or earrings, as a symbol of their beliefs, or find value in the ritual of the Lord's Supper or communion, even if they are unable to specify the deep connection through words.

Erikson (1950) describes adolescence as a transition period from childhood to adulthood, when people examine the various roles they play, and integrate these roles into a perception of self, or identity, in his Stage-5, Identity versus Role Conflict. Fowler assumes that the teen has an ability to think abstractly which allows for a new level of thinking critically in relation to the stories and myths that one has been told in relation to one's belief.

In Kohlberg's (1969) Stage-5, Morality of Contract, of Individual Rights, and of Democratically Accepted Law, the adolescent is moving to an internally controlled morality which parallels Fowler's and Erikson's stages. Teens at this stage in life are moving to a more internally-driven and personally informed way of living. Consequently, developmental factors that lead to Stage-4 Faith, Individuate-Reflective Faith, include beginning to clash with external authority (most often parents in this case); leaving home physically and/or emotionally, causing the examination of self and theology; and the influence of adult models at Stage-4.

According to Fowler (1981) the optimum time to enter Stage-4 is during the traditional college years, age 18-22. Life situations encountered during these years typically cause people to think about their religious and spiritual identity and beliefs. The power of reason and critical analysis comes to the forefront cognitively, and is also often the case in a person's quest for understanding related to the spiritual self as well. In Stage-4 Faith, Individuate-Reflective Faith, the relocation of authority within the self and the interruption of reliance on an external authority both occur (Fowler, 1981). Concurrently, Kohlberg (1969) identified the center for moral decision making during adulthood, Stage-6, Morality of Individual Principles and Conscience, as *internal* ethical principles. Decisions made from this perspective are made according to what is right versus what is written into law, honoring this newly relocated authority within the self, as Fowler described.

Reaching Stage-5 Faith, Conjunctive Faith, is rare before middle age,,largely due to an emerging awareness that reality is more complex than what one's Stage-4, highly rationalized view can contain (Helminiak, 1987). Externally, Conjunctive Faith realizes the validity of *systems other than one's own* and so moves away from seeing a situation as a dichotomy, as seen in Stage 4's either-or thinking. Persons using Conjunctive Faith realize that the deepest truths are inconsistent, resulting in what is often described by others as a sweeter spirit than previous stages. Erikson (1950) describes Stage-7, Generativity versus Stagnation, which is concurrent in the lifespan with Fowler's Stage-5, as a time when a person is concerned with helping, producing for, or guiding the following generation. Both researchers emphasize the external focus of this stage of life. During this stage of life, this search for meaning and purpose often culminates in the extension of oneself for the support and development of others (Canda, 1988). Still, a person in Stage-5 "remains divided" (Helminiak, p. 198). People in Stage-5 faith are living in an untransformed world while experiencing visions of transformation. In some few cases this division leads to radical actualization called Stage 6 faith.

Changes associated with psychological and cognitive development impel a person to focus on the inner or spiritual self (Mulqueen& Elisa, 2000). Exceedingly rare, according to Fowler, Stage-6, Universalizing Faith, incarnates and actualizes the spirit of an inclusive and fulfilled human community, drawn to the familihood of all people (Marra, 2000). This stage constructs an ultimate environment that includes and cherishes all beings (Fowler, 1981). For persons reaching this rare stage of faith development, Fowler suggests that they would be beyond mid-life. Erikson (1950) describes persons of old age as being in a crisis of Ego Integrity versus Despair. Persons in this stage, Stage-8, are looking back over their lives, reflecting, and taking stock of their decisions. For some persons this review leads to a sense of peace, but for others, to a sense of sadness and despair. As people are living longer, more persons are entering into the final stage of development posed by Joan Erikson (1997), Stage-9, and are finding that hope and trust are no longer the firm support they were found to be in previous stages, and that perhaps facing down despair with faith and appropriate humility is the wisest course. Joan Erikson suggests that 'transcen*dance*' might be the "regaining of lost skills, including play, activity, joy, and song, and above all, a major leap above and beyond the fear of death" (p. 127). The components of relationship and unity might suggest some further parallels to Fowler's Stage-6 Faith described above.

Therefore, traditional ways of considering spiritual development draw on the assumptions of general human development. According to stage-based theorists, this growth in authentic self-transcendence that results from the individual's taking responsibility for him or herself, "moves from infant, impulse-dominated self-centeredness to a conformist identity with one's social group and finally to post-conventional self-determination and integration of internal and external reality" (Helminiak, 1987, p. 77). Helminiak proposes Fowler's extensive work around stages of spiritual development as *the* stages of spiritual development, "at least within middle-class American and equivalent cultures" (p. 84). "Movement through these stages reflects qualitative changes in one's view of the world and in all relationships" (Carroll, 2001, p. 14). As has been demonstrated above, it can be useful to consider Fowler's stages of faith in light of other types of development across the lifespan, in order to gain a greater understanding of the common crises, cognitive abilities, conceptual frameworks, and worldviews.

Rabbi Terry Bookman: A Soul's Journey – The Five Stages of Spiritual Growth

Rabbi Bookman (2005) identified five stages, or vantage points, as a part of every soul's journey. These resting spots which allow us the vantage point to "survey the landscape of our lives" (p. xiii) are Beginnings, Commitments, Intimacy, Wanderings and Acceptance. Unlike Fowler's stages of spiritual development based on the possible age-ranges for a person's development, Bookman does not link his descriptions to particular suggested age ranges. Instead, Bookman purports that though we have many beginnings in our lives, the ones which take hold and become the most meaningful and long-lasting, are typically those we have sought intentionally, or embraced with openness, often corresponding with young adulthood, or later.

Rabbi Bookman (2005), unlike Borysenko (1998), Canda (1988), Fox (1999) and others, unapologetically makes connections between spiritual growth and participation in formal religious traditions, teachings and disciplines. He recognizes that helping professionals will likely interact with numerous people who describe themselves as being 'spiritual but not religious.' Bookman notes that "what they usually mean is that they have an awareness, a consciousness of God in their lives and their world, but they find religion, with its rules, rituals, hierarchies, and repetition more an impediment than an enhancement" (p. 52). As a Jewish priest, his understanding of what the Torah directs, "is that spirituality devoid of religion – limits, discipline – ultimately leads to idolatry" (p. 52).

Similarly, "the Torah is equally harsh in its judgment on religion without spirituality calling it hypocrisy and emptiness" (p. 53). Though clients who describe themselves as 'spiritual but not religious' might link this greater awareness and consciousness to God, many others might use terms such as Other, the Greater Good, My Higher Power, and many others. Some clients might share Bookman's conviction of this necessary connection between religion and spirituality, but many will not. Sensitivity to the potential separation of these understandings and practices in the lives of our clients is critical, as we actively assess over time the potential areas of strength, resiliency and possibility clients may find in this realm of his/her life.

Additionally, Bookman's (2005) premise reminds us how critical it is as helping professionals, to listen to the stories of the client systems, to hear and actively use in our responses, the language they assign to the important experiences, revelations, assumptions, and transitions in their lives, and not impose our own language or meaning. For instance, if a helping professional were to take part in a Brief Initial Assessment (Hodge, 2004) beginning with a question such as 'I was wondering if you happened to be interested in spirituality or religion?,' in order to maximize the possible strength of this exchange, and build the trust within the helping relationship, the helping professional must listen carefully for terms utilized, experiences referred to, as well as those left out, pauses, or the change in the speed in which clients communicate their lived truth. If we follow this initial question with a 'standardized' second question which includes terminology or the name of a Higher Power or Godhead in language which does not 'match' that of the client, we will likely find that the client is unable to access and share the kind of information, experiences, or wonderings we are intending to provoke. Depending on the response(s) of clients to initial spiritual assessment questions, further questions can be asked throughout the helping relationship which explore how clients' faith is impacting their experience of the presenting situation, as well as where they receive spiritual support. These discussions can reflect the strength of *community*, sense of hope and possibility which can be strong foundations for growth and transformation, as well as identify potential areas of negative assumptions related to clients' understanding of self and their place in the world which can be further addressed and worked through, leading to healing and wholeness.

During Bookman's (2005) Beginnings stage, people absorb all that they are learning with great enthusiasm and excitement. Commitment follows, as a stage when people realize that any time of spiritual growth necessitates a "temporary narrowing of our freedom followed by work and discipline" (p. xiii). The stage of Intimacy is reached as fleeting moments of connection are experienced, when people know with certainty that they are on the right path, almost as if 'sky-writing' had declared it, and that all is well with their lives. A sense that everything that happens, does so with meaning and purpose, accompanies the days of persons in the Intimacy stage. As obstacles are confronted and people are challenged to give up, the stage of Wanderings occurs. Acceptance, the fifth stage, occurs as a person owns the past, lets it go, draws lessons from it, marvels at the sense his/her life makes, and reaches a state of inner peace.

One of the "criticisms leveled at general stage theories is that such theories are merely descriptions of how specific people change, and that such models are only valid for the one culture out of which they have emerged. The patterns are chiefly due to cultural factors, expectations, roles, and conditioning, or else economics, and do not reflect universal tendencies of human nature outside of the society portrayed" (Irwin, 2002, p. 30). Erikson himself conceded that what a man adds up to must develop in stages, but no stage explains the man (Coles, 1970). Other specific critique of Kohlberg's and sometimes Erikson's work includes potential cultural biases inherent in categorization, limitations imposed by children's developing vocabulary and expression of their ideas, the lack of clear-cut divisions between one category and another, and the idea that the stages must occur in an absolute order.

Dykstra (1981) questions the very foundation of Kohlberg's work. Though he finds Kohlberg to be quite clear about what he thinks morality is and what it takes to be a moral person, Dykstra questions the judgement-based or juridical ethics upon which this image of a moral person is derived. Dykstra contrasts Kohlberg's form of ethics which provide a clear guide for action through its rules and principles for decision making posed by Kohlberg, with 'visional ethics.' Dykstra's visional ethics focuses on questioning what we see and what it is that enables human beings to see more realistically. For visional ethics, action follows vision, and vision depends upon character – "a person thinking, reasoning, believing, feeling, willing, and acting as a whole" (p. 59). Fowler (1986b) himself contends that the contributions of Kohlberg and others are useful only to a point when addressing conceptually the last relational step of faith. This is primarily because Kohlberg favors an objectifying, technical reasoning, which has no room for freedom, risk, passion, and subjectivity, all central in Fowler's final stage of faith development, or letting it go and finding inner peace, as described in Bookman's (2005) final stage, Acceptance.

Alternative Ways of Thinking about Spiritual Development

As social workers, concerning ourselves with "what and how we actually live in this world" can lead to a variety of approaches for defining and understanding spiritual development within ourselves and for those with whom we work (Marra, 2000, p. 72). While recognizing the worth and unique contribution of the stage-based approaches, a number of researchers have proposed expanded or additional ways of considering spiritual development. Carol Gilligan, Joan Borysenko, Matthew Fox, Harry R. Moody and David Carroll and others have approached development from a largely feminist perspective and offer some additional useful ideas for thinking about spiritual development. Further, Wendy Haight incorporates some broader cultural implications for considering the importance of the role of spirituality within the lives of children and all individuals. And, finally, Craig Dykstra's unique process critique, which focuses on the practices and behaviors that he identifies as inherent in spiritual development, will be discussed.

Gilligan, Moody & Carroll, Borysenko, & Fox: Feminist Approaches to Development
An alternative way of thinking invites the participation of voices of those persons often unheard, including persons other than the young, white, heterosexual, Judeo-Christian, able-bodied, male, with sufficient resources and power (Schriver, 2004). Carol Gilligan and others (Taylor, Gilligan, & Sullivan, 1985) have examined the research and findings of many traditional theorists, and concluded that generally the experience of girls and women at best are treated with curiosity, and a brief description inferring 'otherness' in comparison to the 'norm,' defined as or assumed to be boys and men. Gilligan proposes a look at girls as "'different,' mainly to hold it apart from its common mistranslation, 'deficient'" (p. 2). She suggests that to listen to the voices of women is to learn a great deal about what is necessary for more completely understanding the meaning of individual development for both women and men (Gilligan, 1982). Additionally, persons in many minority groups hold a worldview emphasizing the inter-relatedness of the self or the individual with other systems in the person's environment such as families, households, communities, and the ethnic group as a whole, often embracing 'story' as legend, myth and metaphor. "In addition to and in conjunction with the family, religious and spiritual institutions hold and pass along the philosophical standpoints or worldview of the people" (p. 355). Therefore, it is useful to review approaches that embrace a communal spiritual developmental process.

Moody and Carroll (1997) acknowledge the value of the life span transitions and passages identified in extensive psychological research by persons such as Erikson, Levinson, Sheehy, Freud, Spock and others. However, they also recognize that though the models posed by many of these researchers were persuasive, they were somehow incomplete, as cautioned earlier about stage-based theories. What Moody and Carroll, as well as Borysenko (1998) and others realized, is that an "element of the human condition that has always been at the heart and soul of every human culture from primordial time – *the spiritual element*" (p. 8) was omitted from those models. Spiritual as well as psychological and social passages are parallel and occur across a lifetime. The "structure of the great religions of the world – Christianity, Judaism, Taoism, Islam, Buddhism, Hinduism – are all likewise rooted in ideas of progressive developmental passages" (p. 9). Irwin (2002) noted that Kohlberg, Erikson and Jung each, in fact, do utilize language which correlates to spirituality. He observed that these components of morality from a non-dualistic perspective, concern for others rather than oneself, and a release of archetypal images from the collective unconscious, are incorporated in higher, more evolved stages of moral and psychosocial development. If we are to hold a holistic view of our clients at any stage of their development, we must include entry points to consider their spiritual passages, beliefs, connections, wonderings and potential in relation to the work we are engaged in together.

In her bio-psycho-*spiritual* model, Joan Borysenko (2004; 1998) expands the more traditionally accepted bio-psycho-social understanding of individual development. Borysenko's work builds on the assumption that a person's spiritual development is integrally connected to his/her cognitive, physical, and psychosocial learning and transformation. Utilizing the bio-psycho-spiritual feedback loop, she describes this spiral-formation of development through 12 seven-year cycles of renewal and metamorphosis, each one preparing for the next (See Table 2). There are three such cycles in each 'quadrant.' The four quadrants are broadly defined as childhood and adolescence, young adulthood, midlife, and late adulthood. The thirteenth part of the life cycle, death, is perhaps the ultimate act of renewal and growth.

Borysenko explains the evolving capacities of each period, traces the waxing and waning of feminine consciousness, and assures women that midlife is a stage, not a crisis. Thomas (2001) cites similar findings, as she describes a "renewal of spirituality" for many women, as their lives changed the moment they gave birth (p. 93). Though Borysenko's work is grouped within linear age-related stages, her approach is largely focused on the recurring themes of the inter-connectedness between people, nature, and things. A person living in such a way as to embrace the ideals set out by Borysenko would recognize that true intimacy based on respect and love is the measure of a life well lived. This often plays out in the choices made by a person related to work, leisure, living arrangements, and social commitments, as well as forming the underlying motivation for all relationships. As the person grows older, Borysenko (1998) suggests that "this innate female spirituality underlies an often unspoken commitment to protect our world from the ravages of greed and violence" (p. 3). This presentation gives a wonderful example of the spiral-model of spiritual development (see Table 2).

A spiritual metaphor for traditional and alternative paradigms may be found in the familiar themes of 'Climbing Jacob's Ladder' and 'Dancing Sarah's Circle.' Climbing Jacob's ladder, as defined by Fox, is a metaphor based on Jacob's dream recorded in the twenty-eighth chapter of Genesis , interpreted through the lens of a Western-Christianity, male-dominated perspective (Fox, 1999). This Biblical text has been utilized to describe the faith journey as one symbolic of fleeing the earth in an upward climb to God. In this model or metaphor, Fox suggests that "we climb to God by contemplation and descend to neighbor by compassion. Thus compassion is descent; it is also an after-thought, a luxury that one can afford only after a very long life-time of contemplative ascending" (p. 40). According to Fox, a spiritual developmental understanding based on this traditional, hierarchical, competitive, independent, and linear approach to growth will necessarily embrace distinct, clearly defined, and restrictive patterns. Openness to the visual and theoretical understanding of dancing Sarah's circle allows for a wide variety of spiritual experiences, explanations, and attachments of meaning for persons on this journey.

Borysenko (2000) replaces the heroic model of step-by-step progress up Jacob's ladder with the image of women walking and Dancing Sarah's Circle. She suggests that, like all women, the mother of Isaac came to know herself in the deep, intuitive way through the medium of her relationships rather than strictly in terms of a relationship with a transcendent God (2004). Dancing Sarah's Circle is based on the biblical text found in Genesis 18-21, culminating in Sarah, at the age of ninety, giving birth to a surprise son she named Isaac, meaning "God has smiled, God has been kind" (Fox, 1999, p.44). Thus, a spirituality of Dancing Sarah's Circle is one of wonder and joy. Sarah could be surprised, filled with unexpected wonder, and able to laugh. Sarah, then, is a symbol of laughter, creativity, and shalom.

A spiritual developmental understanding based on this alternative notion including a shared experience/ecstasy, interdependence, nurture, circle-like welcome of others, culminating in a love of neighbor that *is* love of God, will necessarily embrace a broader, fluid, circular, dynamic, shared pattern of spiritual growth. Jesus' supper times with his disciples can be seen as a Sarah circle kind of intimacy and his Last Supper experience rings especially true to this dynamic. The sacrament of washing the feet that meant so much to Jesus the night before he died is a patent example of a Sarah circle dynamic. Jesus both washed his disciples' feet *and* had his feet washed with ointment by a woman willing to dry them with her long hair. "All of Sarah's circle dynamic is as much receiving as giving" (Fox, 1999, p. 56).

Within alternative approaches to understanding spirituality and spiritual development, certain concepts are central, such as mutuality, cooperation, harmony between persons, the earth, and God, and participating in significant life events. These are the main tenets of Sarah's Circle. One example of persons working together within this understanding of spirituality is a liberation group. Persons in these groups come together to share their pain of oppression and discrimination thus building a bond, and striving for mutual empowerment. Person's embracing the Sarah's Circle dynamic might take part in cooperatives such as food or clothing or housing, expanding the options, resources and flexibility of all involved. Living in harmony with the environment through interest in solar, wind and water energy systems is another example of people living Sarah's Circle within society. Finally, parents who insist on natural childbirth wherein their child will be welcomed eye to eye by a circle of fully conscious and celebrating, wonder-struck family, offer another way in which persons may choose to live out the tenets held within Sarah's Circle, in full participation of important life events.

Borysenko (1998) believes that "from a spiritual vantage point our major life task is much larger than making money, finding a mate, having a career, raising children, looking beautiful, achieving psychological health, or defying aging, illness, and death. It is a recognition of the sacred in daily life – a deep gratitude for the wonders of the world and the delicate web of inter-connectedness between people, nature and things" (p. 3). Her description of the spiritual realm of a person's life parallels nicely with Canda's (1988) emphasis on seeking a sense of meaning and purpose in life, and striving for mutually fulfilling relationships among individuals, society, and ultimate reality, focusing on the *relational* aspects of persons.

A significant difference between the growth of persons in Borysenko's understanding and Fowler's is that each previous type of interaction, personal experience, and belief process is cherished and viewed as critical, remaining a part of a person's whole, rather than an emphasis on leaving a particular stage behind for another, higher one. Bohannan (1992) comes to a similar conclusion. She states that women experience the sacred as immanent rather than as transcendent, living their lives in the awareness of the sacred around them, and practicing grace and love in the here and now. This rhythmic approach to the understanding of a woman's body, mind, and spirit, is interdependent, creative, and dynamic (Borysenko, 2004).

"No spiritual journey is marked by a straight, unbroken line. Rather, like the path through a Zen garden; there are many twists and turns, even switchbacks, now progressing forward, now (seemingly) regressing" (Bookman, 2005, p. xiii). Bookman speaks of stages of development which are more like familiar places we revisit as we change, grow, and age. An image which represents this repetitive, active, and engaged process is found in the labyrinth, a metaphorical representation of the journey to our own center and back again out into the world, appearing as an oasis of possibility, pathways, and hope (Straughan, 2006). The labyrinth is an ancient symbol that relates to wholeness. It combines the imagery of the circle and the spiral into a meandering but purposeful path, similar to the spiritual pathways and growth experienced by many persons (Johnston, 2007).

The walking of the labyrinth involves intuition, creativity, and even imagery. With a labyrinth, there is only one choice to be made – to enter or not. The choice is whether or not to walk a spiritual path (Johnston, 2007). As people walk into the pathways of the labyrinth, they are encouraged to 'let go' of the things that are weighing on our minds, and 'strip' themselves of outward distractions, in order to be fully present with what they are feeling, knowing and experiencing. Then, when they reach the center, they are to be quiet (in spirit), calm, reflective, prayerful even - repeating silently or out loud, writings that are posted within that inner circle, or that come to mind. Then, once the people on this journey are ready, they are encouraged on their outward return to begin to prepare to 're-enter' the world, by calling to mind people and situations they were connected to, and being actively thoughtful about them (Straughan, 2006). The winding back and forth of the pathways of the labyrinth seem to parallel the images Borysenko (1998), Bookman (2005) and Fox (1999) suggest of the spiral or circular nature of the spiritual journey and growth.

Wendy Haight: Cultural Implications for Spiritual Development
Spiritual socialization can be central to children's healthy development. Haight (1998) found that for some African American children, this foundation is directly tied to resiliency. Despite profound, ongoing stressors, her research recognized significant strength within African American children, their families and communities, often tied to the role of the church in their lives, and of a generally shared spiritual connection. Neumark (1998) suggests that spiritual development cannot be taught or managed, but "children can be encouraged to develop spiritually through being given the opportunity to consider, reflect, dream, and challenge" (p. 22).

Ancestral worldviews are reflected throughout the social institutions responsible for imparting the beliefs and values of the group such as the family, and religious and spiritual institutions. In addition to and in conjunction with the family, religious and spiritual institutions hold and pass along the philosophical standpoints or worldviews of the people (Schriver, 2004). The African-American community, like others, has rich traditions and history that uplift the hurt, comfort the struggling, and celebrate the soul (Hudley, Miller, & Haight, 2003). Church leaders rise to significance in the daily moral life of families and communities. "Individuals, families, and neighborhoods seek their counsel and support, guidance and inspiration. The church is also a fulcrum of much of the social life in the community and exists as a staging area for political and social activism" (Saleebey, 2001, p. 315).

A Rabbi working as a community organizer found that the lives of many low- to moderate-income people of color and working-class ethnic whites revolve around their religious and spiritual beliefs (ben Asher, 2001). As practitioners, we may find that ethnic and cultural diversity among clients is paralleled in spiritual and religious belief systems and practices. Many African Americans hold a worldview with roots in an African philosophical position that stresses collectivism rather than individualism. The worldviews of many Native Americans perceive all aspects of life as interrelated and of religious significance although there is no single dominant religion among the many Native American cultures. Asian/Pacific American families stress a belief system in which harmony is a core value. Latino religious beliefs reinforce a belief system in which the role of the family is a central tenet (Guadalupe, 2005; Harrison, Wilson, Pine, Chan, & Buriel, 1990). Such worldviews as these suggest much more in common with the core concerns of social work. The principles of social systems and ecological thinking found in these worldviews complement the growing emphasis on spirituality and religion within social work practice (Schriver, 2004).

The church often plays an important and supportive role for families of color. Church provides a sense of community and inter-relatedness for many individuals and families. Family and church are so intertwined for some African Americans, for example, that church members may refer to other members as their 'church family.' One's church family may provide such important supports as role models for young family members and assistance with child rearing (Hudley, Miller, & Haight, 2003). Even for African American families that do not belong to a formal church, spirituality may play a significant role. This spirituality is often a strength and a survival mechanism for African American families that can be tapped, particularly in times of death and dying, illness, loss, and bereavement (Boyd-Franklin, 1993; Hudley, Miller, & Haight, 2003). It is important to acknowledge the cultural implications of spiritual development, and the unique roles, meaning, and expectations found within each faith community.

Craig Dykstra: A Process Critique of Spiritual Development

Craig Dykstra (1999) embraces a certain 'strangeness,' a 'peculiarity' of Christian practice, as an asset, not a handicap. He accents the role of families, however defined, and youth, however attracted, in such settings which is a similar focus to Haight's findings related to some African American communities. This openness to 'strangeness' or other ways of thinking about and understanding certain life events, and ascribing meaning to them, fits well within an alternative approach to thinking about spiritual development. Dykstra's approach leaves more room for less traditional ways of expressing one's spiritual journey, which can include meditation, the acknowledgement of a particular geographic space which serves as a spiritual oasis, and the honoring of the God-given life and worth in all living beings.

Dykstra (1999) believes that the development of Christian nurture, rather than following formal 'stages,' relates to themes integral to the Christian story itself, focusing on ways of being and thinking and doing. If one considers spiritual development as a spiral-shaped experience, drawing from the recurring realities of a circle, but honoring the assumed growth and movement that a ladder suggests, it is possible to begin to understand a more thematic approach to this process. Dykstra identifies hunger, life, practices, places, and signs as broad themes recurring in our lives, embracing the mystery or depth of Christian faith, and a variety of methods for practicing this faith.

William Hull (1991) describes Christian salvation as a dynamic process – we were saved, we are being saved, and we will be saved. This somewhat subtle shift from the ladder image to a re-visiting process in cyclical form is quite profound, as the spiral-formation of growth allows one to re-engage with themes throughout life. This approach mirrors our own yearly reliving of the significant events on the liturgical calendar including communion, Lent, Easter, Pentecost, Advent, Christmas, and Epiphany. The process of re-experiencing these pivotal celebrations allows us to find the extraordinary in the 'ordinary.' As we continue to grow, change, understand ourselves, others, and God in different ways, our experiencing of these events is repetitive, yet new.

These alternative approaches to understanding spiritual development allow for the impact of greater societal, political, racial, ethnic, socioeconomic, physical, and emotional factors throughout this life process. Helminiak (1996) argues that if the needs of organisms are not met, the higher levels of psyche and spirit are adversely affected. Inversely, a sick spirit impacts psyche and organism negatively. Young, Cashwell, and Shcherbakova (2000) conclude that spirituality seems to provide a buffer from stressful life events that are perceived as negative, further supporting the value of the spiral-formed developmental impact which sustains the connections to previous life experiences.

Conclusion

The spiritual development approaches discussed in this chapter support the central tenet that "important religious beliefs, rituals, and social structures can play key roles as individuals and families move through the life cycle" (Hugen, 2001, p. 13). Some of the elements identified as significant dimensions of spiritual development are creativity, contemplation, wholeness, connectedness and quest or search for meaning (Guadalupe, 2005). In short, "spirituality is essential to human happiness and mental health" (Elkins, 1999, p. 44).

What occurs between the client and the social worker involves not only the traditional interventions, methods, and skills the social worker applies, but also a two-way exchange of ideas, feelings, beliefs, and values that may or may not be directly addressed or acknowledged. "Whether professionals are 'believers' in the spiritual dimension is important. 'Nonbelievers' may not be fully able to accept clients who consider spirituality and religion to be meaningful and useful within the context of their life experiences" (Sermabeikian, 1994, pp. 178-79). Social workers, therefore, should develop self-understanding regarding personal biases, their own experiences that lead to strong assumptions about others, existential issues and spiritual growth (Canda, 1988; Cascio, 1998; & Russel, 2006). "Self-inquiry must be a disciplined and consistent process of personal and professional growth. Social workers should examine their beliefs, motivations, values, and activities and consider the impact of these factors upon the client's spirituality" (Canda, p. 245).

A spiritual bias can be just as harmful as racism or sexism. When considering the issue of spirit, spiritual, and spirituality, a social worker must also consider his or her assumptions about the process of growth, deepening awareness, and the language and meanings attached to this spiritual development. Whether the philosophical tenets of Climbing Jacob's Ladder or those supporting Dancing Sarah's Circle are embraced, social workers must enter into an awareness of the sacred for themselves and for the persons with whom they work.

References

ben Asher, M. (2001). Spirituality and religion in social work practice. *Social Work Today, 1*(7), 15-18.

Bohannan, H. (1992). Quest-tioning tradition: Spiritual transformation images in women's narratives and 'housekeeping.' *Western Folklore, 51*(1), 65-80.

Bookman, T. (2005). *A soul's journey: Meditations on the five stages of spiritual growth.* Lincoln, NE: iUniverse.

Borysenko, J. (1998). *A woman's book of life: The biology, psychology, and spirituality of the feminine life cycle.* New York: Riverhead Books.

Borysenko, J. (2000). *A woman's journey to God: Finding the feminine path.* New York: Riverhead Books.

Borysenko, J. (2004). *A woman's spiritual retreat: Teaching, meditations, rituals to celebrate your authentic feminine wisdom.* Louisville, CO: Sounds True Publishing.

Boyd-Franklin, N. (1993). Race, class and poverty. In *Normal family processes*, Walsh, F. (Ed.). New York: Guilford.

Brandt, A. (1991). Do kids need religion? *Utne Reader, 43,* 84-88.

Canda, E.R. (1988). Spirituality, religious diversity, and social work practice. *Social Casework: The Journal of Contemporary Social Work,* 238-247.

Carroll, M.M. (2001). Conceptual models of spirituality. *Social Thought, 20*(1/2), 5-21.

Cascio, T. (1998). Incorporating spirituality into social work practice: A review of what to do. *Families in Society: The Journal of Contemporary Human Services, 79*(5), 523-531.

Coles, R. (1990). *The spiritual life of children.* Boston: Houghton Mifflin.

Coles, R. (1970). *Erik H. Erikson: The growth of his works.* Boston: Little, Brown and Company.

Council on Social Work Education. (2000). Curriculum policy statement for master's degree program in social work education. Alexandria, VA: Author.

Dykstra, C. (1999). *Growing in the life of faith: Education and Christian practice.* Louisville, KY: Geneva Press.

Dykstra, C.R. (1981). *Vision and character: A Christian educator's alternative to Kohlberg.* New York: Paulist Press.

Elkins, D.N. (1999). Spirituality. *Psychology Today, 32*(5), 44-50.

Erikson, E. (1997). *The life cycle completed: Extended version with new chapters on the ninth stage of development.* New York: Norton.

Erikson, E. (1950). *Childhood and society.* New York: Norton.

Faiver, C., Ingersoll, R.E., O'Brien, E., & McNally, C. (2001). *Explorations in counseling and spirituality: Philosophical, practical, and personal reflections.* Belmont, CA: Wadsworth/Thomson Learning.

Fowler, J. (1981). *Stages of faith: The psychology of human development and the quest for meaning.* San Francisco: Harper Collins.

Fowler, J. (1986a). Faith and the structuring of meaning. In C. Dykstra, & S. Parks (Eds.), *Faith development and Fowler* (pp. 15-44). Birmingham, AL: Religious Education Press.

Fowler, J. (1986b). Dialogue toward a future in faith development studies. In C. Dykstra, & S. Parks (Eds.), *Faith development and Fowler* (pp. 275-301). Birmingham, AL: Religious Education Press.

Fox, M. (1999). *A spirituality named compassion.* San Francisco: HarperCollins.

Furman, L.D., Zahl, M-A, Benson, P.W., & Canda, E.R. (2007). An international analysis of the role of religion and spirituality in social work practice. *Families in Society: The Journal of Contemporary Social Services, 88*(2), 241-254.

Gilligan, C. (1982). *In a different voice: Psychological theory and women's development.* Cambridge: Harvard University Press.

Guadalupe, J.A. (2005). Spirituality and multidimensional contextual practice. In K.L. Guadalupe, & D. Lum (Eds.), *Multidimensional contextual practice: Diversity and transcendence* (pp. 146-163). Belmont, CA: Thomson Brooks/Cole.

Haight, W.L. (1998). "Gathering the Spirit" at First Baptist Church: Spirituality as a protective factor in the lives of African American children. *Social Work, 43*(3), 213-21.

Harrison, A., Wilson, M., Pine, C., Chan, S., & Buriel, R. (1990). Family ecologies of ethnic minority children. *Child Development, 61*, 347-362.

Helminiak, D.A. (1987). *Spiritual development: An interdisciplinary study.* Chicago: Loyola University Press.

Helminiak, D.A. (1996). *The human core of spirituality: Mind as psyche and spirit.* Albany, N.Y.: State University of New York Press.

Hodge, D.R. (2003). The challenge of spiritual diversity: Can social work facilitate an inclusive environment? *Families in Society, 84*(3), 348-358.

Hodge, D.R. (2004). Why conduct a spiritual assessment? A theoretical foundation of assessment. *Advances in Social Work, 5*(2), 183-196.

Hudely, E.V.P., Miller, P.J., & Haight, W. (2003). *Raise up a child: Human development in an African-American family.* Chicago: Lyceum Books.

Hugen, B., (Ed.). (1998). *Christianity and social work: Readings on the integration of Christian faith and social work practice.* Botsford, CT: North American Association of Christians in Social Work.

Hugen, B. (2001). Spirituality and religion in social work practice: A conceptual model. In Van Hook, M., Hugen, B., & Aguilar, M. (Eds.), *Spirituality within religious traditions in social work practice* (pp. 9-17). Pacific Grove, CA: Brooks/Cole.

Hull, W.E. (1991). *The Christian experience of salvation.* Nashville: Broadman & Holman Publishers.

Irwin, R.R. (2002). *Human development and the spiritual life: How consciousness grows toward transformation.* New York: Kluwer Academic/Plenum Publishers.

Johnston, D. (2007). *The Labyrinth: Walking your spiritual journey.* Retrieved November 28, 2007, from http://www.lessons4living.com/labyrinth.htm.

Joseph, M.V. (1988). Religion and social work practice. *Social Casework: The Journal of Contemporary Social Work*, 443-449.

Jung, C.G. (1933). *Modern man in search of a soul.* New York: Harcourt Brace Jovanovich.

Kohlberg, L. (1969). *Stages in the development of moral thought and action.* New York: Holt, Rinehart & Winston.

Kropf, R. (1991). Faith's last stage may well be leap in the dark. *National Catholic Reporter, 28*(9), 12.

Marra, R. (2000). What do you mean, "spirituality"? *Journal of Pastoral Counseling, 22*, 67-79.Moody, H.R., & Carroll, D. (1997). *The five stages of the soul: Charting the spiritual passages that shape our lives.* New York: Anchor Books.

Moody, H.R., & Carroll, D. (1998). *The five stages of the soul: Charting the spiritual passages that shape our lives.* New York: Anchor Books.

Mulqueen, J., & Elias, J.L. (2000). Understanding spiritual development through cognitive development. *Journal of Pastoral Counseling, Annual*, 99-113.

Neumark, V. (1998). Hole makes whole. *Times Educational Supplement, 4272,* pp. 22-24.

Russel, R. (2006). Spirituality and social work: Current trends and future directions. *Arete, 30*(1), 42-52.

Saleebey, D. (2001). *Human behavior and social environments: A biopsychosocial approach.* New York: Columbia University.

Schriver, J.M. (2004). *Human behavior and the social environment: Shifting paradigms in essential knowledge for social work practice* (4ᵗʰ ed.). Boston: Allyn & Bacon.

Scott, D.G. (2003). Spirituality in child and youth care: Considering spiritual development and "relational consciousness." *Child and Youth Forum, 32*(2), 117-131.

Sermabeikian, P. (1994). Our clients, ourselves: The spiritual perspective and social work practice. *Social Work, 39*(3), 178-83.

Smith, M.H. (1997-1998). Embodied wisdom, embodied faith: Bio-spirituality. *Hungry-hearts,1*(3-4), 1-7.

Spencer, S.W. (1961). What place has religion in social work education? *Social Work,* 161-170.

Straughan, H.H. (2006). *The journey of learning.* Unpublished manuscript.

Taylor, J.M., Gilligan, C., & Sullivan, A.M. (1985). *Between voice and silence: Women and girls, race and relationship.* Cambridge, MA: Harvard University Press.

Thomas, T. (2001). Becoming a mother: Matrescence as spiritual formation. *Religious Education, 96*(1), 88-105.

United Nations Convention on the Rights of the Child. (1991). Ottawa: Ministry of Supply and Services Canada.

Young, J.S., Cashwell, C.S., & Shcherbakova, J. (2000). The moderating relationship of spirituality on negative life events and psychological adjustment. *Counseling and Values, 45*(1), 49-60.

Table 1: Stages of Psychosocial, Moral, and Spiritual Development
Erikson, Kohlberg, and Fowler

Erik Erikson's Eight Stages of Man (Psychosocial Development) *Ninth Stage contributed by Joan Erikson		Lawrence Kohlberg's Six Stages of Moral Development		James Fowler's Six stages of Faith Development	
Stage/Age	Description	Stage/Age	Description	Stage/Age	Description
Stage 1: Basic trust vs. basic mistrust Birth-12/18 months	Infant develops trust, as he or she understands that some people or things can be depended on.			Pre-Stage: Undifferentiated Faith Birth-1 ½ years	Faith characterized by mutuality between infant and nurturers. First pre-images of God are formed prior to language & are feeling-oriented, not reason-oriented.
Stage 2: Autonomy vs. Shame & Doubt 18 months – 3 yr.	Accomplishing various tasks/activities provides children with feelings of self-worth and self-confidence.				
Stage 3: Initiative vs. Guilt 3-6 years	Preschoolers encouraged to take initiative to explore & learn are likely to feel confident in initiating relationships, & pursue career objectives later in life. Preschoolers consistently restricted or punished are more likely to experience emotional guilt, & most often follow the lead of others.	Level 1-Preconventional 4-10 years Stage 1: Punishment & Obedience Orientation. Controls are external. Behavior governed by receiving rewards/punishments. Decisions concerning what is good/bad are made in order to avoid receiving punishment. Stage 2: Naïve Instrumental Hedonism. Rules are obeyed in order to receive rewards. Often favors are exchanged.		Stage 1: Intuitive-Projective Faith 3-7 years	Child constructs ever-shifting world of imitation, fantasy, & imagination. Child thinks only literally. Sees God as person yet realizes imagery falls short.
Stage 4: Industry vs. Inferiority 6-12 years	These children need to be productive & succeed in play and school activities.	Level 2 – Conventional 10-13 years Stage 3: "Good Boy/Girl Morality". Behavior governed by conforming to social expectations. Good behavior is considered to be what pleases others. Stage 4: Authority-Maintaining Morality. Belief in law & order is strong. Behavior conforms to law & higher authority. Social order is important.		Stage 2: Mythic-Literal Faith 6-12 years	Emergence of concrete operational thinking precipitates the transition to this stage, as a child is able to see the world from more than 1 perspective. Child's world is simple, orderly, temporally linear, and dependable.

212 Hope Haslam Straughan

Fowler – Faith Development

Stage 3: Synthetic-Conventional Faith 12-beyond	Emergence of formal operational thinking allows critical reflection on myths central to Stage 2. See God as personal & relational, holding great value to religious symbols.
Stage 4: Individuate-Reflective Faith Young adulthood or beyond (many persons stay between Stage 3 & 4)	Physical separation from home and encounter with new environment; authority moves from outside to inside person. Perception of God similar to Stage 3.
Stage 5: Conjunctive Faith mid-life or beyond	Person must have known life experiences of grief/confusion; deepest truths are inconsistent; sweeter spirit than Stages 3 & 4; lives with ambiguity; views faith from perspective of others; open to change.
Stage 6: Universalizing Faith Adulthood (exceptionally rare)	Characterized by brotherhood of all; focus on love, peace & justice; religion is relational, not conceptual; a radical absorption with unity of all people.

Kohlberg

Level 3 – Post Conventional
(many persons never move to Level 3)

Late adolescence

Stage 5: Morality of Contract, of Individual Rights, and of Democratically Accepted Law
Moral decisions internally controlled. Morality involves higher level principles beyond law and self-interest. Laws considered necessary, subject to rational thought and interpretation.

Adulthood

Stage 6: Morality of Individual Principles & Conscience
Behavior based on internal ethical principles. Decisions made according to what is right vs. what is written into law.

Erikson – Psychosocial Development

Stage 5: Identity vs. Role Confusion Adolescence	This transition period from childhood to adulthood is when a person examines the various roles they play, and integrate these roles into a perception of self, or identity.
Stage 6: Intimacy vs. Isolation Young adult	Young adulthood is characterized by a quest of intimacy. Persons not attaining intimacy are likely to suffer isolation, and were likely to resolve some of the crises of earlier psychosocial development.
Stage 7: Generativity vs. Stagnation Maturity	People are concerned with helping, producing for, or guiding the following generation. People lacking generativity become self-absorbed and inward.
Stage 8: Ego Integrity vs. Despair Old Age	People look back over life and reflect, taking stock in their decisions. For some this leads to a sense of peace (ego integrity) and for others to a sense of sadness and despair.
* Stage 9: Basic Mistrust vs. Trust: Hope Shame & Doubt vs. Autonomy: Will Guilt vs. Initiative: Purpose Inferiority vs. Industry: Competence Identity Confusion vs. Identity: Fidelity Isolation vs. Intimacy: Love Stagnation vs. Generativity: Care Despair & Disgust vs. Integrity: Wisdom Eighties and Nineties	People enter their late 80's and 90's and experience new demands, reevaluations, and daily difficulties. Despair is a close companion due to intense multiples losses, failing physical and cognitive abilities, and lessening autonomy. Old age is a circumstance which places the dystonic elements in a more prominent position than in earlier stages, with syntonic qualities having less potency. The underlined characteristics are possible outcomes of a person in their 80's or 90's struggling with each paired element, which can lead to growth, strength and commitment.

Table 2 Joan Borysenko's Feminine Life Cycle

The Ultimate Act of Renewal & Growth

Quadrant One:
Childhood and Adolescence

Early Childhood
1st period: Ages 0-7
From Empathy to Interdependence
Middle Childhood
2nd Period: Ages 7-14
The Logic of the Heart
Adolescence
3rd Period: Ages 14-21
Snow While Falls Asleep, But Awakens to Herself

Death

Joan Borysenko's
Feminine Life Cycle
In Seven Year Cycles

Quadrant Two:
Young Adulthood

Wisdom's Daughters
10th Period: Ages 63-70
Creating a New Integral Culture
The Gifts of Change
11th Period: Ages 70-77
Resiliency, Loss, and Growth
Recapitulating Our Lives
12th Period: Ages 77-84 and Beyond
Generativity, Retrospection, and Transcendence

A Home of One's Own
4th Period: Ages 21-28
The Psychobiology of Mating and Motherhood
The Age 30 Transition
5th Period: Ages 28-35
New Realities, New Plans
Healing and Balance
6th Period: Ages 35-42
Spinning Straw into Gold

Quadrant Four:
Elder Years

The Midlife Metamorphosis
7th Period: Ages 42-49
Authenticity, Power, and
the Emergence of the Guardian
From Herbs to HRT
8th Period: Ages 49-56
A Mindful Approach to Menopause
The Heart of a Woman
9th Period: Ages 56-63
Feminine Power and Social Action

Quadrant Three:
Midlife

CHAPTER 13

SOCIAL WELFARE IN A DIVERSE SOCIETY: LOVING THE NEIGHBOR YOU DON'T KNOW

James R. Vanderwoerd

Christians the world over are familiar with the second greatest command-ment given by Jesus to "love your neighbor as yourself" (Luke 10:27). Jesus' illustration of the implications of this commandment with the parable of the Good Samaritan (Luke 10:30-36) makes it clear that a neighbor is understood as any person one comes into contact with who is in need. While that may have been clear for first century Jews living in Jesus' time, it is less clear how this commandment can be fulfilled in 21st century societies. How are we to love our neighbors when we do not actually come into face-to-face contact with them? In large, urban, densely-populated, transitory societies, we might be aware of the acute needs of groups of people, but we cannot possibly cross paths with them all. What, then, can it mean to love our neighbor as ourself? Are we to be content with simply showing love only to those with whom we are personally connected? Or, does Jesus' command compel us to go beyond just the needy person before us and extend to the many that we do not and cannot personally know?

One answer to these questions has been to institutionalize and formalize the responsibility for the care and welfare of others via the establishment of the welfare state. At the beginning of the 21st century, however, the idea of the welfare state has come under question in many industrialized societies (Gilbert, 2004), and there have been increasing critiques of the welfare state and whether its advancement can even be considered a success. This debate has important implications for the legitimacy, role, and authority of social work, since it is a profession that depends to a large extent on the welfare state for its existence.

Should Christian social workers defend the welfare state? Should trends such as devolution, faith-based initiatives, and for-profit services be interpreted as threats to be resisted, or do these trends portend an appropriate return to a limited government that makes room for the charitable impulse of voluntary, church-based helping? Foundational to these questions is the question of who is responsible, in a diverse, technologically advanced, multi-cultural society, for the welfare and well-being of those who are most disadvantaged and vulnerable. Past answers no longer suffice—neither the 19th century version, in which indi-viduals were responsible to exercise their charitable obligations to their needy neighbors, nor the 20th century version, in which the state was responsible.

This chapter identifies several key biblical principles that provide a foundation from which to understand a Christian vision for 21st century social welfare. First, a brief discussion of the nature of societies will be described, followed by some implications and principles for how individual Christians, particularly social workers, understand their role in such societies. Next follows a discussion of the mutual rights and responsibilities that flow from this view and its understanding of the nature of humans as God's image-bearers. Finally, the paper explores the implications of this vision for three social welfare policy issues: the role of faith-related social service organizations; the rights of persons who are gay, lesbian, bi-sexual or transgendered (GLBT) to adopt or foster children; and the social welfare roles and responsibilities of business corporations.

Complex Societies

The Salvation Army, Rosie O'Donnell, and BP (British Petroleum) — mention any of these names in casual conversation and one quickly gets a sense of the complexity of 21st century North American society and the widely disparate perspectives that exist among different people. How are we to understand such variation and complexity? Nostalgic hearkening to the "good old days" often portrays a mythical simple society in which it was assumed that everyone agreed about what was right and wrong. But today, people hold different beliefs about different things at different levels. Society is complex, if not downright confusing.

One way Christians have made sense of this confusion and complexity has been to start with an understanding of creation informed by the biblical story. For example, Wolters (1995), working from within the neo-Calvinist tradition, describes in his book *Creation Regained* how God created *all* of existing reality – including different societies – and continues to uphold it all. This biblical understanding of society posits that social structures were not created exclusively by humans, but rather were established by God as part of the created order. However, humans do have a unique role in developing, establishing, and refining these structures in response to God's created order, and can thus choose to do this in obedience or in rejection of God. Further, according to Wolters, these structures have characteristics and properties, similar to the laws that govern physical reality, which God built into them and that establish parameters for their functioning (Wolters, 1985; 1995).

The overall purpose of social structures is to facilitate God's intent for humans in His creation, which is the abundant flourishing of human relationships in harmony—what the Hebrews in the Old Testament called *shalom* (Gornick, 2002). One of our tasks as humans is to seek understanding and knowledge about the characteristics and properties of various social structures so that we might discern God's intent and purpose for them—and for us (MacLarkey, 1991).

To be sure, however, this is tricky business, in part because the Bible is not a social science reference book that provides simple formulas for universal application. God has given humans considerable latitude in developing social structures that are appropriate to specific times and places. It would be too simplistic to suggest that the Bible provides blueprints for particular social arrangements that are universal across the breadth of historical and cultural variation.

Nevertheless, humans are called to develop and utilize social arrangements in a way that is consistent with God's commands and in a way which either contributes to or detracts from shalom. That is, social reality, unlike physical reality, can stray from adherence to God's norms because social structures are established and realized through human effort, and humans, unlike rocks, water, and other inanimate matter, can be obedient or disobedient.

Further, creation is not static, but is continually changing, at least not through the work of humans, who are empowered by God to work in the world to develop it. Humans not only build physical things, but also develop social organizations, practices, and institutions. Societies evolve and change over time through human imagination and intervention; social forms and entities that exist today did not exist yesterday and may not tomorrow. Such variation is understood to be part of God's plan for his creation—albeit distorted and stunted by sin and human failing. Nevertheless, the evolution of societies from agrarian rural to industrial and post-industrial are not seen as diverging from God's will, but rather as the unfolding history of God's kingdom in which humans play a primary role (Kalsbeek, 1975; Koyzis, 2003).

Not all humans, however, acknowledge God, and some outright reject or disobey Him. What are Christians to do about such people? Few would advocate that they be forced to obey God or become Christians, even if this was possible (sadly, this has not stopped some Christians in the past from resorting to coercion, even violently so). We take it for granted that not all citizens in a given nation are Christians, and that even if they were, wide differences of opinion exist about how things ought to be. Further, we recognize that citizens have a right to believe what they want, and to express that belief freely. Indeed, this right is enshrined as the First Amendment in the Constitution of the United States and in Articles 2a and 2b of the Canadian Charter of Rights and Freedoms, and in Article 18 of the United Nations Universal Declaration of Human Rights.

The idea of pluralism is often used to recognize the religious diversity within societies. There are at least three types of pluralism. The first, variously labeled as *confessional pluralism* (Skillen, 1994) or *spiritual or directional diversity* (Mouw & Griffioen, 1993), addresses diversity based on spiritual beliefs, religion, or confessions. This type of pluralism recognizes that individuals and groups within society may legitimately hold varying beliefs and, within the rules of law, act on these beliefs. It is this type of pluralism that makes space for differences in spirituality and religion, and provides guidance for how persons from different religious and confessional (including belief systems that are not explicitly religious) belief systems treat one another.

We also readily acknowledge that the Salvation Army, Rosie O'Donnell and her lesbian partner's relationship with their children, and BP are three very different types of social entities among many more: we attend churches, play on soccer teams, volunteer at the public library, sit on school boards, serve Thanksgiving dinners at the downtown soup kitchen, visit art galleries and museums, enroll our children (and their animals) in 4H clubs, hold memberships in the American Automobile Association, and send donations to Bread for the World. These and a virtually infinite number of other ways in which people can associate and interact are a second type of pluralism referred to as *structural pluralism* or *associational diversity*. Regardless of the specific labels, the underlying idea is a recognition that society consists of a wide variety of types of organizations, and that individuals are free to join and associate together according to their own voluntary choices.

The third type of plurality is labeled as *cultural* or *contextual*. This type of plurality refers to the differences associated with ethnicity, culture, and language. While these may overlap with confessional / directional pluralism, distinguishing between these is important in that it prevents us from making erroneous assumptions that conflate beliefs and culture, for example, that all Muslims are Arab, or that all Indians are Sikhs.

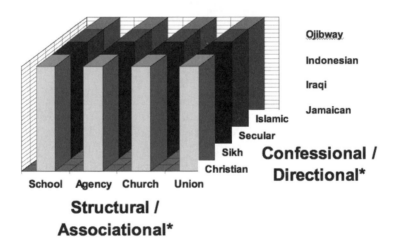

Figure 1. Three Types of Pluralities in Complex Societies
*Note that for each of the three types of pluralities, the four specific labels are only examples, and are not intended to be exhaustive. For example, under structural / associational pluralism, there are many more types of societal structures that could be included such as businesses, professions, families, community theatre groups, self-help groups, bowling leagues, etc.

As shown in Figure 1, a person could belong to particular societal structures (for example a school or a labor union) that specifically operate from within a particular confessional or directional context. Such confessional contexts could be explicitly religious (such as a Christian university, or an Islamic school, or a Jewish social service agency) but could also not be specifically religious. For example, an agency serving women and children who are victims of male violence could be explicitly situated within a secular feminist perspective; or, a labor union could be organized explicitly according to a Marxist-socialist perspective; or a child welfare agency could operate from an explicit anti-oppressive perspective.

Together, these three types of pluralisms capture the idea that people organize and live their lives in terms of their fundamental beliefs about the world (i.e, confessional / directional), in terms of the purpose or function of the grouping (i.e., structural / associational), and in terms of their belonging to various ethnic and cultural groups. Further, this understanding of multiple pluralities allows for the recognition of how fundamental beliefs operate in different social contexts. While we may disagree with other individuals and their choices, we recognize that in a diverse society, imposing our own particular perspectives on others is not a legitimate response when we encounter individuals who make choices different from our own, unless such choices violate established rules of law.

Sociologists use the term *institutions* to make sense of all the different ways in which people organize their lives within society. Institutions are the major building blocks of society and can be understood as the basic ways in which humans organize themselves to meet their needs. Commonly identified institutions include family, marriage, religion, law or justice, government and politics, education, and health.

The idea that society is more than simply individuals pursuing their own self-interests within a set of minimal government regulations (what Enlightenment liberals have called "the social contract"; see Nisbet, 1982) has led to much renewed interest in how individuals work together to offset the alienation and bureaucracy that arise in large institutions, along with the sense of helplessness that comes from simply acting on one's own. *Civil society* and *mediating structures* are terms that are used increasingly to refer to the many ways in which people live, work, play, and relate to one another other than as individuals or as units within large institutions (Berger & Neuhaus, 1996; Wuthnow, 2004).

Of particular interest is how these numerous and different social entities relate to one another and how the overlapping, multiple, and sometimes contradictory claims of these entities can be sorted out. For example, who is responsible for teaching children about sexuality, parents or schools? What role should government have in sorting out such a question? Is government to be "above" parents and schools, telling them what they may or may not do? Or, are parents, schools (and other social entities) independent of government, and thus allowed to do as they wish?

Two prominent Christian theories address these questions: the Catholic concept of subsidiarity, and the neo-Calvinist concept of sphere sovereignty (Chaplin, 1995; Koyzis, 2003; McIlroy, 2003). According to both positions, God's work of creation includes an ordering of the social relationships and organizations of society such as families, marriages, schools, business corporations, unions, sports teams, neighborhood associations, and consumer groups. Both subsidiarity and sphere sovereignty assert that these various social entities exist not simply at the behest of the state, but have a legitimacy and authority that ultimately comes from God.

Further, both positions claim that these entities possess autonomy appropriate to their social space and function. The concept of proximity is an important principle of subsidiarity. According to this idea, it is always preferable for decision-making and control to be held and exercised at the level that is closest (i.e, most proximate) to the situation. Local organizations and institutions, therefore, have the right to govern their own affairs. For example, churches do not need to get government approval over their doctrines, nor do parents need government to tell them what to feed their children. In other words, these various organizations have the right to make decisions without interference from government.

At the same time, however, Catholics and Calvinists both assert a role for government that is, in slightly different ways, overarching of these many other social organizations. Catholic social thought appeals to the idea of the common good and argues that government must provide the context and regulatory framework to ensure that other organizations contribute to, or at least do not directly detract from, the common good (Weigel, 1993). Thus, according to subsidiarity, the key criterion is not protecting the interests of particular organizations or entities, but rather, to ensure the best possible achievement of the common good. In other words, the common good as a principle is more important than the rights of organizations or individuals. Therefore, Catholic social thought always allows—indeed, demands—that higher and more distant entities, such as government, are entitled and have the responsibility to intervene when the common good is threatened by more local organizations.

Similarly, sphere sovereignty argues that each social organization has a specific and central role that is inherently attached to that organization as part of God's creation plan. The term *norm* refers to this role as the ideal standard to which organizations must aspire. Whether a specific organization identifies itself as Christian or not matters less than whether that organization conducts itself consistent with God's norms. The norm for government—that is, its central role and fundamental purpose—is to uphold public justice, that is, to encourage other organizations under its jurisdiction to fulfill their respective obligations and to adjudicate and protect the rights of other citizens and organizations to just and fair treatment in keeping with their unique, God-created norms (Koyzis, 2003; Sherrat, 1999; Skillen, 1994).

The key similarity in both subsidiarity and sphere sovereignty is an understanding that government has a unique, overarching—but also limited—role with respect to all the other types of social organizations. Government is not simply one among other entities, but has special responsibilities and obligations toward all of the citizens and residents within its jurisdiction. All other types of organizations can limit their memberships and therefore can choose whom to serve or include.

While the specifics of each of these viewpoints is beyond the scope of this chapter, the key difference is that subsidiarity tends to a more vertical and hierarchical ordering of social institutions, whereas sphere sovereignty views various social entities as being arranged horizontally (Chaplin, 1995; Koyzis, 2003).

Individuals Within Complex Societies

A Christian worldview also provides an understanding of the nature of humans and their roles and characteristics within diverse, pluralistic, and complex societies. The fundamental characteristic of humans, according to this view, is that we are created as image-bearers of God (see Genesis 1 -2; Middleton & Walsh, 1995, ch. 6). Exactly what that means has been a matter of much debate, but it includes at least that we image God's "we-ness" and his creativity. God said, "Let *us* make man in *our* image, in *our* likeness" (Gen. 1:26, emphasis added). God's plural self-identification alludes to his three-in-one personhood as Father, Son, and Holy Spirit. We can infer from this that God is relational and social, and that we, as His image-bearers, are also relational and social. To be human—to image God—is to be in mutual, harmonious, independent relationships with others; the reverse is also true: when we are isolated from others or when our relationships are constrained, limited, or broken, then we are in some way less than fully human as God intended. The various types of social entities discussed above are an indication of the many ways in which we humans have lived out our relational character.

We are also creative beings with the capacity to envision and imagine. We mirror God by harnessing our talents, gifts, and resources to build and establish physical structures and social arrangements and to make something of ourselves and the world (Crouch, 2008). Further, our being made in God's image as creative beings also carries with it the responsibility to use our creative energy for God's purposes and for others' benefit. Neil Plantinga (1995) describes this as follows:

> [W]e are to become *responsible* beings: people to whom God can entrust deep and worthy assignments, expecting us to make something significant of them—expecting us to make something significant of our lives. None of us simply finds himself here in the world. None of our lives is an accident. We have been called into existence, expected, awaited, equipped, and assigned. We have been called to undertake the stewardship of a good creation, to create sturdy and buoyant families that pulse with the glad give-and-take of the generations. We are expected to show hospitality to strangers and to express gratitude to friends and teachers. We have been assigned to seek justice for our neighbors and, whenever we can, to relieve them from the tyranny of their suffering (p. 197; emphasis added).

As image-bearers of God, we carry both responsibilities and rights. We are responsible, as Plantinga argues, to both God and others. But, we have the right to basic treatment and conditions, not because we deserve them, or only because of our worth as humans, but also so that we have what we need in order to carry out those responsibilities. Responsibility cannot be exercised without adequate resources to enable us to fulfill our calling. Part of what it means to image God's creativeness is that we participate in creation and its unfolding. The capacity to participate is therefore a fundamental ingredient in our life together (Coffin, 2000; Mott, 1996).

What role do individual Christians have in complex societies? Christian sociologist Brad Breems (2001) argues that we must be "critical—curative." To be critical is to be discerning about our contemporary culture and its spirits, and how these complement and diverge from God's intentions. It requires keen observation into the world around us, as well as a regular rootedness in God's ways via Scripture, prayer and meditation. But, to be critical alone is not sufficient. Breems argues we must also be curative—that is, we must use our discernment and insights as a call to action to bring healing (or *shalom*, see Gornick, 2002) where there is brokenness and pain.

To be critical and curative is not only to bring healing to individual hurt and pain, but also to apply God's word of redemption to the structures of society as well. We know that all of creation groans under the weight of sin (Romans 8:21-22), and thus that God's redemption plan includes not only people, but all other parts of creation, including the social organizations and institutions within which we humans live out our social lives together. The apostle Paul says God makes us ambassadors in his reconciliation plan (II Cor. 5: 17-20). This means that we are appointed as God's representatives to carry out his work to fix the brokenness. A lofty mandate, to be sure, but not one that tempts us to conclude that our way is best or right. Richard Mouw (1992) reminds us of the need to avoid triumphalism and take on an attitude of humility and civility, even as we carry on with confidence the work to which we have been called.

Implications in Three Areas

In sum, a Christian worldview provides a framework for understanding humans and their place in an increasingly complex post-industrial society (Poe, 2002; Walsh & Middleton, 1984). Further, this worldview provides a way for Christians to make sense of the conflicting claims in a diverse culture, particularly when so many of these claims are counter to, if not outright inimical, to God's claims. Directional and associational pluralism recognizes that there must be space and allowance for people to associate and conduct themselves in accordance with their own worldview, beliefs, or doctrine, even if others would view such conduct as unacceptable. We also recognize that the impulse we witness in ourselves and our neighbors to associate and gather together for an infinite number of reasons and ascribing to a wide variety of beliefs is evidence of our being made in God's image, even if we believe others' choices to be disobedient to God's will.

Three social welfare policy issues serve as examples of the implications of this framework: the role of faith-based groups in addressing social problems, the rights of persons who are gay, lesbian, bisexual or transgendered (GLBT) to adopt or foster children, and the social welfare responsibilities of business corporations. Although each of these issues merits more attention to be addressed adequately, the purpose here is to show how the Christian worldview sketched above helps us to think about complex social welfare issues.

Faith-based Organizations

Christians disagree about the extent to which faith groups, especially churches, should be responsible for social problems and in particular whether religion should replace government as the primary social institution responsible for addressing the needs of our most vulnerable citizens (Wuthnow, 2004).

Fundamental to these issues is an understanding of the role of government vis-à-vis other social institutions. According to the framework described in the first part of this paper, government has a special responsibility to uphold justice. Mott (1996) elaborates on this by distinguishing between government's obligation to protect people from bad things (what he calls negative justice) and ensuring that people have access to good things (positive justice) in order to allow individuals to fulfill their obligations and responsibilities. Government, therefore, must not surrender its responsibility for the welfare of its citizens, particularly toward those who are most vulnerable. With respect to religious organizations' role in social welfare, government must provide a context that encourages their participation, but does not offload a social welfare responsibility onto religion (Bane, Coffin, & Thiemann, 2000; Daly, 2005).

On the other hand, the practice in both the USA and Canada in the last half of the 20th century has been to marginalize and exclude some religious organizations from social welfare participation unless those organizations are willing to give up some aspect of their faith in order to adhere to a secular, allegedly value-free perspective that is often the price of participation in social welfare provision, especially with public funding (Donaldson & Carlson-Thies, 2003; Monsma, 1996).

Legal and regulatory practice regarding the limitation of public funding of religious organizations in the USA, and similar practices in Canada (despite the lack of an explicit principle of church-state separation; Hiemstra, 2002) has been until recently based on a separationist principle that restricts religious organizations' access to public funding. The implication of structural and confessional pluralism, however, is that a new relationship between government and faith-based organizations becomes possible (Vanderwoerd, 2002). Rather than regarding government aid to faith-based organizations as a violation of the First Amendment, this kind of pluralism would mean that faith-based organizations be given the same opportunity for access to public dollars as other nonprofit organizations.

In other words, organizations should not be prevented from accessing public funding on the basis of their religious beliefs, or because the services for which they seek funding are explicitly religious. Rather, the principle of structural and confessional pluralism would enable various organizations to maintain the integrity of their particular religious beliefs and still participate in particular aspects of public life.

Some legal scholars have suggested that the concept of neutrality (sometimes also referred to as "equal treatment") provides a legal interpretation that acknowledges this pluralism compared to earlier separationist interpretations that operated according to a "no aid to religion" principle (Esbeck, 1997; Monsma, 1993, 2000). The neutrality principle allows for individuals and groups to participate fully in the public square without having to leave their personal religious or secular viewpoints at home. Esbeck (1997), for example, in support of government funding for faith-based social service organizations, suggests that:

> ...the neutrality principle rejects the three assumptions made by separationist theory: that the activities of faith-based charities are severable into "sacred" and "secular" aspects, that religion is "private" whereas government monopolizes "public" matters, and that governmental assistance paid to service providers is aid to the providers as well as aid to the ultimate beneficiaries (p. 21-22).

With the rejection of these first two assumptions, neutrality theory is consistent with the concept of structural and confessional pluralism. Further, this principle suggests an approach which does not violate the intentions of the First Amendment, namely, that government neither advance nor restrict religious belief, but allow its citizens and groups autonomy regarding religious conviction and practice.

Finally, in the interest of protecting religious autonomy, the neutrality principle improves on the separationist interpretation that attempted to divide religious organizations' activities into secular and "pervasively sectarian" categories. Recognizing that religious beliefs are expressed across the spectrum of human life—and not just constrained to either private life or to the church—the neutrality principle allows faith-based organizations (FBOs) to receive public money and still maintain their religious integrity in the particular work they do. The concept of neutrality, therefore, is seen to provide a legal framework that opens the way for government funding of faith-based organizations while remaining true to the intentions of the First Amendment.

The legislative and regulative changes associated with the White House Office of Faith-Based and Community Initiatives represent a level of recognition and space for religious expression in public life that is overdue. Reducing the religious barriers to accessing government funds acknowledges that faith is more than just the private beliefs of individuals, but that it also centrally directs a society's public life. Further, in a diverse country, space must be allowed for the public expression of many faiths, rather than the imposition of either the majority's faith perspective, or an allegedly neutral secular perspective. On this basis alone, the "newer deal," as these developments have been called (Cnaan, 1999), is a welcome advance in social welfare policy.

Despite this promise, unanswered questions remain. First, the claims of superior effectiveness of faith-based organizations in addressing social problems compared to secular alternatives must be subjected to more rigorous evaluation. Appropriate social science techniques must be employed to identify and test the unique characteristics of faith-based services (Boddie & Cnaan, 2006. Such evaluation is particularly necessary to avoid uncritically favoring faith-based organizations over secular services absent other criteria for effectiveness.

Second, it would be a grave mistake to imagine that increasing the participation of faith-based providers with government funds can substitute for a governmental responsibility. Social problems have never been due solely to personal failures or personal sin, and individually focused solutions will never solve the deeper-seated structural and systemic failures that are also implicated in social problems. When God calls his people to be ambassadors of reconciliation it is clear that this reconciliation is not reserved just for personal and individual brokenness, but for *all* creation. Government—faith partnerships should be part of the solution, but can never be the whole solution.

Same Sex Adoption and Fostering

The right of persons who are gay and lesbian to adopt or foster children is even more controversial and contested than the role of religion in social welfare. However, just as associational and directional diversity allow space for religious organizations to participate in social welfare with public funding and support, so also does this principle provide space for gays and lesbians to live out their choices without discrimination.

Many Christians find this position unsettling because it appears to condone or even encourage behavior and practices that they believe are fundamentally contrary to God's intent. It is important to note at the outset that Christians disagree about what God's will is for same-sex relationships (Christian Scholar's Review, 1997; Zahniser & Kagle, 2007). Regardless of one's position on the legitimacy of same-sex relationships, however, the issue here is what government's role ought to be with respect to two other types of social structures: marriage and the family.

The concepts of confessional and structural pluralism, as described above, suggest that we must be willing to accord others the right to live their lives according to their fundamental assumptions and beliefs (whether explicitly religious or otherwise) and for these beliefs to be allowed expression not only in people's choices about religious activities and expression (i.e., confessional pluralism), but also in the way they participate in other social entities (i.e., structural pluralism). Skillen (1994) argues this point as follows:

> The Constitution does not give government the right to confound religion with, or to confine religion to, institutional churches.... If... citizens are given legitimate protection under the Constitution to practice their religions freely (confessional pluralism), then all citizens should be free to conduct family life, schooling, and other social practices (structural pluralism) in ways that are consistent with the obligations of their deepest presuppositions and faiths (pp. 86-87).

The principle of sphere sovereignty provides further parameters on what authority different spheres should or should not exercise. In this case, government's authority is to provide the context for individuals and groups to exercise their responsibilities according to their convictions. Thus, government should not limit or constrain individuals or groups unless there is some direct reason connected to the general welfare or, in Catholic social thought, the common

good. The neutral stance that government takes with respect to religious organizations in social welfare is also called for here: government cannot implicitly
or explicitly endorse a particular arrangement or structure for families unless
and only if there is a compelling reason to do so to serve the common good
(Van Geest, 2002).

The issue here is for government to act in such a way as to enhance public
justice and further the common welfare or good of all without infringing on
the rights of individuals or groups to live according to their own beliefs. In
particular, it is important for government to protect minority groups from having the will of the majority imposed upon them. Indeed, in the Netherlands,
both Protestants and Catholics combined their numbers and argued for space
and protection from secular perspectives, arguing their position on the basis
of sphere sovereignty and subsidiarity. In that country, religious groups get full
access to public funding for schools, agencies, media outlets, and many other
institutions (Glenn, 2000); as well, the Netherlands also provides greater freedom
for same-sex couples to marry.

The importance of the public justice principle becomes apparent if we
engage in a fictional thought experiment and we envision several hypothetical
alternative scenarios unfolding in the future:

- Jews have become the dominant religion, and most of them have concluded that all boys and men should be circumcised; or,
- Muslims have become the majority, and most of them believe that all
  women and girls must wear a *hijab* (the traditional head covering) at
  all times in public; or,
- Christians who interpret the bible literally are in the majority, and
  most of them have concluded that women must keep their hair long.

Now imagine that in any one of these fictional scenarios a couple with
a short-haired wife, or a mother without a *hijab*, or an uncircumcised father
wants to adopt or foster a child. If the appropriate child welfare professionals
have determined that the family would be suitable, are there any grounds for a
state government, in any of the three scenarios above, to pass a law to prevent
short-haired women, non-*hijab* wearing mothers, or uncircumcised fathers from
fostering or adopting? Unless there is some compelling evidence to conclude
that short-haired women, non-*hijab* wearing mothers, or uncircumcised fathers
present a clear danger or harm to children, the answer clearly would be "no."

No matter how much we as individuals might strongly disagree with these
couples' choices about hair length, head coverings, or circumcision, we would
hardly expect the government to pass laws to restrict such choices, even if we
find them morally repugnant according to *our* faith beliefs. The same is true for
gay or lesbian partners who wish to adopt or foster children. There is compelling
(Patterson, 2004)—though disputed (Dailey, 2001)—research evidence that gay
or lesbian parents are no better or worse than heterosexual parents, and that
children of gay or lesbian parents are no more or less likely to become gay or
lesbian or to develop sexual identity problems.

The role of the state is not to attempt to define and enforce morally correct behavior or choices unless it can be clearly demonstrated that such behavior threatens the common good or limits public justice. It *is* the role of the state to provide safe alternatives for neglected, abused, and troubled children whose own parents or families have failed them. Whether homosexuality or head coverings or circumcision or hair length is morally right or wrong is not a matter for public laws, but for churches, synagogues, temples, families, and couples to determine. Governments must provide the liberty and capacity for these groups to make these choices for themselves, not pass laws that impose the choices or beliefs of one group over others.

The task for Christians in social work is to attempt to discern God's norms for the social entity called the family. If our ultimate goal is to facilitate the development of healthy relationships, then that overrides our faith conviction about the morality of same sex partners as adoptive or foster parents. In the three hypothetical examples above, it is clear that appealing to a higher norm leads one to see past the convictions of other groups with whom we disagree about women's hair length, head coverings, or male circumcision as criteria by which to assess the suitability of an adoptive or foster placement.

Business Corporations

People seldom think of business corporations when thinking about social welfare policy or social problems. Nevertheless, the corporation has become a major provider of social welfare benefits in most post-industrial economies, and even further, has enormous influence—both negative and positive—over many people's lives, both directly and indirectly, via its economic activity and decisions (Lodge & Wilson, 2006). Even aside from the substantial role that private corporations play in social welfare, the Christian worldview articulated here leads to the inclusion of this somewhat unusual example.

Business corporations tend to fly under the radar when social welfare is discussed, but here, too, the concept of sphere sovereignty asserts that business corporations are not autonomous, but have their authority and legitimacy in God's creational design for social life. Further, God's creational order provides parameters for how business corporations function in relationship to other social organizations (such as families, schools, unions, nonprofits, and so on) and to government. Antonides (1978) develops this as follows:

A business enterprise must respond to a broader variety of social norms than merely the economic; it must take into consideration a broader variety of interests than merely the financial yardstick of profit. A business enterprise—also a multinational corporation—must take into account the interests of investors, but also the interests of the suppliers of natural resources, of the workers, of the consumers, and of persons and social structures—especially families—that are directly or indirectly affected by the enterprise's productive activity. An economic enterprise is never closed off from its social environment and the slogan "free enterprise" should not blind us to this fact. An economic enterprise must display its own normative structuration—"sphere sovereignty"—in the context of societal/interdependence and intertwinement (p. 178).

A business corporation is one among many types of social structures, with its own unique characteristics and properties or norms. What, then, is the purpose or function of a business corporation? What way does a business corporation represent obedience or disobedience to God's norms? The vast majority of Christians who have wrestled with these questions tend to focus exclusively on the ethical behavior of the persons who own or run the company (Rae & Wong, 2004). Here the emphasis is on developing a set of ethical principles or guidelines which are presumed to distinguish between a Christian or biblical and a so-called secular way of managing a business (Novak, 2004). None of these, however, gets at the underlying question of *what* a business corporation is, and what its purpose is other than to generate wealth or profit.

As with the previous two issues, the foundation laid from the perspective outlined in the first part of the paper provides the basis for understanding the underlying and fundamental aspects of business corporations. Vandezande (1984), drawing on the concept of sphere sovereignty, distinguishes between the business corporation and the business enterprise:

I view the *corporation* as the entity that legally "owns" and administers the financial investments of the shareholders. I view the business *enterprise* as the human work-community that has the organizational obligation to develop and implement stewardly aims and activities. While the corporation is the legal trustee of the shareholders' financial investments, such as land, buildings, machinery, and equipment, it does not own the enterprise. A human work-community and its talents cannot be owned (p. 72).

Bob Goudzwaard (1979), a Dutch Christian economist, in his analysis of capitalism, shows how the biblical emphasis on humans as stewards (Genesis 1-2; Psalm 24) of God's creation provides the origins for the term *economics*. This concept of stewardship is identified as the key characteristic for the business corporation (or *enterprise*, using Vandezande's term) as a social structure. Antonides (1978) develops this further by drawing on the Dutch philosopher Herman Dooyeweerd, whose Christian philosophical framework identified fifteen fundamental aspects of creation and their key characteristics. Included is the economic aspect, for which the key characteristic is the management—or stewardship—of scarce resources (Kalsbeek, 1975; Skillen, 1979).

As Antonides (1978) makes clear, the key criterion on which to evaluate the performance of a business corporation, therefore, is according to the biblical principle of stewardship, rather than profit.

The norm for a business enterprise as an economically qualified societal structure is stewardship. This must be the key guideline in all its activities. The realization of the norm of stewardship entails a careful use and allocation of natural resources, labor, managerial talent, capital, etc., so that an economic surplus is attained as a result of economic productive activity. This economic surplus can be measured in a financial manner in terms of profit. But, as soon as we mention the word profit, a warning is in order because of the loaded history of that term. A business enterprise must respond to a broader variety of social norms than merely the economic; it must take into consideration a broader variety of interests than merely the financial yardstick of profit (p. 178).

Indeed, many in the secular business world have become increasingly aware that profit as "the bottom line" is no longer adequate, and, in the end, has become counterproductive to sound business practice (Batstone, 2003; Norman & MacDonald, 2004). As well, some Christians have begun to acknowledge that the concept of stewardship is fundamental to understanding business corporations and discerning whether their activities and performance are consistent with God's will (Krueger, 1997; Stackhouse,, McCann, Roels, & Williams, 1995).

A Christian worldview that recognizes the God-created diversity of social structures and their norms also brings into focus business corporations when social workers consider the question of how to love one's neighbour in a society of strangers. The acronym TINA—There Is No Alternative—has been used by critics of globalization to draw attention to the way in which the role of corporations and the structures and arrangements of a free market economy are presumed to be off limits when debating such controversial policy issues such as free trade, worker rights, minimum wages, and social benefits. As Christians who confess that Christ's lordship extends to all His creation, we reject TINA and boldly assert instead that "…there are thousands of alternatives" (Kang, 2005, p. 10), and that discerning these means careful examination of business corporations not simply according to the dominant norm of profitability-at-all-costs, but to a broader assessment of how corporations measure up to God's norms for constructive wealth creation (Heslam, 2009).

Conclusion

Social workers operating from the perspective sketched here can no longer afford to focus entirely on the role of government as the sole provider of social welfare, or, in the other extreme, argue that individuals and churches acting charitably are solely responsible. The simple command to "love your neighbor as yourself" turns out to be exceedingly complicated in the context of complex, diverse societies, where most of our neighbors are anonymous strangers. In small, homogenous, self-contained, and independent communities, the practice of loving one's neighbor – and sharing the responsibility for others' welfare – is comparatively easy. As modern industrialized and capitalist nation-states emerged in the 18th and 19th centuries, however, needs born of new social problems outstripped the capacity of the welfare community, welfare family, or welfare tribe (Chatterjee, 1996). The welfare state filled the gap, and by the mid-20th century had all but replaced the family and the community as the primary institution responsible for social welfare. The welfare state has become a way in which we can collectively love our neighbor.

However, under pressure from neo-conservative governments, reduced revenues, and soaring costs, cracks appeared in the welfare state in the closing decades of the 20th century. Social workers—along with other left-leaning groups—reacted predictably by advocating nearly unanimous calls to shore up the welfare state (Mishra, 1999; Klein, 2007; Raphael, 2007). In fact, advocating for social justice has become nearly synonymous with support for government-driven and financed welfare state expansion (Schneider & Netting, 1999), and questioning this is viewed as heresy and abandonment of social work values (Belcher, Fandetti, & Cole, 2004; Chatterjee, 2002; personal communication, October 31, 2002).

At the same time, public support for an advanced welfare state has waned substantially since the 1970s, and there is widespread sentiment that the welfare state has produced an "entitlement" society that fails to reward or encourage responsibility. It is no coincidence that the 1996 welfare reform legislation signed into law by former president Bill Clinton was named the "Personal Responsibility and Work Opportunity Reconciliation Act."

As well, many evangelical Christians have become increasingly vocal in their resistance to the perceived domination of the welfare state, and particularly in the way in which the welfare state as an institution has been part of what is perceived as a sustained "liberal" attack on the traditional structures of society, particularly marriages and families. Thus, we have an impasse where social workers and other professions associated with the "liberal elite" support the welfare state, pitted against conservatives and many religious persons who support a reduced government role and renewed support for traditional approaches to solving compelling social problems (Hodge, 2003 2004; Olasky, 1992; Schwartz, 2000)

The understanding of society described in this paper—drawing on Catholic social thought and Protestant Reformed thinking, particularly in the neo-Calvinist tradition—provides a way to circumvent this standoff and point us in a direction where Jesus' admonition that anyone in need is a neighbor can be implemented realistically in complex, diverse societies. Sphere sovereignty (and the similar Catholic concept of subsidiarity) suggests that society consists of multiple social structures, and that each has a unique function and a legitimate area of responsibility commensurate with its characteristics and in obedience to God's norms.

Although it is true that we can never be absolutely confident that we fully understand these structures and their norms (Mouw, 1992; Wolterstorff, 1995), that should not stop us from trying. A long tradition of Christian scholarship and practice has established public justice and the pursuit of the common good as the special purview of government (Hiemstra, 2005). This means that government has the responsibility to ensure that all persons and groups under its jurisdiction are encouraged and supported to participate and fulfill their responsibilities. This does not mean, however, that government has the only responsibility for social welfare.

Confessional and structural pluralism entail a social order in which persons are able to associate both according to their fundamental beliefs (whether explicitly religious or not) across the full spectrum of social structures, and not simply within the social structure of formal religion via churches, synagogues, mosques, and other bodies of worship. Faith-based organizations, therefore, should have the same access to public funding for social welfare services as secular organizations.

In a similar way, if two persons of the same sex, on the basis of their fundamental beliefs about the world, seek to partner to adopt or foster children, government ought not to restrict such persons from that choice, or at least, from the legal, regulative, and welfare benefits that are available to heterosexual persons who adopt or foster.

Finally, Christians in social work can participate with others to draw attention to the ways in which corporations, as one of many God-created social structures, live up not simply to the norms of the market, but to the higher obligations to which God calls them.

Christians in social work must develop increasing sensitivity to the wide variety of confessions out there, especially when they differ from our own. We know too well our own substantial rifts even within the body of Christ. Our task is to attempt to discern the sources of social brokenness and seek to bring healing by facilitating and equipping other social entities to fulfill the obligations and expectations which God has set for them. Our call as social workers is to exercise compassion—not coercion—in pursuit of shalom.

References

Antonides, H. (1978). *Multinationals and the peaceable kingdom.* Toronto, ON: Clarke, Irwin.

Bane, M., Coffin, B., & Thiemann, R. (Eds.). (2000). *Who will provide? The changing role of religion in American social welfare.* Boulder, CO: Westview Press.

Batstone, D. (2003). *Saving the corporate soul & (who knows?) maybe your own: Eight principles for creating and preserving integrity and profitability without selling out.* San Franciso, CA: Jossey-Bass.

Belcher, J., Fandetti, D., & Cole, D. (2004). Is Christian religious conservatism compatible with the liberal social welfare state? *Social Work, 49*(2), 269-276.

Berger, P., & Neuhaus, R. J. (1996). *To empower people: From state to civil society, 20th Anniversary Edition.* Washington, DC: American Enterprise Institute.

Boddie, S. & Cnaan, R.A. (Eds.). (2006). *Faith-based social services: Measures, assessments, and effectiveness.* Binghamton, NY: Haworth Pastoral Press.

Breems, B. (2001). The service of sociology: Providing a lighter cloak or a sturdier iron cage? In J. Kok (Ed). *Marginal resistance,* (pp. 253-272). Sioux Center, IA: Dordt College Press.

Chaplin, J. (1995). Subsidiarity and sphere sovereignty: Catholic and reformed conceptions of the role of the state, In *Confessing Christ in Doing Politics: Essays on Christian Political Thought and Action,* (pp. 104-129). Potchefstroom, RSA: Institute for Reformational Studies, Potschefstroom University.

Chatterjee, P. (1996). *Approaches to the welfare state.* Washington, DC: NASW Press.

Chatterjee, P., & D'Aprix, A. (2002). Two tails of justice. *Families in Society, 83*(4), 374-386.

Christian Scholar's Review. (1997). *Theme issue: Christianity and homosexuality, 26*(4).

Cnaan, R. (1999). *The newer deal: Social work and religion in partnership.* New York, NY: Columbia University Press.

Coffin, B. (2000). Where religion and public values meet: Who will contest? In M. Bane, B. Coffin, & R. Thiemann (Eds.). *Who Will Provide? The Changing Role of Religion in American Social Welfare*, (pp. 121-146). Boulder, CO: Westview Press.

Crouch, A. (2008). *Culture making: Recovering our creative calling.* Downer's Grove, IL: InterVarsity Press.

Dailey, T. (2001). Homosexual parenting: Placing children at risk. *Insight Issue* No. 238. October 30, 2001. [Available: http://www.frc.org/get.cfm?i=IS01J3].

Daly, L. (2005). Compassion capital: Bush's faith-based initiative is bigger than you think. *Boston Review*, 30, April / May 2005. [Available: http://bostonreview.net/BR30.2/daly.html].

Donaldson, D., & Carlson-Thies, S. (2003). *A revolution of compassion: Faith-based groups as full partners in fighting America's social problems.* Grand Rapids, MI: Baker Books.

Esbeck, C. (1997). A constitutional case for governmental cooperation with faith-based social service providers. *Emory Law Journal, 46*(1), 1- 41.

Gilbert, N. (2004). *Transformation of the welfare state: The silent surrender of public responsibility.* New York, NY: Oxford University Press.

Glenn, C. (2000). *The ambiguous embrace: Government and faith-based schools and social agencies.* Princeton, NJ: Princeton University Press.

Gornick, M. (2002). *To live in peace: Biblical faith and the changing inner city.* Grand Rapids, MI: Eerdmans.

Goudzwaard, B. (1979). *Capitalism and progress: A diagnosis of western society.* Grand Rapids, MI: Eerdmans / Toronto, ON: Wedge.

Heslam, P. (2009). Commercial entrepreneurship for the good of people and planet, in M.W. Goheen & E.G. Glanville (Eds.), *The gospel and globalization: Exploring the religious roots of a globalized world.* Vancouver, BC: Regent College Publishing, pp. 161-178.

Hiemstra, J. (2005). Section I. church, state and the kingdom of god, An overview, *REC [Reformed Ecumenical Council] Focus*, 5(2), 3–49.

Hiemstra, J. (2002). Government relations with faith-based non-profit social agencies in Alberta. *Journal of Church & State,* 44(1), 19-44.

Hodge, D. (2004). Who we are, where we come from, and some of our perceptions: Comparison of social workers and the general population, *Social Work, 49*(2), 261-268.

Hodge, D. (2003). Differences in worldviews between social workers and people of faith. *Families in Society, 84*(2), 285-295.

Kalsbeek, L. (1975). *Contours of a Christian philosophy: An introduction to Herman Dooyeweerd's thought.* Toronto, ON: Wedge Publishing.

Kang, Y. (2005). Global ethics and a common morality. Paper presented at the International Symposium of the Association for Reformational Philosophy, Hoeven, The Netherlands, August 16-19, 2005.

Klein, N. (2007). *The shock doctrine: The rise of disaster capitalism.* Toronto, ON: Knopf Canada.

Koyzis, D. (2003). *Political visions & illusions: A survey & Christian critique of contemporary ideologies.* Downer's Grove, IL: InterVarsity Press.

Krueger, D. (1997). *The business corporation & productive justice.* Nashville, TN: Abingdon Press.

Lodge, G. & Wilson, C. (2006). *A corporate solution to global poverty: How multinationals can help the poor and invigorate their own legitimacy.* Princeton, NJ: Princeton University Press.

MacLarkey, R. (1991). Reformational social philosophy and sociological theory. *Perspectives on Science and Christian Faith, 43,* 96-102.

McIlroy, D. (2003). Subsidiarity and sphere sovereignty: Christian reflections on the size, shape and scope of government. *Journal of Church and State, 45*(4), 739-763.

Middleton, R., & Walsh, B. (1995). *Truth is stranger than it used to be: Biblical faith in a postmodern age.* Downer's Grove, IL: InterVarsity Press.

Mishra, R. (1999). *Globalization and the welfare state.* Northampton, MA: E. Elgar Press.

Monsma, S. (1993). *Positive neutrality: Letting religious freedom ring.* Grand Rapids, MI: Baker Books.

Monsma, S. (1996). *When sacred and secular mix: religious nonprofit organizations and public money.* Lanham, MD: Rowman & Littlefield.

Monsma, S. (2000). Substantive neutrality as a basis for free exercise - no establishment common ground. *Journal of Church and State, 42*(1), 13 - 35.

Mott, S. (1996). Foundations of the welfare responsibility of the government, In S. Carlson-Thies & J. Skillen (Eds). *Welfare in America: Christian perspectives on a policy in crisis.* Grand Rapids, MI: Eerdmans.

Mouw, R. (1992). *Uncommon decency: Christian civility in an uncivil world.* Downer's Grove, IL: InterVarsity Press.

Mouw, R., & Griffioen, S. (1993). *Pluralisms and horizons: An essay in Christian public philosophy.* Grand Rapids, MI: Eerdmans.

Nisbet, R. (1982). *The social philosophers: Community and conflict in western thought.* New York, NY: Washington Square Press / Harper & Row.

Norman, W., & MacDonald, C. (2004). Getting to the bottom of "triple bottom line". *Business Ethics Quarterly, 14*(2), 243-262.

Novak, M. (2004). A theology of the corporation, In S. Rae & K. Wong, (Eds). *Beyond Integrity: A Judeo-Christian Approach to Business Ethics,* (pp. 216-222). Grand Rapids, MI: Zondervan.

Olasky, M. (1992). *The tragedy of American compassion.* Washington, DC: Regnery Gateway.

Patterson, C. (2004). Lesbian and gay parents and their children; Summary of research findings. In *Lesbian and Gay Parenting: A Resource for Psychologists.* Washington, DC: American Psychological Association.

Plantinga, N. (1995). *Not the way it's supposed to be: A breviary of sin.* Grand Rapids, MI: Eerdmans.

Poe, M. A. (2002). Christian world view and social work, In D. Dockery & G. Thornbury, (Eds). *Shaping a Christian Worldview: The Foundations of Christian Higher Education.* (pp.317-334). Nashville, TN: Broadman & Holman.

Rae, S., & Wong, K. (Eds). (2004). *Beyond Integrity: A Judeo-Christian Approach to Business Ethics.* Grand Rapids, MI: Zondervan.

Raphael, D. (2007). *Poverty and Policy in Canada: Implications for Health and Quality of Life.* Toronto, ON: Canadian Scholar's Press.

Schwartz, J. (2000). *Fighting poverty with virtue: Moral reform and America's poor, 1825-2000.* Bloomington, IN: Indiana University Press.

Schneider, R., & Netting, E. (1999). Influencing social policy in a time of devolution: Upholding social work's great tradition. *Social Work, 44*(4), 349-357.

Skillen, J. (1979). Herman Dooyeweerd's contribution to the philosophy of the social sciences. *Journal of the American Scientific Affiliation,* 20-24.

Skillen, J. (1994). *Recharging the American experiment: Principled pluralism for genuine civic community.* Grand Rapids, MI: Baker Books.

Sherrat, T. (1999). Rehabilitating the state in America: Abraham Kuyper's overlooked contribution, *Christian Scholar's Review, 29*(2), 323–346.

Stackhouse, M. McCann, D. P., Roels, S. J., & Williams, P. N. (1995). On moral business: classical and contemporary resources for ethics in economic life. Grand Rapids, MI: Erdsman Publishing Company.

Vanderwoerd, J. (2002). Is the newer deal a better deal? Government funding of faith-based social services. *Christian Scholars Review, 33,* 300-318.

Vandezande, G. (1984). *Christians in the crisis.* Toronto, ON: Anglican Book Centre.

Van Geest, F. (2002). Homosexuality and public policy: A challenge for sphere sovereignty. *Perspectives: A Journal of Reformed Thought, 17*(10), 5-10.

Walsh, B., & Middleton, R. (1984). *The transforming vision: Shaping a Christian world view.* Downer's Grove, IL: InterVarsity Press.

Weigel, G. (1993). *Building the free society: Democracy, capitalism, and Catholic social teaching.* Grand Rapids, MI: Eerdmans and Washington, D.C.: Ethics and Public Policy Center.

Wolters, A. (1985). *Creation regained: Biblical basics for a reformational worldview.* Grand Rapids, MI: Eerdmans.

Wolters, A. (1995). Creation order: A historical look at our heritage, in B. Walsh, H. Hart, & R. Vander Vennen, (Eds). *An Ethos of Compassion and the Integrity of Creation,* (pp. 33-48). New York, NY: University Press of America.

Wolterstorff, N. (1995). Points of unease with the creation order tradition, In B. Walsh, H. Hart, & R. Vander Vennen, (Eds). *An Ethos of Compassion and the Integrity of Creation,* (pp. 62-66). New York, NY: University Press of America.

Wuthnow, R. (2004). *Saving America? Faith-based services and the future of civil society.* Princeton, NJ: Princeton University Press.

Zahniser, J., & Cagle, L. (2007). Homosexuality: Toward an informed compassionate response. *Christian Scholar's Review, 36*(3), 323-348.

CHAPTER 14

WORKING WITH LGBT CLIENTS: PROMISING PRACTICES AND PERSONAL CHALLENGES

Allison Tan

My client is gay. I am a Christian social worker. Now what do I do? This is a scenario many Christians in social work practice will inevitably face at some point in their professional journey. To be sure, Christian social workers are themselves diverse in terms of their own sexual orientations and their beliefs about homosexuality. However, it is well-known that many Christian denominations have historically held a negative view of homosexuality, and this results in many Christian social workers struggling to reconcile their professional and spiritual lives.

If you have not yet encountered lesbian, gay, bisexual, or transgender (LGBT) clients in your practice, it is only a matter of time. Goldfried (2008) found that LGBT individuals and same-sex couples are actually more likely to seek mental health therapy or treatment than heterosexuals. This may be due to the stigma and discrimination they face (Harper and Schneider 2003; Meyer, 2003). The questions about promising practices for working with LGBT clients[1] are far from settled, but I will try here to ask questions and raise important issues to help you wrestle with the personal and professional challenges that come with providing quality, ethical care to LGBT clients.

Through a critical review of the literature and my personal experiences as a Christian social worker, I will utilize two case vignettes to represent the common themes and challenges associated with working with the LGBT population. The first vignette guides the investigation into the literature on promising practices (including a specific focus on 'affirmative practice' and the skills of 'critical consciousness' and 'difficult dialogues') for intervention with the LGBT population. It also addresses literature on the religious and spiritual lives of LGBT individuals. I will conclude with a second case vignette about a Christian practitioner in social work in order to guide discussion about how one social worker might apply her professional role, rooted in her Christian faith, to her work with the LGBT community.

My overarching aim here will be to support Christians in social work who want to work competently with the LGBT population, based on a deep-seated belief in the call of both our faith and our profession to provide quality services to *all* people in a rich, diverse world. Toward that end, it is important first and foremost to be clear about what this chapter is *not*. It is not an attempt to engage in a Scriptural debate or argument around the issues of homosexuality; such a hermeneutical discussion is beyond my expertise and is also not necessarily integral to a discussion of social work's promising practices. This chapter very purposefully does not take sides in the current gay rights debates; the stance I take here is not a political or theological one. Instead, it takes an evidence-based stance – the recommendations and practice-related discussion herein are rooted in the literature. Finally, while I believe every student and practitioner should prepare to serve a diverse range of clients, I know that there are some practitioners who may try to avoid serving LGBT clients as a regular part of their social work practice As I will discuss in more detail later, if there is any client group, LBGT or otherwise, that a social worker feels he or she cannot treat with respect, it is better to ethically and professionally refer the client to someone better able to help, while simultaneously examining one's own professional values, perhaps with a supervisor or mentor.

Promising Practices with the LGBT Population

As we encounter LGBT clients in our practice, many of us will be challenged by the question of how to best serve them. The case vignette below represents a real client I worked with (Kenny, not his real name) as an example of a gay male client seeking social work services. This case will be utilized throughout the chapter to guide our exploration into promising practices for working with LGBT clients.

Kenny, a 29-year-old African American man, has been HIV-positive for about 6 years. In the 3 years Kenny and Mike have been living together, their relationship has nearly always been characterized by a mix of fighting and frustration with one another. When the health center where they both received their medical care began to offer mental health counseling to its HIV-positive clients, Kenny was one of the first to express interest. In his first session, he described his relationship with Mike as 'hopeless' and 'dangerous'. He stated that Mike was often abusive toward him – and also shared that this relationship is not his first abusive one. When the social worker asked why he stayed with Mike, Kenny says, "I am HIV-positive. Who else is going to want to be with me? Even my family doesn't want to talk to me anymore. Mike is all I've got." The social worker was also able to identify Kenny's use of alcohol and marijuana as a means to self-medicate and cope with his problems. Early diagnostic efforts found Kenny to be severely depressed – he did also mention past suicidal ideation.

Counseling sessions focused on the presenting problem Kenny identified – his relationship with Mike. Kenny shared with the social worker a series of severed re-lationships: his mother and a number of other family members had all but disowned him after learning he was gay; he did not identify any close friends and stated that he can't really 'hang out' at the places in his neighborhood because "my people just don't get my lifestyle". Other than his job at a local drug store, Kenny stayed in his apartment by himself or with Mike most of the time. The social worker once gave

Kenny a homework assignment –to think about activities that brought him joy, that he might like to engage in to give his life meaning. The following week, Kenny shared that the only thing he could think of all week that brought him joy was when he used to sing in the church choir. "That brought me joy – I loved it. That gave my life meaning – I really miss it." Kenny went on to share that the church he grew up in and had attended for more than 20 years had asked him to leave when he began to share openly with church members that he was gay and brought a partner with him one week to the worship service.

In thinking about how best to help Kenny, we are also able to explore in more detail promising practices with the LGBT population. Figure 1 outlines the critical review strategy utilized to explore what is known about promising practices for working with LGBT individuals. "LGBT" was combined with four different sets of key phrases to arrive at a solid base upon which to review the literature. This process, while not definitive, does reflect what I was able to find from a transparent and clear search of the extant mental health literature at the time of writing (Fall 2011).

Figure 1: Overview of critical review strategy

Databases Searched: Academic Search Premier (ASP) and OVID

Keywords:

LGBT + 'best practices'	ASP = 3	OVID = 0
LGBT + 'evidence-based practice'	ASP = 0	OVID = 1
LGBT + 'interventions'	ASP = 16	OVID = 25
LGBT + 'therapy'	ASP = 11	OVID = 30
Total number of hits:	ASP = 28,	OVID = 48

The goal of this review was to understand which techniques, interventions, and theoretical orientations are commonly associated with culturally-competent work with this population. These findings can be used by practitioners interested in improving their clinical skills with LGBT individuals like Kenny and are detailed in the "Review of the Literature: Findings" section later in the chapter.

The importance of terminology

It is essential to speak briefly to the term "LGBT population," which is used throughout this chapter to describe lesbian, gay, and bisexual individuals. This term was specifically chosen because it was found to be the one most commonly used in both the popular and research literature, though it is a term that is still considered controversial. Some prominent researchers and practitioners within the field argue against this phraseology because it lumps *all* gay men, lesbian women, and bisexual men and women, along with transgender individuals, into one category (see Fassinger & Areseau, 2008). Additionally, much of the research that claims to represent the LGBT population is actually heavily weighted with lesbian and gay individuals and weakly includes bisexual and transgender individuals, if at all (Fisher, Easterly & Lazear, 2008). Therefore, many researchers are in favor of a more narrow "LGB" term, because transgender individuals are quite different in terms of their needs and often highly underrepresented in the literature (Harper & Schneider, 2003; Israel, Gorcheva, Burnes & Walther, 2008; Smith, 2005). One of the alternative terms to describe this population is "sexual minority clients" (Dworkin & Guttierez, 1992), which also may be seen as controversial. However, the LGBT terminology was selected instead simply because of its prevalence in the literature. In working with a client like Kenny, I would strongly encourage the social work practitioner to ask him what terminology he is most comfortable with and how he wishes to be identified. Using the client's desired language is a vital first step toward building competent social work practice.

Review of the Literature: Findings

Figure 2 below gives an overview of nine of the key studies on LGBT practice and summarizes their influence on this topic; many of their conclusions are referenced throughout the entirety of this chapter.

Key Themes

Perhaps the most crucial theme in the LGBT literature is the consensus in support of the uniqueness of LGBT 'best practices' because of the compounding factors the LGBT client faces; these factors can include stigma, lack of familial support, etc. This research suggests tailoring interventions to meet the unique barriers and needs associated with the LGBT population. While the presenting problem of an LGBT client may not appear significantly different than one of a heterosexual client (i.e. Kenny sought help for relationship problems and general feelings of depression), research indicates that Kenny's presenting problems are likely more severe because of unique factors including his experience of, prejudice, oppression, and homophobia in our society (Dworkin & Guttierez, 1992; Meyer, 2003). In other words, the LGBT client's presenting problems might be similar, but they are confounded and compounded by "specific psychosocial stressors unique to this population" including victimization, harassment, fear of rejection, discrimination, past abuse, and isolation from family and friends (Berg, Mimiaga &

Safren, 2008, 294). Certainly, this is the case for Kenny. These unique barriers and the corresponding importance of tailored LGBT-specific interventions are referenced in the studies in Figure 2.

FIGURE 2: *Key Studies/Contributions*

Source	Research Design/Methods	Major Contributions
Berg, Mimiaga & Safren, 2008	Qualitative/Quantitative study – based on a chart review of 92 gay men in mental health treatment	Demographics and history variables characterizing gay men who seek services; implications for interventions tailored to unique needs of population
Bieschke, Perez & DeBord, 2007	Practice-based book	Concepts of dual marginalization and acculturation; specific guidance for affirmative counseling practices
Israel, Gorcheva, Burnes & Walther, 2008	Qualitative study based on 42 LGBT clients' experiences in counseling	Delineates 'helpful' and 'unhelpful' counseling experiences; includes discussion of variables at the levels of client, therapist, and intervention
Israel, Ketz, Detrie, Burke & Shulman, 2003	Qualitative study – based on feedback from LGBT experts, practitioners, and clients	Outlines specific competencies counseling professionals should exhibit in working with LGBT population
Omoto & Kurtzman, 2006	Review of several large quantitative and qualitative LGBT datasets	Overviews state of LGBT research, including limitations; establishes use of qualitative research as effective with hard-to-reach populations
Romeo, 2007	Qualitative dissertation	Proposes effective workshops for the training of practitioners to work competently with the LGBT population
Ross, Doctor, Dimito, Kuehl & Armstrong, 2007	Quantitative uncontrolled trial – based on 7 Cognitive Behavioral Therapy (CBT) groups	Suggests a model for intervention, which tailors CBT to meet the unique needs of the LGBT population
Smith, 2005	Quantitative dissertation	Creates and validates a scale (LGBT Hardiness Scale) for use in assessment of LGBT client needs
Stone Fish & Harvey, 2005	Practice article – coupling queer theory with family therapy	Emphasizes importance of affirmative counseling techniques; concepts of 'critical consciousness' and 'difficult dialogues'

In one study, 86.4% of LGBT clients engaged in mental health treatment stated the importance of the intervention being LGBT-specific (Ross, Doctor, Dimito, Kuehl & Armstrong, 2007).

One way to think about tailoring interventions to the specific needs of the LGBT population is to approach promising practices as an issue of cultural competence and diversity training. Logan & Baret (2005) outline a set of guidelines for working with the LGBT population as recommended by leaders of the Association for Gay, Lesbian, and Bisexual Issues in Counseling. Some researchers encourage practitioners to view effective practice with the LGBT population as a cross-cultural competency issue (Amadio & Perez, 2008), while others note that a framework for planning interventions with ethnic minority LGBT clients called the Racial Ethnic and Sexual Orientation (RSIC) has been developed (Ohnishi, Ibrahim & Grzegorek, 2006). Considering the identification of promising practices for work with the LGBT population as one component of their overall cultural competence may persuade some practitioners to view this work differently.

Describing effective practice with the LGBT population, Israel, Gorcheva, Burnes, and Walther (2008) polled a set of LGBT individuals currently engaged in mental health treatment regarding examples of 'helpful and unhelpful' counseling experiences. After reviewing their qualitative data, these researchers summarized the key findings in three categories of variables: client, therapist, and intervention. This suggests that promising practices with the LGBT population require consideration of multiple components of efficacy. These three categories will be utilized in the pages that follow to structure the themes emerging not only from this key qualitative study, but also from the entirety of the literature on the subject, as a means to considering how best to serve Kenny.

Client Variables and Characteristics

In the study by Israel and colleagues (2008), the researchers found that the strongest client-level variable associated with 'helpful' experiences in counseling was providing the client with the highest possible level of autonomy. Clients like Kenny are often highly cognitively functioning and feel empowered and valued when they are given independence and autonomy in the counseling session. Considering the challenges some Christian social workers might face in working with the LGBT population, this can become a challenge since giving the LGBT client independence and autonomy often means granting him or her the freedom to discuss all issues, even those that might make some Christian social workers uncomfortable. The use of a Narrative Therapy approach to such practice can also be beneficial.

The largest client-level theme in the literature is the concept of conflict in acculturation. Acculturation refers to the level of assimilation, connection, and sense of belonging or isolation individuals feel toward their cultural groups. It refers to how well Kenny feels he fits in with the various cultures to which he belongs. The caution here for practitioners, then, is to understand the common conflicts LGBT clients may be facing in attempts to acculturate with the LGBT community as well as with their other (sometimes conflicting) cultures. 'Dual acculturation' is often used in the literature to describe the challenge of finding identity in belonging in one's LGBT community *and* one's ethnic culture of origin (Ohnishi, Ibrahim & Grzegorek, 2006). Acculturation may serve as a challenge even beyond sexual orientation and ethnicity (as in the case of Kenny) when one seeks to identify with other groups, including family of origin and religious community (Bieschke, Perez & DeBord, 2007). Harper and Schneider (2003) refer to this as 'double, triple, and quadruple minority status.'

Therapist Variables and Characteristics

Israel and colleagues (2008) also identified a larger set of therapist-related variables associated with 'helpful' experiences in counseling, which includes a therapist who openly shares his or her perspective and opinion, provides positive and encouraging feedback, exhibits strong basic counseling skills, can develop a close and trusting therapeutic relationship, and has specific LGBT training and practice experience. The larger literature base echoes some of these themes and adds some additional therapist-level considerations.

In one qualitative study, Romeo (2007) addresses the need for practitioners to receive updated and on-going training regarding practice with this population by implementing a set of LGBT-focused training workshops for practitioners and seeking to measure behavior changes in the practitioners post-training. This study reported several significant behavior changes, including increased likelihood to seek out and read LGBT-related books, engaging more regularly in conversations with co-workers about LGBT issues, and changing language used in reference to and in practice with the LGBT population.

Another major area of research on therapist preparedness for work with LGBT clients is in the area of self-awareness and self-reflection (Butler, 2010). Kenny, and clients like him, might experience prejudice and discrimination from others on a daily basis; he should be able to expect a competent social work practitioner who will not perpetuate that prejudice in the counseling session. This is a highly important point for practitioners looking to improve competency with this population, as it emphasizes the detrimental effects that unrecognized bias, prejudice, and judgmental attitudes can have on the practice environment. Interestingly, while this is a theme common in the most current literature, it has been emphasized over the past several decades, with one researcher almost two decades ago stating the need for a "call for priority to be placed on counselor awareness" (Dworkin & Guttierez, 1992).

Perhaps the most researched therapist-related factor influencing competent practice with the LGBT population has been the sexual orientation of the counselor and, indeed, there are therapists who identify as both Christian and LGBT. Some researchers emphasize the value of a therapist with the same sexual orientation as the client. One such study reported 95.5% of their respondents stated the importance of their mental health group therapy sessions being facilitated by a therapist who is of the same sexual orientation (Ross, Doctor, Dimito, Kuehl & Armstrong, 2007). Yet, several studies report otherwise; various samples of LGBT clients reported that the therapist/counselor's sexual orientation is not as significant as his or her competence as a counselor (Bieschke, Paul & Blasko, 2007). Interestingly, that same study also found that LGBT clients have a preference for social workers and counselors over psychiatrists.

Another study by Israel and colleagues (2003) presents a specific set of competencies for counselors in working with LGBT clients. One of the strengths of this study is the involvement of LGBT clients who were polled along with expert practitioners. Clients and practitioners were asked about the knowledge, attitudes, and skills necessary for competent practice with the LGBT population. In its entirety, the study rank orders 85 different categories of such competencies. According to those surveyed, the top three characteristics of competent counselors working with LGBT clients are: 1) knowledge about discrimination, oppression, prejudice, homophobia, and heterosexism, 2) a non-homophobic attitude (i.e. not feeling one's sexual orientation is evil and in need of changing), and 3) sensitivity to LGBT client's issues, including ethics and confidentiality and a willingness to listen to all aspects of LGBT life.

Intervention Variables and Characteristics

Regarding variables and characteristics directly related to the actual intervention and/or counseling strategies utilized in 'helpful' experiences, Israel and colleagues (2008) reported LGBT individuals benefited most from counseling conducted from specific approaches or theoretical bases. Those approaches most commonly identified were cognitive behavioral, dialectical behavior, imagery, and relaxation therapies. The study's participants also reported direction and structure to be most 'helpful', citing confrontation, goal setting, and homework as beneficial components of counseling.

Studies have attempted to demonstrate the effectiveness of specific therapeutic interventions with the LGBT population. Several such studies have begun to legitimize adaptations of cognitive behavioral therapy (CBT) for working with LGBT clients (Berg, Mimiaga & Safren, 2008; Ross, Doctor, Dimito, Kuehl & Armstrong, 2007). The latter study mentioned above (Ross et.al) describes a model of CBT adapted to the specific needs of LGBT group work; the model augments traditional CBT work with specific curriculum addressing anti-oppression, the coming out process, and experiences of homophobia. In their intervention trial, a 14-week group saw significant decreases in depression and increases in self-esteem. In the case scenario, the use of "homework" in counseling (common in Cognitive-behavior-oriented therapy) could certainly be helpful to Kenny and his social worker.

Another set of researchers offered theoretical support for the incorporation of liberation psychology (defined as work that seeks to bridge the gap between personal mental health issues and societal oppression) in work with LGBT clients, citing the interwoven nature of personal and social change as uniquely applicable to the LGBT experience (Russell & Bohan, 2007). Other authors suggest the innovation of using art therapy with the LGBT population, based on research indicating the relationship between creative expression and healthy sexual identity development (Pelton-Sweet & Sherry, 2008).

While each of the interventions mentioned above may very well result in some measure of effectiveness in practice with the LGBT population, the most dominant theme in all of the literature on the subject is the concept of 'affirmative' counseling (Amadio & Perez, 2008; Bieschke, Perez & DeBord, 2007; Croteau, Bieschke, Fassigner & Manning, 2008; Dworkin & Guttierez, 1992; Logan & Barret, 2002; Whitman, Horn & Boyd, 2007). Defining affirmative practice is a bit challenging. One understanding of affirmative practice is to value homosexuality and heterosexuality equally (Dworkin & Guttierez, 1992). Another way to consider affirmative practice is by asking the question, "How have you either created barriers or built bridges" for the LGBT community? (Logan & Barret, 2002 42). This discussion of affirmative practice is a major theme in the literature and one of the linchpins of promising practices for working with LGBT clients like Kenny. More discussion of affirmative practice, specifically related to instances of discordant social worker-client beliefs, is provided in a latter section of this chapter.

Bieschke, Perez & DeBord (2007) say this about the definition of affirmative counseling: "Existing definitions tend to reflect more of an attitude than a set of behaviors or specific instructions" (p.7). While this may be true about the nature of affirmative practice, Stone Fish & Harvey (2005) do make some attempt at illustrating what an affirmative approach to family therapy with LGBT youth might look like. They introduce the concepts of 'critical consciousness' (i.e. the work of encouraging family members to evaluate their own ideas about gender and sexual orientation) and 'difficult dialogues' (i.e. bravely facilitating emotionally-charged family conversations).

These techniques reflect a strong support for a model of narrative therapy, which has been presented by some in the social work and counseling fields as particularly applicable and empowering for work with the LGBT population (Walters, 2009). Clients like Kenny might prefer to be given the opportunity to simply 'talk' and, in doing so, he is given a powerful opportunity to create his own story – to describe and define for himself the trajectory of his life and the ways in which his sexuality has impact on his mental health and well-being . The narrative therapy approach may be most applicable in instances where the client's opinions and beliefs are discordant with the practitioner's beliefs and values (which will be addressed further in a later section of this chapter).

Spiritual and/or Religious LGBT Clients

Additionally, a narrative approach may be beneficial in giving clients like Kenny a forum to share experiences and internal struggles in navigating through multiple cultures and social circles. Kenny's story introduces a very important aspect of LGBT life that has, at times, been very misunderstood and even dismissed by helping professionals. Especially for practitioners who hold conservative religious beliefs and values that define homosexuality as sinful, the fact that a gay or lesbian client may also be a committed religious or spiritual person may seem confusing. Yet, there are many (perhaps most) LGBT individuals like Kenny who view themselves as members of both LGBT communities and religious (including Christian) communities. Some work is certainly being done to better understand the challenges these LGBT men and women face, but promising practices for helping clients like Kenny find meaning and acceptance are few. Clearly, bridges must continue to be built between religious communities and LGBT communities (Marin, 2009), as there are members of each group who genuinely seek to understand and engage with members of the other.

Having gleaned multiple important lessons from the literature to inform practice with LGBT clients, we now turn our attention to the second part of the chapter, which focuses on the personal challenges many Christian social workers may experience. At the conclusion of the chapter, we return briefly to the aforementioned literature and draw some overarching conclusions about the promising practices for working with the LGBT population.

History of Research and the LGBT Movement

The current state of research on promising practices for working with the LGBT population is perhaps best understood by examining the history of LGBT research on this area of practice. Harper and Schneider (2003) summarized historical trends in four 'phases' of study.(See Figure 3). Prior to 1973, homosexuality was generally understood as a mental illness and research focused on homosexuality as pathology. In 1973, the Diagnostic and Statistical Manual (DSM) removed homosexuality as a mental illness (Spitzer, 1981), resulting in a significant shift in research efforts. Once views of homosexuality shifted from pathological to a diversity issue, research (and social work practice) began to take a more open-minded and inquisitive stance. The second phase of research then focused on the experience of LGBT life and included broad approaches to understanding experiences of LGBT men and women. As HIV/AIDS emerged, research included HIV risk behaviors, which led to the third phase of research in a new millennium. At that time, the National Institutes of Health (NIH) committed large amounts of grant funding specifically for researching LGBT health issues. This third phase, while health-focused, remained inquisitive in nature; yet, driven by government funding and the medical community, each carrying its own set of values, agendas, and hypotheses. This medical and public health phase of research certainly brought important issues into the public arena, but also perpetuated a certain level of LGBT stigma.

The fourth and current phase of LGBT research is noted not for a change of topic studied, but rather a change in approach. This phase is characterized by a commitment to strengths-based research and to the resiliency of LGBT men and women. Croteau, Bieschke, Fassinger, and Manning (2008) summarized this historical overview by indicating that the pathology-focused research of the past (i.e. aimed at "curing" homosexuality and creating problem-focused interventions) has been replaced by current affirmative approaches to research, which see the problem as institutional and societal rather than individual.

FIGURE 3: Overview of historical trends in LGBT research

WHEN	FOCUS OF RESEARCH	TRANSITION
Phase One: Prior to 1973	Homosexuality as pathology Homosexuality as mental illness	Removal from DSM
Phase Two: 1973-1990	The experience of LGBT life The coming-out process Relationship patterns and practices Effects of discrimination/violence	HIV epidemic
Phase Three: 1985-2000	LGBT health outcomes HIV risk behavior and reduction	Reduced HIV funding and Affirmative practice
Phase Four: 2000-present	Resiliency of LGBT people Strengths of LGBT community Institutional stigma	

The trends in social work practice with the LGBT population can be clearly seen in tandem with these trends in the LGBT research. Clients like Kenny have likely experienced the gamut of attitudes fueled by these trends in various interactions with people in the helping professions. He may remember a time when he was told his sexual orientation meant he was sick or needed to be 'cured'; he may recall a time when a counselor asked pointed, albeit curious, questions about his behaviors and experiences as a gay man; as an HIV-positive gay man, he may certainly have experienced an influx of services and messaging directed toward him in terms of HIV prevention and protection. Hopefully, Kenny will also experience an affirmative social worker able to help him recognize his strength and resilience as he faces his current struggles.

Personal Challenges for Christian Social Workers

Christine is a social work practitioner who works at a faith-based mental health center. She has recently had a number of LGBT clients present in her office for counseling. Two of these recent clients were young, gay men; one came seeking help with depression and the other has severe substance abuse issues. Another of her ongoing clients recently revealed her lesbian sexual orientation in a counseling session.

Christine generally avoids discussion of sexuality with these clients, especially with the gay men (with whom she is especially hesitant). However, because the clients know of Christine's faith and the mission of the agency, several of them have begun to ask her direct questions about her ability to accept them and their sexual orientations. The clients have not expressed any desire to be referred to another counselor or agency. In fact, one of the gay men seems to be quite interested in the faith-based aspect of the health center. The lesbian client comes from a Christian family and has had a generally positive experience with her family's faith community. Yet, Christine admits to feeling uncomfortable addressing sexuality with these clients.

Challenged by how to integrate her own personal beliefs and Christian faith, as well as the faith-based mission of her agency, into the provision of competent care for these clients, Christine recently emailed me to ask for advice. Christine's email spoke of her desire to provide her clients with best practices tailored to their unique needs. She spoke openly about the complete lack of familiarity she and her agency have in working with the LGBT population, calling it "uncharted and daunting territory." Christine also expressed with honesty and humility her feelings of discomfort in talking with her clients about their sexuality. She and her co-workers have talked privately amongst themselves about these challenges and several of them have recognized in themselves a tendency to judge the clients in "their sin."

What is Christine to do? Her particular Christian views are an undeniable part of who she is and what she brings into the helping relationship. She should, first and foremost, be commended for having the self-awareness and professional integrity that led her to ask for help in the first place. Certainly, her situation is not uncommon – in fact, some who are reading this chapter might be able to identify with Christine. So, to broaden the question – what is *any social worker* to do when working with clients whose beliefs or practices are discordant with our own?

Returning to the Literature

In summarizing the current state of LGBT research, Bieschke, Perez & DeBord (2007) identify a 'hot topic': the harm of conversion therapy. Conversion therapy, also called reparative therapy, refers to counseling homosexual clients with the intended purpose of changing their orientation. Regarding conversion therapy, most in the field agree that there is no conclusive evidence that it is effective. In fact, most professional organizations in the helping professions have developed official position statements opposing the use of conversion therapy.

The National Association of Social Workers' position statement on conversion and reparative therapies states clearly the belief ...

> ...that such treatment potentially can lead to severe emotional damage. Specifically, transformational ministries are fueled by stigmatization of lesbians and gay men, which in turn produces the social climate that pressures some people to seek change in sexual orientation. No data demonstrate that reparative or conversion therapies are effective, and in fact they may be harmful (NASW, 2000).

Similarly, the American Psychological Association has concluded that insufficient evidence exists to support the idea that sexual orientation can be altered through therapeutic aims. Therefore, their formal resolution echoes the NASW:

> The American Psychological Association encourages mental health professionals to avoid misrepresenting the efficacy of sexual orientation change efforts by promoting or promising change in sexual orientation when providing assistance to individuals distressed by their own or others' sexual orientation (APA, 2009).

While the aforementioned resolutions cite the inconclusive nature of this literature on conversion therapy, some research does exist which presents compelling data suggesting potential harmfulness (e.g. Halderman, 1994; Shidlo & Schroeder, 2002) and a lack of evidence of any long-term 'success' in changing one's sexual orientation (Bieschke, Paul & Blasko, 2007; Butler, 2010; Shidlo & Schroeder, 2002; Blackwell, 2008). In our case study, it is not clear whether the concept of conversion therapy is one that Christine and her faith-based agency endorse – the email did not indicate one way or the other. Evidence that conversion therapy can be harmful, coupled with the definitive stances against conversion therapy taken by the leading professional mental health organizations, is likely to discourage Christine, and others like her, from suggesting conversion as a therapeutic end.

In contrast to the controversy about conversion therapy, there is some initial literature encouraging social workers to embrace the challenge of reconciling conflicting religious and sexual identities. Rather than see religion as inherently a problem for working with LGBT clients, it should be understood that religious beliefs (like those of both Kenny and Christine) have the potential to be viewed and utilized as both positive or negative forces in social work practice for LGBT men and women (Greene, 2007).

Self-Awareness and Moving Toward Affirmative Practice with LGBT Clients

The first step for any practitioner seeking to ensure his or her competency in practice with diverse clients is to develop one's own self-awareness, and Christine's email requesting help is a very positive first step. The profession of social work demands that practitioners achieve a level of cultural competence (which includes instances of discordant religious and/or spiritual beliefs). The NASW Standards of Cultural Competence set two interrelated standards expressing these challenges (although the standards do not explicitly refer to spirituality and/or religion) (NASW, 2001). Standard One states: "Social workers shall function in accordance with the values, ethics, and standards of the profession, recognizing how personal and professional values may conflict with or accommodate the needs of diverse clients." Standard Two focuses on the development of the social worker's self-awareness: "Social workers shall seek to develop an understanding of their own personal, cultural values and beliefs as one way of appreciating the importance of multicultural identities in the lives of people." How then can Christine best manage her own religious/spiritual beliefs and sort out how to help her LGBT clients?

Establishing an Affirmative Practice

Perhaps the greatest pioneer in the quest to integrate the Christian faith with social work practice was Alan Keith-Lucas. In one of the most widely-read primers for Christian social work students, he articulates very clearly what he saw as the essence of social work practice for Christians:

> As a Christian committed to the dissemination of what I believe to be the truth, my task as a social worker is not so much to convince others of this truth, as to provide them with the experience of being loved, forgiven and cared for so that the Good News I believe in may be a credible option for them (Keith-Lucas, 1985, 35).

This emphasis, not on conversion, but on creating an atmosphere where the client feels loved and cared for, can serve as a significant platform for meaningful social work practice in the face of discordant client/counselor beliefs.

This environment Keith-Lucas suggests also fits well with the literature on the value of affirmative practice with the LGBT population. The practitioner's personal religious and/or spiritual beliefs, if not handled well, could lead the practitioner to create barriers detrimental to the helping process. In this case study, it seems Christine has begun to recognize this danger in her own practice. Engaging in a time of self-reflection and the building of self-awareness can address and prevent these barriers. Guidelines for affirmative practice models can be an important foundation for the competent integration of spirituality into social work practice – especially with LGBT clients.

Affirmative practice is defined by the creation of a respectful space for dialogue in which the values and beliefs of the clinician do not cloud the progress and goals of the client. What is presented in this chapter is intended to equip the social work practitioner with the knowledge and skills to make such a respectful dialogue possible. Yet, for some, these skills will not be enough. For those practitioners who remain challenged by or hesitant toward affirmative practice in this way, the following section discusses avenues for appropriate and ethical referral.

Is it Time to Refer?

If Christine (or any other practitioner like her) is reading this chapter and thinking, "I'm not sure I can do this," there are additional options she can consider that still allow her to be helpful to her LGBT client, though these options are full of ethical and possible legal challenges for the practitioner. For some Christian practitioners, the task of creating such an affirmative environment for LGBT clients may prove to be too difficult. Practitioners who, after a time of honest introspection and self-awareness searching, cannot reach a place of sincere affirmation should take appropriate next steps to ensure that their LGBT client gets the mental health support they need. The challenge for these practitioners is that the fields of social work, counseling, and clinical psychology are far from settled on how best to make such a referral to another counselor. Additionally, considerable academic and legal debate still exists in the field about whether mental health professionals (social workers, counselors, and psychologists) should even feel empowered to make such a referral at all; a number of resources in the field argue that the most ethical response to LGBT clients is for all mental health professionals to provide competent counseling services to LGBT clients regardless of the practitioner's personal views on homosexuality (Hermann & Herlihy, 2006; Janson, 2002; Murphy, Rawlings, & Howe, 2003; Pearson, 2003).

More specifically, much controversy exists with regard to the ethics of making such a referral and/or declining to work with specific clients due to one's own religious beliefs. Several legal cases involving counseling students and full-time employees who have refused to counsel LGBT clients based on the counselors' religious beliefs have resulted in different interpretations. One judgment upheld the termination of the counselor for not agreeing to counsel LGBT clients (*Bruff v. North Mississippi Health Services, Inc., 2001*) while another recent court decision by the 6th Circuit U.S. Court of Appeals (*Ward v. Polite et al., 2012*) held that Eastern Michigan University was wrong to expel a counseling student for declaring her intention to refer LGBT clients to other competent professionals due to her religious convictions regarding homosexuality (Melloy, 2010; Bohon, 2012). Another legal challenge (which is still pending as this book goes to press) has been made recently by a school counseling student at Augusta State University in Augusta, who claims she had her First Amendment rights violated by being required to change her views on counseling LGBT clients (Schmidt, 2010).

While there are no similar legal challenges yet about whether or not social work practitioners or students have an ethical obligation to counsel any and all LGBT clients they encounter in practice, there is one high-profile case in which a social work program was sued and investigated for alleged intolerant practices toward Christian social work students who balked at supporting LGBT issues. The school (Missouri State University) settled a lawsuit brought by a Christian BSW student who said she was pressured to sign a letter for a class project advocating that the state legislature support adoption by gay couples. The university ordered an external review of the program and reviewers found:

> There is an atmosphere where the [NASW] Code of Ethics is used in order to coerce students into certain belief systems regarding social work practice and the social work profession. This represents a distorted use of the Social Work Code of Ethics in that the Code of Ethics articulates that social workers should respect the values and beliefs of others (Sowers & Patchner, 2007).

Whether or not specific challenges to ethical practice with LGBT clients by Christian social workers have been mounted within the field of social work to date, we must acknowledge the controversy, as well as the likelihood, that these tensions are going to persist in the field for the near future. As of this writing (early 2012), no definitive position has been taken by the major counseling professional associations (in psychology, counseling, and social work) on the ethics of making these referrals. More clarity from both the law and the mental health professions is needed in this area to guide professionals (both religious and secular) in how to navigate these difficult issues.

The question I would ask Christine is: 'Where do you, as a practitioner, stand in your ability to help LGBT clients?' This question of the social worker's ability and competence to serve a particular population applies to every client/ worker relationship, not just LGBT clients. If Christine cannot genuinely ensure that her personal values and beliefs will not be imposed upon the LGBT client, it is, in my opinion, best for the client to be referred to another service provider who can provide competent and ethical service. I would strongly encourage all Christian practitioners to prepare for such possibilities by developing and maintaining a list of appropriate referral sources in the local area; purposefully seeking out networking opportunities to meet with and get to know practitioners in one's community with experience working with the LGBT population can also be helpful. Likewise, in order to effectively respond to a client like Kenny, practitioners should also familiarize themselves with the various faith communities in the area, identifying particularly gay-affirming church congregations.

I recognize that this process of referral can be difficult, especially if the practitioner's comfort level engaging in conversation with the LGBT client is low. Yet, the language used to communicate the reason for the referral to another service provider must be carefully chosen and articulately spoken. If she reaches a point of referral, Christine should be sure to state the reason for referral clearly, directly, and non-judgmentally. She may wish to say something like, "I have been thinking about our progress thus far, and I feel that you might benefit from a counselor with more experience working with LGBT clients." This statement puts the focus on providing the client with the best possible care, rather than on the counselor's personal discomfort or beliefs. When the social worker is not prepared to create an affirming space for dialogue, choosing to refer a client with discordant beliefs and practices, while developing one's own self awareness around the issues, may be in the best interests of the client.

In Summary

For some who read this chapter, concluding at this point will be, perhaps, unsettling. This chapter does not conclude with a neatly wrapped package of evidence-based interventions, nor does it conclude with permission granted to Christian practitioners to 'save' their LGBT clients. Much gray area remains. Still, it is my hope that this chapter serves to stimulate further thinking and discussion among Christian social workers like Christine who are engaged in work with LGBT men and women, and to equip those practitioners with new literature to consider in the process.

Ultimately, Christian practitioners like Christine will best serve her LGBT[2] clients by developing an ability to engage in genuine dialogue about the client's history of oppression and the baggage that history may bring into the helping relationship. As such, the solutions to the LGBT client's situation are rarely exclusively clinical in nature; there are social and spiritual ends that must also be addressed (as in the case of Kenny and his exclusion from the Church). Finally, should the practitioner feel unable to provide the type of affirmative practice suggested in this chapter, the best step might be to sensitively and positively refer the client elsewhere, while continuing to examine his or her ability to provide all clients "with the experience of being loved, forgiven and cared for." (Keith Lucas, 1985, 35).

References

Amadio, D.M., & Perez, R.M. (2008). Affirmative counseling and psychotherapy with lesbian, gay, bisexual, and transgender clients. In Negy, C. (Ed). *Cross-cultural psychotherapy: Toward a critical understanding of diverse clients (2nd ed.)*. Reno, NV: Bent Tree Press.

American Psychological Association. (2009). Resolution on the appropriate therapeutic responses to sexual orientation distress and change efforts. Retrieved from http://www.apa.org/about/governance/council/policy/sexual-orientation.aspx.

Berg, M.B., Mimiaga, M.J., & Safren, S.A. (2008). Mental health concerns of gay and bisexual men seeking mental health services. *Journal of Homosexuality, 54*(3), 293-306.

Bieschke, K.J., Paul, P.L., & Blasko, K.A. (2007). Review of empirical research focused on the experience of lesbian, gay, and bisexual clients in counseling and psychotherapy. In Bieschke, K.J., Perez, R.M., & DeBord, K.A. (Eds). *Handbook of counseling and psychotherapy with lesbian, gay, bisexual, and transgender clients (2nd ed.)*. Washington, DC: American Psychological Association.

Bieschke, K.J., Perez, R.M., & DeBord, K.A. (Eds.) (2007). *Handbook of counseling and psychotherapy with lesbian, gay, bisexual, and transgender clients*. Washington, DC: American Psychological Association.

Blackwell, C.W. (2008). Nursing implications in the application of conversion therapies on gay, lesbian, bisexual, and transgender clients. *Issues in Mental Health Nursing, 29 (6)*, 651-65

Bohon, D. (2012, January 31). Court rules for Christian counseling student in religious discrimination case. *The New American.* Retrieved from http://thenewamerican.com/culture/faith-and-morals/10712-court-rules-for-christian-counseling-student-in-religious-discrimination-case.

Bruff v. North Mississippi Health Services, Inc., 244 F.3d 495 (5th Cir. 2001).

Butler, C. (2010). Sexual and gender minorities: Consideration for therapy and training. In Butler, C., O'Donovan, A., & Shaw, E. (Eds.), *Sex, sexuality and therapeutic practice: A manual for therapists and trainers.* New York: Routledge/Taylor & Francis Group.

Croteau, J.M., Bieschke, K.J., Fassinger, R.E., & Manning, J.L. (2008). Counseling psychology and sexual orientation: History, selective trends, and future directions. In Brown, S.D., & Lent, R.W. (Eds.) *Handbook of counseling psychology, 4th Edition.* Hoboken, NJ: John Wiley & Sons, Inc.

Dworkin, S.H. & Gutierrez, F.J. (1992). *Counseling gay men & lesbians: Journey to the end of the rainbow.* American Association of Counseling and Development: Alexandria, VA.

Fassinger, R.E., & Arseneau, J.R. (2008). „I'd rather get wet than be under that umbrella“: Differentiating the experiences and identities of lesbian, gay, bisexual, and transgender people. In Bieschke, K.J., Perez, R.M., & DeBord, K.A. (Eds). *Handbook of counseling and psychotherapy with lesbian, gay, bisexual, and transgender clients (2nd ed.).* Washington, DC: American Psychological Association.

Fisher, S.K., Easterly, S., & Lazear, K.J. (2008). Lesbian, gay, bisexual and transgender families and their children. In Gullotta, T.P., & Blau, G.M. (Eds.) *Family influences on childhood behavior and development: Evidence-based prevention and treatment approaches.* New York, NY, US: Routledge/Taylor & Francis Group.

Goldfried, M.R. (2008). Integrating knowledge of lesbian, gay, and bisexual issues in clinical practice and training. *The Behavior Therapist, 31(7)*, 131-132.

Greene, B. (2007). Delivering ethical psychological services to lesbian, gay, and bisexual clients. In Bieschke, K.J., Perez, R.M., & DeBord, K.A. (Eds). *Handbook of counseling and psychotherapy with lesbian, gay, bisexual, and transgender clients (2nd ed.).* Washington, DC: American Psychological Association.

Halderman, D. (1994). The practice and ethics of sexual orientation conversion therapy. *Journal of Counseling and Clinical Psychology, 62*, 221-227.

Harper, G.W., & Schneider, M. (2003). Oppression and discrimination among lesbian, gay, bisexual, and transgendered people and communities: A challenge for community psychology. *American Journal of Community Psychology, 31(3/4)*, 243-253.

Hermann, M.A. & Herlihy, B. R. (2006). Legal and ethical implications of refusing to counsel homosexual clients. *Journal of Counseling & Development, 84 (4)*, 414-418.

Israel, T., Gorcheva R., Burnes, T.R., & Walther, W.A. (2008). Helpful and unhelpful therapy experiences of LGBT clients. *Psychotherapy Research, 18(3)*, 294-305.

Israel, T., Ketz, K., Detrie, P.M., Burke, M.C., & Shulman, J.L. (2003). Identifying counselor competencies for working with lesbian, gay, and bisexual clients. *Journal of Gay & Lesbian Psychotherapy, 7*, 3-21.

Janson, G. R. (2002). Family counseling and referral with gay, lesbian, bisexual, and transgendered clients: Ethical considerations. *The Family Journal, 10 (3)*, 328-333.

Keith-Lucas, A. (1985). *So you want to be a social worker: A primer for the Christian student.* North American Association of Christians in Social Work: St. Davids, PA.

Logan, C.R., & Barret, R. (2005). Counseling competencies for sexual minority clients. *Journal of LGBT Issues in Counseling, 1(1)*, 3-22.

Logan, C.R., & Barret, R.L. (2002). *Counseling gay men and lesbians: A practice primer.* Brooks/Cole Thomson Learning: Pacific Grove, CA.

Marin, A. (2009). *Love is an orientation: Elevating the conversation with the gay community.* Intervarsity Press: Downers Grove, IL.

Melloy, K. (2010). Anti-gay counseling student sues Ga. University for 'discrimination. *Edge.* Retrieved from http://www.edgeorlando.com/index.php?ch=news&sc=&sc3=&id=108527&pf=1.

Meyer, I, H. (2003). Prejudice, social stress, and mental health in lebian, gay, and bisexual populations. Conceptual issues and research evidence. *Psychological Bulletin, 129,* 674-97.

Murphy, J.A., Rawlings, E. I., & Howe, S.R. (2003). A survey of clinical psychologists on treating lesbian, gay, and bisexual clients. *Professional Psychology: Research and Practice, 33 (2),* 183-189.

NASW (National Association of Social Workers). (2000). Position statement on reparative/conversion therapies. Retrieved from http://www.socialworkers.org/diversity/lgb/reparative.asp.

NASW (National Association of Social Workers), (2001). *Standards for Cultural Competence.* Washington, DC: NASW.

Ohnishi, H., Ibrahim, F.A., & Grzegorek, J.L. (2006). Intersections of identities: Counseling lesbian, gay, bisexual, and transgender Asian-Americans. *Journal of LGBT Issues in Counseling, 1*(3), 77-94.

Omoto, A.M., & Kurtzman, H.S. (Eds.) (2006). *Sexual orientation and mental health: Examining identity and development in lesbian, gay, and bisexual people.* Washington, DC: American Psychological Association.

Pearson, Q. M. (2003). Breaking the silence in the counselor education classroom: A training seminar on counseling sexual minority clients. *Journal of Counseling & Development, 81 (3),* 292-300.

Pelton-Sweet, L.M., & Sherry, A. (2008). Coming out through art: A review of art therapy with LGBT clients. *Art Therapy, 25*(4), 170-176.

Romeo, A.N. (2007). Challenging heterosexism and homophobia: Qualitative research to improve health professionals' behaviors. *Dissertation Abstracts International Section A: Humanities and Social Sciences,.68*(3-A), 892.

Ross, L.E., Doctor, F., Dimito, A., Kuehl, D., & Armstrong, M.S. (2007). Can talking about oppression reduce depression? Modified CBT group treatment for LGBT people with depression. *Journal of Gay & Lesbian Social Services, 19*(1). 1-15.

Russell, G.M., & Bohan, J.S. (2007). Liberating psychotherapy: Liberation psychology and psychotherapy with LGBT clients. *Journal of Gay & Lesbian Psychotherapy, 11*(3/4), 59-75.

Schmidt, J. (2010). Augusta State U. is accused of requiring a counseling student to accept homosexuality. *The Chronicle of Higher Education.* Retrieved from http://chronicle.com/article/Augusta-State-U-Is-Accused-of/123650/.

Shidlo, A., & Schroeder, M. (2002). Changing sexual orientation: A consumers' report. *Professional Psychology: Research and Practice, 33*(3), 249-259.

Smith, M.S. (2005). The development and psychometric evaluation of a rapid assessment instrument measuring hardiness in lesbian, gay, bisexual, and transgender persons. *Dissertation Abstracts International Section A: Humanities and Social Sciences, 67*(10-A), 3983.

Sowers, K. & Patchner, M. (2007). School of Social Work site visit report. Retrieved from Missouri State University website: www.missouristate.edu/provost/socialwork.htm.

Spitzer, R.L. (1981). The diagnostic status of homosexuality in DSM-III: A reformulation of the issues. The American Journal of Psychiatry, 138(2), 210-215.

Stone Fish, L., & Harvey, R.G. (Eds.) (2005). *Nurturing queer youth: Family therapy transformed.* New York: W.W. Norton.

Walters, H. (2009). *Empowering people who are gay and lesbian in the context of Christian community: The use of narratives to bridge the social divide between personal faith and institutional oppression.* Presented at North American Christians in Social Work Annual Conference: Indianapolis, IN.

Ward v. Polite, No. 10-2100, 2012 WL 251939 (6th Cir. 1/27/12).

Whitman, J.S., Horn, S.S., & Boyd, C.J. (2007). Activism in the schools: Providing LGBTQ affirmative training to school counselors. *Journal of Gay & Lesbian Psychotherapy,* 11(3/4), 143-154.

Notes

1 In this chapter we will discuss primarily lesbian and gay clients, and briefly mention transgender and bisexual individuals. However, transgender and bisexual individuals will not be discussed in this chapter due to their very specific issues. We have chosen to use the LGBT terminology throughout because of its prevalence in the literature and because a few points of discussion (for example the struggle with stigma) would apply to all four groups.

2 Although this chapter has discussed lesbian and gay clients primarily, I believe that many of the promising practices suggested here may be cautiously applied to bisexual and transgender clients as well.

CHAPTER 15

SPIRITUAL ASSESSMENT: A REVIEW OF COMPLEMENTARY ASSESSMENT MODELS

David R. Hodge and Crystal R. Holtrop

Spiritual assessment is increasingly recognized as a fundamental dimension of service provision (*Hodge & Limb, 2010a*). Despite this fact, most social workers appear to have received minimal training on the topic (*Canda & Furman, 2010; Sheridan, 2009*). The lack of attention devoted to spiritual assessment represents a significant oversight. To highlight the importance of spiritual assessment, we will briefly discuss four rationales related to ontology, ethics, strengths, and autonomy.

Spirituality is often central to clients' personal ontology. In other words, spirituality can be the essence of their personhood, the lens through which they view reality. Accordingly, spirituality may inform attitudes and practices in many areas, including child rearing, communication styles, diet, marriage arrangements, medical care, military participation, recreation, schooling, and social interactions (*Hodge, 2004b; Van Hook, Hugen & Aguilar, 2001*). For many individuals, religion is the most important facet of their lives (*Newport, 2006*). Further, for African Americans, women, the elderly, the poor, and many other populations of significance to social workers, spirituality is particularly salient (*Newport, 2006; Smith & Faris, 2005; Taylor, Chatters & Jackson, 2007*). The provision of respectful services to these groups is often contingent upon practitioners' awareness of clients' spiritually based beliefs and practices. In order to provide effective services, social workers must develop some understanding of clients' spiritual worldviews (*Hodge & Bushfield, 2006*).

A second rationale stems from the profession's ethical mandates. Spirituality is often expressed in distinct spiritual traditions or faith-based cultures (*Van Hook et al., 2001*). The NASW Code of Ethics (*2008*) stipulates that social workers are to demonstrate competence and sensitivity toward faith-based cultures (1.05b) and recognizes the strengths that exist among such groups (1.05a). Similarly, the NASW Standards for Cultural Competence in Social Work Practice (*2001*) recognize the importance of developing cultural competency in the area of spirituality and religion. In short, ethically sound practice entails obtaining the knowledge to exhibit spiritual sensitivity to clients.

Social workers are increasingly recognizing the importance of strengths (*Saleebey, 2009; Smith, 2006*). Reviews have consistently found a generally positive association between spirituality and a wide number of beneficial characteristics *(Koenig, McCullough & Larson, 2001; Koenig, 2007)*. More specifically, various measures of spirituality and religion have been associated with higher levels of well-being, happiness and life satisfaction; hope and optimism, purpose and meaning in life, self-esteem, martial stability and satisfaction, social support, and faster recovery from depression *(Johnson, 2002; Koenig et al., 2001; Koenig, 2007)*. Unfortunately, these strengths often lie dormant. Spiritual assessment provides a vehicle to identify and tap clients' spiritual assets to help them in ameliorating their problems *(Hodge, 2004b)*.

Finally, there is the issue of client autonomy. Many clients desire to integrate their spiritual beliefs and values into the helping relationship *(Rose, Westefeld & Ansley, 2008)*. According to Gallup data reported by Bart *(1998)*, 66% of the general public would prefer to see a professional counselor with spiritual values and beliefs and 81% wanted to have their own values and beliefs integrated into the counseling process. Further, research suggests that spirituality tends to become more salient during difficult situations *(Ferraro & Kelley-Moore, 2000; Pargament, 2007)*, when individuals may be more likely to encounter social workers.

In sum, spiritual assessment provides social workers with a means to understand clients' spiritual strengths, beliefs, and values—in short—their worldview. Not only is such knowledge often critical for culturally competent practice, in many instances it is an ethical imperative. Spiritual assessment provides a mechanism to identify clients' spiritual resources and honor their desire to integrate their beliefs and values into the clinical dialogue.

In light of the importance of spiritual assessment, this chapter reviews a number of recently developed assessment approaches and provides examples of how they may be applied in practice with Christian clients. Our intent is not to provide an exhaustive review of various assessment methods, but rather to review a specific family of assessment instruments. These four instruments were developed to complement one another in the hopes of providing social workers with a set of assessment tools for use in numerous settings with a variety of clients. Rather than being interchangeable, one approach may be ideal in one context while another tool may be better suited to address a different client-to-practitioner interface. Readers are encouraged to obtain the original articles in which the instruments first appeared, which have since been collated into book form with added content *(Hodge, 2003)*, and to become familiar with the strengths and limitations of each assessment instrument *(Hodge & Limb, 2010b)*. The assessment tools may be used with clients from an array of different spiritual traditions. Recently, efforts have been made to validate each of the tools for use with Native American clients *(Hodge & Limb, 2009a; Hodge & Limb, 2009b; Hodge & Limb, 2010c; Limb & Hodge, 2007; Limb & Hodge, 2011)*. In this chapter, however, we will be using Christian clients to illustrate the instruments.

After defining spiritual assessment, spirituality, and religion, four assessment instruments are reviewed—spiritual genograms *(Hodge, 2001b)*, spiritual lifemaps *(Hodge, 2005e)*, spiritual histories *(Hodge, 2001a)*, and spiritual ecomaps *(Hodge, 2000; Hodge & Williams, 2002)*. A brief overview of the assets and limitations of each method is provided and, for the three diagrammatic instruments, case examples are supplied to familiarize the reader with the instrument. A brief discussion on conducting an assessment concludes the chapter.

Definitions

Spiritual assessment is defined as the process of gathering and organizing spiritually based data into a coherent format that provides the basis for interventions *(Hodge, 2001a)*. The subsequent interventions may or may not be spiritually based. As implied above, a spiritual assessment may be conducted for the purposes of using traditional, non-spiritual interventions in a manner that is more congruent with clients' beliefs and values.

Spirituality is defined as an existential relationship with God (or perceived transcendence) *(Hodge, 2001b)*. Religion flows from spirituality, expressing the spiritual relationship in particular beliefs, forms, and practices that have been developed in community with other individuals who share similar experiences of transcendent reality *(Hodge, 2005d)*. Thus, in keeping with the understanding of many other social workers, spirituality and religion can be conceptualized as overlapping but distinct constructs *(Canda & Furman, 2010; Hodge & McGrew, 2006)*.

Spiritual Genograms

In a manner analogous to traditional genograms, spiritual genograms provide social workers with a tangible graphic representation of spirituality across at least three generations *(Hodge, 2001b)*. Through the use of what is essentially a modified family tree, they help both practitioners and clients understand the flow of historically rooted patterns through time. In short, spiritual genograms are a blueprint of complex intergenerational spiritual interactions.

In keeping with standard genogram conventions *(McGoldrick, Gerson & Petry, 2008)*, the basic family structure is commonly delineated across at least three generations. Typically, squares represent males and circles denote females. In some cases, triangles or other geometric shapes can be used to designate individuals who have played major spiritual roles but are not members of the immediate biological family *(Hodge, 2001b)*.

To indicate clients' spiritual tradition, colored drawing pencils can be used to shade in the circles and squares *(Hodge, 2001b)*. Color coding provides a graphic "color snapshot" of the overall spiritual composition of the family system. Various colors can be used to signify religious preference (Buddhist, Christian, Hindu, Jewish, Muslim, New Age, none, etc.), or more specifically, when the information is known, denomination (Assemblies of God, Brethren, Catholic, Southern Baptist, Presbyterian, etc.). For example, a circle representing a female Southern Baptist could be colored red, a member of the Assemblies of God might be colored orange, a Muslim might be colored brown, and an individual whose affiliation and beliefs are unknown could be left uncolored. A change in an adult's religious orientation can be signified by listing the date of the change beside a circle which is drawn outside the figure and filling in the space between the circle and the figure with the appropriate color, a procedure which indicates the stability or fluidity of the person's beliefs over time. Using a similar approach, changes in orientation might also be noted by coloring the vertical segment connecting the child with the parents.

If needed, the color scheme can also be used to incorporate information on commitment (devout vs. nominal) and theology (conservative vs. liberal) *(Hodge, 2001b)*. For example, yellow might be used to signify a devout, conservative Methodist while gray could be used for a nominal Methodist. Alternatively, symbols, which are placed beside the appropriate circle or square, could be used to indicate the degree of commitment or theological orientation. An open set of scriptures, for instance, might be used to indicate a devout person. Social workers can explain the options to clients and allow them to select the colors and symbols that they perceive best express their worldview.

Spiritually meaningful events can also be incorporated, such as water and spirit baptisms, confirmations, church memberships, and bar mitzvahs *(Hodge, 2001b)*. Symbols drawn from the client's spiritual journey can be used to signify these events. For instance, a cross might be used by a Christian to indicate reaching a point of conversion, a dove might be used by a Pentecostal to depict a deeper work of the Holy Spirit, or a sunbeam might used by a New Age adherent to symbolize a time of profound spiritual enlightenment. In addition, short summary statements can be used to denote significant events or personal strengths.

In addition to depicting religious beliefs, it is also possible to include an affective component *(Hodge, 2005c)*. In other words, felt spiritual closeness between family members can be illustrated on spiritual genograms. Lines with double-headed arrows can be used to symbolize a relationship in which individuals experience a close reciprocal spiritual bond. The thickness of the line can indicate the intimacy or strength of the relationship. In situations where the relationship is more hierarchical and less reciprocal—as might occur with a grandparent mentoring a grandchild—a single arrowhead can be used to depict the flow of spiritual resources. Finally, spiritual conflict can be portrayed with a jagged line, similar to a lightening bolt, drawn between the two individuals.

Case Example

Diagram 1 (following page) indicates what a relatively straightforward spiritual genogram might look like for a couple, Mark and Beth, who are experiencing marital problems. In place of the colors that would normally be used with a spiritual genogram, patterns (for example, dots, diagonals, waves) are employed to depict various denominations.

After three years of marriage, Mark, 26, and Beth, 23, requested counseling after the recent birth of their daughter, Megan. Her birth renewed their interest in church attendance as they both desired to have Megan baptized and raised with spiritual values. However, they disagreed on practically everything else—

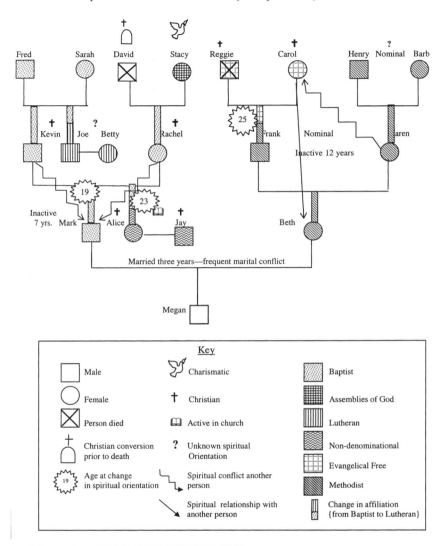

Diagram 1.

how to spend money, parent their daughter, where to go to church, and how to accomplish household tasks. Mark and Beth's inability to resolve conflict was due to a power struggle over whose family of origin's rules they were going to follow. Due to their conflict over which church to attend, the therapist developed a spiritual genogram to enhance their traditional genogram.

During Mark's childhood, his nuclear family and his paternal grandparents attended the Baptist church that was 3 blocks away from their house. His family shared a tradition of going to Mark's paternal grandparents' house every Sunday after church. Although Mark knew that Aunt Betty and Uncle Joe attended a

Lutheran church regularly, he had never heard them talk openly about their faith at family gatherings and was unsure how important it was to them. His maternal grandmother attended an Assemblies of God church before she was placed in the nursing home. He recalled his grandmother sharing a story about how she prayed for 30 years that her husband would become a Christian, and that her prayers were answered shortly before her husband died.

During his adolescence, Mark perceived his parents' rules as old-fashioned and rigid and rebelled against them. As soon as he left home, Mark stopped attending church, much to his parents' chagrin. His sister, Alice, left the Baptist church when she was 23 years old and started attending a non-denominational church where she met her husband, Jay. Alice and Jay are still actively involved in this church and frequently share information with Mark and Beth about family activities that are occurring there. As Mark shared this information, the therapist drew a cross by the names of his parents, paternal grandparents, maternal grandmother, sister, and brother-in-law to indicate that they were Christians. She put a question mark next to his aunt and uncle due to Mark's lack of clarity about their level of commitment to their faith. In order to signify Alice and Jay's devout faith and active participation in their church, the therapist drew an open Bible near their names. She colored their circles and squares different colors to indicate the various denominations represented in Mark's family. Uncle Joe's and Alice's rectangles that attach them to their respective parents have two colors, indicating that they switched from attending the Baptist church to a different denomination.

Beth's family attended a Methodist church when she was young. However, their attendance dwindled to Easter and Christmas as Beth became active in school activities. She knew that her parents both believed in God, but did not see this belief influencing their lives. However, Beth had fond memories of sitting on her paternal grandmother's lap as she listened to her grandmother, Carol, read Bible stories to her. She also recalled attending Vacation Bible school which was sponsored by the Evangelical Free church her grandmother attended. She assumed that "Grandma Carol" was a committed Christian because she overheard her mother complain about "how religious Grandma Carol was" and observed her mother rebuff Grandma Carol whenever she offered to pray for the family. To signify Beth's mother's underlying conflict towards Grandma Carol over spiritual matters, the therapist drew a jagged arrow between their circles. Although her paternal grandfather died before Beth was born, she recalled her Grandma Carol fondly referring to her husband as "a fine man who loved people and the Lord."

Although Beth stated she believes in God, she acknowledged that she presently refers to God primarily when she is swearing angrily at Mark. However, as the conflict between Beth and Mark continued to escalate, she started contemplating "giving God a try." She was open to attending a church as long as it was not Mark's parents' church. She thought his mother already interfered with their marriage far too much. The therapist colored Beth's maternal grandparents' and parents' circles and squares red to represent the Methodist denomination. Due to their nominal interest in spiritual matters, Beth and Mark agreed that the therapist should not draw a cross by their names. She did draw a cross by Grandma Carol's name and by her paternal grandfather's name, and also drew an arrow from her Grandmother Carol to Beth, indicating the spiritual influence she had on Beth.

With the multi-colored spiritual genogram directly in front of them, Mark and Beth were struck by the diversity of denominations represented in their extended families. This new perspective helped them see beyond their original, narrowly defined choices of Baptist vs. Methodist that Mark and Beth clung to out of loyalty to their families of origin. The therapist encouraged the couple to interview members of their extended family, asking questions concerning their faith, their religious practices, and the strengths and limitations of their church and denomination. Beth and Mark discovered that the new perspectives gained from the interviews helped them be more evaluative in their decision-making process and moved them beyond their stalemate.

Assets and Limitations

Although spiritual genograms can be effective assessment instruments in a number of situations, they may be particularly useful when the family system plays an important role in the client's life or when the client presents with problems involving family members or family of origin issues (Hodge, 2005a). For example, spiritual genograms might be used with interfaith couples experiencing spiritually based barriers to intimacy to expose areas of difference and potential conflict as well to highlight the respective spiritual strengths each person brings to the relationship. Similarly, spiritual genograms could also be used with couples from similar backgrounds to increase their level of intimacy.

Conversely, spiritual genograms may be an inappropriate assessment instrument in situations where historical influences are of minor importance (Hodge, 2005a). Further, even in situations where generational influences are pertinent, many clients do not connect past events with current difficulties. Accordingly, clients may view genogram construction and between-session tasks as an ineffective use of time. Proceeding with such interventions before clients appreciate their usefulness can reduce treatment adherence and jeopardize outcomes. Consequently, in some contexts it may be best to use assessment approaches that do not focus on the generational aspects of spirituality.

Spiritual Lifemaps

While spiritual genograms chart the flow of spirituality across at least three generations, spiritual lifemaps depict clients' personal spiritual life-story (Hodge, 2005e). More specifically, spiritual lifemaps are a pictorial delineation of a client's spiritual journey. In a manner analogous to renowned African writer Augustine's (354-430/1991) *Confessions*, spiritual lifemaps are an illustrated account of clients' relationship with God over time—a map of their spiritual life.

At its most basic level, a drawing pencil is used to sketch various spiritually significant life events on paper *(Hodge, 2005e)*. The method is similar to various approaches drawn from art and family therapy in which a client's history is depicted on a "lifeline" *Tracz & Gehart-Brooks, 1999)*. Much like road maps, spiritual lifemaps tell us where we have come from, where we are now, and where we are going.

To assist clients in the creative expression of their spiritual journeys, it is usually best to use a large sheet of paper (e.g., 24" x 36") on which to sketch the map *(Hodge, 2005e)*. Providing drawing instruments of different sizes and colors are also helpful as is offering a selection of popular periodicals and various types and colors of construction paper. Providing these items, in conjunction with scissors, glue sticks, and rulers, allows clients to clip and paste items onto the lifemap.

Spiritually significant events are depicted on a path, a roadway, or a single line that represents clients' spiritual sojourn *Hodge, 2005e)*. Typically, the path proceeds chronologically, from birth through to the present. Frequently the path continues on to death and the client's transition to the afterlife. Hand drawn symbols, cut out pictures, and other representations are used to mark key events along the journey. In keeping with many spiritual traditions, which conceive material existence to be an extension of the sacred reality, it is common to depict important lifestage events on the lifemap (for example, marriage, birth of a child, death of a close friend or relative, or loss of a job). While it is often necessary to provide clients with general guidelines, client creativity and self-expression should typically be encouraged.

To fully operationalize the potential of the instrument, it is important to ask clients to incorporate the various crises they have faced into their lifemaps along with the spiritual resources they have used to overcome those trials *(Hodge, 2005e)*. Symbols such as hills, bumps, potholes, rain, clouds, and lightning can be used to portray difficult life situations. Delineating successful strategies that clients have used in the past frequently suggests options for overcoming present struggles.

Case Example

Diagram 2 (following page) provides an example of what a spiritual lifemap might look like on a smaller scale. Tyrone, a 42 year-old black male, was recently diagnosed with terminal cancer. The doctor confirmed his worst fears that the cancer was inoperable, and predicted that Tyrone had approximately 6 months to live. A medical social worker on the oncology ward met with Tyrone to help him process the shock of his prognosis and prepare for what appeared to be a premature death. Shortly into their conversation, the social worker discovered that Tyrone was actively involved in the Third Missionary Baptist Church. Tyrone's eyes lit up as he shared that he began playing guitar in the church's music ministry 10 years ago, a couple of years after he became a Christian. It soon became clear to the social worker that Tyrone's faith was a significant strength and could help him cope with his present crisis. In order to help Tyrone identify

Diagram 2.

effective coping strategies, the social worker encouraged Tyrone to develop a spiritual lifemap. Tyrone's creativity and musical interests seemed to indicate that this assignment would be a good fit for his personality.

Tyrone's parents divorced when he was 9 years old. He and his 2 older sisters lived with his mother and periodically visited his father. His mother was actively involved in a Pentecostal church and sang in the church choir. When Tyrone reached adolescence, his anger toward his absent father began to mount and was acted out in rebellion toward his mother. Out of desperation, his mother arranged guitar lessons for Tyrone to creatively redirect his anger and build his self-esteem. Tyrone established a lifelong mentoring relationship with his guitar teacher, Jerome, who consistently believed in him and spawned a passion for a variety of musical styles including blues, jazz, gospel, and rock. When he graduated from high school, he joined a band and played in clubs for the next 9 years. Disillusioned with God for not answering his childhood prayers for his father, Tyrone started experimenting with drugs and alcohol to numb his emptiness inside.

By age 27, Tyrone had successfully recorded a CD with his band and was gaining local notoriety. Life was good. He was doing well financially and he enjoyed dating several different women. However, this season was short-lived. By age 30, he was significantly in debt and was emotionally broken. After 3 years of dating, Tyrone's girlfriend, Janet concluded that Tyrone was more committed to his band than to her and she broke up with him. He coped by increasing his alcohol consumption, which hurt his performance and created conflict with his band members. After a particularly heated argument, Tyrone sought solace from Jerome, his former guitar teacher. Through this renewed friendship, Tyrone began examining his life, his priorities, and the source of his emptiness and bitterness. He forgave God for what he perceived to be abandonment (a replication of his father's abandonment) and he experienced a profound sense of God's love and acceptance. Tyrone soon realized that it was he, not God, who had abandoned divine and human love out of bitterness and despair.

Tyrone started attending the Third Missionary Baptist church. Upon Jerome's advice, Tyrone took a break from playing guitar and immersed himself in Bible study, prayer, and Christian books to help him sort out his unresolved hurts, develop effective anger management skills, and evaluate his life goals. He also developed significant relationships with other men in a Promise Keepers group. He watched several men in the group weather severe trials by clinging onto God's promises and by receiving love and support from their friends. He gradually learned that no matter what happens in life, God is good, faithful, and in control. After a 2-year hiatus, Tyrone began playing guitar in church. Using his talents to worship God gave him a sense of meaning and joy that was deeper than any he had experienced before. Completing the spiritual lifemap helped Tyrone reflect on his life, his pit and peak experiences, the lessons he had learned, and the people who had blest him. Most importantly, he identified key people that would support him through his present illness and pray for God to heal him. While discussing the lifemap with his social worker, Tyrone began to clarify the goals he still wanted to accomplish, like mentoring some young boys in church who were growing up in single parent homes. Through this reflective assignment, he also made the decision to write some songs as a creative way to express his pain, cry out to God, and receive strength and comfort.

Assets and Limitations

Of the assessment methods reviewed in this chapter, spiritual lifemaps are perhaps the most client-directed. Consequently, there are a number of unique advantages associated with the use of this diagrammatic model *(Hodge, 2005a)*. By placing a client-constructed media at the center of assessment, the message is implicitly communicated that the client is a competent, pro-active, self-directed, fully engaged participant in the therapeutic process. Additionally, individuals who are not verbally oriented may find pictorial expression more conducive to their personal communication styles.

The relatively secondary role that social workers play during assessment also offers important advantages *(Hodge, 2005a)*. For many clients, spirituality is a highly personal, sensitive area. Most social workers have had limited training about various spiritual worldviews, in spite of the central role spirituality plays in human behavior *(Canda & Furman, 2010; Sheridan, 2009)*. Consequently, there is the distinct risk that social workers may offend clients and jeopardize the therapeutic relationship through comments that are inadvertently offensive, especially with the use of more practitioner-centered, verbally-based assessment approaches. The pictorial lifemap affords practitioners the opportunity to learn more about the client's worldview while focusing on building therapeutic rapport by providing an atmosphere that is accepting, nonjudgmental, and supportive during assessment *(Hodge, 2005e)*.

In terms of limitations, some social workers may feel so removed from the process that this assessment approach makes poor use of therapeutic time *(Hodge, 2005a)*. Indeed, in the time-constrained, managed care world in which many practitioners work, in some cases it may be advisable to use the lifemap as a homework assignment *(Hodge, 2005e)*. Another significant limitation is that many clients, such as those who are more verbal, those that are uncomfortable with drawing, or those who prefer more direct practitioner and client involvement, may find the use of a largely non-verbal, pictorial instrument to be a poor fit.

Spiritual Histories

A spiritual history represents a narrative alternative to a spiritual lifemap *(Hodge, 2001a)*. Instead of relating the client's spiritual sojourn in a diagrammatic format, the client's spiritual story is related verbally. In a process that is analogous to conducting a family history, the client is provided an interactive forum to share his or her spiritual life story.

To guide the conversation, a two-part framework is used *(Hodge, 2001a)*. As can been seen in Table 1, the first part consists of an initial narrative framework. The purpose of these questions is to provide practitioners with some tools for structuring the assessment. The aim is to help clients tell their stories, typically moving from childhood to the present.

It should also be noted that the questions delineated in Table 1 are offered as suggestions *(Hodge, 2001a)*. Social workers should not view them as a rigid

Table I. Guidelines for conducting spiritual histories

Initial Narrative Framework

1. Describe the religious/spiritual tradition you grew up in. How did your family express its spiritual beliefs? How important was spirituality to your family? Extended family?

2. What sort of personal experiences (practices) stand out to you during your years at home? What made these experiences special? How have they informed your later life?

3. How have you transitioned or matured from those experiences? How would you describe your current spiritual/religious orientation? Is your spirituality a personal strength? If so, how?

Interpretive Anthropological Framework

1. Affect: What aspects of your spiritual life give you pleasure? What role does your spirituality play in handling life's sorrows? Enhancing its joys? Coping with its pain? How does your spirituality give you hope for the future? What do you wish to accomplish in the future?

2. Behavior: Are there particular spiritual rituals or practices that help you deal with life's obstacles? What is your level of involvement in faith-based communities? How are they supportive? Are there spiritually encouraging individuals that you maintain contact with?

3. Cognitive: What are your current religious/spiritual beliefs? What are they based upon? What beliefs do you find particularly meaningful? What does your faith say about trials? How does this belief help you overcome obstacles? How do your beliefs affect your health practices?

4. Communion: Describe your relationship to the Ultimate. What has been your experience of the Ultimate? How does the Ultimate communicate with you? How have these experiences encouraged you? Have there been times of deep spiritual intimacy? How does your relationship help you face life challenges? How would the Ultimate describe you?

5. Conscience: How do you determine right and wrong? What are your key values? How does your spirituality help you deal with guilt (sin)? What role does forgiveness play in your life?

6. Intuition: To what extent do you experience intuitive hunches (flashes of creative insight, premonitions, spiritual insights)? Have these insights been a strength in your life? If so, how?

Table from Hodge (2001)

template that must be applied in every situation, but rather as a fluid framework that should be tailored to the needs of each individual client. In other words, the questions provide a number of possible options that can be used to facilitate the movement of the narrative and to elicit important information.

The second part of Table 1 consists of an interpretive framework (*Hodge, 2001a*) based on the anthropological understandings of Chinese spirituality writer Watchman Nee (*1968*). In addition to soma, Nee envisions a soul, comprised of affect, will, and cognition, and a spirit, comprised of communion, conscience, and intuition. Although human beings are an integrated unity and, consequently, the six dimensions interact with and influence one another, it is possible to distinguish each dimension. As is the case with other human dimensions, such as affect, behavior, and cognition, the dimensions of the spirit also can be discussed individually.

Communion refers to a spiritually based relationship (*Nee, 1968*). More specifically, it denotes the ability to bond with and relate to God. Conscience relates to one's ability to sense right and wrong. Beyond a person's cognitively held values, conscience conveys moral knowledge about the appropriateness of a given set of choices. Intuition refers to the ability to know—to come up with insights that by-pass cognitively based, information-processing channels.

As is apparent in Table 1, the questions in the interpretive anthropological framework are designed to elicit information about each of the six dimensions. The questions are not meant to be asked in any specific order. Rather, they are provided to help social workers draw out the richness of clients' spiritual stories. As clients relate their spiritual narrative, they may tend to touch upon some of the dimensions listed in the interpretive anthropological framework. Social workers can pose questions drawn from the framework to more fully explore clients' spiritual reality in the natural flow of the therapeutic dialogue.

Assets and Limitations

There is some evidence that information is stored and organized as a narrative in the mind (*Hodge, 2001a*). Accordingly, assessment methods that are congruent with this reality work with, rather than against, clients' mental thought processes. Indeed, for verbally oriented persons, spiritual histories may provide the best assessment method. The non-structured format allows clients to relate their stories in a direct, unfiltered manner. For example, whereas genograms require clients to circumscribe their spiritual reality upon a generational chart, assessment with spiritual histories allows clients to choose the relevant material to be shared (*Hodge, 2005a*).

However, not all clients are verbally oriented and some may find that a narrative assessment places too much attention on them in light of the sensitive, personal nature of spirituality (*Hodge, 2005a*). Some clients find it helpful to have a specific framework. Given the amorphous, subjective nature of spirituality, physical depiction may help concretize the client's strengths (*Hodge, 2000*). In other words, the process of conceptualizing and depicting one's spiritual journey may help to focus and objectify spiritual assets, which can then be discussed and marshaled to address problems. Still another limitation is the time spent exploring portions of the client's spiritual history that may have limited utility in terms of addressing the present problem the client is wrestling with.

Spiritual Eco-maps

In contrast to the above assessment tools, spiritual eco-maps focus on clients' current spiritual relationships *(Hodge, 2000; Hodge & Williams, 2002)*. The assessment instruments previously mentioned are united in the sense that they all are designed to tap some portion of a client's spiritual story as it exists through time. Spiritual genograms, lifemaps and histories typically cover one to three generations of a client's spiritual narrative. Spiritual eco-maps, on the other hand, focus on that portion of clients' spiritual story that exists in space. In other words, this assessment approach highlights clients' present relationships to various spiritual assets.

In keeping with traditional eco-gram construction *(Hartman, 1995)* the immediate family system is typically portrayed as a circle in the center of a piece of paper. Household family members can be sketched inside the circle, with squares depicting males and circles representing females *(Hodge, 2000)*. Alternatively, separate eco-maps can be drawn for each individual *(Hodge & Williams, 2002)*.

Significant spiritual systems or domains are depicted as circles on the outskirts of the paper, with the names of the respective systems written inside the circles. The circles are placed in a radius around the family circle, which may consist of a single figure representing the client. While clients should be encouraged to depict the domains that are most relevant to their spiritual worldviews, there are a number of spiritual systems that are strengths across many spiritual traditions.

More specifically, social workers should generally seek to explore clients' relationships with God, rituals, faith communities and encounters with angels, demons, and other spiritual visitations *(Hodge, 2000)*. One's relationship with God is widely regarded as a key strength, as are rituals, or codified spiritual practices such as devotional reading, meditation, prayer, scripture study, singing hymns, worship, "practicing the presence" of God by focusing on God's presence and active involvement in daily affairs. Faith communities refer to various church and para-church communities that individuals may associate with on a regular basis, such as church services, fellowship groups, mid-week Bible studies, youth groups, and singles associations.

As suggested above, social workers should also seek to incorporate into the eco-map any spiritual system that has meaning to the client *(Hodge, 2000)*. For example, one may wish to explore clients' relationship to their parents' spiritual traditions or their relationship to individuals who hold a position of significant spiritual leadership in their lives, such as a pastor, spiritual mentor, or elder. The goal should be to delineate on the eco-map all the spiritual systems that are relevant to the client's present spirituality.

The heart of the spiritual eco-map is the depiction of relationships between the family system and the spiritual systems, which are represented by various types of sketched lines *(Hodge, 2000)*. Thicker lines represent stronger or more powerful relationships. A dashed line represents the most tenuous relationship, while a jagged line denotes a conflicted one. An arrow is drawn on the line to indicate the flow of energy, resources, or interest. As is the case with the other diagrammatic instruments profiled above, short, descriptive encapsulations, significant dates, or other creative depictions, can also be incorporated onto the map to provide more information about relational dynamics.

When using eco-maps with individuals, the appropriate type of line is drawn in between the family system (the figure representing the client) and the spiritual systems. When working with families, lines are drawn to the family system as a unit when the family shares a particular relationship in common, or more frequently, connections are drawn to individual family members depicting the various unique relationships between each family member and various spiritual systems.

A Case Example

In an abbreviated manner, Diagram 3 depicts how a spiritual eco-map might be used with the Martinez family, consisting of Miguel and Maria, and their two children, Angie, 16, and Tony, 10. The Martinez family sought counseling as part of a relapse prevention plan for Angie who had recently been released from an in-patient alcohol treatment program. The goal of counseling was to reduce the conflict and distrust that existed between Angie and her parents. Angie thought her parents were overly strict, and her parents felt betrayed by Angie's chronic lying. In addition, Miguel and Maria removed Angie from public school and enrolled her in a Christian school in an attempt to prevent her from associating with her peer group that frequently abused alcohol.

Angie and her parents were embroiled in a heated conflict as Angie complained that the Alcoholic's Anonymous (AA) groups that her parents insisted she attend were "stupid and a waste of time." Due to Angie's prior deceitfulness and poor decision-making, her parents did not trust Angie's assessment of the AA groups and were adamant that she needed to continue attending two groups per week to help her maintain her sobriety. In order to address this dilemma, the therapist developed a spiritual eco-map with the family to explore the family's spiritual worldview and resources and identify spiritually based alternatives to AA attendance. The family was receptive to this because AA had substantiated the benefits of spirituality in treating alcoholism.

The Martinez family was currently attending St. Vincent's parish. Maria had grown up in this parish and knew many of the parishioners. She and Miguel had attended Cursillo, a weekend retreat that guided participants as they explored a deeper relationship with God, and they continued to participate in Cursillo's on-going groups. Maria, in particular, stated that she had received a great deal of support and prayer from this group when she and Miguel discovered Angie's struggle with alcoholism. Tony had been an altar boy for a couple years and looked

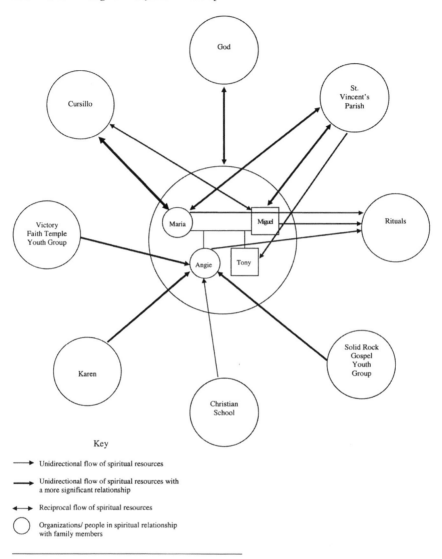

Diagram 3.

forward to seeing his friends at his Christian education class. In the past, Angie had viewed attending mass with disdain and thought that her peers at their parish were "stale." However, after attending in-patient treatment and switching to the Christian school, Angie slowly began to develop an interest in spirituality. Upon invitation from her new friends at school, Angie attended several local youth groups. Specifically, she enjoyed the "cool music" at Solid Rock Gospel Church, and liked the youth pastor, Dan, and his wife, Karen, at Victory Faith Temple. The therapist asked Miguel and Maria if they would be comfortable replacing the AA groups with the youth groups. Although they both wished Angie would attend the Catholic youth group at their parish, they agreed to give it a try and the family contracted to evaluate the youth groups' effectiveness in two months.

The therapist asked the Martinez family if they practiced any family rituals at home. Maria stated that she and Miguel each individually spent some time reading scripture and praying. Angie surprised her parents by stating that, after a conversation with Karen, she had recently started reading a devotional book when she felt upset and praying when she felt tempted to drink. Miguel shared that they discontinued their attempt at family devotions a year ago after a major fight arose between Angie and him. The therapist asked if they would be interested in initiating family devotions again. However, in order to break the conflict pattern of the parents lecturing and Angie bristling at their rigid rules, the therapist encouraged structuring the family devotional time as an open forum in which all family members would be free to share their perspectives and struggles. Miguel and Maria might share how their faith guides their decision-making and helps them deal with life's pain and hardships. Angie and Tony might share what they were learning in youth group, school, and Christian education class. This weekly ritual could potentially reassure Miguel and Maria that Angie was learning productive coping skills, build trust between family members, and help them forgive past grievances.

In congruence with the AA model, the therapist asked Angie if she could identify anyone on the spiritual eco-map that she respected and would like to be her sponsor who would provide support, guidance, and accountability for her. Angie stated that Karen had shared her life story in youth group, and was sure that Karen would be understanding, nonjudgmental, and helpful to her.

By developing the spiritual eco-map, the therapist was able to use the Martinez family's current spiritual resources to help them identify new solutions to their problems. Before this counseling session, Miguel and Maria had briefly heard Angie mention Karen's name, but their distrust and concern that the youth groups were not Catholic had prevented them from hearing the positive influence Karen and the groups were having in Angie's life. The process of developing the spiritual eco-map allowed Angie to openly share for the first time that her new-found faith was helping her stay sober and that the youth groups were helping her grow spiritually. As a result, the family moved past their stalemate, broke down barriers to communication, and began establishing trust.

Assets and Limitations

The main asset of spiritual eco-maps is that they focus upon clients' current spiritual strengths (*Hodge, 2005a*). For social workers seeking to operationalize clients' spiritual assets to help clients solve their problems, this assessment approach may be ideal. The time spent in assessment is focused upon tapping into present spiritual resources.

In some cases, clients may find it less threatening to have a concrete object that functions as the focus of subsequent conversation. As is the case with all diagrammatic instruments, spiritual eco-maps provide an object that can serve as the focal point of discussion. The design of eco-maps, however, with their focus on environmental systems rather than, for example, clients' life stories, helps remove the emphasis from the client as an individual. In short, while other approaches may implicitly emphasize clients, devoid of their contexts, spiritual eco-maps explicitly stress the spiritual systems in clients' environments (Hodge, 2005a).

Spiritual eco-maps suffer from the same limitations as other diagrammatic instruments relative to verbally based spiritual histories. In addition, in at least some situations, the focus on current spiritual assets may result in a limited assessment that overlooks salient historical factors. In some contexts, social workers may wish to explore historical resources by using, for example, a spiritual genogram.

Conducting an Assessment

Knowledge of how to conduct an assessment is also important (Hodge & Limb, 2010a). Developing familiarity with various assessment tools is only part of the assessment process. Practitioners must also know how to use these tools in an appropriate, spiritually sensitive manner. Although a detailed discussion of the mechanics of conducting a spiritual assessment is beyond the scope of this chapter, a few important points will be highlighted.

Social workers should be aware that many clients may be hesitant to trust practitioners. Some clients may be concerned that practitioners will not treat with honor that which is held to be sacred (Richards & Bergin, 2000). Consequently, due to the highly personal nature of spirituality, it is appropriate to procure clients' consent before engaging in a spiritual assessment (Hodge, 2006). Additionally, social workers should explain a particular assessment instrument to ensure that the client is comfortable with the particular approach before engaging in an assessment.

To a great extent, clients' apprehension can be alleviated by expressing genuine support. Adopting an attitude of interest and curiosity toward the client's belief system is an appropriate therapeutic stance (Patterson, Hayworth, Turner & Raskin, 2000).

Social workers can also demonstrate spiritual sensitivity by obtaining knowledge of common spiritual traditions (Hodge, 2005b). For example, if one works in an area where Latter Day Saints and Pentecostals are prominent spiritual traditions, then seeking out information on LDS (Ulrich, Richards & Bergin, 2000) and Pentecostal traditions (Dobbins, 2000) can assist social workers in exhibiting spiritual sensitivity with these populations. Ideally, in the process of attempting to understand clients' spiritual worldviews, social workers should seek to envision life through the particular worldview of the client (Hodge, 2004a).

In their attempts to understand the worldviews of clients, social workers should develop their understanding of the oppression people of faith often experience in the larger secular culture (Smith, 2003). It is important for social workers to recognize that the dominant secular culture often marginalizes or otherwise de-legitimizes devout faith in many influential settings, such as network news *(Kerr, 2003)*, fictional television *(Clarke, 2005)*, colleges and universities *(Cnaan, Wineburg & Boddie, 1999; Hodge, Baughman & Cummings, 2006; Rothman, Lichter & Nevitte, 2005)* and other cultural-shaping "knowledge sector" forums *(Hunter, 1991)*. In other words, people who are secular experience a certain privilege that is foreign to people of faith *(Hodge, 2009)*. Social workers should reflect on how living in a culture that often ignores, devalues, and even ridicules believers' most cherished beliefs and values affects the psychology of people of faith *(Ressler & Hodge, 2003)*.

Developing their understanding of clients' worldviews can assist social workers in respecting clients' spiritual autonomy. The focus of practice should not be on determining whether clients' spiritual beliefs are right or wrong, but rather on how their values animate their lives and assist them in coping with difficulties. The social worker's job is not to accept or reject clients' spiritual values but to understand them and help them use their beliefs and practices to assist clients in overcoming their problems *(Hodge, 2006)*.

In some cases, however, social workers may believe that clients' spiritual beliefs are problematic. In such situations, social workers should not attempt to change clients' values in an area that lies outside the realm of their professional competence. Rather, practitioners should collaborate with or refer such clients to clergy *(Gilbert, 2000)*. Given that this is the clergy's area of professional competency, pastors, priests, and other spiritual specialists are better equipped to ascertain the appropriateness of a given set of beliefs and practices *(Hodge, Bonifas & Chou, 2010)*. It is critical, however, that practitioners respect clients' spiritual autonomy by forming collaborative relationships with clergy that share the same denominational and theological orientation as the client. It would be unethical to covertly attempt to subvert clients' values by, for example, referring a client who holds traditional beliefs to a liberal pastor.

In keeping with their roles as social workers, practitioners should remain focused on empowering clients to address their problems. During the assessment process, social workers might keep two questions in mind. First, during past difficulties, how have clients culled from their spiritual frameworks various resources to address previous problems? Second, what types of unaccessed resources are available in this framework that can be marshaled to address current problems? Social workers can attempt to link clients with untapped resources to help them solve their problems. Practitioners might, for example, suggest particular interventions either drawn from, or consistent with, clients' spiritual worldviews.

More specifically, social workers might employ a modified form of cognitive therapy in which unhealthy beliefs are identified and replaced with positive beliefs drawn from the individual's spiritual belief system *(Hodge, 2008)*. Similarly, practitioners may explore the possibility of reframing current problems as opportunities for spiritual growth *(Jankowski, 2002; Pargament, 2007)*. In attempting to foster the adoption of more productive patterns of behaviors, spiritual rituals may be employed as "exceptions" to unproductive behavioral patterns *(Hodge, 2000)*. Decision-based forgiveness interventions may be useful in some contexts *(DiBlasio, 1998)* while existential, brevity of life interventions may be appropriate in other situations *(Hodge, 2005e)*. Some evidence also suggests that intercessory prayer may assist clients in the recovery process *(Hodge, 2007)*. In each individual setting, the unique spiritual beliefs of the clients and the theoretical orientation of the social worker will indicate which interventions are selected. In any setting, however, the goal should be to help clients use their spiritual strengths to address their issues and concerns.

Conclusion

In order to provide services that are sensitive to clients' spiritual worldviews, social workers must conduct spiritual assessments to have some awareness of clients' spiritual realities. Similarly, to help clients tap into their spiritual strengths to address the problems they wrestle with, it is necessary to undertake an assessment of clients' strengths. A single assessment approach, however, is unlikely to be ideal in all situations; diverse needs call for a variety of approaches. If the profession of social work is to take seriously its mandate to provide culturally sensitive services that build upon clients' unique strengths, then in many cases performing a spiritual assessment is an imperative.

References

Augustine. (354-430/1991). Confessions (H. Chadwick, Trans.). New York: Oxford University Press.

Bart, M. (1998, December). Spirituality in counseling finding believers. Counseling Today, 41(6), 1, 6.

Canda, E. R., & Furman, L. D. (2010). Spiritual diversity in social work practice: The heart of helping (2nd ed.). New York: Oxford University Press.

Clarke, S. H. (2005). Created in whose image? Religious characters on network television. Journal of Media and Religion, 4(3), 137-153.

Cnaan, R. A., Wineburg, R. J., & Boddie, S. C. (1999). The newer deal: Social work and religion in partnership. New York: Columbia University Press.

DiBlasio, F. A. (1998). The use of a decision-based forgiveness intervention within inter-generational family therapy. Journal of Family Therapy, 20(1), 77-94.

Dobbins, R. D. (2000). Psychotherapy with Pentecostal Protestants. In P. S. Richards & A. E. Bergin (Eds.), Handbook of psychotherapy and religious diversity (pp. 155-184). Washington, DC: American Psychological Association.

Ferraro, K. F., & Kelley-Moore, J. A. (2000). Religious consolation among men and women: Do health problems spur seeking? Journal of the Scientific Study of Religion, 39(2), 220-234.

Gilbert, M. (2000). Spirituality in social work groups: Practitioners speak out. Social Work with Groups, 22(4), 67-84.

Hartman, A. (1995). Diagrammatic assessment of family relationships. Families in Society, 76(2), 111-122.

Hodge, D. R. (2000). Spiritual ecomaps: A new diagrammatic tool for assessing marital and family spirituality. Journal of Marital and Family Therapy, 26(1), 229-240.

Hodge, D. R. (2001a). Spiritual assessment: A review of major qualitative methods and a new framework for assessing spirituality. Social Work, 46(3), 203-214.

Hodge, D. R. (2001b). Spiritual genograms: A generational approach to assessing spirituality. Families in Society, 82(1), 35-48.

Hodge, D. R. (2003). Spiritual assessment: A handbook for helping professionals. Botsford, CT: NACSW.

Hodge, D. R. (2004a). Spirituality and people with mental illness: Developing spiritual competency in assessment and intervention. Families in Society, 85(1), 36-44.

Hodge, D. R. (2004b). Why conduct a spiritual assessment? A theoretical rationale for assessment. Advances in Social Work, 5(2), 183-196.

Hodge, D. R. (2005a). Developing a spiritual assessment toolbox: A discussion of the strengths and limitations of five different assessment methods. Health and Social Work, 30(4), 314-323.

Hodge, D. R. (2005b). Social work and the house of Islam: Orienting practitioners to the beliefs and values of Muslims in the United States. Social Work, 50(2), 162-173.

Hodge, D. R. (2005c). Spiritual assessment in marital and family therapy: A methodological framework for selecting between six qualitative assessment tools. Journal of Marital and Family Therapy, 31(4), 341-356.

Hodge, D. R. (2005d). Spiritual ecograms: A new assessment instrument for identifying clients' spiritual strengths in space and across time. Families in Society, 86(2), 287-296.

Hodge, D. R. (2005e). Spiritual life maps: A client-centered pictorial instrument for spiritual assessment, planning, and intervention. Social Work, 50(1), 77-87.

Hodge, D. R. (2006). A template for spiritual assessment: A review of the JCAHO requirements and guidelines for implementation. Social Work, 51(4), 317-326.

Hodge, D. R. (2007). A systematic review of the empirical literature on intercessory prayer. Research on Social Work Practice, 17(2), 174-187.

Hodge, D. R. (2008). Constructing spiritually modified interventions: Cognitive therapy with diverse populations. International Social Work, 51(2), 178-192.

Hodge, D. R. (2009). Secular privilege: Deconstructing the invisible rose-tinted sunglasses. Journal of Religion and Spirituality in Social Work: Social Thought, 28(1/2), 8-34.

Hodge, D. R., Baughman, L. M., & Cummings, J. A. (2006). Moving toward spiritual competency: Deconstructing religious stereotypes and spiritual prejudices in social work literature. Journal of Social Service Research, 32(4), 211-232.

Hodge, D. R., Bonifas, R. P., & Chou, R. J. (2010). Spirituality and older adults: Ethical guidelines to enhance service provision. Advances in Social Work, 11(1), 1-16.

Hodge, D. R., & Bushfield, S. (2006). Developing spiritual competence in practice. Journal of Ethnic and Cultural Diversity in Social Work, 15(3/4), 101-127.

Hodge, D. R., & Limb, G. E. (2009a). Spiritual histories and Native Americans: A mixed method validation study. Journal of Social Service Research, 35(4), 285-296.

Hodge, D. R. & Limb, G. E. (2009b). Establishing the preliminary validity of spiritual eco-maps with Native Americans. Clinical Social Work Journal, 37(4), 320-331.

Hodge, D. R., & Limb, G. E. (2010a). Conducting spiritual assessments with Native Americans: Enhancing cultural competence in social work practice courses. Journal of Social Work Education, 46(2).

Hodge, D. R., & Limb, G. E. (2010b). A Native American perspective on spiritual assessment: The strengths and limitations of a complementary set of assessment tools. Health & Social Work, 35(2), 121-131.

Hodge, D. R., & Limb, G. E. (2010c). Native Americans and brief spiritual assessment:

Examining and operationalizing the Joint Commission's assessment framework. Social Work, 55(4), 297-307.

Hodge, D. R., & McGrew, C. C. (2006). Spirituality, religion and the interrelationship: A nationally representative study. Journal of Social Work Education, 43(3), 637-654.

Hodge, D. R., & Williams, T. R. (2002). Assessing African American spirituality with spiritual eco-maps. Families in Society, 83(5/6), 585-595.

Hunter, J. D. (1991). Culture Wars. New York: BasicBooks.

Jankowski, P. J. (2002). Postmodern spirituality: Implications for promoting change. Counseling and Values, 47(1), 69-79.

Johnson, B. R. (2002). Objective hope. Philadelphia, PA: Center for Research on Religion and Urban Civil Society.

Kerr, P. A. (2003). The framing of fundamentalist Christians: Network television news, 1980-2000. Journal of Media and Religion, 2(4), 203-235.

Koenig, H. G. (2007). Spirituality in patient care (2nd ed.). Philadelphia: Templeton Foundation Press.

Koenig, H. G., McCullough, M. E., & Larson, D. B. (2001). Handbook of religion and health. New York: Oxford University Press.

Limb, G. E., & Hodge, D. R. (2007). Developing spiritual lifemaps as a culture-centered pictorial instrument for spiritual assessments with Native American clients. Research on Social Work Practice, 17(2), 296-304.

Limb, G. E., & Hodge, D. R. (2011). Utilizing spiritual ecograms with Native American families and children to promote cultural competence in family therapy. Journal of Marital and Family Therapy, 37(1), 81-94.

McGoldrick, M., Gerson, R., & Petry, S. S. (2008). Genograms: Assessment and intervention (3rd ed.). New York: W.W. Norton & Company.

NASW Code of Ethics. (2008). Retrieved 05/01/2010, from http://www.socialworkers. org/pubs/code/code.asp.

NASW Standards for Cultural Competence in Social Work Practice. (2001). Retrieved 23/02/2010, from http://www.socialworkers.org/practice/standards/NASWCultur-alStandards.pdf.

Nee, W. (1968). The spiritual man. (Vols. 1-3). New York: Christian Fellowship Publishers.

Newport, F. (2006). Religion most important to Blacks, women, and older Americans. Retrieved 06/06/2009, from http://www.gallup.com/poll/25585/religion-most-important-blacks-women-older-americans.aspx.

Pargament, K. I. (2007). Spiritually integrated psychotherapy: Understanding and addressing the sacred. New York: Guilford Press.

Patterson, J., Hayworth, M., Turner, C., & Raskin, M. (2000). Spiritual issues in family therapy: A graduate-level course. Journal of Martial and Family Therapy, 26(2), 199-210.

Ressler, L. E., & Hodge, D. R. (2003). Silenced voices: Social Work and the oppression of conservative narratives. Social Thought, 22(1), 125-142.

Richards, P. S., & Bergin, A. E. (Editors). (2000). Handbook of psychotherapy and religious diversity. Washington, DC: American Psychological Association.

Rose, E. M., Westefeld, J. S., & Ansley, T. N. (2008). Spiritual issues in counseling: Clients' beliefs and preferences. Psychology of Religion and Spirituality, S(1), 18-33.

Rothman, S., Lichter, S. R., & Nevitte, N. (2005). Politics and the professional advancement among college faculty. The Forum, 3(1), 1-16.

Saleebey, D. (Editor). (2009). The strengths perspective in social work practice (5th ed.). Boston: Pearson/Allyn & Bacon.

Sheridan, M. (2009). Ethical issues in the use of spiritually based interventions in social work practice: What we are doing and why. Journal of Religion and Spirituality in Social Work, 28(1/2), 99-126.

Smith, C. (2003). The secular revolution. Berkeley: University of California Press.

Smith, C., & Faris, R. (2005). Socioeconomic inequality in the American religious system: An update and assessment. Journal for the Scientific Study of Religion, 44(1), 95-104.

Smith, E. J. (2006). The strength-based counseling model. The Counseling Psychologist, 34(1), 13-79.

Taylor, R. J., Chatters, L. M., & Jackson, J. S. (2007). Religious and spiritual involvement among older African Americans, Caribbean Blacks, and non-Hispanic Whites: Findings from the National Survey of American Life. Journal of Gerontology, 62B(4), S238-S250.

Tracz, S. M., & Gehart-Brooks, D. R. (1999). The lifeline: Using art to illustrate history. Journal of Family Psychotherapy, 10(3), 61-63.

Ulrich, W. L., Richards, P. S., & Bergin, A. E. (2000). Psychotherapy with Latter-day Saints. In P. S. Richards & A. E. Bergin (Eds.), Handbook of psychotherapy and religious diversity (pp. 185-209). Washington, DC: American Psychological Association.

Van Hook, M., Hugen, B., & Aguilar, M. A. (Editors). (2001). Spirituality within religious traditions in social work practice. Pacific Grove, CA: Brooks/Cole.

SECTION 4

CHRISTIANS IN SOCIAL WORK PRACTICE:
CONTEMPORARY ISSUES

CHAPTER 16

THE HELPING PROCESS AND CHRISTIAN BELIEFS: INSIGHTS FROM ALAN KEITH-LUCAS[1][2]

Helen Wilson Harris

"Helping is not a technique. It is an investment of one's self" (Keith-Lucas, p. 17). That statement begins our journey into understanding the nature and approach of our professional helping according to one who has written most practically and profoundly about the nature of the helping relationship in social work. Clinician, consultant, and author Alan Keith-Lucas devoted much of his professional life to understanding and communicating what actually makes a difference when "professional helpers" encounter those we call clients and patients and consumers. The buzz word today is "evidence-based practice." How do we as social workers engage our clients in ways that produce change? Alan Keith-Lucas taught that there are principles of helping that are essential to effectiveness and to positive outcomes. "This is a difficult and skilled business. If we are going to attempt it, we need to have some skill in help-ing." (Keith-Lucas, p. 31).

The work of Alan Keith-Lucas continues to inform and inspire practice in child welfare more than ten years after his death. At a recent national conference of the North American Association of Christians in Social Work (NACSW), focus was given to the writings and teaching of AKL as pertinent in practice today. A number of themes emerged in the discussions of professional social workers and in the special edition of the Journal of Social Work and Christianity devoted to the celebration of 100 years since Keith-Lucas' birth.

Theme 1: The ethical integration of Christian faith and social work practice is possible, though not without its challenges. Social workers at the annual conference who knew Keith referenced his ground breaking writing that recognized the contribu-tions of Christianity and Christians to the development of the social work profession. Ressler referred to this quote: "It must be intellectually rigorous, conducted by people who are amateurs neither in religion nor social work. It will have to deal with the 'hard paradoxes' rather than the 'easy correspondences'" (p. 248). Powell recognized that Keith believed and taught that "our Christian faith should greatly enhance our ability to be of help to those we seek to serve; sincere Christian faith provides us with a source of inspiration, insight and skill" (p. 262). Sherwood identified Keith's belief that "our fundamental assumptions about values and the nature of persons are always a matter of faith and worldview, whether religious or secular…." (p. 270). Harris summed up

Keith's commitment to the concept that good helping by the Christian always proceeds from the concepts of grace and forgiveness (p. 297).

Theme 2: Helping in social work practice is grounded in respectful relationships. This is a fundamental concept throughout Keith's writings about faith and practice. It is fascinating to see the parallels between Keith's theology and social work values. It was Keith who first wrote about the concept of client self determination, identifying it with God's gift of choice and unconditional love. Powell highlights this statement from Giving and Taking Help: one principle of good helping is that "helping people find their own way is better than controlling them, however subtly" (p. 266). Sherwood follows up on this theme of respect and self determination by identifying "the importance of respectful relationships in which the client is the 'expert,' valuing client self-determination rather than manipulation or control" (p. 270). Even with mandated clients, Keith recognized that they must be given the right to "decide what to do with the help offered" (p. 274). Harris notes that Keith understood these as "shared values of both secular social work and religion, including the worth and dignity of all human beings, a commitment to self determination, the need for kindness and understanding, and the importance of ethical and just principles" (p. 296).

Theme 3: All good helping involves three interlocking concepts of reality, empathy and support. In fact, these concepts were part of Keith's definition of helping before he came to faith in Christ and were part of his ability to understand God as Father, God as Savior, and God as Holy Spirit (Ressler, p. 247). Harris identifies the following description of Keith's triune helping model:

> *I have tried to show that these are the three ways in which God works with us, as Father, the One who plans the circumstances of our lives and gives us rules for living; as the Son who shared our life and 'was tempted in all ways as we were," so that He understands our troubles, and as the Spirit who is always with us. (p. 297).*

This concept became part of an organizing paradigm on the helping relationship. Kuhlman summed it up this way:

> It distinguishes 'help' from 'control, focuses on the 'helping relationship,' and attempts to specify the 'helping factor,' that is, the combination of 'reality, empathy, and support' in order to make the basic principles of helping accessible to a wide variety of professionals and non-professionals. (p. 314).

Theme 4: Child Welfare Services are much more appropriately named and directed as Family Services. "Keith thought that residential care could be creatively used to benefit both children and families. It should be family centered.....(Powell, p. 259). Keith believed that we would do better to focus on "patching up homes rather than patching up children" (p. 261). The social workers at the conference who knew Keith recognized in his work the precursor to the current kinship care movement, summed up in this comment by Harris: "Instead of trying to rescue children from poor or dysfunctional families, Alan Keith-Lucas recommended that families be understood as important to their children and a resource for planning for care for the child" (p. 299).

These speakers, authors, and in many cases colleagues of Alan Keith-Lucas identified on the 100th anniversary of his birth the inspirational, prophetic messages that still inform social work practice and helping today. The time-honored and practice-validated principles of this visionary leader are worth remembering and emulating.

I am more motivated than ever to share the timeless wisdom of this leader with social workers who are newly trying to integrate their faith and practice and those who are discouraged with the effort.

I first met Alan Keith-Lucas more than 30 years ago. I was a caseworker at the South Texas Children's Home where "Keith" (as he asked to be called) was a consultant who was invited by our administrator to the campus periodically to help us figure out this thing called faith-based residential child care. Dr. Keith-Lucas (I know, Keith) was, on first inspection, an odd looking man with his thin brushy goatee, his tweed jacket with the patched pockets, and his unlit pipe in one hand. His "older adult" look and his British accent gave him a distinguished air though he never seemed formidable to me. I went to the first meeting with him more than a little skeptical that this "outsider" could offer any insight of value to those of us who lived and worked among these children every day. He captured my imagination and my respect by the end of our first five minutes together. Here was a man who read and wrote widely, thought deeply, and loved children simply and completely. He was able in a few days on the campus to connect with the most intractable of the children. He delivered with kindness insights into the attitudes and behaviors of the staff (including me, I confess) that allowed us to look with new eyes into the hearts and potential of children instead of the scars from their damaged lives. He drew as much from Uncle Remus stories as he did from scripture. He, like another great teacher and minister to children, communicated through stories the most amazing truths. He was unorthodox in many ways. Keith saw and responded to the wounded child inside each of us. Remarkably, he left us with the tools to do the same for every child in our care as well as their parents and families.

I continue to regularly read what Alan Keith-Lucas wrote and left behind and I ask my students to do the same. He was a visionary, prophetic social worker, and educator. He wrote, in some cases 50 years ago, about concepts beginning to be understood and used in child care and in social work practice today. Keith's understandings and articulations are life changing. His understandings of the helping relationship, of the importance of the whole person with all of his or her history, of the value of concrete services, of the lifelong impact of separation and loss, of the Biblical mandate to love and respect others including (perhaps especially) those different than we are changed me and continues to change others more than ten years after his death.

I do not propose in this chapter to improve on what Keith has written about the helping relationship. I propose to gather from his works clarifying insights that provide the reader with both a glimpse and deep baptism into the wisdom Alan Keith-Lucas offers us as we discover more about being a helper in a relationship with those in the world who are wounded and to whom we are called.

In his book, Giving and Taking Help, Alan Keith-Lucas asks us to consider anew our motivation and our preparation for entering into a helping relationship with others. He asks us to move away from formulaic helping and tells us that *focusing on the application of a particular technique can result in poor outcomes if we have forgotten the main thing, the client. That, more than anything, sums up his central premise: The client is the expert of his/her own experience. The client is the specialist in the helping relationship, the person who must, in the end, make the decisions and be invested in the process. Keith explains that we begin as helpers by respecting our client's right and ability to make the choices that lead to change. It is the client who must live out the choices that are made and the results that are set in motion. So the client must be engaged in making active choices. An active, willing choice is one that brings with it commitment and the energy and potential to deal with life's circumstances. What then is the helping person's role? It is in relationship and in remembering that the relationship is mutual; the helper and the "helped" are mutually engaged in a relationship focused on choice and change. But having a helping relationship does not mean a having a social relationship like a friendship or a relationship that is focused on being pleasant. Yes, effective helping professionals care deeply about their clients; but that caring means both not prescribing what the other person should do and being willing to stay engaged in the helping relationship even when the circumstances and the decisions are difficult.*

Keith-Lucas tells us: "The defined purpose of the helping relationship is to help a person or group to make choices about a problem or situation and about the help they are willing to take about it." (p. 51) This by necessity means learning how to hear what the client is saying to us and believing that only the client can make a real choice about what course of action will have meaning to him or her. Even in situations where the social worker also represents the "agenda" or interests of the agency, there can be no significant helping without the client's engagement and involvement. It is possible through effective helping to secure that engagement and involvement, to break through the barriers of distrust and agency power and prescription. It works when we let go of the notion of social control and engage in the kind of helping in which clients understand their own responsibility for their lives and the impact of their decisions on the lives of others. Keith-Lucas compares helping a client to trying to move a stalled trolley up against a coiled spring. All of the pushing in the world will only increase the "resistance" and likelihood of ending up further away from the stated goal. Instead, our role as helpers, according to Keith, is to help "uncoil the resistance" or in effect, address the negative experiences and negative feelings that may be keeping the client from being able to make progress. Keith presents a fascinating model for working with clients who have experienced loss of all kinds. He addresses the most important question in helping those who have experienced loss: What makes the difference in coming out of the crisis or loss experience with resilience and mastery instead of despair and lifelong disengagement? Every client encounters tragedy and loss. Keith adapts the "standard" grief and loss model to clarify that those who overcome and are able to turn tragedy into triumph are those who are empowered to address the loss and the feelings that come with it, a phenomenon he calls "protest." The helping person is then, not the person who makes everything seem fine, but the person who permits, even facilitates, the expression of the pain and outrage generated by the loss. The theme again of the helping relationship is authenticity and acceptance of clients even when they are crying or angry or tired or unpleasant.

What follows is the substantive text from Chapter 5 and Chapter 10 from the 1994 Revised Edition of Giving and Taking Help, *in Dr. Keith-Lucas' own words. Some of the original text has been abridged in order to make space for materials from both chapters. My comments and reflections are in italics. I do this in the belief that Keith's work will be transforming in the life of the social worker who is called of God to professional helping. I'm not sure anyone can improve on Keith's words. My reflections are intended to lift up the concepts and add my own voice and experience to his.*

Keith has much more to say about the nature of helping than I have been able to capture here. This material has been chosen because it captures one of his core ideas—that all good helping involves the skillful use of reality, empathy, and support—and that these dimensions of helping reflect the very nature of God.

The Helping Factor (*Giving and Taking Help*, Chapter 5)

Various Theories

There must be something which the helping person brings into the relationship through which help is actually given. The relationship we have discussed cannot do this by itself. It is resultant and not something that can be created apart from what goes on between helper and helped. We cannot set up such a relationship and then sit back and expect help to flow from it without some positive action or contribution on our part. *Helping happens when we invest ourselves in the lives of others, when we are engaged with them in the "here and now" as they understand it. We bring ourselves to the process understanding that we may well be changed as much as the person we are committed to helping. This active participation is the key to effective helping.*

Quite clearly, too, the helping factor is something more than the material things with which help often deals, such as money, a job, housing or medical care, although it is a mistake to think that these things are unimportant. It was one of the misapprehensions of many nineteenth-century helpers that to give material things was wrong, or at best, a necessary evil. *Many helping persons today seem to miss the tremendous importance of "concrete helping." The model of Jesus as helper includes many examples of his provision of material needs, his ability to meet the needs presented to him in the moment.*

A job, a house, an opportunity are very important to people. They may be completely necessary to the solution of their problems. Yet, there is something more to helping than this. While there are obvious situations in which they are all that are needed, in which case helping would seem to consist solely in their provision, in the majority of situations something else has to happen, either in the actual giving or possibly before it, if a person is to make full use of them. And even then their mere provision can be done in such a way that their use is enhanced or limited. The dignity of the application procedure, the concern shown for details, the promptness of their provision, even the setting in which they are given, all contribute to or deduct from their helpfulness.

There have been many attempts to isolate or define the primary helping factor. The nineteenth century, by and large, relied on moral exhortation, friendliness, and encouragement. Later a more rationalist approach relied on careful case study and appropriate treatment, which in general meant manipulation of the environment and the supplying of influences which the helped person was thought to lack. A little later, in the late twenties and early thirties of this century, it was believed that listening alone was perhaps the primary helping factor. The helper became little more than a mirror against which the helped person projected his concerns.

Knowing "Why"

With the advent of psychoanalysis, interpretation of unconscious motives was given first place. It was believed that the rationality of the conscious brain, brought face to face with the apparently infantile reasoning which the unconscious seems to employ--its tendency, for instance to identify wholly unlike things—would reject this irrationality in favor of sensible behavior. Insight would lead to change.

So deeply is this concept ingrained that many people will uphold that one cannot modify one's behavior unless one knows exactly why one has misbehaved in the first place, which is clearly not always so. Some understanding of one's motives may be very helpful in coming to a decision but many of a person's most fruitful decisions and commitments are made without knowing exactly why.

The belief that understanding motive is critical to behavior change once caused a class of mine to insist that the purpose of an interview with a delinquent girl [called Mary Ann] we were studying could be no other than to find out "why" she ran away from home. They were quite shocked when I said that this might be quite helpful, if it could ever be known, although I doubted that it would ever tell us more than the precipitating factor. The actual causality would be probably almost infinitely complex and involve many factors outside both their and Mary Ann's control, a recognition which is being increasingly made by students of epidemiology. If they were interested in trying to create conditions in the community which would minimize delinquency, such an analysis might have value.

But this was not the purpose of the interview as it was held. It could have only one purpose. That would be to find out ways by which Mary Ann would be able to handle her impulse to run away again.

I do not mean that the epidemiological approach, the desire to control or alter conditions so that other Mary Anns might not need to run away, is something with which a social worker should not be concerned. I do mean that to help Mary Ann in the here and now, the knowledge of her action's complicated causality is probably not enough. Even if Mary Ann could say, and even be convinced, that she ran away because of any number of factors, there is still her will, her image of herself, her fears, and the reality of her present situation to take into account. Humans are not simple rational creatures, and a fourteen-year-old girl perhaps not always an exemplar of logical thinking.

If Mary Ann were a very sick child, or if her impulse was such that it was uncontrollable by any conscious act on her part even with some change of attitude on the part of her parents, psychotherapy with interpretation might have been necessary. The need for this would have shown up, perhaps, in a more total disorganization than this girl was presenting, or in her failure to make use of the helping process that most people can use to some extent. Even here her problems might have been solved by psychiatric treatment not involving interpretation.

Her particular behavior might be amenable to conditioning or to drug therapy. This solution would involve a "why" or a sort-knowledge at least that her condition could become manageable if certain tensions were relieved, which is not so much a "why" as a "how." Sometimes by handling one factor in a complex situation a person may be brought to a condition below, as it were, the critical point at which symptoms appear.

However, a preoccupation with causality would have failed to engage Mary Ann's capacity to face her situation and to do something about it herself. It is all very well to know that one behaves badly because one has been rejected or unloved. There is no doubt that to be rejected makes it harder to behave well. But it does not remove the responsibility of a person to do something about his behavior.

Reality, Empathy, and Support

Doing something about her impulse to run away is what Mary Ann needs to struggle with now. To help Mary Ann do this the worker must start with the reality of the situation, the fact that she has done something illegal; the possibility that the judge might send her to a correctional school, or let her go home only under supervision, which she might find difficult to bear; even the fact that she might find it impossible not to run away again. In order to decide what she wanted, what she could bear, what use she could make of whatever was decided, and what help she needed to do this, Mary Ann would need to be held to facing these facts and possibilities.

She would also need to be free to discuss and explore her feelings about them, and in fact be reassured that her expression of these feelings would not get her into trouble. Part of these feelings might be anger, at her parents, at the judge, or at the probation officer. The last is particularly true if the worker has done her job in holding Mary Ann to the reality of the situation; but since this anger is something which Mary Ann cannot help feeling about the situation, and since to repress it, or "bottle it up" will only make it more important and harder to deal with, it may need to be expressed.

Lastly, if Mary Ann is to take help in her situation, she must know that the worker will be available to her, will not turn against her when she is troubled, and will provide as far as she can what Mary Ann needs to carry out her decisions.

This situation may serve, despite its particularity, to help us see what it is that the helping person must convey to any person in trouble. What has to be conveyed can be phrased as a "statement" which the helping person makes, although it is much more than this. It is not simply something said. It is something conveyed by words, feeling, and action. But in terms of a statement it could be phrased in three sentences, as follows:

"This is it." (Reality)

"I know that it must hurt." (Empathy)

"I am here to help you if you want me and can use me," or more succinctly, "You don't have to face this alone." (Support)

These three sentences in turn may be expressed in terms of what is actually offered through them. In this form the helping factor is composed of three complex, interrelated and important elements which we may call *reality, empathy, and support.*

These three elements are always necessary in any helping process and the three together do, in fact, constitute the helping factor. I know of no piece of helping that cannot be analyzed in these terms, and no piece of unsuccessful helping that does not show a weakness in at least one of these elements. Reality has been partial or empathy and support conditional.

We will examine first each principle by itself and then try to bring them together. The order in which they are presented here does not necessarily mean that one introduces them, in helping, serially or in this order. One may start with an expression of empathy or even of support, and in any case they are interwoven. One does not stop where another starts. But if there is an order, reality often does come first.

Reality

Reality means a number of things, some of which have already been touched on. It means, first, not discounting another's problem, not taking it away from him by believing it unimportant. This is a thing we are particularly likely to do to children, whom we cannot believe, for some reason, feel as deeply as we do. How often we say, "Oh, they'll soon forget it," or "They're too young to be affected much," when everything that we really know about them points to the fact that their despair, their fear, and their anger are not only intense but can leave permanent scars. To be real, on the other hand, means to face the problem with someone in all of its ugliness or terror. It means doing him the honor of taking his problem seriously. And, with children in particular, but with adults also, this is the first requirement if a relationship is to grow.   Another form of taking away a person's problem is to solve it for him or to insulate him from it. We either produce a quick solution or we help him to evade it, to forget it, not to come into contact with it often to spare him the pain or disturbance.

But, while it might be necessary to allay some forms of disturbance temporarily, disturbance has about it some of the qualities that are now recognized in a fever. It used to be good medical practice to allay all fevers. Now there is growing understanding that a fever is the body's way of fighting an infection. A child once, in a children's home, was very much disturbed by her mother's visits. The social worker suggested solving the problem by restricting the mother's visits. The child said, with a good deal of anger, "What you don't understand is that this is something I need to get disturbed about."

People need their problems if they are to solve them for themselves. Sometimes they need to be disturbed. Not to permit them to become so, when they are trying to tackle their problems, is to encourage nonchoice.

False Reassurance as "Nonreality"

A common form of nonreality is reassurance. False reassurance, is an attempt to palliate reality by telling the person in trouble that "things will be all right" when there is no reason to think that this will be so, or when the present hurts so much that this is wholly unimportant. We can recognize obvious cases of it. No wise parents today would tell their child that the dentist won't hurt. The dentist very well may hurt, and the parent be proved a liar. But we still, some of us, will tell a child that he will be happy in a foster home when this may not be so and when in any case all he can think of at the moment is his pain at leaving his own parents.

We use this kind of reassurance for two reasons. In the first place, we cannot stand the child's present unhappiness and are willing, although we may not know it, to try to dispel it even at the cost of greater unhappiness later. And, in the second, we are apt to be a little defensive because a foster home, in this case, or some other service, is what we have to offer him and we do not like the idea that he might not like the only thing that we have to give him. It makes us feel very inadequate. I have seen a welfare worker "reassure" a client that the termination of her grant does not really matter, since she ought to be able to get support from a recently located absent husband, when her lights and gas were to be turned off that afternoon. False or unrealistic reassurance does not strengthen a person's ability to handle his problem. It effectually disarms him and robs him of the anger or despair he may need to deal with it.

Another reason for false reassurance is our natural protectiveness toward those we consider vulnerable or lacking in real strength. We feel that the person we are helping would be hurt by coming face to face with the truth. There may be some instances in which the helped person could not possibly face the truth, but more often the helping person is only too glad to have a good reason not to face the helped person with the truth. The genuine cases where the truth is so horrible that it would be more harmful than helpful are rather rare.

Protecting People from the Truth

To protect someone from the truth is to make a very serious judgment about him. It is to say that he is incapable of being helped with his real problem. As a minister expressed it to me once, it is to deny him his chance for an "abundant life," fully experienced.

The truth, too, is often much less harmful than what the imagination puts in its place. Some years ago I was approached by a teacher who was concerned about a fifteen-year-old boy, the adopted son of an apparently stable and loving family, who had begun to run away. There seemed to be nothing in the home to suggest a need to escape from it, and although the boy was adolescent, he did not appear to be particularly rebellious. The boy was plainly running "to" rather than "from," and when I was told that the town he was running to was his birthplace, I was fairly safe in assuming at least tentatively that he was doing what so many children away from their own parents have to do, which was the answer the question, "Why did my parents give me up?

I therefore asked the teacher why the boy's parents had done so and was told that the boy was illegitimate. It was quite hard for her to take when I suggested that if she wanted to help the boy, someone had better tell him the truth. To her surprise the boy was greatly relieved. As the boy expressed it, "Of course she had to find another home for me." Later the boy confessed that he had been for several years tortured by two alternative fantasies, one that his parents were murderers; the other that he had an unbearable odor. We are much too ready to assume that another person cannot bear the truth. Only when an untruth has become so necessary to a person that he or she cannot live without it is it wise not to face the truth. We must remember, however, that reality is only one of the three helping elements. It cannot be introduced without empathy and support.

Reality as Difference

We sometimes call a piece of reality deliberately introduced into a helping situation a piece of difference. It may be a fact. It can conceivably be an opinion, although we need to be careful that it is not a prejudice or a personal point of view irrelevant to the helped person's need. Unskilled workers are, as we have said, full of inappropriate difference, and they introduce pieces of difference in inappropriate ways. *We do this when we blame others for their situations and preempt their problem solving with advice and with prescriptive instruction. Inappropriate difference is what happens when we set ourselves up as good and moral and imply that others could be too if they were just like us.*

How do we know when difference is appropriate? I would suggest at least four criteria for appropriate difference. The first, and perhaps the most important, of these is that there is sufficient likeness – understanding, common purpose – to assure the helped person that the difference is not a personal attack. People can, after all, say things to other people who know that they love them that they could not possibly say to a stranger.

Secondly, the difference must be expressed in the helped person's terms. Often the most useful little bits of difference can be expressed by using the helped person's own words. A welfare worker was interviewing a deserting father, who rather naturally was trying to excuse his desertion. His statement was that he could not bear not being master in his own house. "You know," said the worker, "that's the strangest way I've ever heard of being master in your own house, to run away from it."

Thirdly, there is a somewhat elusive quality about the person who is ready to accept difference. There is an element of challenge, of projecting an image and watching to see how you are going to respond to it. This was very obvious in the deserting father's words. This is perhaps the least concrete of our criteria. It is a sense one gets, an understanding of the process of image projection, a knowledge that a projection is being made for a purpose. The helped person is really saying, "Will you buy this image of me?" and if you do, you only strengthen the image and make the real self less accessible.   The last criterion has to do with empathy and support. It is briefly that one has no right to introduce difference or reality unless one is prepared to help the person one is helping with the shock. Reality by itself is harsh. It is only reality approached with empathy and support that is a true helping process. Indeed we might restate the whole method of help as "facing people with reality with empathy and support." To face someone with reality and leave them to handle it alone is cruelty, not help.

Problems in Using Reality

The fear of not being able to handle the repercussions is one of the chief obstacles to introducing appropriate difference. Obviously to tell even a small percentage of those one is trying to help that they are unpleasant people would be a poor rule in practice. In most cases it would result in the very reverse of helping. It could only be done when the worker is sure that the client recognizes her desire to help. Just as people can tell "home truths"- in itself an interesting term- to those who are sure of their love and interest, so a helper can risk difference with someone who trusts her. Sometimes one can pick up an inherent contradiction in what the seeker for help may say or do. Sometimes one may have to say to someone, "You say you enjoy doing this but you don't sound like it." Body language, too, often betrays what a person is feeling. So does tone of voice. The classic example is that of the counselor who told a mother that her child needed more loving if he were to behave better. The mother came to the next session dragging the child into the office and said, "You were wrong. I've half killed this brat loving him and it hasn't helped a bit."

Playing Devil's Advocate

Another form of difference which can sometimes be of help, providing again that it is kept within a framework of likeness, consists in the speculative assumption of exactly the opposite of what the helped person is asserting, so that he may gain strength in demolishing your argument. This is, in fact, the function of the devil's advocate in a canonization procedure. What a devil's advocate says is, in effect, "Have you considered the possibility that we're on the wrong track altogether? Let's look at that possibility." This is a form of difference that can only be used when the helped person is fairly sure of himself; when, in fact, all that he needs is to move from a tentative statement to a forthright claiming of what he knows and believes.

Reality and "Tact"

Reality also means being direct. Helping persons, unfortunately, have acquired something of the reputation of being rather "wily birds" who tread delicately and never quite say what they mean. This is sometimes described as "tact" or "consideration" but so easily becomes either evasion or a way of gently manipulating someone else to do what you want him to do and at the same time think that it was his own idea. One area in which the reality of the situation needs to be very clearly expressed is that of the helping relationship itself. It includes what will or may happen, the probable consequences of actions, the authority and rights each person has in the situation, who can tell whom to do what, and the conditions under which help is being offered. Concealed power is both unfair and generally unhelpful. The worker from the juvenile court who minimizes its authority and presents it only as wanting to be "of help" without making clear that it will enforce this "help" is trying to buy relationship at the cost of the truth, and she will end up having neither.

Do Not Justify Reality

A further requirement of reality is that it must be presented as it is, without attempts at justification. The moment one does this to reality, one robs it of its primary helping value, which is that it exists outside both helper and the helped person and is something that they can both look at together, as a fact, and without a predetermined mental attitude toward it. To justify, or to explain, means that one claims the reality as "good" and that the helped person is wrong in being angry at it. It raises the possibility that it could be different and nearly always ends in a wrangle between the helped and the helping person about what might be instead of about what is. Helper and helped person need to be on the same side of reality.

The Right to Fail

But there is one use of the word "reality" which helpers should avoid. Unfortunately, the word is often used in professional social work literature to mean the social worker's estimate of the client's capabilities. A course of action is seen to be unreal if, in the social worker's opinion, the client is attempting something beyond his power. But this assessment, although it may be common sense, is not reality for the client. It is merely a judgment on him. What is real is what such plans would cost him and the very real possibility that he might fail. As David Soyer points out, people have the right to fail and may not in fact be satisfied with a second best until the impossible has been attempted. Sometimes, too, people surprise one. To elevate into reality a diagnosis, however careful, is presumptuous and is, in all too many cases, a disguised form of protectiveness.

Being Nice

Reality is perhaps the hardest of the three elements to hold to for any sensitive person. None of us likes to be the bearer of bad news. We do not like seeing people hurt, and reality often hurts. Americans in particular find great difficulty with it, since American culture puts a high premium on considerateness and on not "hurting people's feelings," which makes plain speaking very difficult. If anyone doubts this – and paradoxically many Americans think of themselves as outspoken – one need only compare American and British book reviews or political comment. There is a deep tradition in our culture of being "nice." face reality with someone often feels like being "mean," although it can be ʾously helpful. Even professions which have something of a tradition of ʾ" and no nonsense" about them have apparently developed a need ʾelves gentle and understanding.

Empathy

In order to help someone else with reality, one has to show empathy for him. Empathy is the ability to know, or to imagine, what another person is feeling and, as it were, to feel it with him without becoming caught in that feeling and losing one's own perspective. It is not, let us be very clear, a way of softening reality. Empathy needs to be clearly distinguished from two other responses to people in trouble, sympathy and pity. The three responses have sometimes been described as feeling "like" someone (sympathy), feeling "with" someone (empathy), and feeling "for" someone (pity), but I find these prepositions somewhat difficult. The real difference between them lies in the amount and the kind of difference from the helped person that the helping person maintains.

In sympathy there is little difference. The helping person feels as does the person she is helping. She shares the same feelings, identifies herself with his interests, becomes aligned with him, loves and hates the same things. The helper who feels empathy on the other hand, understands the feelings that the other has about the situation, knows, as we have said, that "it must hurt," but does not claim these feelings herself. The helper who feels pity also retains her difference. She does not get overwhelmed by the troubled person's feelings. Emphasis is on the difference between her and the person she is helping, and the likeness, or understanding, is for the most part, lost. Sympathy, as we have described it, is not entirely useless. There is some value in the precept to "rejoice with those that do rejoice and weep with those who weep." It is good to know that one is not alone and there are others who feel as you do. This may seem like an exaggerated sympathy. But this is one of sympathy's problems. We often hear it said that one can have too much sympathy for such and such a person (or such and such a group of persons). This is perfectly true. Sympathy can very easily become a weak emotion, and it can confirm a weak person in his weakness. Empathy is both a strong and a strengthening emotion. Because of the difference that the person who has empathy retains, she never condones or confirms weakness but enlists the troubled person's feelings in the attempt to overcome it. One cannot have too much empathy. But – and here, perhaps is the rub- empathy very easily slops over into sympathy. Sympathy is much the easier emotion. It is very easy to get caught in someone else's feeling system and to begin to identify with it.

An Act of the Loving Imagination

I have spoken of empathy as an emotion, and purposely so. It is, of course, formally an act, but an act based on feeling. The best description I know of it is an "act of the loving imagination."

Both "act" and "imagination" are important words here. Empathy is much more than knowing intellectually what another must be feeling. It always involves the ability to enter into this feeling, to experience it and therefore to know its meaning for the other person and the actions that are likely to flow from it.

There is in fact a paradox here which it is very hard to explain in ordinary, rational terms. Both to feel and to know is necessary if the purposes of empathy are to be fulfilled. Nothing carries less conviction, or is likely to fall so wide of the mark, as an attempt at empathy that is purely intellectual. The purpose of empathy is to convey feeling, not knowledge. But because feeling is communicated by so much more than words – by gestures, tone of voice, facial expression, and bodily posture, which are too complex to be capable of dissimulation – an assurance of feeling can only be communicated if this feeling actually exists.

In my experience, the facility of empathy can be trained, if not fully taught. While there are certainly people who have a natural empathy for others, there are also those who can release a great deal of loving imagination once they can free themselves from stereotyped reactions to people and once they become aware of their tendency, in some situations, to respond negatively, or sympathetically rather than empathically.

To learn empathy one has to be free from the kind of blocks that are thrown in one's path by liking and disliking people, by lining oneself up either for them or against them, instead of just caring about them, whether one likes or dislikes them. And this comes largely from self-knowledge. It is not so much that a person stops liking and disliking as it is that he or she learns to control the consequences of such feelings. Empathy also depends on knowledge, and on encounters with people who are quite different from oneself.

Knowledge of social conditions and some of the causes of feeling can also be of help. But empathy does not in fact need to be too precise. There is always something of the tentative about it, an acknowledgment that feeling must be present, and probably within a given range, and an invitation to the helped person to express his feeling more precisely. That is why the statement which we have used to typify empathy is not, "I know how it hurts," but "I know that it must hurt."

The empathy which is needed, at least in the beginning of a relationship, is largely directed toward the struggle through which the helped person is going, his fear of help, his wanting and not wanting to get well, the frustrations of his efforts to solve his problem by himself, and this is common human experience, although not always recognized as such. There are times when one can convey empathy in a subverbal manner, but generally it needs to be expressed verbally. I find that many young helping people can feel empathically, but they find it difficult to put their feeling into words.

Support, No Matter What

The third element in the helping factor is support. This has two aspects, material and psychological. Material support, the means to accomplish the task, may or may not be present in the helping situation. It is not generally part of either psychotherapy or problem-related counseling. When it does occur in these, it takes the form of technical know-how of some kind, whether this be marital techniques or where to find a school for one's child. In some helping it is, however, the most visible part and is thought of by many people as all that there is to help. It is what helping gives, whether this be money, opportunity, or know-how. Nor, as we have said, can it ever be considered unimportant.

People need money, opportunity, education, and technical assistance to implement their decisions.

But people also need psychological support. They need to know that they are accepted and that the helping person will not give up on them. She will not be shaken in her desire to help. Even if helping proves impossible, she will still care about the person she is helping, "no matter what."

Support Even When Help is Not Possible

Particularly she will not desert the person she is trying to help because that person disappoints her or makes what she believes to be an unwise or immoral decision. It is true that there are two or possibly three situations in which this decision or failure may mean an inability on the part of the helping person to go on being the primary helper. One situation occurs when the decision, or some limitation in the helped person, removes him from contact with the particular source of help with which he has been working. A student may fail and be required to leave a school; a child's behavior may be such that for the protection of others he must leave a Children's Home; or a client may no longer be eligible for assistance. There is also always the possibility that the helped person's problems may be such that no one knows at present how he can be helped. His resistance to help may be so strong or his ability to act so lacking that no skill that we have at present would be enough to provide any help. He may need, for his own protection or that of society, to be institutionalized, or control measures may have to be substituted for help. This decision would, however, have to be made with the greatest reluctance and with the knowledge that the helped person had not so much proved himself unhelpable as we unable to help him.

But even should one of these conditions separate helped person and helper, the principle of support means that the separation is not accompanied by rejection. The helping person still cares. She still respects and is concerned about what happens to the other. Sometimes indeed it is in this very act of separation that helping really begins. I once knew a child in a Children's Home for whom all attempts to help her had seemed unsuccessful. When she faced trial in another city, the housemother, rather than rejecting her, asked the administrator to allow her to support the child through the trial. It was, not unnaturally, to the housemother who had shown concern for her at her worst that this child turned later in life. It was she whom she consulted over the problems of working and marriage. And six years later when her younger sister, who had remained at the Children's Home, became restless, she offered her sister a home and help.

It goes without saying that support is also hard to practice. It is very easy to reject those who have let one down, especially where this has been accompanied with anger, blame, or ingratitude. Hard, but possible

To Support is Not to Condone

It is extremely difficult for human beings to get away from the idea that to care about a person in trouble is to condone what he has done. It does not seem sufficient to allow someone to suffer the consequences of his act or to take his punishment for it. We seem to need to reinforce societal sanctions by disassociating ourselves from those who have offended against them, instead of seeing these people as those who need our help the most. Part of this is reaction against unrealistic helping. To be concerned about a delinquent is not to approve of delinquency. Nor is it to excuse it, to throw all of the blame onto conditions or onto society. Poor conditions and poor heredity undoubtedly make it harder for acceptable decisions to be made, but not all people make such decisions under these strains. The helper whose support is a disguised form of exculpation, who believes that the delinquent had no choice but to act as he did, is being unrealistic. She is indulging rather than helping.

But, in part, our unwillingness to try to help rather than to punish the delinquent is our fear of ourselves. It is a strange reflection on how delicately balanced our "good" and "bad" decisions must be that we get so angry at the bad ones. This anger has its roots in fear. We fear that we, too, may be tempted. It has long been known to psychiatrists that those who are most violently opposed to some social ill are often those to whom it is secretly most attractive, and that the faults we see in others are often the ones we are most prone to ourselves.

Support may be indicated in a number of ways. Sometimes the mere fact of being there is sufficient. Sometimes it is indicated by physical contact, particularly with a child. Sometimes it includes a direct offer of help, or making clear that one is available. Sometimes it is a matter of giving someone an introduction, of "breaking the ice" for him in facing a new experience. One must, however, remember that the statement is not simply, "I am here to help you," but "I am here to help you if you want me and can use me." Support is at its best when it is consistent but unobtrusive and it must be always be unconditional.

Using the Elements

Reality, empathy, and support, then, are the three elements of the helping factor. They still do not tell us how to help in any given situation, which is perhaps something no one can tell another, but they do give us some idea of how we need to approach the problem. But even here they are not prescriptions. No one can go into a helping situation saying to herself, "I will be real. I will be empathic. I will offer support." The very effort would distract her from listening to the person she wanted to help.

But they do offer a way of looking at our own helping efforts. In every helping situation that has gone wrong, or been less than productive than one hoped, it is good to ask oneself three questions:

1. Have I been able to face reality with this person, or have I glossed over the truth or offered false reassurance?
2. Have I been able to feel and express real empathy, or has empathy been lacking, or limited ("You can share your feeling with me as long as you don't feel so and so")?
3. Have I offered real support, or has it been conditional support ("I will continue to try to help you as long as you don't do this or that")?

An honest answer to these three questions often shows us what has gone wrong.

All three elements are necessary to each other. Reality without empathy is harsh and unhelpful. Empathy about something that is not real is clearly meaningless and can only lead the client to what we have called nonchoice. Reality and empathy together need support, both material and psychological, if decisions are to be carried out. Support in carrying out unreal plans is obviously a waste of time. The three are in fact triune, and although in any one situation one may seem to be predominant, all three need to be present. *Alan Keith-Lucas found significant connections between the concepts of reality, empathy and support and the roles of the Trinity in Father, Son and Holy Spirit. Effective helping requires all of the components of relationship with the God who provides ultimate helping.*

The Triune God and Triune Helping

God the Father, the Creator, is in Christian thought certainly the author of reality—both the reality of things and that of the moral and natural law, as well as of the laws of causality and consequence. God is also the Wholly Other, the One who is different, who is "God, not man."

Biblical history, as Christians read it, certainly suggests that this reality was not enough. Human beings alone could not, of their own will, face reality and change in relation to it. There was needed an act of empathy, and there is no more characteristic or total act of empathy than that described in the Incarnation – God who became human and yet remained God, "who in every respect has been tempted as we are, yet without sinning." Indeed, the whole theology of "very God and very man," the refusal to consider Jesus as either less than God and not wholly human, or part human, or part God and part human, the insistence that he is a single person, is a struggle with the problem – how a person can feel another's pain and yet remain separate from it. Both require the concept that in doing two apparently different things at the same time, one does not do either less completely.

Again, the name given to the Spirit, both in the King James Version and in the Prayer Book, is the Comforter. Although the word "comfort" has suffered a weakening of meaning since the seventeenth century, its derivation is from *cum*, meaning " with" and *fortis*, meaning "strong." A comforter is therefore one who is "strong with you," and there is no better one-sentence definition of support.

Reality, empathy, and support—Father, Son, and Holy Spirit—the analogy may seem blasphemous at first. It is, however, logical that if the person asking for help is analogous to the recipient of grace, then the helping person must, as far as it is possible for a finite, fallible being to do so, model her helping on the actions of God. Help becomes in a new sense the expression of one's religion, not just as the term is often used, one's general but unspecified goodwill toward others, but what one actually believes. It follows, too, that the helping process is real, that it is not merely a collection of pragmatic principles, that it deserves much closer study than it has received to date, and that where we have got it right, it is much more than a set of useful techniques.

How Might We Distinguish a Christian Helper from A Secular One?

A Christian of Grace will not…

- Pass judgment because she is conscious of herself as a sinner dependent on grace.
- Practice direct evangelism or witness unless involved with members of her own faith or people who are seeking a Christian solution to their problems as witnessing is often not good helping. People rarely change and grow because they are told that they should. Most people one helps do not as yet trust the helper. The best witnessing occurs in service responding to the client when the client is ready to deal with spiritual matters. Many clients' life experience has been such that they have no reason to believe the Word of God. If one's only knowledge of having a father is that he beats one or deserts one, how can one believe in a Heavenly Father?
- Focus on spiritual help rather than tangible concrete help. Christianity is the only religion whose founder prayed for daily bread, and in Matthew 25, Jesus did not say, "I was in need of counseling and you counseled me," but "I was hungry, thirsty and naked."
- Ask if someone deserves to be helped. Jesus was more concerned with the character of the person who gives aid than the character of the person who receives aid.

Qualities of a Christian Helper…

- Looking for evidence of grace in those she helps
- Steadfastly standing by people and caring even when help seems impossible
- Standing by her values despite current culture
- Holding institutions accountable for justice, kindness, and walking humbly with God
- Staying tough enough to deal with reality with clients
- Continuing to exhibit true humility and willingness to learn, grow and discriminate new practice trends

Drawing it all Together

In the last several chapters of Giving and Taking Help, Alan Keith-Lucas helps us to understand that not everyone is called and gifted to helping, particularly professional helping as articulated here. Helping persons are human persons with our own needs and interests. This makes self awareness or "self knowledge" even more important as we consider our own areas of prejudice and personal challenge when working with clients. Awareness of our "similarities and differences" is the beginning of good helping. Helping persons use specific knowledge, values and skills, but not to the exclusion of spontaneity and natural helping. Keith identifies that helping persons particularly need courage to be real with clients, to take risks that they won't be liked, to give clients the right to fail. We also need the kind of humility, awareness of sameness, that lets us relate to clients without judging their differences and that keeps us grounded in serving others, knowing that ultimately our treatment of others as persons worthy of respect and care will bear fruit. It is not necessary that we "like" all of our clients. It is necessary that we care and that our concern includes respect rather than control as Powell, Sherwood, and Ressler so powerfully pointed out in their recent writing about his work.

Understanding the nature of the helping relationship and process allows us then to incorporate specific guidelines for our professional helping. Keith suggests that we always start with what the client is asking us for rather than what we think they should be asking for from us. We must tune in then to the feeling behind or underneath the words even before the client articulates them. Good helping means not taking the client's feelings personally and recognizing that feelings are neither good nor bad – they simply are. So we focus on the issues rather than denying the feeling by reframing the situation. Real helping, according to Keith, means letting clients choose even when the choice includes failure and then continuing in the helping relationship to formulate the reality, the problem, the alternatives, and the opportunities. Clients can become overwhelmed by the enormity of their reality. Partializing the problem or concern allows them to focus on work that can be done now and in subsequent meetings when the helper and helped can explore how well the choices and resultant actions are working out. This evaluation of practice with the client allows modification of the plan of action in response to ongoing results. So the helper, rather than offering imperatives and control, may offer advice that the helped can consider and that can be modified as needed. This early definition of client self determination is essential to the Christian social worker.

For Keith, helping another person is more like consultation than it is diagnosis and treatment. The helper comes alongside the person who is facing a difficult reality and helps the person figure out exactly what it is and what the available options might be, including what they each would take or cost to pursue. The helper tries to support the person in making what Keith calls "choice" rather than "non-choice" responses to the difficult situation. "Choice" responses come in two basic kinds: (1) To fight against the difficulty and to change it (when change is possible); or (2) To accept and constructively use the difficulty (when change is not possible). "Non-choice" responses come in two parallel basic kinds: (1) To deny the reality of the difficulty and seek ways to avoid it; or (2) To "accept" the difficulty in a way that leaves the person crushed. The helper can neither fully know when change is possible nor take responsibility for what the helped person is able to choose and do.

The key to helping is not the answer to "why?" but the answer to 'given your current circumstances, what next?" When we help clients to modify choices and decisions that aren't working and celebrate those that are, we bring with us movement toward long term success for those clients. Helpers cannot help everyone and must use self awareness and assessment to know when to refer clients for more specialized help. Even in those cases, the helper can often assist with immediate needs while the referral is being made. Keith-Lucas also identifies ways in which the principles of helping contribute to positive outcomes in more adversarial settings including court, business, arguments among colleagues and in therapeutic settings including work with children and families. His bottom line: "The helping process, in fact, works." (p. 157.) Recent attention both to his principles and his practice affirms the importance of work with families and the importance of respect for clients in all circumstances.

The values that drive the helping process, according to Alan Keith-Lucas, are centered in the value of each person and the person's freedom to choose without being judged, leading to the use of feelings and relationship to help people find "their own way." He finds those values for himself grounded in and growing out of Judeo-Christian values, even as he acknowledges that the values of the helper have significant influence over the process. Helpers are frequently agents of social systems with power; the helper's willingness to empower clients rather than exacerbate the power differential is key to successful helping.

Alan Keith-Lucas describes God, the Father, as the author of reality; Jesus, the Son with us, as empathy; and the Holy Spirit as comforter and supporter. The use of the helping factors of reality through empathy and support sums up the professional use of self that is taught in so many helping programs and models the integration of Christian faith and professional helping practice.

Notes

[1]Readers wishing to cite this work should do so understanding and noting that a substantive portion of this chapter is taken from the following work: Keith-Lucas, Alan. (1994). Chapters 5 and 10, *Giving and Taking Help*. Revised Edition. (Editor: David Sherwood). St. Davids, PA: The North American Association of Christians in Social Work. The original work was published in 1972.

[2]Note of thanks and acknowledgement: Special thank you to Dr. David Sherwood who edited Giving and Taking Help, and reviewed this manuscript and whose commitment to respecting Keith's words and wishes made this chapter possible.

CHAPTER 17

ETHICAL INTEGRATION OF FAITH AND SOCIAL WORK PRACTICE: EVANGELISM

David A. Sherwood

As I sat down to write this, I couldn't help but think of the old adage, "Fools rush in where angels fear to tread." Probably right. However, it seemed like it might be useful, at least as a conversation starter, to take a stab at trying to apply Christian and social work values, ethics, and practice principles to some of the controversial issues that seem to raise questions for most of us. I want to focus on the relationship between professional social work practice and evangelism.

I need to warn you from the beginning, on the other hand (my naturally cautious side coming out), that I do not propose to state the definitive Christian position on anything. What I do propose to do is to try to think through the application of Christian and social work values and practice principles to working with clients regarding evangelism in ways that maintain integrity for both our clients and ourselves.

Not Just an Issue for Christians

The first point I want to make is that this matter of trying to figure out how to have integrity and competence in the handling of our own beliefs and values as we work respectfully and ethically with clients is not just an issue for Christians. Every single one of us comes to our work profoundly influenced by assumptions, beliefs, values, and commitments that we hold in part on faith. That is part of what it means to be a human being. Our reason and our science can only take us so far, but they can never take us to the bottom line of values and meaning. "Facts," to the degree that we can ever really discern them, never answer the "so what" question. Values are never derivable from facts alone.

The first level of self-disclosure and informed consent that every social worker owes is critical personal self-awareness. This can be spiritual, religious, ideological, or theoretical—any "meta-narrative" that we use to make sense out of our experience of life. "Hello, my name is David and I'm a Christian." Or, "I'm a Buddhist," "I'm an agnostic," "I'm an atheist," "I'm a logical positivist," "I'm a behaviorist," "I'm a post-modernist." Or a Punk or a Goth or a Democrat or a Republican, for that matter. I'm not saying that we should greet our clients this way, but I am saying that we need to be aware of our beliefs and be self-critical in regard to how they affect our work.

What are my fundamental assumptions, beliefs, and values? How do they affect my practice? The way I interact with my clients? My selection of theories and interpretation of facts? It is not simply a matter of *what* I believe (important as that is), but *how* I believe it, how I handle my beliefs, which in itself comes back around to the nature of my value commitments.

Lawrence Ressler frequently tells the story of his MSW class at Temple University with Jeffrey Galper, who announced at the beginning of the semester, "I am a Marxist, and I teach from a Marxist perspective." I hope this meant that he had achieved this critical personal self-awareness that I am talking about and that his self-disclosure was in the service of facilitating informed consent on the part of his students. The proof of the social work practice pudding, of course, would be in his conscientiousness in not imposing this view on his students, his willingness to permit or even facilitate disagreement. Of course, the more deeply held the beliefs and the greater the disagreement, the more difficult it is to support self-determination. This is true even when self-determination is one of the core values believed in.

So—integrating faith and practice is not just a Christian thing. It is a human thing. Those who don't understand this basic truth are the ones who may pose the greatest risk of all of "imposing their beliefs on others," precisely because they may think that they are not susceptible to the problem (Sherwood, 2000). However, the rest of my comments are going to be addressed primarily to Christians in social work, even though I think the basic principles will apply to those who are not Christians. Many of us may feel tempted to "evangelize" in more way than one.

Addressing Spiritual and Religious Issues with Clients is Not (Necessarily or Normally) Evangelism

"Talking about God" with clients is not necessarily or normally evangelism. This is an important distinction. For too long social workers (secular and otherwise) have tended to "solve" the problem of evangelism by avoiding spirituality and religion and offering a blanket condemnation—"Thou shalt not discuss spiritual and religious issues with clients." If you do, it is automatically presumed that you are "imposing your own values on clients." This happens in spite of overwhelming evidence that issues of meaning and purpose are central in the lives of clients, that spirituality and religion have great importance to many people, and that religiously-based groups, congregations, and organizations are vital sources of support for people (as well as barriers, at times).

Well, sometimes social workers do impose their values (religious, political, or otherwise) on clients and it is an ethical violation when they do. I would stress that when this happens it is a violation of Christian ethics as well as social work ethics. But deliberately avoiding spiritual and religious issues is professional incompetence. The presumption has often been that spiritual and religious issues should simply be referred to chaplains or other clergy. In what other important area of life would social workers condone such a policy of withdrawal and referral? How can we say we deal with the whole person-in-environment while ignoring one of the most important dimensions of people's lives (for good or ill)? Or how can we claim competence in dealing with diversity while ignoring or misunderstanding such a fundamental kind of diversity (Sherwood, 1998)?

The short answer is that we can't and shouldn't ignore spiritual and religious issues. The key is that we must do it from a client-focused and client-led perspective. This normally means that we may not ethically engage in evangelism with our clients. Exceptions would typically be when we are practicing in a faith-based context with a clearly identified Christian identity and with clients who clearly express informed consent. Even then, it is not transparently obvious that evangelism would be appropriate. I hope I can make it clear why I say this.

Proclamation versus Demonstration of the Gospel

A perhaps simplistic but none-the-less useful distinction is this: It is always ethical and appropriate to demonstrate the gospel to our clients, but it is seldom ethical to proclaim the gospel to them in our professional role as social workers.

The Bible describes evangelism in the sense of demonstrating or living out the gospel as the calling of every Christian. "Therefore be imitators of God, as beloved children, and live in love, as Christ loved us and gave himself up for us" (Ephesians 5:1-2). "We know love by this, that he laid down his life for us—and we ought to lay down our lives for one another. How does God's love abide in anyone who has the world's goods and sees a brother or sister in need and yet refuses help" (I John 3:16-17).

The profession of social work provides us all with unique opportunities to demonstrate the gospel of Christ—to give to our clients the grace-filled gift of knowing what it feels like to be treated with love and justice, what it feels like to experience caring, grace, forgiveness, trustworthiness, honesty, and fairness, what it feels like to be treated with respect and dignity as a person with God-given value. Often our clients have few opportunities in their lives to be in a respectful, non-exploitive relationship. The power of this experience can be transforming. It can even be a form of "pre-evangelism," preparing the soil for the good seed of the gospel proclaimed.

We do not all have the same part to play in God's work in a person's life. The New Testament frequently talks about varieties of gifts among the various parts of the body, and evangelism is one of them (Romans 12:3-8, I Corinthians 12:4-31, Ephesians 4:11-16). "What then is Apollos? What is Paul? Servants through whom you came to believe, as the Lord assigned to each. I planted, Apollos watered, but God gave the growth" (I Corinthians 3:5-6). As Alan Keith-Lucas has said (1985, p. 28):

> Paul said that faith was the gift of the Spirit, which is true, but what we can do as social workers—and we do have a wonderful opportunity to do so—is to show such love and forgivingness that a confused and desperate person can understand the Spirit's message when it comes.

A consideration of the Parable of the Sower may be helpful here. The seed only grows to maturity when there is good ground to receive it. But stony or even shallow ground can be converted to good ground by the addition of nutrients (love) or ploughing (facing reality) or breaking up of clots (getting rid of blocks) and perhaps what social workers can do for the most part is to be tillers of the ground, rather than the Sower, who must in the long run be God Himself. It is true that certain men and women, powerful preachers or prophets, may act, as it were, for God as sowers, but even they have for the most part audiences that have some readiness to listen.

On the other hand, explicit evangelism of clients (proclamation) in professional social work is almost always unethical. Why? What are the values and ethical principles involved?

Values and Practice: The Principle/Practice Pyramid

Christian and social work values largely agree at the level of principles. However, we may disagree on both the foundational assumptions/worldviews which support the principles, the rules/strategies for prioritizing the values principles when they conflict, and the practice implications of the value principles.

It helps me to conceptualize these relationships in the form of a "Principle/ Practice Pyramid." The base of the pyramid is formed by our fundamental worldview and faith-based assumptions (religious or not) about the nature of the world, what it means to be a person, the nature of values, and the nature of knowledge.

On top of and growing out of this foundation sits our core values or principles. As a Christian I understand these to be the "exceptionless absolutes" of love and justice. The social work Code of Ethics might say (and Christians would agree) that this includes service, social justice, dignity and worth of the person, importance of human relationships, integrity, and competence.

On top of and growing out of this "principle" layer are the moral rules that guide the application of the principles to various domains of life. These are "deontological" parameters that suggest what we ought to do. Biblical examples would be the Ten Commandments, the Sermon on the Mount, and other Biblical teachings that help us to understand what love and justice require in various spheres of life. In the social work Code of Ethics, these would be the specific standards relating to responsibilities to clients, colleagues, practice settings, as professionals, the profession, and the broader society. These rules can guide us, but they can never provide us with absolute prescriptions for what we should do on the case level.

At the top of the pyramid sit the specific cases in which we are required to use the principles and rules to make professional judgments in the messiness of real life and practice. It is here that we will find ourselves in the most likelihood of conscientious disagreement with each other, even when we start with the same values, principles, and rules. The short answer for why this is true is that we are fallen (subject to the distortions of our selfishness, fear, and pride) and finite (limited in what we can know and predict). And even more challenging, our principles and rules start coming into conflict with each other on this level. It is here that we have to resolve ethical dilemmas in which any actual action we can take is going to advance some of our values (and the rules that go with them) at the expense of some of our other values (and the rules that go with them).

The Use and Limits of the Code of Ethics (and the Bible): Ethical Judgments Are Required Because Legitimate Values Come into Conflict

Ethical analysis and decision making is required when we encounter an ethical problem and at the case level we cannot maximize all values simultaneously. In my paradigm, the definition of an ethical problem or dilemma is that we have more than one legitimate moral obligation that have come into some degree of tension in the case that we find ourselves dealing with.

For example, I believe in client self-determination (one legitimate moral obligation) and I believe in the protection of human life (another legitimate moral obligation). Most of the time these values do not come into conflict. However, now I have a client who is threatening to kill his wife. I now have an ethical problem in which any action I take will compromise one or more of my moral obligations. Values and ethical principles can and do come into conflict on the case level.

It is important to realize from the beginning what the Bible and Code of Ethics can do for us and what they cannot. They can give us critical guidance and direction, but they can never give us prescriptive formulas that will tell us exactly what to do in every case, precisely because in the particular instance not all of the values can be fully achieved and not all of the rules can be completely followed. The Code of Ethics (1999, pp. 1, 2-3) says it very well:

> Core values, and the principles that flow from them, must be balanced within the context and complexity of the human experience...
> The Code offers a set of values, principles, and standards to guide decision making and conduct when ethical issues arise. It does not provide a set of rules that prescribe how social workers should act in all situations. Specific applications of the Code must take into account the context in which it is being considered and the possibility of conflicts among the Code's values, principles, and standards.

Sometimes one of these biblical rules or Code of Ethics standards may have to give way to another in order for us to come as close to love and justice as the situation allows. At the case level, we are always going to have to take responsibility for making judgments that prioritize our values and approximate the good we seek as closely as we can.

Ethics and Evangelism

So, what are some of the core values and ethical principles from the Bible and the Code of Ethics that relate to evangelism with clients? I'll try to list a

306 David A. Sherwood

few and give some comments, although several of them overlap and interact with each other. And I would say that they all fall under the Biblical absolutes of love and justice.

1. The Great Commission:

Well, what Christians call the "Great Commission" is certainly one of these core values, the reason we are exploring this issue in the first place. While the imperative "Go therefore and make disciples of all nations" (Matthew 28:19) was given to Jesus' original disciples, the New Testament makes it quite clear that bearing testimony to the good news about Jesus' healing and saving work on behalf of humankind is in some sense the responsibility of all of us who are disciples of Jesus Christ. And if the gospel of Christ is true, what could be more important for people to hear? This value is real for us and explains why we struggle with the question of evangelism in our professional roles.

2. My Calling and Role:

Remember our discussion above about demonstration and proclamation? While it is true that not only evangelists bear witness to the gospel, it is also true that our particular calling and role in a given situation has a great impact on what it is appropriate for us to do. If you are convinced that your calling from God is evangelism in the sense of direct proclamation, then you should be an evangelist and not a social worker (or a nurse, or a car salesman, or a loan officer). Under what auspice are you working? What are the functions associated with your role? My father-in-law for many years demonstrated the grace and love of Christ in his role as a bank teller at the Potter's Bank and Trust in East Liverpool, Ohio, including taking money out of his own pocket to make sure that certain poor customers were able to get at least a little cash at the end of the month. But he could not, and did not, use his position to hand them tracts with the cash. As a social worker you may at times find it appropriate to share your faith directly, but most of the time you won't.

3. Self-Determination:

From the first chapter of Genesis on, the Bible presents a picture of human beings endowed with the gift and responsibility of choice with consequences. We are presented with the paradox and mystery (on our level of understanding) of God's sovereignty and our freedom. God is depicted as calling us, but not coercing us, warning us, but not protecting us. Conscience and commitment cannot be compelled, even though external behavior might be. Self-determination is also a standard of the Code of Ethics (1999, p. 7), growing out of the principle of the inherent dignity and worth of the person. If ever a social work value stood on a theological foundation it is belief in the inherent dignity and worth of every person. While I may have my perceptions of what might be best for my clients, I have no right to compel or manipulate them to that end. I do have a responsibility to help facilitate their ability to exercise their self-determination, including the exploration of available alternatives and their possible consequences, so that their choices are as informed as possible. God grants us the fearful dignity of self-determination; we can hardly try to deny it to our clients, explicitly or implicitly.

4. *Informed Consent:*

A fundamental component of informed choice is informed consent, another standard of the Code of Ethics (1999, pp. 7-8). Informed consent essentially means that people should know what they are getting into and agree to it. This principle interacts intimately with the next one— integrity. Informed consent is one of the key determinants of whether or not evangelism with clients is ethical. Related concepts are agency auspice and client expectations. Why are clients coming to your agency or to you? What expectations do they have? Is there anything upfront that would lead them to understand that the sharing of your religious beliefs or evangelism would be a likely part of their experience with your agency or you? I have found that even in explicitly faith-based agencies there surprisingly few times when direct evangelism is the appropriate focus or outcome of interaction with clients. Christian clients struggle with the same kinds of issues as other clients. Sometimes we can help them sort through how their beliefs are resources or barriers for them. But sometimes religious clients want to use "religious talk" to avoid coming to grips with their issues. There would be almost no cases in a public or secular private agency when direct evangelism an appropriate focus or outcome of interaction with clients.

5. *Integrity:*

Honesty and integrity are core Biblical and social work values. A number of "rules" derive from this value, such as truth-telling, trustworthiness, and keeping agreements. Some of the standards in the Code of Ethics deriving from this principle come under the general heading of "Conflicts of Interest' (1999, pp. 9-10). These rules are particularly relevant to the question of engaging in evangelism with clients. These rules say, "Social workers should be alert to and avoid conflicts of interest that interfere with the exercise of professional discretion and impartial judgment" (1999, p. 9). They speak to the importance of setting clear, appropriate, and culturally sensitive boundaries and being careful of dual or multiple relationships with clients. Of particular relevance to the issue of evangelism is the standard that says, "Social workers should not take unfair advantage of any professional relationship or exploit others to further their personal, religious, political, or business interests" (1999, p. 9).

So, What about Evangelism?

The main reason that evangelism in the context of a professional social work relationship is normally unethical is that it almost always involves the risk of exploitation of a vulnerable relationship. It usually involves taking advantage of our professional role and relationship with our clients. It lacks the integrity of informed consent. And even when there seems to be a certain consent or even request from the client to go through the evangelistic door, it is the social worker's responsibility to be the boundary keeper. I am not saying that there can never be a legitimate open door under any circumstance, but I am saying that the social worker, acting in the professional capacity, bears a heavy weight of responsibility to avoid taking advantage of the client's vulnerability.

I think most Christians have little difficulty understanding the analogous rule in the Code of Ethics which says, "Social workers should under no circumstances engage in sexual activities or sexual contact with current clients, whether such contact is consensual or forced" (1999, p. 13). We also understand that it is the social worker's responsibility, not the client's, to maintain these boundaries. I hope no one is offended by my comparison of sexual exploitation to evangelism. Clearly there are significant differences. I believe in evangelism and I do not believe in sexual exploitation. However, we also need to understand the way in which evangelism in the context of a professional relationship does have some significant likeness to sexual exploitation, or any other taking advantage of the professional role.

For example, evangelizing a client coming to a public Rape Crisis Center would be unethical and, I would say, un-Christian. She is in a physically and emotionally vulnerable situation, there is nothing about the sign on the door that would lead you to believe that her coming is even giving implied consent to evangelism, and she is trusting you for specific kinds of help. The nature of your role and relationship means that you have a special responsibility not to exploit that role. What you can most certainly do with her is to give her the opportunity to experience what it is like to receive "grace," love and justice; what it is like to experience respect, caring, support, trustworthiness, honesty; what it is like to not be taken advantage of.

It would also probably be going much to far to ask her, "Are you a Christian?" Even if she said no, and you quietly moved on, the question would hang in the air, coming from a representative of the Rape Crisis Center to a person in a state of vulnerability who had a very particular reason for coming to this agency. How would she read that? How would it affect her response?

However, it might be quite competent and ethical professional practice to use a more appropriate probe that could be stated in "non-religious" terms— "This must be hard. Is there anything in your life that helps you get through things like this?" Then if she mentions something about her spiritual or religious beliefs, you are in a position to make a better judgment about how you might help her, even perhaps including engaging spiritual and religious resources. That could be good "spiritually-sensitive" social work practice (Sherwood, 1998).

Even then, you would be faced with the necessity of using good assessment skills, discernment, and judgment. For example, you would think that praying with clients in Christian agencies would be obviously the right thing to do. However, some clients are "religious" manipulators, and consciously or unconsciously use the appearance of spirituality to avoid dealing with hard issues. When a client says, "Let's just pray about that," or "I think we just have to trust the Lord," you have to try to discern whether doing that is helpful or their way of avoiding dealing with their anger, fear, abusive behavior, or whatever else they may need to face.

No Prescriptions, but Guidance

You will have probably noticed that I have avoided words such as "never" or "always" in what I have said. This is quite deliberate, and goes back to my earlier comments about what ethical principles and rules can do for us and what they can't. They can give us meaningful guidance but they can't give us simple formulas to prescribe our response to every situation. Although I might have come close to it, I have not argued that evangelism is never compatible with our professional role as social workers. I have tried to suggest ethical considerations as we try to make our best judgments about how we relate to our clients.

Morally and practically, a sense of certainty is highly attractive. Who doesn't want to be sure that they are "right" and that they are doing the right thing? But that level of certainty is often not available to us as human beings. And yet we do have to decide and act. These judgments always require prioritizing our values based on the best understanding we can achieve at the time regarding the relevant values involved and the potential consequences of the choices available to us.

Ultimately, how we respond in these hard cases has more to do with the moral virtue or character that we have developed, by God's grace and through God's Spirit, than it does with the specific facts and theories we have learned. Lord, help us to be people who hunger and thirst for your "more excellent way" (I Corinthians 12:31).

Note

This chapter is a revised version of an article first published in 2002 in *Social Work & Christianity*, *29(1)*, 1-12.

References

Keith-Lucas, Alan. (1985). *So you want to be a social worker: A primer for the Christian student*. Botsford, CT: North American Association of Christians in Social Work.

NACSW. (1999). *Code of ethics*. Washington, DC: National Association of Social Workers.

Sherwood, David A. (2000). Pluralism, tolerance, and respect for diversity: Engaging our deepest differences within the bond of civility. *Social Work & Christianity*, *26(2)*, 101-111.

Sherwood, David A. (1998). Spiritual assessment as a normal part of social work practice: Power to help and power to harm. *Social Work & Christianity*, *24(2)*, 80-89.

CHAPTER 18

MOVING MOUNTAINS: CONGREGATIONS AS SETTINGS FOR SOCIAL WORK PRACTICE

Diana Garland and Gaynor Yancey

There is a huge role for ministry in social work. It goes back to social work roots. The biggest challenge is for social work to take a step back and learn the culture of that community—the congregation. Then social work can move mountains (Caiden, a congregational social worker).

Beth was originally employed as a part-time college minister in the congregation where she now serves as associate pastor; the senior pastor quickly saw the value Beth could bring if she were full time on the congregational staff. The pastor launched a partnership with a denominational agency to employ Beth in a full time capacity, with some of her time dedicated to serve in the community as the agency's representative. Over time, however, the congregation will gradually phase in her entire salary and the agency will phase out. Beth oversees the congregation's community ministry, benevolence ministry, and tutoring ministry in a nearby school. She is supervising social work interns from the state university who are serving with her in a congregational setting. She sees herself as a "minister whose skill set is social work." Beth incorporates the work she is doing into the weekly worship of her congregation. She loves preaching and someday wants to be a senior pastor; she has two masters-level degrees: a Master of Divinity (M.Div.) and a Master of Social Work (MSW).

Carl began his work as a denominationally-affiliated missionary in an inner city of the Northeast. He planted a congregation, which began in a café and then moved to an abandoned gay bar. He has the MSW, M.Div., and Doctor of Ministry degrees. He sees himself as a pastor primarily, although his social work education is invaluable to him. Many of his congregants have chronic mental illness; some are homeless. A day treatment facility for persons with mental illness is located across the street from his church. There is great ethnic diversity in the congregation, reflecting the surrounding community. Carl directs numerous children's programs and other activities in the community center that is also his congregation. Mission teams from churches in other states hear about Carl's congregation and present challenges when they come intending to "help those in need." Carl works to empower his congregation to minister to the mission teams, aiming to make the relationship between the visitors and his congregation mutual.

Earl was teaching in a college and serving as an elder[1] in his congregation when he learned 11 years ago that his congregation wanted to hire a counselor. He talked to the other elders and they hired him. He provides counseling to those in the congregation, although never to those he also serves as elder. He had to limit the congregational involvement of one man who was acting in sexually inappropriate ways with children. Based on that experience, he has developed policies designed to protect children from the potential of abuse in the congregation's programs. He has started sexual addictions support groups. He also leads Bible studies and educational programs that deal holistically with a variety of life challenges such as parenting, caring for older adult parents, and chronic illness. He is known as a social worker but his title is "counselor minister." He sometimes struggles with serving people in his own faith community and the resulting boundary issues from that relationship.

****

Some of us remember preschool Sunday school and Vacation Bible School leaders teaching us what a church is, using their own hands as a model: "Put your hands together, lacing your fingers together pointing down to your feet, with your first fingers pointing up to the sky, and make your thumbs touch each other. You have made a church!" They went on into the sing-song little rhyme: "Here is the church, here is the steeple." They turned their hands over, now with fingers pointing heaven-ward, and we copied the action and said the rhyme together exuberantly: "Open the doors, and here are the people," and we wiggled our finger-people, upright, the church now unfolded. This interactive exercise was meant to teach us an important lesson – churches are not buildings or places, but rather, the people themselves who gather to worship and live their faith in service together.

Jesus referred to his followers as "my church" (NRSV, Matthew 16:18). Denominations may also refer to themselves as a "church," such as the Presbyterian Church (USA). The concept of church, or the followers of Christ across time and place, takes expression locally as a "congregation," the people who come together regularly and voluntarily for worship at a particular location (Ammerman, 1997; Chaves, 2004; Warner, 1994; Wind & Lewis, 1994). A congregation is the be-steepled gathering of wiggling people we symbolized with our preschool hands. The two key characteristics of congregations in the United States are that they are *voluntary* and they are *communities*. The people of a congregation gather regularly for worship, religious education, and companionship, as well as to serve both one another and "neighbors" locally and globally (Luke 10:25-37). The congregation functions as a primary community for their members, providing a feeling of belonging and an opportunity for mutual need-meeting (Ammerman, 2002; Garland, 2008).

Srs. Mary Vincentia Joseph and Anne Patrick Conrad were the first to publish in the social work literature about this setting for social work practice, using the term "parish social work" (Joseph & Conrad, 1980). The term "church social work" has also been used to refer to social work in congregations as well as in denominational and para-church agencies and programs (Garland, 1992), before the term "faith-based" came into popular parlance (e.g., Governor's Advisory Task Force on Faith-Based Community Service Groups, 1996). We have chosen to use the term "congregational social work" to be congruent with the growing congregational studies literature (e.g., Ammerman, 1997, 2001, 2005; Chaves, 2004). As the examples of Beth, Carl, and Earl illustrate in the opening vignettes, a congregational social worker provides professional services and leadership, part-time or full-time, in and through a congregation, whether the employer is the congregation itself or a social service or denominational agency working in collaboration with congregations.

Characteristics of Congregations

The research base describing and informing congregations' involvement in social services has grown over the past 25 years.[2] There are several characteristics that, together, make congregations a unique setting for social work practice: (1) they are host settings for practice; (2) they are social communities; (3) they are voluntary organizations; (4) they have a distinctive culture; (5) they spin off programs and services; and (6) they are advocates for justice and care for vulnerable populations.

1. Congregations are host settings for social services.

Churches are not primarily social service agencies. Instead, they are *host settings*. In a social work context, host settings are organizations that have purposes other than or broader than the provision of social services, though those broader purposes can be enhanced by what the social service professions can offer. For example, hospitals and schools are also "host settings" for social work. They are not social service agencies, but their purposes – treating illness and educating students – are furthered by social services. Hospital social workers help plan for care after a patient leaves the hospital, and help families deal with the crises of difficult diagnoses and with making care plans. School social workers address family and community factors that keep children from succeeding in school. The services of social workers presumably help both schools and hospitals to accomplish their primary objectives.

If social workers in a host setting forget that they are there to help the organization achieve its goals, and instead try to transform the setting into a *primary* setting, one whose central purpose is providing the social services needed by individuals and families in the community, the host setting may object and even withdraw from social work involvement. Hospital social workers can address the needs of patients and their families, and may even be able to advocate for their needs with community structures and even the hospital itself. They probably cannot expect the hospital to support their spending time working with street gangs in order to decrease the violence in the community, however. Even though such work may be indirectly related to the health of patients and their families, the hospital will probably see working with gangs as peripheral, not an activity to invest in if it means less energy is directed toward the direct care needs of patients and their families.

Serving people and advocacy for social justice are central to the mission of the church. The admonition that God expects us to meet the needs of others (e.g., Matthew 25) and to "seek justice" (e.g., Micah 6:8) is common throughout scripture. Congregational social workers must keep in mind, however, that service and advocacy are important for the church because they point to the kingdom of God, because they are the fulfillment of Jesus' teachings, and because engaging in them grows the faith of Christians. The social service and social action of congregations are anchored in and reflective of the church's mission (Garland, 2010; D. R. Myers, Wolfer, & Garland, 2008; Rusaw & Swanson, 2004).

The volunteer service of church members is a tremendous resource to social services in our society; it has been estimated that churchgoers donate about 1.8 million hours of services in the United States annually, and it is well documented that congregations provide a wide array of social services to their communities (Cnaan et al., 2002; Cnaan et al., 2003; Filteau, 1993) . Because of their engagement, societal leaders may view congregations as resources to be mined for addressing the needs of communities, seeking their resources of money and volunteers for their social service programs. For example, a signature of the faith-based initiatives of federal and state governments has been governmental leaders calling on congregations to become social service providers. At least one state governor suggested that if every congregation would "adopt" a family receiving governmental financial aid, our country could end the need for welfare programs, despite the evidence that congregations do not have the capacity to replace public responsibility for the complex social welfare challenges in our society (Chaves, 2003, 2010; Chaves & Wineburg, 2009; De Vita, 2005; Farnsely, 2004; Farris, Nathan, & Wright, 2004; Wineburg, 2005; Working Group on Human Needs and Faith-Based and Community Initiatives, 2003; Wuthnow, 2004). Many congregations are inundated with requests from organizations needing volunteers and financial support. Moreover, exhortations from government leaders to become involved are almost never the catalyst for congregational engagement. Instead, the engagement has to be sought because leaders within the congregation see the engagement as an important expression of the congregation's mission (Garland, 2010).

2. Congregations are social communities.

A *community* is the set of personal contacts through which persons and families receive and give emotional and interpersonal support and nurturing, material aid and services, information, and new social contacts. The people in a community know us. They are people we can borrow from or who will take care of a child in an emergency. They are the ones from whom we can obtain news and gossip so that we know the significant and not so significant information that gives shape to our lives. *All* persons, both children and adults, need community. Because children are so dependent on others for their survival, their vulnerability in the absence of community is more apparent. Even self-sufficient adults living alone seek the company of others, if only for recreation and social support. We all need community when we become ill, injured, or feel threatened. In our world of increasing independence and loss of neighborhoods as social networks, of more adults living alone and more children in single-parent households, congregations can be a social community for people in a way that social service agencies can never be (Brueggemann, 1996; Garland, 1999a, 1999b, 1999c; Saleebey, 2004).

3. Churches are voluntary organizations.

A hallmark of American society is that religious participation is voluntary. If people do not like what is happening in one congregation, they simply move to another, or stop participating altogether. In some denominations, the congregation's financial assets and facilities belong to the denomination. However, in other denominations, even the congregation's participation in the denomination is voluntary. If the congregation does not like what the denomination is doing, it may choose to withdraw and to affiliate with another denomination, to remain independent, or simply to withhold its financial support from the denomination.

Dealing with conflict and maintaining interpersonal relationships have much greater import for social workers in congregations than those in other professional settings. Volunteers do the work, and supervising and consulting with volunteers is dramatically different than supervising and consulting with employees. Volunteers have to continue to see the significance of what they do in order to be motivated; there is no paycheck at the end of the week that keeps them coming even when they are tired and discouraged. Dealing with difficulties in the work of volunteers requires considerable skill and sensitivity.

4. Congregations have distinctive cultures.

Congregations have distinctive cultures; they have their own language, non-verbal symbols, norms, and patterns of relationships. They have historical identities that shape their current understanding of themselves. Like families, congregations develop over time, going through stages that shape the community's life together (Ammerman, 2002, 2005; Carroll, Dudley, & McKinney, 1986; Garland, 1994). The Bible, theology, and doctrine are central repositories of beliefs and values that are central to a congregation's culture. For example, the concepts of the "family of God" and Christian hospitality provide a foundation for social action in behalf of homeless and isolated persons and social ministry programs designed to include them in the community. Biblical teachings on the value and role of children provide impetus for child welfare services and child advocacy. Understanding these distinctive characteristics of the congregational context is just as important for effective professional practice as it is to understand the culture, history, and current life experiences of an ethnic community as a practice setting.

5. Congregations spin off programs and services.

Sometimes church start ministries that take on lives of their own, outgrowing the congregational settings where they began. Many child care centers, schools, and social services programs may be started by a congregation and continue to use the congregation's facilities, but they may seek incorporation as an independent organization (Garland & Chamiec-Case, 2005). For example, All Saints Church in Los Angeles began an AIDS ministry when few programs for AIDS patients and their families existed. Over time, the church was able to obtain funding from government and private sources outside the congregation. As volunteers outside the congregation began working with the AIDS ministry and as the program grew, it became incorporated and independent of the church. Releasing programs and services to become independent entities may allow them to pursue funding sources not available to the congregation, hire staff members outside of the faith community, or protect the congregation from legal liability for the work of the organization.

6. Congregations are advocates for justice and care for vulnerable populations.

Congregations not only care for those in need around them, but they can advocate for just treatment of vulnerable persons – those in poverty, immigrants, vulnerable elderly, and children. Many social movements, such as the ending of the African slave trade, protection of children by child labor laws, and civil rights for women and for African-Americans, began and were carried by congregations or by members of congregations who were motivated by their faith. Jesus made the declaration of Jubilee, a radical economic redistribution designed to end poverty (Leviticus 25:10-28), central to his mission and identity and called his followers to continue that mission. The salvation proclaimed includes not only deliverance from sin and physical healing, but also it involves a gift of economic and social well-being for the poor and powerless (Luke 4:16-21). Jesus taught his followers to "seek" the kingdom of God (Matthew 6:33), to yearn for the justice of God's ways to be their ways. Seeking justice means tackling the social structures that lead to poverty, violence and discouragement in the lives of God's children (Hessel, 1992; Singletary, 2005).

Describing Social Work in Congregations

The characteristics of congregations delineated above suggest that congregations make fertile soil for social work practice. Indeed, social workers have been working in congregational settings since the beginning of the profession more than a century ago. The first social workers – "friendly visitors," "deaconesses," and "home missionaries" – were women in congregations (Garland, 1994; Myers, 2006; Scales, 2000). Social work became the route into ministry for women who were denied access to clergy roles.

Our Research on Social Work in Congregations

Over time, social workers also began to be added to the professional staffs of congregations. In 1987, one of us (Garland) attempted to define the field in a survey of 21 such social workers (1987, 1992). More than 20 years later, a second study used the research instrument from the 1987 study and surveyed 30 congregational social workers who responded to an e-mail notice about the study sent to members of the North American Association of Christians in Social Work (NACSW) (Northern, 2009). The congregational social workers surveyed had a variety of job titles, as well as job responsibilities, ranging from direct practice to social ministry leadership. They saw themselves as social workers, although others in the congregation often did not recognize their professional identity.

In order to understand better the current realities of congregations as settings for practice, we have built on these surveys by conducting qualitative research using in-depth telephone interviews of social workers employed full-time or part-time in congregations.

Research Subjects

We sent information about the research project on the electronic listserves of three organizations: NACSW, the National Association of Deans and Directors of Schools of Social Work (NADD), and Baccalaureate Program Directors of Social Work (BPD). The NACSW listserve posting asked for social workers employed full-time or part-time in a congregational setting to volunteer for the study. We asked social work deans and directors to identify any alumni in this practice setting. Based on these three electronic postings, we made contact with 114 self-identified congregational social workers in Christian and Jewish settings. We interviewed by telephone the first 28 who contacted us as part of this first study in a series of research studies on congregational social work. The 28 congregations represented are located in 21 states and represent 10 denominations. [3]

The Interview

Telephone interviews ranged from 26 to 120 minutes, with an average length (mean) of 68 minutes. The two authors conducted all the interviews, encouraging interviewees to tell stories and follow their own thoughts. Interview questions evolved as we conducted the early interviews and learned what other questions emerged, and how we could ask questions that better elicited the detailed descriptions of social work in congregations we were seeking. Sample questions include: What programs and areas of responsibility do you have? How does the church see you or identify you? How do other social workers in the community see you? What do you especially enjoy about your work? Like least? How does the concept of calling or vocation relate to your work? We probed for stories and specific examples to illustrate what they told us.

At the conclusion of the interview, we asked demographic questions and entered responses into a separate database. Those data included denominational affiliation of the social worker and of the congregation, the official title of the social workers, educational degree(s) and year(s) of graduation, gender, ethnicity, age, number of years in social work practice, number of years working with congregations, and number of years in the current position.

We audio recorded the telephone interviews and then transcribed each interview. The interviewer assigned each subject, location, and congregation pseudonyms prior to transcription, and those pseudonyms were used in place of actual names during the transcription in order to protect the identity of subjects and their congregations. Tapes were erased after transcriptions were completed. We placed transcriptions in an encrypted computer with names and code names in a separate file from the transcripts.

Analyzing the Data

We inserted each transcript into a database and used the software package, Atlas-Ti, to code the data. We developed codes that identified the themes in the interviews, developing code families as we worked, returning to old codes and renaming and sorting them as we progressed through the transcripts. Both authors, along with two graduate social work students, coded each transcript. We independently coded two transcripts and then compared the extent to which we applied the same code to the same interview quotation. Our inter-rater reliability was established at 85%; that is, we both applied the same code to the same segment of the transcript 85% of the time. We developed 439 codes that we applied to 1531 interview segments in the 28 transcripts.

After completing the initial coding, the investigator who conducted the interview also wrote a brief case description of the interview subject; the three case descriptions at the beginning of this chapter are excerpts from these descriptions. We used these descriptions as a reference when studying the data, to put quotations in the larger context of the social workers' stories.

Findings

The social work degrees these professionals hold are: the BSW (n=3), MSW (n=21), and PhD (n=4). We asked for the names of the schools in which they completed their BSW and/or MSW. Ten of the respondents completed their professional education in religiously-affiliated college or university settings; 17 studied in public or non-sectarian private universities. Most also have obtained formal theological education in addition to their social work education (n = 19).[4] Ten also have master degrees in religion or ministry, one has a doctoral degree in ministry, four have certificates in theology, two have undergraduate degrees in religion, and two are currently enrolled in divinity programs.

Nineteen of the respondents are female; 9 are male. The median age is 36; the mean age is 46. The sample is overwhelmingly White, with one African-American and one Jewish respondent.

These social workers have been serving professionally for an average (mean) of 16 years, with a range of 2 to 34 years. They have been working an average (mean) of 9.5 years in congregations, with a range of 1 to 26 years. Many had worked in the same congregation for most of their careers, with an average of 7 years of service in their current congregational setting, and a range of 1 to 26 years.

Professional Identity

A number of the interviewees said that the congregation knows and sees them as a social worker, even though they have different job titles. Their titles are quite diverse and include the following: Associate Pastor, Christian Counselor, Church Counselor, Clinical Therapist, Consultant, Counselor Minister, Executive Director (n = 3), Director, Director of Community Ministries (n = 3), Director of Social Outreach, Director of Special Ministries, Mission Outreach Coordinator, Pastor (n = 4), Pastor of Care Ministries, Social Worker, Spiritual Director, and Youth Minister.[5]

Most of our respondents value licensure. For example, Inez bears the title "Christian counselor" for her congregation. She noted that she displays her state social work license prominently and makes sure that clients know her professional role. We began asking subjects if they were licensed after the first 5 interviews. Of the remaining 23 interviewees, 18 were licensed and 5 were not.

Professional Roles

We wondered what roles congregants and the larger community envisioned social workers taking in the congregation. Several respondents talked about how they became recognized as a leader with valuable expertise as the congregation experienced their work over time; we labeled this "emerging role legitimacy." As Beth described this process in her congregation, she commented wryly and somewhat proudly that now "the congregation calls on me for everything."

Despite the fact that only one of the interviewees actually carries the official title "social worker," many of their roles are familiar in other social work settings. The social work roles we identified include change agent, clinician/counselor, connector/networker, and researcher. Even Adam, with the title "pastor," said, "the majority of the time I am utilizing my social work skills." Jeanie said that what she is doing is "strengths-based social work; it is old-fashioned social work where I identify needs and find solutions." Nevertheless, two role expectations seem distinctive to congregations: that of minister/pastor and of friend/community member.

Minister/Pastor

The fact that most of these social workers carry titles that contain words such as "minister," "ministries," "pastor," and "missions" rather than "social worker" is not devaluing of the social work profession and identity. Rather, it is an expression of the congregation's mission and organizational character as a host setting for social work practice. Congregations are "communities of faith," a collection of people attempting to practice their religious beliefs through the service that the social worker leads. A number of these social workers are responsible for leading the local and global missions of their congregations, and the social services they provide or facilitate are the current expression of that missions focus. The impetus for service lies in the congregation's religious beliefs about God and what it means to be faithful.

Friend/Community Member

In congregational social work, the roles are often not only dual, but often multiple, ropes of intertwined threads that include not only the professional relationship, but also the expectation that the social worker be a member of the community that both gives and receives from others. That expectation may be expressed in the assumption that the social worker will join the congregation, contribute financially, serve as a volunteer (choir member, Sunday school teacher), and share personal life as well as professional competence with others in the congregation.

Leading Programs and Services

These social workers provide leadership in a wide variety of programs of a congregation. Initially, we tried to organize those programs by the target of service – those that are designed to serve members of the congregations versus those designed for people outside the congregation in the geographic community and beyond. Quickly, we learned that dichotomy did not work for two reasons. First, the congregants are themselves community members, as well as the reverse – congregational activities and services draw members of the surrounding community into the congregation. In addition, many programs involve congregants serving persons in the larger community or in communities in other geographic locations ("mission" trips beyond the local community), so that the program simultaneously is addressing the human needs of those served as well as discipling and mentoring congregants to "love thy neighbor" through service.

When asked who they served, these social workers identified a wide variety of people and groups. We have organized these target populations by broad categories, illustrating that the populations served are almost as broad as social work itself. They include persons who represent:

- Diverse ages: children and youths, college students, families, older adults
- Diverse locations: persons in other countries or other regions in this country, persons in the same urban area but in communities outside the congregation's neighborhood
- Diverse life circumstances: women, parents, gangs, persons who are gay or lesbian
- Diverse physical or emotional life challenges: deafness, developmental disabilities, mental illness, physical illness, substance abuse
- Diverse current problems and crises: domestic violence, living with HIV/AIDS, homelessness, food insecurity, imprisonment (or a family member imprisoned), poverty

The programs that congregations provide address human needs (feeding programs, child care), intervene in crisis (social support), create community (activity programs, recreation, educational services), lead spiritually (religious instruction), educate (family and life skills classes), counsel (clinical services, marriage preparation), and collaborate with other organizations in the area.

Core Social Work Tasks

These programs and services call for a wide variety of what we have named social worker "tasks," i.e., the actual daily activities of the social worker. Many of these tasks are similar across the widely differing congregational activities, such as administering programs or recruiting and managing volunteers. We identified the core tasks of congregational social work that span the various programs and services as: (1) organizing people and systems; (2) administering programs, services and one's own resources of time and energy; (3) assessing; (4) advocating; (5) developing and maintaining relationships; (6) thinking creatively and critically; (7) leading and serving groups; (8) establishing boundaries and safety; (9) teaching, mentoring, and supervising; (10) obtaining resources; (11) evaluating and researching; (12) preaching and other public speaking; and (13) developing knowledge and skills specific to the community in which they are serving.

1. Organizing people and systems

Several of these social workers spoke of creating or organizing systems and programs by bringing people together to address an issue or a task. For example, when Kelly was concerned about anti-Semitic content broadcast by their local radio station, she organized volunteers to provide alternative content and develop a broad strategy of community education. In addition, Kelly and the volunteers successfully advocated for the radio station to adopt new rules about what could be broadcast.

- These social workers described organizing such varied services as:
- single mothers' support groups
- an interfaith organization involving congregations providing shelter for homeless persons,
- refugee resettlement
- chapters of Sexual Addictions Anonymous
- a support group for children whose parents are divorcing
- day camp for community children
- a ministry providing social workers in public agencies with groceries to distribute to families
- a survivors' skills group for women focusing on home and auto maintenance
- international short-term mission trips.

2. Administering programs, services, and one's own resources of time and energy

Almost all of these social workers are doing a wide variety of activities, including leading persons and programs. They train and support volunteers, plan and lead educational and activity groups, and chair community committees and boards. For example, in his role as Pastor of Care Ministries in a very large congregation, Daniel is responsible for 12 different areas of ministry, from the congregation's counseling center to the food pantry. He is also responsible for staff assignments to lead weddings and funerals, and to visit members who are hospitalized or experience trauma or transition.

The following are some of the administrative activities these social workers engage in: preparing and managing budgets; supervising staff; training, managing, and supporting volunteers; setting criteria for receiving services; leading the defining of the mission, goals, objectives development of the congregation or its programs; leading others in developing and staying connected to the vision for their work; forming, developing, and working with governing or advisory boards; and planning events such as missions fairs, yard sales in the community, and one-time mission outreach programs and trips. A key task, then, is balancing multiple roles and responsibilities. The social worker has to decide what to do, what to delegate, what not to do, and set priorities. Adam used a circus performer illustration:

> When I was a kid you often saw the guy with the plates on the poles and he would be spinning all the plates and one would go falling. That's what I feel like all the time. I get one moving and I have to get to the next one but also go back to the last one.

The challenge is not only the knowledge and skills for widely varying tasks, but the balancing of those tasks so that the most important (valued) tasks are not neglected in responding to emergent situations. Moreover, the work expands in response to the social workers' demonstrated abilities and interests, so that, over time, they take on more diverse and expansive responsibilities. Therefore, administration includes the social worker's own time, energy, focus, and skills – the professional self – and not simply the programs and services. The more fluid and autonomous the role, the more self-management is needed.

3. Assessing

Congregational social workers conduct assessments of resources and challenges in the communities their congregations serve as well as the client systems that are part of their practice. Several of these social workers have conducted or led volunteers in conducting comprehensive community assessments.

4. Advocating

They also work at the community and social policy level as an advocate for groups and communities unable to advocate for themselves. For example, Ben, the full-time pastor of an ethnically diverse nondenominational Christian congregation, keeps his eyes on policies that affect the community and the congregants that he serves. The African American male dropout rate is high in his city, so he attends school board meetings and city council meetings, advocating for policy changes that will support African American boys staying in school. Becky, who ministers with the deaf community, consults with agencies in the city to make sure that the deaf community receives the services they need. "Empowerment" was a term these social workers commonly used.

5. Developing and maintaining relationships

The heart of the work of these social workers, not unlike professionals in other contexts of social work practice, is building relationships with congregants, clients, volunteers, community members, community leaders, and between community organizations. They described developing relationships across lines that normally divide the community and using their relationships to forms bridges and collaborations. Carl, the inner city pastor, described how he learned to pull his community together:

> I've learned that I have to work with everybody, regardless of whether they are Christian or not. We have to work together. Pastors who don't have a social work degree are unwilling to cross that line; I think they don't trust God, and I trust God. I trust that God will accomplish God's purposes. They get caught up on the theology and that prevents them from helping people.

Perhaps even more challenging than working across political, cultural, and ethnic lines in a community is to work with other congregations of the same faith tradition. For example, Kelly says of her work, "We're the only organization in town that tries to get all of the Jewish players to make nice, not just fragment and do their own thing, but to try to work as a community."

These social workers talked about engaging the communities they serve. They must learn the nuances of communication in the community and be able to speak the language and be sensitive to the culture of congregational life.

6. Thinking creatively and critically

These social workers bring creative and critical thinking to the work of the congregation. For example, Carl, pastor of a small congregation in the heart of an impoverished inner city, is helping the volunteers who come to serve in their inner city neighborhood to identify the strengths of the community and not see only the needs. Adam helped the volunteers in a homeless feeding program to learn ways to communicate respect for those they served in small acts, such as not stacking loaded plates of food on top of one another but to serve as they would serve guests in their home. At the denominational level, Fay suggested that the denomination should not tell congregations what social justice issues to engage and how, but rather, allow congregations to develop their own agenda for their own context.

It was evident that for several of these social workers humor was the creative way they manage and reframe the unexpected. For example, Carl described one of his parishioners who is a client at the day treatment program for persons with chronic mental illness, across the street from the congregation:

One day, Steve was knocking on the door and said, "I want Jesus for my savior. And I want to be a minister." We talked, and I asked what he meant by wanting to be a minister. He said, "When you take your robe off, I want to fold it. When you need a drink, I'll bring you water." One Sunday he brought eight rolls of toilet paper. I asked what he was doing with all that toilet paper. He said that when he bought it, there were all those rolls and he only needed one so he brought the rest to the church. That's what we all ought to do: keep only what we need and give the rest away. Little things like that happen, and God teaches me so much. I started coughing one Sunday during worship and he asked if I needed a drink of water. So he brought me orange stuff in a glass. I asked what it was and he said "Slimfast; I figured you needed that more than water." I'm a little large.

Beth noted that she has gained a reputation for knowing how to handle the unexpected, the out of the ordinary – to bring creative problem solving to virtually any situation. She sees that as the "social work skill set:"

> I jokingly say I'm the minister of all things weird. If anything strange happens in our building, I am the person to call. On Sunday, a man's electric wheel chair stalled out on the way up the hill, and they called on me. I think it's a compliment. It says "We trust you."

Beth brings a fresh perspective to the expectation that she can handle anything and everything; she sees it as a sign of being seen as trustworthy.

7. Leading and serving groups

Much of the activity in congregational life takes place in groups, and these social workers spend much of their time leading and serving in groups. They lead and facilitate educational groups designed to provide knowledge, values, and skills for facing life challenges, as well as support groups. They lead or serve on task groups, such as committees, boards, coalitions, task forces, and action groups.

8. Establishing boundaries and safety

Social workers have multiple roles with congregants and community members; they may find themselves expected to be counselor, worship leader, religious teacher, neighbor, and friend – all with the same people. They juggle the contradictions that come when their community is also their employer.

Dual relationships – professional relationships and friendships – cannot be avoided; they are expected and so these social workers have sought ways to manage relationships that protect community members, clients and themselves from exploiting those dual roles. Codes of ethics primarily deal with the more blatant boundary violations, such as engaging in a sexual relationship with a client. They do not provide guidelines for the daily challenges that may arise in congregational social work, however, such as sitting with one's own family across a church supper table from a client's family. Several of these social workers described the ways they related informally as a friend or in friendly ways with those they serve.

An extensive example below from Chris shows how complicated relationships can become, and the complexity that may result for social workers as they decide how to think about relationship boundaries. Chris spent two hours taking a homeless client, Michael, in his own car to an appointment at the mental health center to get his medication for schizophrenia renewed, a task normally expected of a family member or friend.

> The psychiatrist was very grateful that I was there, to help facilitate communication between the two. After the appointment, we went to lunch and talked over sandwiches.

Chris went on to explain that one of Michael's difficulties was maintaining his medication, but not taking too much so that he runs out by the end of the month. So the congregation's community center locks the medication in the safe for him, and Michael comes to the community center and dispenses himself a week's worth of medication at a time. That way, if he loses his medication, he only loses a week of medication and not two months' worth, which was what he had been carrying around with him. The dispensing arrangement also makes Michael responsible for his own health management. Chris mused that he is not technically Michael's case manager, but they are even closer than that; "I am his minister and friend." That relationship, and the medication dispensing strategy, developed over time; then a crisis came in their relationship. Chris had seen that Michael was in a process of "spiraling down" into a self-destructing pattern of not taking care of himself and not taking his medication:

> I sat him down and said, "Michael, this is your choice to do this and to make some of the decisions you've been making, but we're not going to sit by and watch you do it. I'm either going to be here to help you and for us to work together on this, or you're going to have to do this somewhere else, and you can't come to church here."

Michael continued to refuse to take his medication and was ignoring the other conditions Chris had placed on congregational participation. So Chris acted:

> I had to say, "You can't be here." And that was one of the hardest things that I've done since I've been at this church, to tell someone that they can't come to church.

Three months passed, and when Michael did not return, Chris went looking for him in the woods, where he knew Michael camped:

> He knew that he wasn't allowed to attend worship until he was ready to meet with me again and for us to renegotiate the conditions of his church involvement. And he knew that my door was open, that he could come and meet with me to renegotiate that, but he hadn't come through the door. So I went back out there and found him. I actually taped a note on a tree in the woods on a path that I knew he took, and he found it and he showed back up.

Chris's "conditions" for Michael's involvement are the behavioral expectations required for service one would expect in a social service agency, but they are less common in congregational life, and in the relationship between friends.

A number of these social workers have the responsibility of ensuring the physical safety of the community; they deal with physical threats and consider ways to prevent or respond to sexual and physical abuse in the community. Others described their tasks to be not only securing physical safety but also creating an environment of emotional security conducive to discussing difficult topics from religious doubts to sexual orientation. For example, when the issue of gay marriage became a divisive topic in her congregation's denomination, Caiden developed a Bible study curriculum that she led over a six week period, providing opportunity for congregants to study commentaries on relevant biblical passages and discuss how what they learned together related to their beliefs and attitudes.

9. Teaching, mentoring, and supervising

Like Caiden, several of these social workers provide religious instruction, including teaching from the Bible and the tenets of the religious faith. Inez says about the fact that she is designing a 16-session Bible study course, "It doesn't really fall under social work but I'm doing it, so I guess it is." Others clarified how they see religious education as professional social work practice. For Ben, it is because of the population group served: he leads a Bible study in the state correctional institution, as well as a transitional re-entry father's group for prisoners. For Gordon and others, it is the topics they address. In his work with adolescents, Gordon tries to address topics about which adolescents are curious, or with which they are struggling, helping them to explore what God might have to say about topics such as pornography and sexual orientation.

Many of these social workers are engaged in leading or supporting volunteers who lead educational programs within the congregation and larger community that resemble those found in other social service agencies. They educate for basic life skills such as financial management, car repair and "survival skills for women," personal hygiene, sex education, job interviewing, parent education, grief support groups, nutrition and cooking, smoking cessation, preparation for the "General Education Diploma" test for those adults who dropped out of high school and now want to finish their secondary education in preparation for college, self esteem and body image for adolescent girls, karate, and, basically, whatever would engage the community and strengthen the coping and resilience of individuals, families and the community.

10. Obtaining resources

Volunteers are some of the most significant resources that congregational social workers are responsible for within their congregations. A number of social workers are also involved in grant writing and financial development. Several described how they had to find and manage space in the congregation or the larger community for the programs and services of the congregation.

11. Evaluating and researching

Another important task that only a few of these social workers mentioned is evaluating the relative effectiveness of the work. Chris remembered a favorite social work professor telling a story: a person drowning in the river is rescued. If a second person is drowning, the rescuer will jump in the river again to save this second person. But if he has to rescue a third person, then the rescuer will subsequently march upstream to see who is throwing people in the river. Chris went on:

> Every so often, we sit back and say, are we putting on band-aids or are we really making a difference? We need evaluation tools.

He described how he has used a single-system research design to evaluate programs, measuring the state of the community prior to and then after program implementation. The fact that only a few of these social workers talked about evaluating their practice or conducting research on the effectiveness of the congregation programs for which they carry responsibility suggests that this evaluation and research needs much more attention, particularly since social work in congregations is still being defined.

12. Preaching and other public speaking

Almost half of these social workers said that they preach or otherwise make public presentations and speeches that serve to set the congregation's direction, call the congregation or the community to action, or provide spiritual leadership and guidance. Some are in staff positions for which this is a major responsibility, such as pastor or associate pastor; they preach virtually every week. Others preach occasionally, from once a month to once a year, often topically, on issues particularly relevant to social work – the relationship of faith and service, poverty and hunger, and advocacy for children.

13. Developing knowledge and skills specific to the community

Another major task for these social workers is developing and using knowledge, values, and skills that are required to be culturally competent in this setting. For some, cultural competence involves the dimensions of human life one expects to be relevant to professional social work, such as the cultures of the ethnic groups represented in the congregation and geographic community. There are also demands for cultural competence that are beyond the purview of the typical social work curriculum. For example, to be a competent Bible study leader, these social workers need knowledge about biblical texts and religious traditions.

Challenges

Respondents described the following challenges they have experienced in congregational settings.

The freedom, and responsibility, of deciding where and whom to serve

Congregational social work is very different than practice in an agency setting where a social worker often has a job description and a referral system that assigns clients. Because congregational settings are novel contexts for social practice, many of these social workers are defining their own work parameters, deciding where to focus their resources of time, finances, and volunteers. Deciding whom to serve is a perennial challenge – and opportunity.

Recruiting and working with volunteers

A central responsibility for many of these social workers is engaging and equipping volunteers for service through the congregational programs described earlier, so it is understandable that working with volunteers brings its own category of challenges. Chris, the pastor of an inner city church, is determined that his members will have the opportunity to serve, even though many live in poverty and are accustomed to being on the receiving side of social services. He illustrates the challenges:

> I find that our volunteers hide food around the church so they can come back and get it later. I have to deal with our own volunteers getting into fights with one another. There is so much of that, because they have so many crises in their life."

Equipping volunteers to make meaningful contributions is also a challenge, as David explained:

> There is a continuum: the easiest thing to do is to collect things to give away. The other end [of the continuum] is relationship. It seems difficult to get people to share their lives with others who will share their lives.

Managing interpersonal conflict

Relationships are the heart of social work; relationships with clients, colleagues, or community leaders. In every setting, then, relationships often create the most significant challenges. Congregations are both voluntary organizations and communities, meaning that they are held together – or not – by the relationships among the staff and congregants. David identifies helping people work through conflict in his congregation as a primary responsibility of his, and therefore, he has searched for the underlying hurts and unmet expectations that lead to conflict. He gave as an example the war over styles of worship, often expressed most graphically in the styles of music, as arguably the most heated and common of conflicts in congregations today. Says David: "I'm surprised by the extent of the conflict; I think some of that is grief expressing itself with seniors who see that the church is different from what it once was."

Another common conflict is over use of the congregation's building space. Kylie described their programming of basketball for five year olds in a large room in the church basement. The congregation's trustees were "upset" that the building might be damaged by the children's rough play. Kylie intimated that perhaps there were underlying issues; the program targets children in their neighborhood, children of a lower socio-economic level than the long-term members of the congregation. Chris experienced similar conflict when a group in the congregation proposed that their congregation use their building as an extreme weather shelter for persons who are homeless.

> Even with all of the contact [through our] ministries with persons that are homeless over the past several years, it was still a process

and struggle for the church as a whole to embrace that ministry. . . . We heard people at general church membership meetings say things like, "They're going to clog up the toilets; what if they hide in the closet and jump out the next morning."

The challenges expressed in interpersonal conflict thus range from whether or not to risk chipped paint on the walls if the neighborhood children are allowed to use the building to differences in theology. Because the congregation is a community, if the resulting conflict is not resolved through some process that reaches either consensus or tolerance for diverse opinions, the congregation risks the loss of members who simply can decide to drop out of this congregation or drop out of organized religious life altogether. In other social service settings, conflict may be tolerated; staff may not agree with the policies and decisions of management, but they learn to cope. In a congregation, people may simply leave.

The relationship of service and evangelism

Congregations are not social service organizations; rather, they are religious communities that gather for worship, for religious education, and for mutual support. "Worship" is the adoration of the divine, and for the Abrahamic religions of Christianity, Judaism, and Islam, that worship includes service to others, who are the presence of God in our midst. When we serve persons who are poor, or hungry, or alone in the world, we have served the King of Heaven (e.g., Matthew 18:5; 25:40. Therefore, religious education includes not only classroom learning of religious teaching but engagement in expressing that teaching through service. It is in those aspects of congregational life that social work provides leadership and service. Most congregations believe that they have truth that others can benefit from knowing and a lifestyle that others can benefit from living. Therefore, their understanding of service may include teaching others their faith and attracting new followers and members. That mission is appropriate for congregations as organizations, even though religious proselytizing may be considered inappropriate in a relationship between a social worker and a client.

Catarina describes how she has dealt with the congregation's mission of religious education; she has attempted to teach members that there are different ways of presenting the Christian faith. Instead of beginning with Bible teaching she suggests to the congregation that they build relationships with persons in the neighborhood through the services the congregation offers. "And then, little by little," she says, "through the exercise class, or the parenting class, or the nutrition class, parents start wondering, 'Why is this church doing this?'"

Policies and practices that are grounded in religious beliefs and values

Another challenge comes from the fact that congregations' beliefs and values derive, directly or indirectly, from interpretations of sacred texts and historical religious traditions. The beliefs and values of some persons and groups can be in direct opposition to the beliefs and values of others interpreting the same texts and traditions. Beliefs and traditions translate into policies and practices, and sometimes those policies and practices create challenges for the social worker. Some examples include appropriate leadership roles for women, and the acceptance (or not) of persons who are in various life circumstances: gay or lesbian, divorced, cohabiting, or parenting and unmarried. To illustrate, Daniel's congregation does not allow women to serve in leadership roles or to teach in Sunday School, except to teach other women and young children. From Daniel's perspective, these boundaries on women's roles are oppressive and not grounded in his own interpretation of the Bible. He has managed to place a few lay women in leadership positions in educational and support groups with one caveat: "I was given autonomy as long as the women who are leading aren't 'feminists.'" As Daniel said, the challenge is not working through interpersonal conflict, but deciding how to work in a setting in which your values conflict with organizational values.

> You've got to be careful. You've got to talk the way you're supposed
> to. You learn that…. If you want to work in the church, you've got
> to figure that out.

For Daniel, the struggle is deciding whether to leave or make compromises on some issues in order to continue to make a contribution, even a contribution toward change in the organizational culture that is so challenging for him. Of course, such struggles take place in other host social work settings as well. However, social workers in religious organizations and congregations may have additional dilemmas because they often believe they have experienced God's calling to this work, and that the work expresses their own faith. Moreover, the dissonance they are experiencing between their professional beliefs and values and the beliefs and values of others is taking place not only in their workplace, but also within their own communities.

Outcomes for the Social Worker
The congregational social workers we interviewed described how serving and leading in an organizational context has impacted their own careers and personal lives.

Beliefs and values shaped
Although many of them sought the opportunity to serve through a congregation as a way of living their own beliefs and values, they in turn found their beliefs and values to be challenged and shaped by the work. Adam finds himself learning from those he serves:

> For some reason, there tends to be a homosexual population of
> homeless persons here that's pretty large, and … there were several
> transsexual, transgender folks that would come to the service.
> Then I noticed that several of them were not homeless, but this is
> just where they come to worship…. One guy who dresses like a
> woman would always sit in the back and I would say "come sit up

here." He would say "No, I'm not worthy." I would say, "Sure you're worthy; God loves you just like he loves me. There is no distinction. Show me where that [his dress defining him as unworthy] is in the Bible." Those things impact you and change you.

Satisfaction, gratitude, and fulfillment

Gratitude for the work and satisfaction in it was a common theme described by most of these social workers. They find their work meaningful and fulfilling, but it was not just the positive outcomes in the lives of those they serve that were satisfying. Chris illustrates this in his description of how he forbade a man from coming onto the church property who was a potential threat to the safety of others. The very difficulty of that task, and his ability to handle it, knowing that he had protected vulnerable children, was satisfying:

> It was probably during the painful process of kicking the person out of the church, as strange as that sounds, because I got the sense that I didn't see anybody else around who would have had the skill set to get the church to that point responsibly.

These social workers derive great satisfaction in seeing their fingerprints on the lives of others; they see and are told of the difference they have made in people's lives. The sense of efficacy that comes with having the knowledge and skills to tackle the task, and being recognized for their knowledge and skills, is rewarding.

Some of them have been at the work long enough to see the impact they have had across generations. For example, Adam is now seeing "forechildren" (a play on the term "forefathers") in the program. The children in the programs he leads today have parents that were the first children he served years ago.

Loving and being loved; finding community

If dual relationships create significant professional challenges, their flip side is that many of these social workers feel embraced and even loved as valued members of the congregations they serve. For example, a woman honored Carl's years of work to complete his Doctor of Ministry (DMin) degree by saying he needed four bars on his robe rather than the three that symbolize doctoral studies completion; he was touched by her pride in her pastor's doctoral degree.

Adam is raising his children in the community he serves. He described with emotion how his children have been watched over and cared for by the adolescents in the programs his congregation offers. Two respondents indicated how gratifying it is to see service they have modeled subsequently valued by their own children.

Community respect and legitimacy

Many of these social workers experience respect from the larger community because of their work. They sense that others see them as fulfilling a "legitimate" role of leadership. Role legitimacy is particularly significant since a social worker's role in a congregation is often ill defined initially. Carl described feeling "honored" by those he serves:

> It's an honor to be pastor of homeless people, people whom others wouldn't choose. When I walk the street, they call me "Pastor Carl." Someone hollers across the street across traffic, Hey, Pastor Carl!" There won't be a lot of honor in heaven for me, because I get it here.

Summary

Congregational social work takes place in a convergence of sometimes conflicting conditions that make it a challenging and deeply rewarding context for professional practice. A congregation is both an organization where the social worker works and a social community where the social worker lives and experiences mutual support and care. The social worker's own personal religious beliefs and values are expressed, strengthened, and challenged by the work setting. The professional values and beliefs of social work are used in a setting where service is the expression of religious mission more than it is a response to a systematic social service needs assessment. The language of the community is religious more than social scientific. These characteristics of congregations as work settings make them fertile ground for meaningful work that brings together the social worker's personal faith and professional calling. In the quotation which began this chapter, Caiden described the "huge role" social work can have in congregational life when these factors are understood:

> *The biggest challenge is for social work to take a step back and learn the culture of that community – the congregation. Then social work can move mountains.*

References

Abbott, S. D., Garland, D. R., Huffman-Nevins, A., & Stewart, J. B. (1990). Social workers' views of local churches as service providers: Impressions from an exploratory study. *Social Work and Christianity, 17*, 7-16.

Ammerman, N. T. (1997). *Congregation and community*. New Brunswick: Rutgers University.

Ammerman, N. T. (2001). *Doing good in American communities: Congregations and service organizations working together*. Hartford: Hartford Institute for Religious Research.

Ammerman, N. T. (2002). Still gathering after all these years: Congregations in U.S. cities. In A. Walsh (Ed.), *Can charitable choice work? Covering religion's impact on urban affairs and social services* (pp. 6-22). Hartford: The Leonard E. Greenberg Center for the Study of Religion in Public Life.

Ammerman, N. T. (2005). *Pillars of faith: American congregations and their partners*. Berkeley: University of California Press.

Brueggemann, W. G. (1996). *The practice of macro social work*. Chicago: Nelson-Hall.

Carroll, J. W., Dudley, C. S., & McKinney, W. (Eds.). (1986). *Handbook for congregational studies*. Nashville: Abingdon.

Chaves, M. (2003). Debunking the assumptions behind charitable choice. *Stanford Social Innovation Review, 1*(2), 28-36.

Chaves, M. (2004). *Congregations in America.* Cambridge: Harvard University Press.

Chaves, M. (2005, November 4). *All creatures great and small: Megachurches in context. H. Paul Douglas Lecture.* Paper presented at the Religious Research Association, Rochester, NY.

Chaves, M. (2010). Does anyone remember the faith-based initiative? *Faith and Leadership: Where Christian Leaders Reflect, Connect, and Learn.* Duke Divinity School. Retrieved from http://www.faithandleadership.duke.edu/. DOI: January 8, 2010.

Chaves, M., & Anderson, S. (2008). Continuity and change in American religion, 1972-2006. In P. V. Marsden (Ed.), *Social trends in the United States, 1972-2006: Evidence from the General Social Survey.* Princeton, NJ: Princeton University Press.

Chaves, M., & Wineburg, B. (2009). Did the faith-based initiative change congregations? *Nonprofit and Voluntary Sector Quarterly, 39*(2), 343-355.

Clerkin, R., & Gronbjerg, K. (2003, March 6). *The role of congregations in delivering human services.* Paper presented at the Roundtable on Religion and Social Welfare Policy, Washington, DC.

Cnaan, R. A., Boddie, S. C., Handy, F., Yancey, G., & Schneider, R. (2002). *The invisible caring hand: American congregations and the provision of welfare.* New York: New York University Press.

Cnaan, R. A., Boddie, S. C., & Yancey, G. I. (2003). Bowling alone but surviving together: The congregational norm of community involvement. In C. Smidt (Ed.), *Religion as social capital: Producing the common good* (pp. 19-31). Waco, TX: Baylor University Press.

De Vita, C. J. (2005, November 18). *Devolution of the faith-based initiatives: Understanding what has changed in government contracting.* Paper presented at the 34th Annual Conference, Association for Research on Nonprofit Organizations and Voluntary Action (ARNOVA), Washington, DC.

Farnsely, A. E. I. (2004). What congregations can and can't do: Faith-based politics. *Christian Century, 121*(17), 27-33.

Farris, A., Nathan, R. P., & Wright, D. J. (2004). *The expanding administrative presidency: George W. Bush and the faith-based initiative.* Albany, NY: The Roundtable on Religion and Social Welfare Policy.

Filteau, J. (1993). Churches play critical role in national social welfare. *Intercom* (June-July), 5.

Garland, D. R. (1987). *Social workers on church staff.* Louisville KY: National Institute for Research and Training in Church Social Work, The Southern Baptist Theological Seminary.

Garland, D. R. (1987). Social workers on church staff. Louisville KY: National Institute for Research and Training in Church Social Work, The Southern Baptist Theological Seminary.

Garland, D. R. (Ed.). (1992). *Church social work.* Philadelphia: The North American Association of Christians in Social Work.

Garland, D. R. (1994). *Church agencies: Caring for children and families in crisis.* Washington, DC: Child Welfare League of America.

Garland, D. R. (1995). Church social work. In *Encyclopedia of Social Work.* Washington, DC: National Association of Social Workers.

Garland, D. R. (1998). Church social work. In B. Hugen (Ed.), *Christianity and Social Work: Readings on the integration of Christian faith and social work practice* (pp. 7-25). Botsford, CT: NACSW.

Garland, D. R. (1999a). Community: The goal of family ministry. *Christian Ethics Today,* 5(1), 16-17.

Garland, D. R. (1999b). *Family ministry: A comprehensive guide.* Grand Rapids: Intervarsity Press.

Garland, D. R. (1999c). Making connect-the-dot community work. *Faithworks, 2*(2), 26-17.

Garland, D. R. (2003a). Being Christian means being micro *and* macro. *Catalyst, 46*(1), 3-4.

Garland, D. R. (2008). Christian social services. In *Encyclopedia of Social Work* (8th ed.). Washington, DC: National Association of Social Workers.

Garland, D. R. (2010). *Inside out families: Living faith together.* Waco: Baylor University Press.

Garland, D. R. (Ed.). (1992). *Church social work.* Philadelphia: The North American Association of Christians in Social Work.

Garland, D. R., & Chamiec-Case, R. (2005). Before--and after--the political rhetoric: Faith-based child and family welfare services. *Social Work and Christianity, 32*(1), 22-43.

Garland, D. R., Myers, D., & Wolfer, T. A. (2005). The impact of volunteering on Christian faith and congregational life: The Service and Faith Project from http://www.baylor.edu/~CFCM/

Garland, D. R., Myers, D. M., & Wolfer, T. A. (2008). Social work with religious volunteers: Activating and sustaining community involvement. *Social Work, 53*(3), 255-265.

Garland, D. R., Myers, D. M., & Wolfer, T. A. (2009). Protestant Christian volunteers in community social service programs: What motivates, challenges, and sustains them. *Administration in Social Work, 33*(1), 23-39.

Garland, D. R., Myers, D. M., & Wolfer, T. A. (in press). "Learning to see people as God sees them: Outcomes of community service for congregational volunteers." *Review of Religious Research.*

Garland, D. R., Sherr, M., Dennison, A., & Singletary, J. (2008). Who cares for the children? *Family and Community Ministries: Empowering Through Faith, 22*(1), 6-16.

Garland, D. R., Sherr, M., Singletary, J., & Gardner, L. (2008). Congregations who care for children. *Family and Community Ministries: Empowering Through Faith, 22*(2).

Garland, D. R., & Singletary, J. E. (2008). Congregations as settings for early childhood education. *Early Childhood Services, 2*(2), 111-128.

Garland, D. R., Wolfer, T. A., & Myers, D. R. (2008). How 35 congregations launched and sustained community ministries. *Family and Community Ministries: Empowering Through Faith, 35*(3), 229-257.

Governor's Advisory Task Force on Faith-Based Community Service Groups. (1996). *Faith in action: A new vision for church-state cooperation in Texas.* Austin: Governor's Correspondence Office, P. O. Box 12428, Austin, TX 78711.

Hessel, D. T. (1992). *Social ministry.* (Revised ed.). Philadelphia: Westminster Press.

Joseph, M. V., & Conrad, A. P. (1980). A parish neighborhood model for social work practice. *Social Casework: The Journal of Contemporary Social Work, 61*(7), 423-432.

Myers, D. R., Wolfer, T. A., & Garland, D. R. (2008). Congregational service-learning characteristics and volunteer faith development. *Religious Education, 103*(3), 369-386.

Myers, L. E. (2006). "You got us all a-pullin' together": Southern Methodist deaconesses in the rural South, 1922-1940. In M. Walker & R. Sharpless (Eds.), *Work, family and faith: Rural southern women in the twentieth century.* New York: Columbia University Press.

Northern, V. M. (2009). Social workers in congregational contexts. *Social Work & Christianity, 36*(2), 265-285.

Rusaw, R., & Swanson, E. (2004). *The externally focused church.* Loveland, CO: Group Publishing.

Saleebey, D. (2004). "The Power of Place": Another look at the environment. *Families in Society, 85*(1), 7-16.

Scales, T. L. (2000). "All That Fits a Woman": Training Southern Baptist Women for Charity and Mission, 1907-1926. Macon, GA: Mercer University Press.

Singletary, J. E. (2005). The praxis of social work: A model of how faith informs practice informs faith. *Social Work & Christianity, 32*(1), 56-72.

Warner, S. (1994). The place of the congregation in the contemporary American religious configuration. In J. P. Wind & J. W. Lewis (Eds.), *American congregations* (Vol. 2). Chicago: The University of Chicago Press.

Wind, J. P., & Lewis, J. W. (1994). *American congregations* (Vol. 2). Chicago: The University of Chicago Press.

Wineburg, B. (2005, November 18). *Unintelligent design: Federal intervention strategies into local communities.* Paper presented at the 34th Annual Conference, Association for Research on Nonprofit Organization and Voluntary Action (ARNOVA). Washington, DC.

Working Group on Human Needs and Faith-Based and Community Initiatives. (2003). *Harnessing civic and faith-based power to fight poverty.* Washington, DC: Search for Common Ground.

Wuthnow, R. (2004). Saving America? Faith-based services and the future of civil society. Princeton, NJ: Princeton University Press.

Yancey, G., Rogers, R., Garland, D. R., Netting, F. E., & O'Connor, M. K. (2003). *Methodological challenges in identifying effective practices in urban faith-based social service programs.* Paper presented at the Independent Sector Spring Research Forum, The Role of Faith-Based Organizations in the Social Welfare System, March 6-7, Bethesda, MD.

Notes

1 Congregations vary in their governance structures. Many have boards of volunteers who are the decision-making group for the congregation; these volunteers may be called deacons, trustees, elders, or other such titles. Some strictly serve in the governance of the congregation; in other congregations, these volunteers also provide "shepherding" or pastoral care during times of illness or other family and individual crisis.

2 For examples of the development of congregational social work, see (Abbott, Garland, Huffman-Nevins, & Stewart, 1990; Chaves, 2004, 2005; Chaves & Anderson, 2008; Chaves & Wineburg, 2009; Clerkin & Gronbjerg, 2003; Cnaan, Boddie, Handy, Yancey, & Schneider, 2002; Cnaan, Boddie, & Yancey, 2003; Garland, 1994, 1995, 1998, 1999b, 2003a , 2008; e.g.,Garland, 1992; Garland, Myers, & Wolfer, 2005; Garland, Myers, & Wolfer, 2008, 2009, in press; Garland, Sherr, Dennison, & Singletary, 2008; Garland, Sherr, Singletary, & Gardner, 2008; Garland & Singletary, 2008; Garland, Wolfer, & Myers, 2008; Yancey, Rogers, Garland, Netting, & O'Connor, 2003).

3 These 28 social workers are located in 21 different states, ranging from California to Connecticut. Only 6 states were represented by more than one subject; there were three from Texas and two each from the states of Indiana, Maryland, Minnesota, Ohio, and Tennessee. They represented 10 religious groups, with the

largest being Baptist (n = 11), then nondenominational Christian (n = 5), and Catholic (n = 3), which are also the three largest religious groups in the nation (Chaves, 2004). Other denominations included Church of Christ (n = 2) Methodist (n = 2), and one each from Assemblies of God, Full Gospel, Jewish, Lutheran, and Presbyterian congregations.

4 We are missing data for two subjects.

5 We are missing data on title for one subject. An additional three see themselves primarily as social work faculty in a university or college partnering with the congregation they serve.

CHAPTER 19

ETHICALLY INTEGRATING FAITH AND PRACTICE: EXPLORING HOW FAITH MAKES A DIFFERENCE FOR CHRISTIANS IN SOCIAL WORK

Rick Chamiec-Case

Introduction

Over 25 years ago I was a new, eager, and inexperienced MSW student in my first practicum placement. This first placement was in a state mental health hospital with locked psychiatric wards secured by large, heavy metal doors. I was assigned to work with adolescents, many of them victims and perpetrators of sexual abuse. Many had a history of suicide attempts, and most were considered a threat to themselves and others.

To be honest, I didn't have much of an idea what I was doing, especially considering the complex challenges posed by these clients. But I was fresh and enthusiastic and raring to go, committed to being a positive, encouraging influence in the lives of these boys and girls. I was also pretty naïve.

So when I was singled out and asked to meet with several senior treatment team members at the hospital, I assumed it was because they saw something special in me and that I showed unique potential to become an outstanding social worker! It turns out, however, that what they were really interested in was the fact that I was a dual degree student—and that the other program in which I was enrolled was a master's program at Yale Divinity School. What this said to them was that in addition to being a social work student, it was likely that I was "religious." The members of this senior treatment team wanted to communicate to me a clear and direct message: They told me that, while they didn't hold my being a person of faith against me, it would be unacceptable to let my faith directly influence how I practiced social work in their institution.

Now 25 years later, it seems clear to me that those treatment team colleagues had a particular picture in their minds about what it would mean for my faith to have an influence on my social work practice. And clearly it was not a pretty picture, one that likely featured me running roughshod over the beliefs and values of the clients in their hospital or treating them insensitively or disrespectfully if they had religious beliefs and values that differed from my own. I can understand how with *this* particular picture in mind, the members of the treatment team felt so strongly that I would have to "check my faith at the door" if I were to practice in their program setting.

In my current role as Executive Director of the North American Association of Christian Social Workers (NACSW) and with 25 years of practice and teaching experience, I have learned that the issue of integrating faith in social work practice is much more varied and complex than my intern supervisors imagined when they warned me about letting my faith affect my work in their program. There is, in fact, a wide variety of ways in which the faith of Christians in social work can have an impact on their social work practice, most of which are positive and healthy —and even potentially add significant value to their work. At the same time, I have discovered that social work practice, in turn, often has a vital impact on how Christian social workers understand and live out their faith. In an attempt to organize the many ways faith and practice can potentially interact with each other, this chapter will explore three broad categories for organizing a variety of approaches to ethically integrating Christian faith and social work practice.

But before launching into a description of these three categories and some of the integration approaches that fall under them, there are a couple of preliminary questions that need to be explored to provide some context for this discussion: a) What exactly does the "integration of faith and practice" mean? and b) What key factors influence the ways in which Christian faith and social work practice are integrated?

Defining the Integration of Faith and Practice

The *Merriam-Webster Dictionary* suggests that to integrate is "to form, coordinate, or blend into a functioning or unified whole ... " or "to unite with something else" ("Merriam-Webster online", 2006). The project of integrating Christian faith and social work practice is based on the twin possibilities that: a) faith has something of real use and value to contribute to social work practice and b) social work theory and practice has something of real use and value to contribute to Christian faith. Therefore, for the purposes of this chapter, "integration" will be defined quite broadly to mean any way in which the faith of Christians in social work influences, shapes, or contributes to their understanding and practice of social work, as well as any way that social work theory and practice has a similar impact on how Christian social workers understand and live out their Christian faith.

Key Factors that Influence the Integration of Faith and Practice

Even if we accept this is what integration *means*, it soon becomes clear that there is a wide diversity of views about *how* faith and social work should and do interact with each other. Part of the reason for this diversity of views is that there are a number of factors that potentially influence the ways Christians in social work integrate faith and practice. Based on discussions with hundreds of social workers in my work with NACSW over the past 15 years, I have outlined below in Table 1 the most salient of these factors.

Table 1: Key Factors that Influence the Integration of Faith and Practice

Factor	Example Differences	Example Influence on Integration
1. Social worker's understanding of Christian faith and theology, which is shaped to a large degree by the denominations or faith traditions to which they have been exposed/of which they are a part (Mathisen, 2003). "While Christians … are not controlled by the religious ways of life they have inherited … their work will almost always be shaped to some degree by those commitments. Different traditions of faith … provide us with different questions to pursue, different hunches about where relevant information may be found, and different sentiments regarding which answers seem more appropriate than others" (Jacobson & Jacobson, 2004, p. 77). Christians "will arrive at different integrative stances because their religious presuppositions about theology, practice, worship, and spirituality differ ." (Gingrich & Worthington, 2007, p. 347).	1. Christians in social work come from different denominational backgrounds (for example, Baptist, Roman Catholic, or Lutheran) or see Christian faith through different theological lenses (for example, conservative, moderate, or liberal perspectives).	1a. The focus on Scripture in the integration process for Christians in social work from Protestant backgrounds is often more heavily emphasized than for those from other denominational backgrounds, which often place significant weight on the role of Christian tradition and experience in supporting Christian beliefs and values. 1b. The focus on more cognitive models of integration for Christians in social work from the Reformed tradition may be more heavily emphasized than for those from, for example, the Mennonite tradition, which places an especially strong emphasis on integration efforts focused on doing or living out Christian faith.

Factor	Example Differences	Example Influence on Integration
2. Social worker's understanding regarding the relationship between Christian faith on the one hand, and "secular" knowledge, learning, and culture on the other.	2. Niebuhr, in his classic Christ and Culture (Niebuhr, 1975), sketches out five different perspectives about the relationship between Christian faith and secular learning and culture, which he labels: a) Christ against Culture (in which Christian faith is opposed to or in direct conflict with the learning, culture, and values of the wider secular society); b) The Christ of Culture (which suggests that there is widespread, fundamental agreement between Christian faith and the learning, culture, and values of the wider secular society); c) Christ above Culture (which suggests that although much can be learned from nature and secular culture, there are at least some truths which persons cannot learn or even envision apart from God's gracious gift of revelation through Christ); d) Christ and Culture in Paradox (in which there are irreconcilable tensions between religious and scientific assumptions and methods for discovering truth that will not be resolved in this present world, yet which maintains that neither religious nor scientific truth should be discarded); e) Christ the Transformer of Culture (in which the fallen nature of persons is understood to lead to significant distortions in secular culture and learning, so that Christian faith must transform all learning and culture leading to the eventual coming of the kingdom of God on earth).	2a. Christians in social work influenced by the Christ against Culture perspective will tend to be much more cautious about including insights from secular social work theories and secular theorists (for example, Freud's description of the prominent role of the unconscious, from which follows a largely deterministic view of human behavior) in the integration process, as compared with those who are influenced by the Christ of Culture perspective, who will tend to be much more open about embracing the insights of a wide range of secular social work theories and theorists as they seek to integrate faith and practice. 2b. Christians in social work influenced by the Christ and Culture in Paradox position will tend to be more comfortable holding in tension beliefs like that - i) people created in God's image are agents responsible for their actions on the one hand, as well as the claim that ii) human behavior can be fully explained as the product of persons' natures and environments on the other - than those who are influenced by the Christ the Transformer of Culture position, who will tend to evaluate theories from the starting point of basic beliefs or assumptions that are consistent with core Christian beliefs and values (like that people created in God's image are agents responsible for their actions), and reject or seek to transform theories based on beliefs that are incongruent with these core Christian beliefs and assumptions.
3. The type (auspices) of the organization in which the social worker practices	3. Social workers practice in a wide range of organizations/ organizational auspices including federal, state, or local government programs, private secular organizations, faith-based organizations, congregations, private practice (for profit or not for profit), and so on.	3. Clients seeking or being referred to services in different types of organizations will likely have different expectations regarding whether and how faith or spirituality will be reflected/included in the services they are receiving (for example, government-operated services as contrasted with services provided in a religiously affiliated organization or congregation). These different expectations, in turn, have important implications regarding clients' preferences and informed consent for the inclusion of faith or spirituality in these services.

Factor	Example Differences	Example Influence on Integration
4. The social work method or level at which the social worker focuses	4. Social workers' clients/client systems vary considerably, and can include individuals, families, groups, organizations, or communities. In addition, their practice methods can be as diverse as direct practice at micro, mezzo and macro levels, social work education, research, administration and management, work at the policy level, etc.	4. The interaction of the social workers' faith or spirituality with the faith or spirituality of the client varies considerably depending on whether the client/client system is an individual, a group, an organization, or a community, as well as whether the social worker's primary method would be described as clinical/counseling, casework/referral, advocacy/policy development, administration, or social work education.
5. The types of services and client population(s) with which the social worker practices	5. Social workers provide a wide variety of types of services such as child protective services, health/medical/hospice services, housing or residential services, income maintenance support, private practice, etc. as well as work with many different populations including clients with mental health issues, aging issues, clients struggling with addictions, clients with developmental disabilities, clients caught in the corrections/legal system, and so on.	5a. The inclusion of faith or spirituality in practice is often more prevalent in social work services like hospice care, in which acute questions about the meaning and purpose of life and death, etc., are more likely to surface than in other types of services. 5b. The inclusion of faith or spirituality in practice is often more prevalent in certain fields like addiction services in which interventions like 12-step programs (which usually include a spiritual component) have been widely accepted and its benefits clearly documented for a number of years in that field.

Proposed Categories for Organizing Approaches to Integration

The next section of this chapter will explore three basic categories that can be used to organize a wide variety of approaches to integrating Christian faith and social work practice, arguably without compromising the integrity of either one. The three broad categories presented in this chapter are:

- Category 1. Approaches that emphasize how faith *motivates, strengthens, inspires or sustains* Christians in social work;
- Category 2. Approaches that emphasize how faith influences the way Christians in social work *understand* social work practice, and vice-versa;
- Category 3. Approaches that emphasize how faith influences the way Christians in social work *do* social work practice, and vice-versa.

Category 1: Integration Approaches that Sustain, Inspire, and Motivate

The first broad category for organizing approaches to integration includes models that emphasize how faith motivates, strengthens, inspires, or sustains Christians in social work. In much the same way that airline attendants encourage passengers to strap on an oxygen mask to themselves first (since a passenger who passes out is of no help to anyone else!), social workers that learn to tap the resources of their faith to nourish and fortify their own spirits are in a position to be that much more effective and able to persevere in their work, with the ultimate beneficiaries being their clients.

#1 The Calling and Coping Model of Integration focuses on the vital contribution of many social workers' faith to inform, drive, confirm, or clarify their decisions for choosing the vocation of social work as a career (Eun-Kyoung & Barrett, 2007). As described by Beryl Hugen in his "Calling: A Spirituality Model for Social Work Practice" (Hugen and Scales, 2008), this model of integration emphasizes a profound connection for Christians in social work between answers to questions about the meaning and purpose of their lives and faith, and their reasons for choosing and remaining in social work as their vocation.

In addition, many Christians in social work firmly believe that God calls them to social justice and to serving people who are hurting. This belief motivates, nurtures and sustains their commitment to meet the rigorous demands of social work practice. They find Biblical support through passages such as Deuteronomy 15:7-11, from the Law; Job 29:11-16, and Proverbs 14:31, from the Wisdom literature; Psalm 82:1-4, from the Poetic books; Isaiah 58:6-11, and Jeremiah 22:11-17, from the Major Prophets; Amos 8:4-7, from the Minor Prophets; Matthew 25:31-46, and Luke 4:16-21 from the Gospels; and James 1:26-27, from the Epistles. Their faith supports their ability to remain energized and fully invested in their work.

#2 The Wonder and Worship Model of Integration focuses on Christian social workers' *responses* to the progress and positive change that occurs in the lives of their clients or client systems. Specifically, this model emphasizes the sense of wonder or awe sometimes experienced by social workers of faith as they see glimpses of God's

grace and work of healing and transformation in and through their work—ultimately leading to a response of heartfelt praise and worship (Glanzer, 2008, p. 47).

Category 2: Integration Approaches that Emphasize Understanding

The second category for organizing approaches to integration includes models that emphasize different ways the faith of Christians in social work shapes, influences, and contributes to how they *understand* various aspects of social work theory and practice, and vice versa. Models under this category bring out different ways in which people of faith in social work tend to view social work from a Christian perspective or through a Christian lens, or how they tend to view their Christian faith from a social work perspective or through a social work lens.

#3 The Latent Model of Integration suggests that how Christians understand social work is inherently influenced by their faith, even when they are not necessarily *consciously* aware of it or *deliberately intending* to do something they would call integration —and yet their faith is still nonetheless "unconsciously embodied" (Jacobson & Jacobson, 2004, p. xi) in their work. This model of integration proposes that the core beliefs and values of all social workers, including Christians, will invariably find a way to "seep through" into their understanding of social work--sometimes in ways about which they are largely unaware, at least until they take time to reflect on it.

The name for this model is taken from C.S. Lewis's essay on "Christian Apologetics" in *God in the Dock* (1970) Writing about the influence of Christian faith on literature, but with clear implications for other disciplines like social work, Lewis suggests that "What we want is not more little books about Christianity, but more little books by Christians on other subjects—with their Christianity latent" (Lewis, 1970, p. 93). The Merriam-Webster On-Line Dictionary (http://www.merriam-webster.com) defines latent as "present but not visible, apparent...." What does it mean to suggest that to a certain extent, Christians sometimes come to their understanding of social work "with their Christianity latent?"

Let me try to illustrate. Early in my career I was working for an agency that operated group homes for adolescents with developmental disabilities. Straight out of college with a degree in philosophy, I knew very little about either residential care or developmental disabilities. But I remember with remarkable clarity my strong resistance to a component of the treatment plan for one of the more challenging residents in that system. According to the terms of this resident's behavior plan, he was not allowed to go home to visit his family on weekends unless he met a number of prerequisite behavioral targets during the course of the week. Simply put, if his behavior was not "good enough" during the week, there would be no family visit for him on the weekend. In spite of my lack of work experience in this field, I was fiercely opposed to this component of the resident's behavior plan. Although I couldn't have clearly articulated at that time why I felt this strategy was likely to cause more harm than good, upon reflection many years later, I began to understand my strong reaction. It had to do with the fact that this component of the behavior plan clashed irreconcilably with how I believe God treats us, and in turn, how God asks us to treat each other. At the heart of my understanding of Christian faith is this: If God required us to meet a series of "prerequisite behavioral targets" before He would allow us to have a relationship and fellowship with Him, we would all be in serious trouble! Instead, it is only *because* God loves us first that we are able to begin becoming the kind of people who live and behave in the ways God intends for us. As I understand it, this is what the Christian concept of grace is all about. It seems clear to me now that my Christian faith had a strong impact on my opposition to this component of this resident's behavior plan, but not in a way that was conscious, intentional or overt —I came to this issue with my Christianity latent.

Several *Cognitive Models of Integration* emphasize ways in which Christian beliefs and values shape, blend with, and influence—in a more intentional way— Christian social workers' *understanding* of social work practice, as well as the way social work theories and values reciprocally impact Christians' understanding of their faith. Some examples of cognitive models of integration include: a) the *selective attention* model of integration; b) the *reinforcement* model of integration; c) the *parallel findings* model of integration; d) the *filtering* model of integration; e) the *accommodation* model of integration; f) the *generative* model of integration; and g) the *synthesis* model of integration. For the sake of brevity, these seven models are summarized below in Table 2 in the next few pages that follow, along with one or more example for each model.

Category 3. Approaches Emphasizing what Christians in Social Work Do

The final category of integration approaches includes models that emphasize how the faith of Christians in social work shapes the way they *do* social work practice, and vice-versa. With regard to this third category, it is helpful to distinguish between a) models in which there is little or no interaction between the spiritual beliefs and values of the social worker and those of the client/client system, and b) models in which interaction between the spiritual beliefs and values of the social work and those of the client/client system is an essential component of the integration process. This distinction has sometimes been referred to in the integration literature as the difference between "explicit" and "implicit" integration, with the former emphasizing "a more overt approach <to integration> that directly and systematically deals with spiritual or religious issues ... and uses spiritual resources like prayer, Scripture or sacred texts, referrals to church or other religions groups ... and other religious practices," and the latter "a more covert approach that does not initiate the discussion of religious or spiritual issues" (Tan, 1996, p. 368). I prefer focusing on the degree of *interaction* between the spiritual beliefs and values of social workers and those of their clients. Doing so keeps front and center the relevance of the faith and central beliefs of both social worker and client systems in the helping relationship. The importance of achieving a delicate balance in such interactions is one of the most important considerations related to providing ethical social work practice.

Table 2: Cognitive Models of Integration

Model	Description	Example(s)
Model #4: Selective Attention Model	Focuses on the way that a) Christian beliefs and values influence Christians to focus on particular aspects of or certain priorities within social work practice; or reciprocally b) how social work values and experiences influence a Christian's understanding of particular aspects of or emphases within her theology/tradition or reading of Scripture.	a) Christian's beliefs and values often play a significant role in motivating a social worker to develop a heightened interest in social justice (Eun-Kyoung & Barrett, 2007) or to serve populations that are traditionally marginalized and underserved in our society (Canning, Pozzi, McNeil, & McMinn, 2000, p. 205). b) Social work values and experiences can heighten a Christian in social work's sensitivity to and understanding of passages of Scripture and strands of theology that focus on advocating for those that are poor and marginalized in their communities.
Model #5: Reinforcement Model	Focuses on how what persons learn from either the Christian faith or from social work practice can serve to strengthen, reinforce, support, refine, or complement the other. In this model, one discipline is generally seen as being primary, with the other serving to reinforce or refine that primary discipline (in contrast to model #10, the synthesis model, in which the two disciplines are viewed more as co-equals).	a) Mary Ann Brenden describes a process through which the Colleges of St. Catherine/St. Thomas sought "to more intentionally and systematically integrate Catholic Social Teaching (CST) into their social work curriculum" (Brandsen & Hugen, 2007, p. 354) with the result that CST appreciably "strengthened the social justice content" (p. 354) of their social work programs. b) Groundbreaking research over the past 15-20 years has confirmed a strong, positive correlation between many forms of spirituality/religion on the one hand, and health/mental health on the other (George, Larson, Koenig, & McCullough, 2000). The empirical confirmation of this correlation, long affirmed by almost all faith traditions, provides an example of how "modern learning at its best might ... reinforce ... the truths of faith" (Glanzer, 2008, p. 45).
Model #6: Parallel Findings Model	Emphasizes that because Christian faith and social work practice each have their own distinctive sources and methodologies for discovering knowledge —as well as their own underlying worldview assumptions and overarching purposes - what can be discovered within each discipline is valid and credible, but primarily within its own context and within its own separate sphere. "The truth of each discipline is to remain separate and contextualized within the discipline from which it came. . . this approach gives more equivalent acceptability to the data from each discipline, and integration involves establishing linkages between each discipline's truths" (Eck, 1996, p. 109).	a) Operating from a Christian perspective, one might come to the conclusion that the meeting of a valued outcome in the life of a particular client or community reflects divine influence or the positive impact of prayer for that client or community. Operating from a social work perspective, one might come to the conclusion that the meeting of this same valued outcome is a direct result of, for example, a course of cognitive behavioral therapy or a creative community outreach intervention. b) Shostrom and Montgomery maintain that at the core of human beings is "an innate guidance system energized by the power of God's love" ((1978) in (Eck, 1996)), whereas Freud maintains with equal conviction that the id driven by the biological urges of the libido is what lies at the core of human beings.

Model	Description	Example(s)
Model #7: Filtering Model	Focuses on the use of core Christian beliefs and values that act as filters to help Christians sort out from among various social work theories and practice interventions available in the literature those that they are able and willing to embrace. These filtering decisions are based primarily on the congruence of these various theories and interventions with their core Christian beliefs and values (Brandsen & Hugen, 2007; Chamiec-Case, 2008; Jones, 2006).	The core Christian belief that people are made in God's image and are therefore morally responsible agents might prevent a Christian in social work from fully embracing some theories of human behavior (like B.F. Skinner's, for example) that do not leave a legitimate place for human agency: "My religious, specifically Christian, understanding of the human person ... made in the image of God <requires that> humans must ... in some way be seen as capable of meaningful agency ... such that the search for reductionistic laws to explain human behavior will always be incomplete" (Jones, 2006, p. 254).
Model #8: Accommodation Model	Focuses on the ways Christian faith and social work practice can be reconciled with and therefore make a contribution to the other, but only after one or the other is in some way changed, altered, reconstructed, reinterpreted, transformed, or subsumed within the other to deal with initial or apparent tensions or inconsistencies: "Data from the other discipline must be altered to become acceptable as data for the process of integration" (Eck, 1996, p. 104).	a) Example where Christian faith is accommodated: For many Christians, the position common within social work that human nature and society is essentially good at its core needs to be altered or reinterpreted to reflect the understanding that although we can find some good in people (who are made in God's image) and society (through which God extends common grace to God's world), at the same time, deeply-rooted estrangement and alienation from God and each other and its damaging implications affects every aspect of our humanity, and at every level (individual, family, community, and society) (Bowpitt, 1989). b) Example where social work practice is accommodated: For many in social work, a Christian's belief about prayer would likely be reinterpreted to emphasize aspects about prayer that can be verified empirically (for example, that prayer is an expression of a person's innermost needs and desires in her life that can be useful in promoting personal growth), as opposed to a Christian understanding of prayer as an act in which the prayer asks a loving God to be active and involved in the client's life and healing
Model #9: Generative Model	Emphasizes using core Christian beliefs and values in the development and application of new, fresh insights, theories or interventions that support social work practice —that is, insights, theories and interventions that would likely not be found in the social work literature apart from the core Christian beliefs upon which they are based. Referring to the application of this model in psychology, Eck suggests that the generative model "seeks to rebuild psychology from the ground up by changing its foundational presuppositions to be more consistent with a Christian worldview" ... attempting "to build psychological science on explicitly Christian presuppositions (Eck, 1996, p. 107).	a) In his "Who Cares?" (2008), Jim Vanderwoerd proposes the use of several biblical principles to serve as a foundation for the development of a view of social welfare from a Christian perspective. A couple of these biblical principles Vanderwoerd uses include: a) that God creates and upholds all the different societies that have and do exist; and b) that the purpose of societies/social structures is to facilitate God's intent for humans in creation — which is to have abundantly flourishing relationships in harmony. b) In their "Invitation to the Table," Yangarber-Hicks et al. suggest that Christian themes of "servanthood, obedience, and mutuality in relationship" provide a stark "contrast to contemporary clinical and developmental guides to self-fulfillment or self-actualization" (Yangarber-Hicks et al., 2006, p. 344), and as such, serve as innovative starting points for developing a unique understanding of human behavior and development.

Model	Description	Example(s)
Model #10: Synthesis Model	Emphasizes the mutual influence of and reciprocity between the contributions of faith and social work in the integration process. In this model, knowledge from both Christian faith and social work are considered fully valid or co-equal. As such, the task of integration is to "... create a unified set of truths that mirror the wholeness and unity of God's created and revealed truths" (Eck, 1996, p. 109) that ... broadens the understanding that comes from either <discipline> ... in isolation. ... The truths of God's revealed Word and created world are a unified whole regardless of their data source. The vastness of God's unified truth goes far beyond the scope of any one discipline ... (Eck, 1996, p. 110) Jacobson refers to this process as "crossfertilizing," that is, a "process of weaving the insights of faith and science into new, creative, and scientifically contemporary visions of God and the world" (Jacobson & Jacobson, 2004, pp. 16-17). Badley (1994) refers to this as the fusion model, because it focuses on the fusion of the two disciplines into something new and distinct, something richer or more nuanced than either discipline could be on its own.	Many core values - such as: a) the importance of serving others (particularly those that are who are vulnerable and oppressed); and b) the dignity and worth of persons - are considered core values of both the Christian faith and the social work profession (NASW, 2008), with each discipline contributing a unique perspective or focus that adds depth, nuance, and richness when brought together. With regard to a) the core value of service, social work contributes a unique sensitivity to and knowledge of cultural and ethnic diversity as it relates to service, and has extensive experience applying this knowledge in the provision of effective, culturally sensitive practice. Christian faith, at the same time, provides a compelling and inspiring model of a life characterized by an ultimate commitment to service (Jesus in Matthew 20:28 says about his own life that he "did not come to be served, but to serve, and to give his life as a ransom for many" (New International Version). With regard to b) the core value of dignity and worth of persons, social work, on the one hand, helps unpack this value through the application of the "strengths perspective," a commitment to focusing on their assets, abilities, and potential for growth of all persons, groups, and communities, a perspective that empowers and enhances persons' capacity to achieve valued outcomes in their lives. Christian faith, on the other hand, contributes a powerful rationale for embracing this value, maintaining that people have worth because they are created by God in God's image (Genesis 1:27) and are therefore deeply loved by their Creator —Who particularly reinforces the worth of those who are marginalized in society by identifying closely with them: "Truly I tell you, whatever you did for one of the least of these brothers and sisters of mine, you did for me" (Matthew 25: 40, New International Version).

3a. Approaches to Integration Emphasizing Minimal Interaction Between Social Workers' Faith and Clients' Spirituality

#11 *The Excellence and Integrity Model of Integration* suggests that the faith of Christians in social work often drives their efforts to deliver high-quality services—primarily because their ultimate goal is to honor God (Brandsen & Hugen, 2007). This model encourages top quality, ethical social work practice consistent with the Scriptural admonition that "Whatever you do, work at it with all your heart, as working for the Lord, not for human masters. ... It is the Lord Christ you are serving" (Colossians 3: 23-24, New International Version).

#12 *The Life of Service Model of Integration* emphasizes Christians in social work seeking to demonstrate "loving witness through service" in the delivery of their social work practice. This model suggests that integrating faith and practice primarily consists of acts of loving service with the goal of bringing about good in the world and improving the lives of others (Jacobson & Jacobson, 2004). The focus of integration in this model is not so much on analyzing *intellectually* how faith contributes to social work practice (like in the cognitive models of integration), but rather on putting faith into action by humbly serving others. The Mennonite tradition suggests that Jesus' washing of the disciples' feet at the Last Supper is an inspiring example of selfless service: "basin and towel is the classic image here" (Wolfer, 2011, p. 156) and something he exhorts his followers to imitate in their own lives.

Often this life of "following Jesus in the way of service and obedience"(Wolfer, 2011, p. 158) is modeled for us by Christians who exemplify what it means to live out their faith by serving others. These Christian exemplars serve "to help others have spiritual and religious models as well as to provide inspiration and direction" (Yangarber-Hicks et al., 2006, p. 343), and can inspire us to imitate the way faith has made a difference in their work. This is true whether they are persons we know well (co-workers or colleagues), or people about whom we have read or heard (notable figures like Mother Teresa or Martin Luther King Jr, for example).

#13 *The Virtues Model of Integration* suggests that Christians in social work engage in a variety of Christian practices that manifest specific virtues with a direct and beneficial impact on the delivery of their social work practice. The major emphasis of this model is not just on what social workers *do*, but even more fundamentally on who they *are* (and *are becoming*), and how their developing characters permeate all aspects of their life, including their work. According to this model, "integration [is] essentially focused on reflecting Christian characteristics [such as] honesty, compassion, humility, and care" (Ripley, Garzon, Hall, Mangis, & Murphy, 2009, p. 6) in relationships with clients and colleagues. This model suggests that taking seriously on-going virtue and character formation potentially contributes to the value Christians in social work bring to their practice as they strive to become conformed to the image of Christ, who is viewed as the "primary source for fulfilled humanity and ... the *telos* of human development" (Yangarber-Hicks et al., 2006, p. 344).

#14 *The Intrapersonal Model of Integration* (Tan, 2009) focuses on Christians in social work engaging in one or more spiritual disciplines that help them focus and prepare for their social work practice. The emphasis here is on social workers engaging in spiritual disciplines that *do not* involve any direct interaction with their clients or client systems.

Some examples of intrapersonal integration might include social workers: a) engaging in private prayer or meditation, or visiting a place that is sacred to them as an intentional strategy for preparing for interactions with their clients or client groups; b) privately reflecting on passages of Scripture or other religious texts that serve to encourage or inspire them, help them cope more effectively with situational anxiety or work-related stress, or enable them to focus their energies and attention and thereby increase the effectiveness of their work; c) participating in other forms of individual or corporate worship, especially when the content, liturgy, or expression of that worship reinforces the purpose and value of their work; d) exploring or celebrating their faith through various forms of art, music, dance, poetry, theatre, and so on. Other examples might include social workers silently praying (before, after, or during their work) for their client's well-being and progress (Walker, Gorsuch, Siang-Yang (2004), p. 71), for God to guide their efforts, or for strengthening their relationships with clients.

3b. Integration Approaches Emphasizing Interaction Between Social Workers' Faith and Their Clients' Spirituality

Up to this point, the approaches to integration discussed in this chapter have focused on ways that faith can serve to motivate, strengthen, and inspire social workers, or contribute to how social workers understand the theories and principles that undergird their social work practice and vice versa. Given the level of concern expressed by some within the social work profession (and the treatment team 25 years ago in my internship) that expressions of Christian faith can pose irreconcilable differences with social work values (Dressel, Bolen, & Shepardson, 2011; Spano & Koenig, 2007; Todd & Coholic, 2007), it is important to emphasize that the first 13 models outlined here arguably do not appear to raise any significant ethical tensions or concerns.

There are, however, models of integration which do, in fact, have the potential to raise ethical concerns—those in which the faith of social workers *interacts* in some way with the spiritual beliefs and values of their clients/client systems or colleagues/supervisees. We now turn our attention to these.

An obvious question one could raise at this point is this: if there are a variety of "safe" (low or no risk) integration models at the disposal of Christians in social work, why not simply stick with these "safer" models and assiduously avoid any approaches to integration in which the spiritual beliefs and values of the social worker *interact* with those of their clients? Here's why: social workers have a strong commitment to "starting where the client is." Because religion and spirituality are important to many of their clients[1], most social workers feel compelled to incorporate clients' spiritual and religious interests, strengths, and beliefs in the helping process when this an important dimension in their clients' lives. To attempt to steer clear of clients' spirituality and religion– just to "play it safe"—could seriously impede social workers' efforts to "start where the client is," therefore detracting from competent, client-centered practice.

Put another way, the social work profession is "defined historically, ethically, and empirically by practice that intentionally accounts for contextual factors that shape clients' problems, resources and strengths" (M. Williams & Smolak, 2007, p. 26). Since a majority of Americans define themselves as "religious" or belong to a faith community (Chaves, 2004), faith, religion and spirituality are often critical contextual factors in the lives of our clients, and as such, cannot and should not be downplayed or ignored by competent social workers.

Conducting thorough spiritual assessments is an important strategy for gathering information about clients' spiritual interests, strengths, beliefs, resources and current challenges. Fortunately, the vital role of spiritual assessment in generating the information needed for culturally-sensitive and competent services has received increasing attention and support in the social work literature in recent years (D. Hodge, 2003a, , 2003b; D. R. Hodge, 2007; Nelson-Becker, Nakashima, & Canda, 2007; Parker, Larimore, & Crowther, 2002). Spiritual assessment puts the primary focus in the helping process on the spiritual and religious beliefs and values *of the client*, an emphasis consistent with the social worker's commitment to starting where the client is.

Role of Social Workers' Faith

At the same time, the faith of Christians in social work plays an important role in shaping how they view the world, and how they understand and practice social work—often at a deep level. Expectations by some in the profession that in order to be ethical practitioners, Christians in social work should be required to "check their faith at the door," unrealistically assume that they—or any social workers for that matter—are capable of bracketing the core beliefs and values that form a crucial part of their self-identities. One of the valuable contributions of post-Enlightenment thought—endorsed also in many Christian circles (Plantinga & Wolterstorff, 1983)—is that none of us is able to step outside of and leave behind our most basic and fundamental beliefs about the world around us. To require that of Christians in social work—or any social worker for that matter—is seriously misguided. Further, even if it were possible for Christians in social work to shed their core beliefs and values (which it is not), to do so would negate the vital role that faith often plays in forming and sustaining their passionate commitment to the values and purposes of social work.

As a result, the question is not *whether* the faith of Christians in social work interacts with the spiritual beliefs and values of their clients, but rather *how thoughtfully, competently, and ethically* Christians in social work handle these interactions. Christians who make a commitment to become social workers agree in good faith to abide by the ethics and standards of the social work profession, which includes a responsibility not to (even inadvertently) unduly impose or let their own beliefs and values overwhelm those of their clients. An important aspect of maintaining this responsibility is for Christians in social work to be keenly aware of their own spiritual and religious beliefs and values, and the different ways they can potentially impact their work. It is only when they are conscious and mindful of their own beliefs and values that Christians in social work can be intentional about how to integrate them into the helping relationship. The challenge for Christians in social work—and indeed for all social workers—is to "figure out how to have integrity and competence in the handling of our own beliefs and values as … [they] work respectfully and ethically with clients" (Sherwood, 2008, p. 409).

#14 *The Spiritual/Religious Sensitivity Model of Integration emphasizes* Christians in social work drawing upon their own experience of faith to heighten their sensitivity to and understanding of the spiritual or religious interests, strengths, and concerns of the clients, client systems, and colleagues/supervisees (Gingrich & Worthington, 2007; Okundaye, Gray, & Gray, 1999) with whom they work. There are a number of ways that the integration of Christian faith has the potential to contribute to spiritually and religiously sensitive practice (M. Williams & Smolak, 2007) including:

a) helping Christians in social work *grasp the relevance and meaning of spirituality in the lives of their clients* (by reflecting on the relevance and meaning that spirituality has had in their own lives);

b) motivating Christians in social work to *carefully explore and support the potential contributions of their clients' spirituality* to assist their clients' efforts to meet valued outcomes (by recalling the contributions faith has made in their own lives);

c) assisting Christians in social work to *understand the language, beliefs and values which are part of their clients' spiritual worldviews* (by comparing and contrasting them with their own spiritual beliefs and values, which are a part of their own spiritual worldview);

d) helping Christians in social work *be open to taking their clients' spiritual beliefs and values on their clients' terms* (Jones, 2006; Reber, 2006) (since the Christian faith affirms that there is, in fact, something real and ultimate that transcends the natural world).

It is worth noting that Christians in social work have played an important role in developing resources for the larger social work profession related to providing more spiritually and religiously sensitive social work practice (see, for example, the following resources (Ellor, Netting, & Thibault, 1999; Furman & Chandy, 1994; D. Hodge, 2003b; Hugen & Scales, 2008; Scales, Wolfer, Sherwood, Garland, Hugen, & Pittman, 2002; Van Hook, Hugen, & Aguilar, 2001).

The importance of social workers increasing their spiritual and religious sensitivity and competence has become increasingly recognized within the social work profession in light of the growing evidence in the research literature that clients' spirituality often serves to "positively influence the behavioral and emotion health of families and individuals" (Miller, Korinek, & Ivey, 2006, p. 356;) Pargament, 1997; N. R. Williams, 2004). At the same time, an essential aspect of spiritually sensitive practice is a social worker's responsibility to evaluate whether clients' experiences with faith, spirituality, or religion have been positive and healthy (providing a valuable resource supporting strength, hope and healing), or, as unfortunately is sometimes the case, negative or even toxic (where religion or spirituality have been used as tools of oppression or abuse to control or cause pain and hurt).

Let me briefly outline an example of the spiritual/religious sensitivity model. In his article, "Constructing Spiritually Modified Interventions: Cognitive Therapy with Diverse Populations" (D. R. Hodge, 2008), David Hodge, a Christian social work scholar, proposes a strategy for modifying or adapting cognitive behavioral therapy (CBT) in a way that he argues is spiritually and religiously sensitive to clients whose spiritual worldviews are in conflict with some of the values underlying traditional cognitive behavioral therapy. Hodge's argument goes something like this:

- Every social work intervention is informed by an underlying set of values and worldview (no interventions are value-free) (p. 179).
- The use of interventions whose underlying values and worldview are incongruent with clients' values may have limited effectiveness, and/ or be offensive/disrespectful of the clients' autonomy (or even cause some harm) (p. 179).
- Many western counseling interventions—such as cognitive behavioral theory—have been strongly influenced by "Enlightenment-based" values and worldview assumptions such as individualism, independence, self-actualization, and secularism (p. 180-181).
- Many clients embrace spiritual value systems and/or transcendent worldviews that are incongruent with some of these Enlightenment-based values and worldview assumptions: "Islam, for instance, tends to affirm values such as spirituality and community as opposed to secularism and individualism" (D. R. Hodge, 2008, p. 182).
- For these clients who do not share Enlightenment-based values and worldview assumptions, interventions like traditional, western cognitive behavioral therapy may pose significant value conflicts, and therefore may have limited effectiveness and/or be offensive to and/or disrespectful of the these clients.
- Therefore, to address these potential value conflicts in a way that exhibits spiritual and religious sensitivity, "practitioners trained in western cognitive procedures might consider constructing spiritually modified interventions with clients who affirm spiritual worldviews" (D. R. Hodge, 2008, p. 183).

Hodge's development of a number of modifications to CBT in this article that are sensitive to Muslim clients underscores the point that it is the spiritual beliefs and values of the client that remain the primary focus in the helping relationship, even though much of the motivation for Christians in social work to be spiritually and religiously sensitive to their clients is driven by the social worker's faith.

#15 *The Christian Intervention Model of Integration* emphasizes that there might be situations—especially when working in certain organizational contexts like Christian congregations or Christian faith-based organizations —in which Christians in social work will interact with individuals or groups that self-identify as Christians, and present with an active interest in or even request services and interventions which intentionally draw upon Christian beliefs, values and practices. Closely related to the spiritual and religious sensitivity model, the Christian intervention model focuses on the development and implementation of interventions that are explicitly Christian in design and are *understood and desired (or even requested) to be as such by the client*. Even within this model, though, it is important to emphasize that it must be the Christian beliefs and values as understood by the client that remain the primary focus and driver of the helping relationship.

Some examples of types of interventions that are explicitly Christian in design include a) adaptations of already-existing secular theories and techniques using Christian language, values and concepts - for example, spiritually-modified cognitive therapy for Christians (D. Hodge, 2003b; Propst, 1988), hope-focused marriage and enrichment (Worthington, 2005), and Christian PREP (Stanley & Trathen, 1994); b) original interventions developed from a base of explicitly Christian beliefs and values - for example, inner healing (Gingrich & Worthington, 2007); and c) incorporating Christian practices or disciplines in a helping relationship - for example, supporting clients' efforts to meditate or pray (or praying with them), encouraging the use of passages of Scriptures or other spiritual, religious, or sacred writings that might encourage, teach, or help clients to cope more effectively with challenges in their lives, helping clients to tap the resources of their faith through various forms of art, music, dance, and poetry, for strength and empowerment, and so forth. A recent study (Wade, Worthington, & Vogel, 2007) provided some promising evidence that when working with clients who have a high level of Christian commitment, "the use of explicitly Christian interventions (interpretations of Scripture, assignment of scriptural readings, prayer for the client) is helpful at promoting improved mental health outcomes" (Gingrich & Worthington, 2007, p. 352).

It is important to note that one of the potential challenges associated with the Christian intervention model is the risk that without appropriate precautions, the social workers' Christian beliefs and values might inadvertently overshadow or dominate those of the client:

> One danger in providing religious and spiritual interventions is that the lack of formal training to supplement therapists' personal religious or spiritual experience creates a risk of therapists imposing their own values or applying religious and spiritual interventions inappropriately (Walker, Gorsuch, & Siang-Yang, 2004, p. 77).

To help address this risk, it is crucial that Christians in social work who develop interventions with clients that are explicitly Christian in design: a) carefully weigh their clients' potential diminished information processing and decision-making abilities due to a heightened state of vulnerability; and b) exercise vigilance with regard to the disproportionate power social workers have in their relationships with clients. Each of these considerations has important implications with regard to their clients' abilities to provide informed consent for and participate authentically in interventions that are explicitly Christian in design.

#16 *The Bridging Model of Integration* emphasizes the role that Christians in social work can play as bridges between the faith community and the social work/ social services community. For although these two communities often share a similar commitment to reaching out to people in need, often they find it difficult to understand, trust and work cohesively with one another. The bridging model of integration focuses on social workers of faith taking advantage of their affiliations with and understanding of both communities to help bring them together to more effectively help people and communities flourish and meet valued outcomes.

The following represents an example of a Christian in social work serving as a bridge between the social services community on the one hand, and faith-based organizations and congregations on the other. During the late 1990s, Bill Raymond, an MSW- level social worker, was the executive director of Good Samaritan, a faith-based organization located in Ottawa County, Michigan. As part of its "Project Zero," Ottawa County officials approached Good Samaritan about partnering to help individuals receiving welfare to obtain employment. Under Bill's leadership, Good Samaritan, which had long-standing relationships with many congregations in the area, mobilized over local 50 churches and helped these churches develop teams of trained mentors to work with interested welfare recipients. The Ottawa County welfare office, after screening clients in their system, would refer appropriate candidates to Good Samaritan, which would facilitate matches between the Ottawa County clients and church mentor teams, as well as provide on-going training and support for these teams. This partnership, in which Bill served as a key bridge builder between government officials and a wide range of congregations from the faith community, contributed to Ottawa County becoming "the first locality in America to put every able-bodied welfare recipient to work" (Sherman, 1999).

Concluding Thoughts on Integrating Christian Faith and Social Work Practice

In recent decades "increasing numbers of contemporary social work practitioners have expressed their needs to integrate their spirituality and faith into their professional activities" (Eun-Kyoung & Barrett, 2007, p. 3), a phenomenon that is by no means unique to social work, since in many fields and types of work "there has been a growing awareness that people's religious faith should inform and impact their life at work" (Russell, 2007, p. 72). There are a number of important reasons for this vital interest in the integration of faith and practice. First, as described earlier in the chapter, for many Christians in social work, faith forms a core part of their identities, and is not something that can simply be "checked at the door" when they do their work. Trying to bracket their faith from their social work practice would feel stilted and inauthentic, leading to an unsatisfying and unproductive disconnect between their personal and professional selves. Hughes, speaking about the integration of faith and scholarship, but with obvious implications for this discussion, suggests that:

> ... if we have any hope of becoming psychologically healthy human beings, we must integrate every aspect of our lives around a core identity that stands at the center of our self-understanding. ... It is simply unthinkable that I should practice my teaching and my scholarship in one corner of my life, and practice my Christian faith in another so that never the twain shall meet...I must find some way to integrate these two core dimensions that define who I am at the most basic levels of my life" (2005, pp. xv; 97).

Second, for many Christians in social work, faith is a powerful asset that provides motivation, supports resilience, and strengthens their ability to cope with the many challenges and stresses associated with being a social worker. For many people of faith, tapping the resources of their faith can be an extremely powerful strategy for sustaining their ability to be the best social workers they can possibly be.

Third, many Christians in social work believe that the content of their faith provides valuable perspective and unique insight - for example, about the depth of the struggles associated with the human condition, or the transforming potential of self-giving love—that is typically not a part of their social work training, but which can be extremely helpful when applied thoughtfully to their social work practice (Jacobson & Jacobson, 2004).

Fourth, within the profession of social work, it has been increasingly recognized that for many clients, faith or spirituality is an important part of their lives, and as such, needs to be openly recognized and acknowledged in their work with such clients (Eun-Kyoung & Barrett, 2007). For Christians in social work, this recognition and affirmation is heightened by the strength and support they have personally experienced through their own faith and their participation in a faith community. As such, learning how to ethically integrate faith and practice can play a valuable role in supporting their efforts to provide spiritually and religiously sensitive social work practice with their clients.

This chapter's description of the ethical integration of Christian faith and social work practice in not intended to be "the final word" on this subject—far from it. There is still a great deal that we need to learn about the reciprocal influence of Christian faith and social work practice on each other. For example, there is currently very little empirical research evaluating outcomes associated with the integration of faith and practice. There needs to be careful empirical work focused on which models of integration are currently in use, by whom, under what circumstances, in which settings, under whose auspices, with which populations, and to what measurable effect. In addition, much of the integration literature addresses how faith contributes to social work practice. But much less attention has been paid to the potential ways that social work theory and practice contribute to how Christians in social work understand, experience, and practice their faith. Finally, more efforts need to be made to explore what the distinctive theologies and practices of the various Christian denominations and traditions (Baptist, Mennonite, Presbyterian, Lutheran, Episcopalian, Roman Catholic, Quaker, etc.) contribute to our understanding of the integration of faith and practice. It is my hope that this chapter will serve as both a resource and an impetus for continued discussion about the many ways faith can make a positive, healthy difference in the work of Christians in social work committed to the ethical integration of Christian faith and professional social work practice.

References

Arnold, R. M., Avants, S. K., Margolin, A. M., & Marcotte, D. (2002). Patient attitudes concerning the inclusion of spirituality into addiction treatment. *Journal of Substance Abuse Treatment, 23,* 319-326.

Badley, K. (1994). The faith/learning integration movement in Christian higher education: Slogan or substance? *Research on Christian Education, 3,* 13-33.

Bowpitt, G. (1989). *Social work and Christianity*. Edinburgh: Handsel Press..

Brandsen, C., & Hugen, B. (2007). Social work through the lens of Christian faith: Working toward integration. *Social Work & Christianity, 34*(4), 349-355.

Canning, S. S., Pozzi, C. F., McNeil, J. D., & McMinn, M. R. (2000). Integration as service : Implications of faith-praxis integration for training. *Journal of Psychology & Theology, 28*(3), 201-211.

Chamiec-Case, R. (2008). Exploring the filtering role of Christian beliefs and values in the integration of Christian faith and social work practice. In B. Hugen & L. Scales (Eds.), *Christianity and social work: Readings on the integration of Christian faith and social work practice* (Third ed., pp. 93-104). Botsford, CT: NACSW.

Chaves, M. (2004). *Congregations in America* Cambridge, Massachusetts: Harvard University Press.

Dressel, A., Bolen, R., & Shepardson, C. (2011). Can religious expression and sexual orientation affirmation coexist in social work? A critique of Hodge's theoretical, theological, and conceptual frameworks. *Journal of Social Work Education, 47*(2).

Eck, B. E. (1996). Integrating the integrators: An organizing framework for a multifaceted process of integration. *Journal of Psychology and Christianity, 15*(2), 101-115.

Ellor, J. W., Netting, F. E., & Thibault, J. M. (1999). *Understanding religious and spiritual aspects of human service practice*. Columbia, S.C.: University of South Carolina Press.

Eun-Kyoung, L., & Barrett, C. (2007). Integrating spirituality, faith, and social justice in social work practice and education: A pilot study. *Journal of Religion & Spirituality in Social Work, 26*(2), 1-21.

Furman, L. D., & Chandy, J. M. (1994). Religion and spirituality: A long-neglected cultural component of rural social work practice. *Human Services in the Rural Environment, 17*(3/4), 21-26.

George, L. K., Larson, D. B., Koenig, H. G., & McCullough, M. E. (2000). Spirituality and health: What we know, what we need to know. *Journal of Social & Clinical Psychology, 19*(1), 102-116.

Gingrich, F., & Worthington, E. L. (2007). Supervision and the integration of faith into clinical practice: research considerations. *Journal of Psychology and Christianity, 26*(4), 342-355.

Glanzer, P. L. (2008). Why we should discard "the integration of faith and learning": Rearticulating the mission of the Christian scholar. *Journal of Education & Christian Belief, 12*(1), 41-51.

Hodge, D. (2003a). The intrinsic spirituality scale: A new six-item instrument for assessing the salience of spirituality as a motivational construct. *Journal of Social Service Research, 30*(1), 41-61.

Hodge, D. (2003b). *Spiritual assessment: Handbook for helping professionals.* Botsford, CT: North American Association of Christians in Social Work.

Hodge, D. R. (2007). The spiritual competence scale: A new instrument for assessing spiritual competence at the programmatic level. *Research on Social Work Practice, 17*(2), 287-295.

Hodge, D. R. (2008). Constructing spiritually modified interventions: Cognitive therapy with diverse populations. *International Social Work, 51*(2), 178-192.

Hugen, B., & Scales, T. L. (2008). *Christianity and social work: Readings on the integration of Christian faith and social work practice (3rd ed).* Botsford, CT: NACSW.

Hughes, R. T. (2005). *The vocation of a Christian scholar: How Christian faith can sustain the life of the mind* (Revised Edition ed.). Grand Rapids, MI: William B. Eerdmans Publishing Company.

Jacobson, D., & Jacobson, R. (2004). *Scholarship and Christian faith: Enlarging the conversation.* New York: Oxford.

Jones, S. L. (2006). Integration: defending it, describing it, doing it. *Journal of Psychology & Theology, 34*(3), 252-259.

Lewis, C. S. (1970). *God in the dock: Essays on theology and ethics* Grand Rapids, MI: Eerdmans.

Mathisen, J. A. (2003). Integrating world views with social roles: supplying a missing piece of the discussion on faith-learning integration. *Journal of Psychology and Christianity, 22*(3), 230-240.

Merriam-Webster online. (2006). Retrieved February 20, 2006, from http://www.m-w.com/

Miller, M. M., Korinek, A. W., & Ivey, D. C. (2006). Integrating spirituality into training: The spiritual issues in supervision scale. *American Journal of Family Therapy, 34*(4), 355-372.

NASW. (2008). NASW code of ethics. Retrieved April 1, 2010, from http://www.naswdc.org/pubs/code/code.asp

Nelson-Becker, H., Nakashima, M., & Canda, E. R. (2007). Spiritual Assessment in Aging: A Framework for Clinicians. *Journal of Gerontological Social Work, vol, 48*(3-4), 3-4.

Niebuhr, H. R. (1975). *Christ and Culture.* New York: Harper and Row.

Okundaye, J. N., Gray, C., & Gray, L. B. (1999). Reimaging field instruction from a spiritually sensitive perspective: An alternative approach. *Social Work, 44,* 371-383.

Pargament, K. (1997). *The psychology of religion and coping.* New York: The Guilford Press.

Parker, M., Larimore, W. L., & Crowther, M. (2002). Should clinicians incorporate positive spirituality Into their practices? What does the evidence say? *Annals of Behavioral Medicine. Special Issue: Spirituality, Religiousness, and Health: From Research to Clinical Practice, 24*(1), 69-73.

Plantinga, A., & Wolterstorff, N. (1983). *Faith and rationality: Reason and belief in God.* Notre Dame: Univ. of Notre Dame Press.

Propst, R. (1988). *Psychotherapy in a religious framework: Spirituality in the emotional healing process.* New York: Human Sciences Press.

Reber, J. S. (2006). Secular psychology: What's the problem? *Journal of Psychology and Theology, 34,* 205-216.

Ripley, J. S., Garzon, F. L., Hall, M. E. L., Mangis, M. W., & Murphy, C. J. (2009). Pilgrims' progress: Faculty and university factors in graduate student integration of faith and profession. *Journal of Psychology and Theology, 37*(1), 5-14.

Russell, M. L. (2007). The secret of marketplace leadership success: constructing a comprehensive framework for the effective integration of leadership, faith, and work. *Journal of Religious Leadership, 6*(1), 71-101.

Scales, T. L., Wolfer, T., Sherwood, D., Garland, D., Hugen, B., & Pittman, S. (2002). *Spirituality and religion in social work practice : decision cases with teaching notes.* Alexandria, Va.: Council on Social Work Education.

Sherman, A. (1999). Faith in communities: Implementing "Charitable Choice" - Transcending the separation between church and state [Electronic Version]. *Philanthropy.* Retrieved September 27, 2011, from http://www.centeronfic.org/v2/equip/publications/articles/ImplementingCharitableChoice_1999.html.

Sherwood, D. (2008). Ethical integration of faith and social work practice: Evangelism. In B. H. L. Scales (Ed.), *Christianity and social work: Readings on the integration of Christian faith and social work practice (3rd ed)* (pp. 409-418). Botsford: CT: NACSW.

Shostrom, E. L., & Montgomery, D. (1978). *Healing love: How God works within the personality.* Nashville, TN: Abingdon.

Spano, R., & Koenig, T. (2007). What is sacred when personal and professional values collide? *Journal of Social Work Values and Ethics, 4*(3).

Stanley, S. M., & Trathen, D. (1994). Christian PREP: An empirically based model for marital and premarital intervention. *Journal of Psychology and Christianity, 13,* 158-165.

Tan, S.-Y. (1996). Religion in clinical practice: Explicit and implicit integration. In E. P. Shafranske (Ed.), *Religion and the clinical practice of psychology* (pp. 365-390). Washington, DC: American Psychological Association.

Tan, S.-Y. (2009). Developing integration skills: The role of clinical supervision. *Journal of Psychology and Theology, 37*(1), 54-61.

Todd, S., & Coholic, D. (2007). Christian fundamentalism and anti-oppressive social work pedagogy. *Journal of Teaching in Social Work, 27*(3/4), 5-25.

Van Hook, M., Hugen, B., & Aguilar, M. A. (2001). *Spirituality within religious traditions in social work practice.* Pacific Grove, CA: Brooks/Cole.

Vanderwoerd, J. R. (2008). Who cares? Social welfare in a diverse society. In B. Hugen & L. Scales (Eds.), *Christianity and social work: Readings on the integration of Christian faith and social work practice* (Third ed., pp. 179-198). Botsford, CT: NACSW.

Wade, N. G., Worthington, E. L., & Vogel, D. L. (2007). Effectiveness of religiously tailored interventions in Christian therapy. *Psychotherapy Research, 17,* 91-105.

Walker, D. F., Gorsuch, R. L., & Siang-Yang, T. (2004). Therapists' Integration of Religion and Spirituality in Counseling: A Meta-Analysis. *Counseling & Values, 49*(1), 69-80.

Walsh, R. (2000). *Essential spirituality: the 7 central practices to awaken heart and mind.* New York: Chichester.

Williams, M., & Smolak, A. (2007). Integrating faith matters in social work education. *Journal of Religion & Spirituality in Social Work, 26*(3), 25-44.

Williams, N. R. (2004). Spirituality and religion in the lives of runaway and homeless youth: coping with adversity. *Journal of Religion and Spirituality in Social Work, 23*(4), 47-66.

Wolfer, T. (2011). Following Jesus in social work: Learning from Anabaptist theology and practice. *Social Work and Christianity, 38*(2), 146-174.

Worthington, E. L. (2005). *Hope-focused marriage counseling: A brief approach* (Revised edition). Downer's Grove: IL: InterVarsity Press.

Yangarber-Hicks, N., Behensky, C., Canning, S. S., Flanagan, K. S., Gibson, N. J. S., Hicks,

M. W., et al. (2006). Invitation to the table conversation: A few diverse perspectives on integration. *Journal of Psychology and Christianity,* 25(4), 338-353.

Note

[1] Recent research has confirmed that spirituality and religion continue to be important to a majority of people in our society, and an extremely relevant consideration in helping relationships. For example, 87% of Americans identify themselves with a religious group or community (Chaves, 2004), and 81% of clients surveyed indicated that they wanted to have their spiritual practices and beliefs included in any counseling services (Walsh, 2000)(see also (Arnold, Avants, Margolin, & Marcotte, 2002).

CHAPTER 20

EVIDENCE-BASED PRACTICE: CAN PRACTITIONERS REALLY BE VALUES-NEUTRAL?

Allison Tan and Michael S. Kelly

Much has been written in the past decade about the implementation of the evidence-based practice (EBP) process in social work. This growing body of literature discusses the barriers that prevent social workers from engaging in the EBP process. In this chapter, a summary of this literature provides a starting point for a new discussion regarding the complications created by the practitioners' personal values and religious or spiritual beliefs. We propose what we believe is an important addition to the EBP decision-making model—that of practitioner transparency and self-awareness—to account for the reality that practitioners are not and cannot purport to be "values-neutral" in their incorporation of EBP principles.

Furman (2009) asserts that because EBP is strongly associated with the scientific process, EBP is "value-free and accepted on face value" (p. 82). This quote suggests that, as long as the practice interventions we utilize are rooted in science, our own personal values and beliefs are somehow neutralized—tempered by the "value free" nature of the scientific, evidence-based practice (EBP) process. Consider the last time you engaged with a client for whom you felt a level of personal attachment or affinity; was the work you did (and the interventions you chose) totally devoid of your own personal feelings about him or her? By contrast, consider the last time you engaged with a client or patient who you knew was involved in a pattern of behaviors you objected to on moral grounds; was your service to that client entirely unaffected by your personal values? In instances like these, can we trust that by searching for solutions within the empirical literature and tempering those findings with the circumstances of the client as well as our own clinical experience (i.e. the EBP process), we are ourselves remaining "values-neutral"? This chapter begins with a brief review of the EBP process along with some related literature documenting one type of barrier associated with failure to successfully implement EBP. We will then return to this question, locating it in a context of Christians practicing social work, ultimately seeking to clarify the role practitioner values and beliefs do play in our practice with diverse populations.

Evidence-Based Practice

The evidence-based practice model of decision-making, which originated in the field of medicine (starting as EBM or evidence-based medicine), is perhaps best understood through the pictorial illustration below.

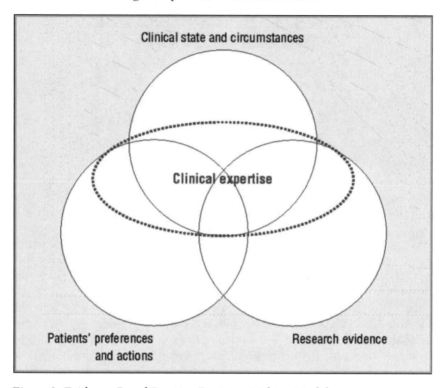

Figure 1: Evidence-Based Practice Decision-Making Model
(Used with permission; Haynes, Devereaux, & Guyatt, 2002)

EBP decision-making integrates what is known from the research evidence, the clinical state of the client[1], and the client's own preferences and actions – all of which is to be informed by the expertise of the practitioner. Regarding the *research evidence*, EBP adheres to a hierarchy of evidence that values systematic reviews and randomized controlled trials (RCTs) over less rigorous experimental designs. This evidence hierarchy encourages greater generalizability of research evidence and promotes a scientifically-oriented process that values rigor over anecdotal evidence (Gibbs, 2003 Kelly, Raines, Stone, & Frey, 2010). The second element of the EBP decision-making model, the *clinical state* of the patient or client must then be used to balance such evidence. The practitioner must carefully assess the level of fit between the research and the individual's situation; for

---

1   Although the model uses the word "patient" to describe the individual seeking services, we will use the term more common in social work: "client."

example, is the client too old, too sick, too uncooperative, or too complicated to apply what is known from the literature (Evidence-Based Medicine Working Group, 1992)? It has been documented that engaging in this step allows for a collaborative process with beneficial results for both clinical outcomes and the client-practitioner relationship (Freeman & Sweeney, 2001). The third aspect of EBP decision-making might be the most innovative. More authoritarian models of clinical care may integrate evidence and clinical circumstances but rarely include the *patient's own preferences* into treatment planning. Doing so calls for "techniques of behavioral science to determine what patients are really looking for" (Evidence-Based Medicine Working Group, 1992, p. 2422).

These components of EBP seem to be a natural fit for social work, as EBP urges the social work practitioner to not simply defer to the evidence, but rather to engage in a client-centered process to determine the best course of action for the individual (Sheyett, 2006). In fact, the originators of the EBP decision-making model have, in the last decade, offered an alternative term to describe the intent of their model; in explaining the intersection of the aforementioned three elements (informed by clinical expertise), Haynes, Devereaux, and Guyatt (2002) state that the EBP process "was developed to encourage practitioners and patients to pay due respect – no more, no less – to current best evidence in making decisions. An alternative term that some social workers may find more appealing is *research enhanced health care*" (p. 1349, emphasis added). As such, the EBP process deemphasizes the intuition of the practitioner (Evidence-Based Medicine Working Group, 1992; Gambrill, 2007) by instead encouraging a systematic integration of multiple sources of information in order to arrive at an evidence-informed solution. For social workers, the idea of "research enhanced health care" fits with the Council of Social Work Education's (CSWE) mandate for social workers to engage in "practice-informed research and research-informed practice (CSWE, 2008, Educational Policy 2.1.6).

Despite the seeming congruence of EBP with social work practice, it is necessary to acknowledge the well-documented challenges and barriers that can prevent more practitioners from engaging in the EBP process of decision-making. Some of these barriers are logistical and competency related: practitioners frequently report difficulty in accessing, assessing, interpreting, and applying empirical evidence into their practice (Haynes & Haines, 1998). While such claims may in fact be valid given the scientific rigor of the EBP process, other barriers and reasons cited by practitioners for their underuse of EBP relate more to the perception that EBP ties the hands of practitioners (Haynes, Devereaux & Guyatt, 2002), making them unable to draw on their own practice wisdom (Freeman & Sweeney, 2001). One study exploring this perception noted "how resistant practitioners are to withdrawing established treatments from practice even once their utility has been disproved" (Haynes & Haines, 1998, p. 274). Related specifically to the field of social work, some have identified this tension as a potential ethical debate between EBP and the values of the social work profession – specifically the tendency to value empirically-supported knowledge over the autonomy of the client (Furman, 2009). While all of these barriers and perceptions raise important questions related to the underutilization of EBP, we wish to raise one more.

Is Evidence-Based Practice Values-Neutral?

There is growing literature on the challenges the EBP process might present to social work values and the National Association of Social Workers (NASW) Code of Ethics (Gambrill, 2007; Gibbs & Gambrill, 2002; Scheyett, 2006). It is true that little was included in the original EBP model regarding professional values. However, there is also nothing specifically depicted in the EBP decision-making diagram about practitioners' *personal values*. Does this mean that we are to believe that practitioner values and beliefs are absent from the EBP process? From its inception, the attraction of the EBP model has been its move away from "authority driven" clinical decision-making (i.e. choosing certain interventions simply because that is what has always been done). However, there seems to have been an accompanying sentiment that EBP ensures that decisions will not be *personally value-driven* either. As such, the EBP process has developed a reputation as being value-free on the part of the practitioner. Gibbs and Gambrill (2002), two of the staunchest advocates for EBP in social work, applaud EBP as distinct from traditional teaching methods that tend to "mix evidence indiscriminately to support a particular position" (Gibbs & Gambrill, p. 462), stating that EBP "controls for clinician bias" (Gibbs & Gambrill, p. 463). However, we know that being values-neutral is a challenge for all social workers, reflected in a rich literature of social workers struggling with moral and ethical challenges (Clark, 2006).

The EBP process is rooted largely in the preferences, rights, and values of the client. Toward that end, the literature describes ethically-appropriate EBP responses to work with highly religious clients (Hasnain, Sinacore, Mensah, & Levy, 2005; Huppert, Siev & Kushner, 2007). We know that a client's religious values, morals, and beliefs can impact preferences for treatment, sometimes by conflicting with empirically-supported interventions. Still, the literature is largely silent when it comes to instances where religious or other moral beliefs of *the practitioner* may yield additional challenges. The EBP process "encourages us to ask, 'How good is the evidence?' and 'Could I be wrong?'" (Gambrill, 2007, p. 449). These are brave questions often left unaddressed as practitioners half-heartedly engage in an EBP-like process while holding tightly to their own values and comfort zones when selecting interventions.

The remainder of this chapter will address this challenge, recognizing that practitioner values and behavior *do* affect the outcomes of care (Evidence-Based Medicine Working Group, 1992). By offering some additions to the traditional EBP decision-making model, we hope to provide a more accurate portrayal of what must happen in order to engage in the scientific EBP process in a way that accounts for the values of practitioners rather than incorrectly assuming the process to be "values-neutral."

New Additions to Conventional Evidence-Based Practice

The additions proposed here build on the traditional EBP decision-making model (Figure 1) based on the understanding that practitioners cannot normally be purely "values-neutral" in their work with clients. In order to ensure that the fidelity of the EBP process is maintained as its originators intended, the model must include intentional elements that remind practitioners to consciously address their own values as well as the values of clients. While these additional elements may have been implied in the original model, we argue for stating and illustrating them clearly so that the practitioner's personal morals, values, and beliefs are not unconsciously impacting the course of treatment. Embedded in these additions is the high value we must place on our own professional integrity; that is, our commitment to search the evidence against our favored views and to consider well-argued alternative views (Gambrill, 2007). This new EBP decision-making model is intentionally "value laden" because we believe that proper EBP process is not as easy as simply "informing" or disregarding our own values, beliefs, tendencies, and intuition. Therefore, by adding in new elements of intentional *self-awareness* and *transparency*, we can maintain our professional integrity while at the same time acknowledging the value laden

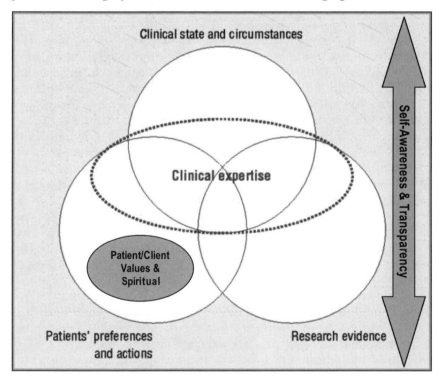

Figure 2: Value-Laden Evidence-Based Practice Decision Making Model
(Adapted from Haynes, Devereaux, & Guyatt, 2002)

nature of work with diverse populations. As seen in Figure 2, the competencies of self-awareness and transparency need to be practiced throughout the entire process of EBP decision-making. There are implications for skillful integration in each aspect of the EBP model. In the remaining discussion of this chapter, we attempt to illustrate what self-awareness and transparency might look like in each of the three main elements of the EBP decision-making process: research evidence, the clinical state, and client preferences.

Regarding the *research evidence* component of the EBP decision-making process, the incorporation of self-awareness and transparency on the part of the practitioner is critically important for maintaining the fidelity and scientific rigor of the EBP process. There is a danger, largely ignored in the existing literature on EBP, of practitioners – consciously or unconsciously – limiting the scope of their research within the context of their own values and clinical preferences. In other words, the practitioner may not look for the potential disconfirming evidence that might challenge existing preconceptions of the social worker or the client (Raines, 2008). To address this danger, our adapted EBP decision-making model stresses the importance of practitioner self-awareness in the course of the search of the research literature. Gibbs and Gambrill (2002) have briefly described ethical reviews of the literature: "Ethical reviewers seek all published and unpublished research that meets standards for inclusion in a review, regardless of whether that research supports or refutes their assumptions" (p. 470). We argue that the only way to truly ensure that one's search of the literature is so inclusive is to engage in an ongoing process of self-awareness. The danger of limiting our search within our own values becomes even more challenging when the process of searching the literature fails to yield conclusive research findings.

When empirically-supported interventions cannot be located, the guidance in existing EBP literature instructs practitioners to inform clients of the lack of evidence in the literature and then suggests that "helpers describe *their hypo-thetical views* about problem-related factors and related service implications" (emphasis added, Gibbs & Gambrill, 2002, 460). While our experience with EBP tells us that this is sometimes necessary, we have some discomfort with the likelihood that – especially given the inherent power imbalance between the social worker and the client–that the client may blur the practitioner's "hypo-thetical views" with the idea of evidence. In order to ensure that, in the absence of empirically-supported interventions, the personal biases and values of the practitioner do not wrongly communicate empirical support and certainty to the client, the need for transparency and humility is crucial. Transparency at this point in the EBP process requires that practitioners articulate those "hypo-thetical views" in a way that leaves no confusion between preference and fact.

The need for self-awareness and transparency also holds strong implications for the understanding of the *clinical state*, the next component of the EBP decision-making process. For those in the social work profession, we are called to employ culturally-competent practice with diverse populations in which the dignity and worth of each individual person is supremely valued, regardless of any personal characteristics or lifestyle. However, if we allow ourselves a moment of complete humility and honest self-awareness, each of us can recall at least one client or group of clients for which our own personal judgment conflicted with our client's life choices. Especially when we are considering the role of values, beliefs, and morals (and even more so when we think specifically of religious beliefs and values), practitioners must acknowledge those biases. If one of the three components in arriving at EBP decisions for intervention with clients is the clinical state of the client, then we must take the time to identify and acknowledge when our personal values, beliefs, and morals have an impact on the way we interpret and judge a client's situation. For example, some practitioners have personal values, whether related to their religious beliefs or not, regarding homosexuality, abortion, addiction, childbearing, childrearing practices, health, and hygiene. When considering the role of self-awareness in regard to the clinical state, we are simply reminding practitioners to be aware of those biases because no practitioner is as "values-neutral" as we purport to be. The use of transparency regarding these judgments may be problematic and should be engaged in very carefully. While referral of a client may be necessary, it may not be appropriate to be entirely transparent with the client regarding the practitioner's judgment of the client's lifestyle or behavior choices.

There are important implications of both transparency and self-awareness within the realm of the third component of the original model – *client preferences and actions*. Much has been written in recent years about the need for spiritual assessment in clinical social work practice (see Hodge, 2001). Some studies have estimated that between 43% and 62% of mental health clients identify religion and/or spirituality as playing highly beneficial roles in their lives (Sheridan, 2004). Given the potential value a client's spirituality may give to his or her clinical experience, "a sensible clinician, whether or not he or she is spiritual in any way, will realize that any purpose-giving, optimistic belief system that is relevant to a client, must, as a matter of sound practice, be acknowledged, explored, and reasonably integrated into the clinical process" (Hoyt, 2008, p. 225). As such, we are suggesting the addition of one more element to the original EBP decision-making process. Within the context of the client preferences and actions piece of the decision-making process, we argue for the central importance of an intentional time of assessment of the client's own values and spirituality. Engaging in an assessment of the client's values and spirituality relates directly to the practitioner's own processes of self-awareness and transparency by a) opening the door for a clinical process that ensures clients will not be "caught between secular and spiritual outlooks" (Gotterer, 2001, p. 187), b) increasing the transparency of the decision-making process by inviting in this important element of the client's life, and c) providing the practitioner with valuable information about the client that may or may not align with the values, beliefs, and morals he or she holds dear. Understanding the beliefs and values of the client, the practitioner can then compare his or her own beliefs and values in order to identify points of connection or discordant beliefs (Tan, 2010). Especially when discordant belief patterns exist between the practitioner and the client, if left unchecked, the EBP decision-making process becomes skewed, biased, and more unscientific than we may realize.

Implications and Next Steps

We do wish to acknowledge one particular setting in which the value-laden EBP decision-making process proposed here may be problematic. Little has been written about the challenges inherent in the provision of EBP-driven services within the context of a faith-based social service agency. Recognizing this gap in the literature, we urge those in the faith-based arena to research their specific interventions in order to develop empirical support for them. We have ethical concerns about knowingly providing non-empirically supported treatment interventions without being clear with our clients that that's what we're doing. However, many faith-based agencies do not yet have established literature to validate their services. Developing this research base will result in huge strides forward to legitimize the powerful work being done in faith-based organizations, while also serving as a challenge to those service providers who may be utilizing interventions with no empirical support. Inherent in this call for further research are two potentially controversial obstacles. First, we must be ready to address what faith-based practitioners are to do when the EBP process yields an intervention their agency cannot implement within the context of their mission. Second, we must begin to consider whether or not there are interventions that should be established within the literature as effective for a client who identifies as atheist and other interventions deemed effective for highly-spiritual clients. These are large research tasks to undertake; yet we feel compelled to make the case for their relevance in applying our value-laden EBP decision-making process to a broad audience.

By adding self-awareness and transparency to the EBP decision-making model, practitioners and clients alike may feel more secure that clinical decisions are more scientifically rigorous and bias-free. Practitioners are *not* "values-neutral" in our work with clients, especially when faced with particularly diverse populations and behaviors that carry with them an element of spiritual, moral, or other personal bias. Helping professions of all kinds, including social work and medicine, have an ethical responsibility to engage in a truly transparent EBP process – one in which we present *all* treatment options found in the literature, regardless of practitioner or client values and preferences. By engaging in an ongoing process of self-awareness, we can begin to work toward "tempering" our own values. We can never truly shelve our personal values, morals, and beliefs, but we can account for them by following the value-laden EBP decision-making process suggested here.

References

Clark, C. (2006). Moral character in social work. *British Journal of Social Work, 36 (1)*, 75-89.

Council on Social Work Education. (2008). *Educational policy and accreditation standards*. Retrieved from http://www.cswe.org/Accreditation/2008EPASDescription.aspx.

Evidence-Based Medicine Working Group. (1992). Evidence-based medicine: A new approach to teaching the practice of medicine. *JAMA, 268*(17), 2420-2425.

Freeman, A.C., & Sweeney, K. (2001). Why general practitioners do not implement evidence: Qualitative study. *British Medical Journal, 323*, 1-5.

Furman, R. (2009). Ethical considerations of evidence-based practice. *Social Work, 54*(1), 82-84.

Gambrill, E. (2007). Views of evidence-based practice: Social workers' code of ethics and accreditation standards as guides for choice. *Journal of Social Work Education, 43*(3), 447-462.

Gibbs, L. E. (2003). *Evidence-based practice for the helping professions: A practical guide with integrated multimedia.*. Pacific Grove, CA: Brooks/Cole.

Gibbs, L., & Gambrill, E. (2002). Evidence-based practice: Counterarguments to objections. *Research on Social Work Practice, 12*, 452-472.

Gotterer, R. (2001). The spiritual dimension in clinical social work practice: A client perspective. *Families in Society, 82*(2), 187-193.

Hasnain, M., Sinacore, J.M., Mensah, E.K., & Levy, J.A. (2005). Influence of religiosity on HIV risk behaviors in active injection drug users. *AIDS Care, 17*(7), 892-901.

Haynes, R.B., Devereaux, P.J., & Guyatt, G.H. (2002). Physicians' and patients' choices in evidence-based practice. *British Medical Journal, 324*, 1349-1350.

Haynes, R.B., & Haines, A. (1998). Barriers and bridges to evidence-based health care practice. *British Medical Journal, 317*, 273-276.

Hodge, D.R. (2001). Spiritual assessment: A review of major qualitative methods and a new framework for assessing spirituality. *Social Work, 46*(3), 203-212.

Hoyt, C.A. (2008). What if the spirit does not move me? A personal reconnaissance and reconciliation. *Social Work, 53*(3), 223-231.

Huppert, J.D., Siev, J., & Kushner, E.S. (2007). When religion and obsessive-compulsive disorder collide: Treating scrupulosity in ultra-orthodox Jews. *Journal of Clinical Psychology, 63*(10), 925-941.

Raines, J. C. (2008). *Evidence-based practice in school mental health*. New York: Oxford.

Scheyett, A. (2006). Danger and opportunity: Challenges in teaching evidence-based practice in the social work curriculum. *Journal of Teaching in Social Work, 26*(1), 19-29.

Sheridan, M.J. (2004). Predicting the use of spiritually-derived interventions in social work practice: A survey of practitioners. *Journal of Religion and Spirituality in Social Work, 23*(4), 5-25.

Tan, A. (2010). Our clients' spirituality…and our own: Implications for best practices in social work. *Praxis, 10*, 6-12.

CHAPTER 21

INTERNATIONAL SOCIAL WORK: A FAITH-BASED, ANTI-OPPRESSIVE APPROACH

Elizabeth Patterson

With increased global awareness and interdependency, there is great opportunity for social workers to combine their Christian callings and social work skills through international social work efforts at home and abroad. Social work practice, biblical principles and theories of Christian missions offer parallel principles that can shape international social work practice. However, throughout history we have the seen the reality of shamefully oppressive international social welfare practices in the name of Christian faith. As we combine Christian faith and social work values in this era of globalization, anti-oppressive practice can inform our approach in order to combat unintentionally oppressive practice. My involvement in the process of the development of a faith-based NGO in Romania will provide a case study to challenge Christian social workers toward anti-oppressive practices.

Defining International Social Work

The International Federation of Social Workers (IFSW) defines international social work by stating:

> The social work profession promotes social change, problem solving in human relationships and the empowerment and liberation of people to enhance well-being. Utilising theories of human behaviour and social systems, social work intervenes at the points where people interact with their environments. Principles of human rights and social justice are fundamental to social work (IFSW, n.d.)

The goal of IFSW is to provide a general definition of social work that transcends individual cultures and nations in order to be relevant in international contexts. More specifically to international practice, Healy's (2008) definition of international social work embraces globalization in both local and global contexts, stating that international social work is:

> ...international professional action and the capacity for international action by the social work profession and its members. International action has four dimensions: internationally related

domestic practice and advocacy, professional exchange, international practice, and international policy development and advocacy" (Healy, 2008, p. 10).

Healy further defined this work as "...international professional action by the social work profession that promotes human rights and social justice within the values and ethics of the profession and Christian faith principles." and noted dimensions are a good starting point, but I believe a Christian faith-based consideration of international social work should include aspects of human rights and social justice principles and the influence of faith on the Christian social worker's practice. Therefore, I suggest my own definition of international social work for Christians:

> " ...international professional action by the social work profession that promotes human rights and social justice within the values and ethics of the profession and Christian faith principles."

Justification for Faith Based International Social Work

Section 6.01 of the NASW Code of Ethics states:

> Social workers should promote the general welfare of society, from local to global levels, and the development of people, their communities, and their environments. Social workers should advocate for living conditions conducive to the fulfillment of basic human needs and should promote social, economic, political, and cultural values and institutions that are compatible with the realization of social justice (NASW, 2008).

This statement reminds us of our ethical obligation as social workers towards not just local, but also global society. This statement, when combined with foundational principles of social work practice of the dignity and worth of the person, service, cultural competence and self-determination, emphasizes the importance of social work practice in global contexts that exhibits sustainable, culturally empowering practices.

Biblical foundations and theory of Christian missions combine Christian principles with social work values. Both the Old and New Testament biblical narratives reveal the importance of caring for those in need, including foreigners. Numerous scriptures in the Old Testament call for justice for the poor and oppressed and call for fair treatment of foreigners (including Exodus 23:5, Leviticus 23: 22, Isaiah 1:17, Leviticus 25:35, Psalm 82:3, Proverbs 14:31). Jesus bridges the gap between the Old and New Covenant by declaring Isaiah 61 in Luke 4: 18-19, "The Spirit of the Lord is on me because he has anointed me to proclaim good news to the poor. He has sent me to proclaim freedom for the prisoners and recovery of sight for the blind, to set the oppressed free, to proclaim the year of the Lord's favor (NIV)." Jesus preached and lived a lifestyle of a kingdom of God that was available for all people and defied cultural norms. He reached out to marginalized cultures and people that Jews typically did not engage. He then commanded his disciples to "Go into all the world and preach the gospel (Mark 16:15, NIV)." This gospel, or good news, brings both salvation of a kingdom to come and justice for the poor and oppressed in the current realm. Joining together this Great Commission commandment with our social work values encourages Christian involvement in faith-based international social work.

Principles of missions that have developed out of these biblical mandates also inform a Christian perspective on international social work practice. International Christian missions usually involves entering a culture different from one's own. Theories of missions emphasize the importance of understanding the culture one is entering for effective relationship building and of not automatically identifying dominant cultural values as Christian values (Smith, 1998). Practice of missions also emphasizes the indigenization and contextualization of the church, which strives to mirror social work principles of culturally sensitive self-determination and empowerment. Ideally, this model of missions should indicate that both social work and Christian missions focus on working with and training local cultures to do sustainable work in their own cultural context (Eitel, 1998; Tennent, 2010). International social workers and Christian missionaries both should have the goal of "working themselves out of a job" through a process of empowerment towards developing local leadership to sustain culturally relevant work (Gray, 2006; Tennent, 2010). As we move towards a model of international social work practice that is ethical and faith-based, it is important to first examine the history of international social welfare so we can learn from our past as we develop new international social work paradigms.

History of International Social Welfare and the Christian Church

Ancient cultures were largely homogenous. When in need, people took care of their own family and community groups (Queen, 1922), but when foreigners crossed into new lands, kindness to strangers was considered a virtue in many early cultures and religions, including Hebrew Law (Harnack & Hermann, 1907; Trattner, 1994). Old Testament documents record religious mandates to look after the widow, orphan and foreigner. Social policies existed to meet the needs of the poor, such as the harvest principle of gleaning and the year of the Sabbath and Jubilee that redistributed wealth (Exodus 22-23, Leviticus 25).

Although there were ancient traditions and policies that encouraged just treatment of out groups, cultural groups still conquered territories to acquire more land, often oppressing inhabitants and even enslaving those they conquered. Slavery continued to be acceptable practice in the days of the early Christian Church. However, the early church was open to all social classes, including slaves, and encouraged mutual aid, sharing of resources, visiting of prisoners, and the entertainment of strangers while also emphasizing the importance providing for one's own needs (Hnik, 1938; Queen, 1922).

More formal systems of charity developed with the breakdown of relationships within communities and increased migration. As Christianity spread and became more influential under Constantine, charitable practices developed. Xenodochia were established as relief institutions aiding groups needing care, such as the aging, sick, orphans, widows and those in poverty. During this time the power of the bishops in Rome increased. Mackenzie (2010) suggests that the Catholic Church serves as an example of an early international charitable organization with centralized power in Rome joining the church throughout the Western World.

Although much Christian charity was done in the name of religion, there has also been much oppression in the name of major world religions, including Christianity (Krehbiel, 1937). Under religious auspices, the Crusades created a Holy War for Christian dominance of the Holy Land, killing tens of thousands along the way (Parry, 1965). As the world expanded through further exploration, international oppression in the name of religion, wealth and power continued. By the 15th and 16th centuries, Western European countries were colonizing lands they had discovered, including what we now call North America, often in the name of Christian faith and missionary zeal (Parry, 1965; Wallace, 1930).

In the 1500's, the Protestant Reformation took place, also impacting systems of charity in countries where Protestant ideas spread internationally. As Protestantism grew, monasteries diminished. The Protestant church revolted against the corruption within the system of papal indulgences and did not offer an alternative method of charity, emphasizing grace and hard work rather than the giving of alms and good works (Harnack & Hermann, 1907; Hnik, 1938; Queen, 1922). These philosophical attitudes that influenced religious charity, along with societal changes that created more poverty led to the development of public relief systems, starting in France, Germany, and Switzerland, then moving to England and eventually the U.S. (Queen, 1922).

As industrialization took place and North America was colonized, those who captured and oppressed slaves justified their actions as a means of personal and economic development (Leiby, 1978). Settlers sought new land at the expense of indigenous people, justifying the oppression as a colonization effort to convert the "savages" to Christianity and modify their culture, while providing new wealth for both themselves and their colonizers (Osterhammel, 1997). Eitel (1998) suggests that "biblically inspired adventurism coincided with secular trends... Economic and political interests stimulated Western powers to engage in imperialistic expansionism (p. 306)". As industrialized countries advanced their own wealth, there became a greater gap between rich and poor nations (Magdoff, 1978).

With both land and industrial expansion of the Americas, massive immigration during the Industrial revolution brought more European immigrants to North America. A greater diversity of cultures came to North America and new culture groups worked together for the first time (Jennissen & Lundy, 2011; Leiby, 1978). Conditions in cities worsened as populations grew. Recent immigrants often suffered the most as they adjusted to the new land while being displaced from their own cultures and families (Queen, 1922).

International Influence on the Development of Social Work

In the late 19th and early 20th centuries, private charities, many religious in nature, were developing to provide direct services for those in need (Friedlander, 1975; Healy, 2008; Queen, 1922). Some of these charities spread across borders internationally and have continued their international influence to this day. These charities include City Missions, Young Men's Christian Association (YMCA) and Young Women's Christian Association (YWCA), and the Salvation Army. Many of these organizations developed systems for providing services to the poor that were precursors to later professional social work methods. During the latter part of the 19th century, religious motivations often shaped social welfare ideologies and work among private charities in Western Europe and North America (Hnik, 1938; Young & Ashton, 1956). The Social Gospel movement emphasized the importance of meeting social needs as an important part of carrying out the gospel of Jesus Christ, both in domestic and international work (Harnack & Hermann,1907; Rauschenbusch,1922). While this movement was being formed, it influenced religious charities and their work, including the work of City Missions in urban slums. City Missions contributed to the development of social services by providing more than immediate relief; they created restaurants, lodging houses, sewing workrooms and nurseries (Leiby, 1978; Valverde, 2008).

Historically grounded in the City Mission philosophy, The Young Men's Christian Association (YMCA) and Young Women's Christian Association (YWCA) took root in England and spread internationally, working with immigrant populations in the U.S. as well as internationally (Leiby, 1978; Morse, 1918; Rice, 1947; Sims, 1936). The Salvation Army, established first in England as a church with primarily evangelistic intentions, quickly developed charitable purposes as it reached out to marginalized groups. The Salvation Army work spread to North America and other parts of the world, continuing the mission to reach the poorest of the poor (Leiby, 1978; Valverde, 2008).

Meanwhile, the rising middle and upper class bourgeoisie developed nonsectarian charities without formal religious ties (Valverde, 2008; Queen, 1922). Although these agencies were mostly secular in nature, their leaders often had religious motivations and international involvement (Beauman, 1996; Holden, 1922; Richmond, 1930a). Starting in Europe and then moving to North America, both the charity organization societies and settlement house movements worked with immigrants to the U.S. while also spreading their influence internationally during the early development of social work. Jane Addams, who showed deep concern for culturally sensitive practice, also collaborated with early social justice pioneers from other countries visiting Hull House. She also traveled to Europe and Russia and was involved in the international peace movement, leading to her Nobel Peace Prize in 1931 (Addams, 1920, Addams,1922; Addams, 1910; Bruno, 1957; Jennissen & Lundy, 2011).

As this brief historical analysis indicates, throughout the last two millennia there have been oppressive practices coexisting alongside genuine charitable works within international relations. However, as social welfare services developed in the past two centuries, they have often included service to immigrant populations in the U.S. as well as international populations abroad. The profession of social work also developed in the early 20th century through international learning and mutual exchange of information between nations. Once professional social work took root, the U.S. and Western Europe became dominant forces in the development of social work practice internationally as social work theories and models spread to developing nations (Healy, 2008). In recent years globalization has resulted in new opportunities for international social work.

International Social Work Today

Globalization
   Although international interdependency has been a part of society for centuries, since the 1990's, globalization has increased at an exponential rate (Ife, 2000). Modern day globalization encompasses a greater breakthrough in information, technology, and cultural domains (Mizrahi & Davis, 2008), creating the notion of an increasingly smaller world. Social problems such as human trafficking, global health epidemics, and poverty are no longer contained within national borders or even global regions. This makes global issues local and local issues global (Dominelli, 2004; Ife, 2000; Payne & Askeland, 2008). Globalization allows a greater opportunity for more people to take advantage of travel opportunities to spread the gospel through evangelism, aid, and development efforts.
   One example of the onset of globalization is the fall of communism that took place in the 1990's in the former Soviet Union and other parts of Eastern Europe. The rest of the world became aware of the social problems that arose during the communist era (Healy, 2008; Perry, Berg, & Krukones, 2011). Social work educators and professionals were called upon to help develop the social welfare system and social work educational systems (Bridge, 2004; Horwath & Shardlow, 2004; Walsch, Griffiths, McGolgan, & Ross, 2005). Christian missions and churches flooded these areas to spread the gospel through evangelism and assistance with physical needs.
   These and other opportunities to develop social work in other parts of the world have provided chances to share the gospel, meet human needs in tangible ways, and to share social work resources and knowledge. However, there are real concerns that these new opportunities might result in social workers repeating imperialistic, colonialist practices of times past in a culturally incompetent way (Kendall, 1995). As the U.S. has become a dominant force in both professional social work and in missions internationally, we must ask ourselves: are we repeating culturally imperialistic models of practice or exhibiting empowering social justice principles?

Repeating Colonialist Practices?
   There is much literature that encourages social workers to engage in international social work practice during this era of globalization. However, at the

same time, there is much literature cautioning against the oppressive practices that may exist within international social work practice today (Fox, 2010; Gray, 2005 Midgley, 1997; Jonsson, 2010; Payne & Askeland, 2008). In fact, some believe that globalization has brought about more opportunities for international social work, but has benefited the rich nations much more than poor nations. Perhaps it has further perpetuated the risk of colonistic practices in international social work (Fox, 2010; Jonsson, 2010; Midgley, 1997; Morely, 2004). Colonialist practices take place when Western models are offered to developing nations without being adapted in a culturally relevant manner.

The Western world, with a longer history of social work education and social programs, may have resources to aid less developed regions of the world, yet the history of colonization and cultural imperialism need to be recognized if these efforts are to empower rather than oppress (Cox & Pawar, 2006). Sadly, colonialist tendencies can even permeate the social work profession as well as Christian international work and missions, despite the values and ethics of social work that would go against this notion of power and dominance. Midgley (2007) states that these "unequal international power relations have a direct impact on inequality and the welfare of ordinary people around the world" (p. 614). This is particularly true in international social work, when people from Western nations interact with those from less developed communities. Post-communist countries of Eastern Europe provide a great example of this danger of cultural imperialism. When the fall of communism opened up avenues for teaching social work, it was often assumed that experts from the West had the knowledge to bring social work expertise to these nations (Horwath, J. & Shardlow, 2004; Cox & Pawar, 2006).

I recently was reminded of this in a meeting about international social work when a young, articulate social worker who had recently finished her MSW joined our conversation. She had deep knowledge of international social welfare issues and stated that she did not believe in the "missionary" mindset of international social work. Although we may not share the same faith, and her remark may seem negative towards my involvement in international social work in a missions setting, I understood what she meant and agreed with the meaning behind her statement. Missionary efforts have often been accused of oppressing cultural groups internationally. This saddens me, as I believe that both social work values and missions theory embrace cultural empowerment. However, I am aware that both international social work and missions endeavors have often exhibited oppressive practice approaches.

Should these oppressive tendencies stop us from international practice? Definitely not. Both biblical mandates and the values and ethics of social work call us towards international service. We must intentionally work towards empowering models of practice that truly exhibit biblical, missions and social work principles that promote dignity and worth of the individual, self-determination, and culturally relevant practice. Anti-oppressive practice is a model that I believe Christian social workers can apply.

Anti-Oppressive Practice

Power and Oppression

Anti-oppressive practice is a common method in English-speaking countries that recognize oppression, including Canada, Great Britain and Australia. However, anti-oppressive practice has not been as common among social workers from the United States (VanWormer, 2004).. Anti-oppressive social work acknowledges the power differentials that pervade society and the oppressive structures that exist at various levels of society, further marginalizing people outside dominant cultures (Darlymple & Burke, 2006 Dominelli, 2002; Mullaly, 2002). Mullaly (2002) takes a critical approach to anti-oppressive practice, putting emphasis on the structural inequalities that exploit and oppress the less dominant groups, stating that:

> ...both the structural forces and human agency are integral in developing an understanding of oppression and anti-oppressive practices. Both structures and individuals are able to exercise power. However it is patently obvious that a social institution will be able to exercise more power than an individual, and that an individual from the dominant group will, for the most part, be able to exercise more political, social, and economic power than members of a subordinate group (p. 20).

Anti-oppressive practice also recognizes that these acts of oppression do exist at personal, cultural and societal levels (Mullaly, 2002). Oppression is described at the personal level as "thoughts, attitudes and behaviors that predict negative prejudgments of subordinate groups (p. 52)." This oppression is usually based on stereotypes and often happens at a subconscious level. When traveling internationally, westerners often assume a stereotypical viewpoint of those from the culture, whether positive or negative, and often need to set aside these viewpoints to learn and understand the reality and deeper meaning of their actions.

Anti-oppressive practice theory also acknowledges the power differential between the social worker and the client system and the potential for the social worker to be unintentionally oppressive (Clifford & Burke, 2009; Mullaly, 2002; Dominelli 2002). When social workers and students from developed countries host people from other countries in mutual exchange or travel to other countries to practice or educate, they normally go with the best intentions, hoping to make at least a short term difference and perhaps a lasting change. By bringing Western ideologies and interventions to international social work education, practice, and policy, social workers often oppress while intending to empower.

Social workers must be aware of the power differentials that exist between dominant nations and developing nations at the personal, cultural and societal levels and the potential oppression felt by those from nations with less power and privilege. Healy (2008) notes the criticisms of the International Federation of Social Workers (IFSW) and International Association of Schools of Social Work (IASSW) codes of ethics. Some would argue that there is a "Western bias" to these codes in that they leave out the values of less individualistic, community oriented societies.

Anti-Oppressive Connections to Christian Faith: Freedom for the Oppressed

So how does anti-oppressive practice fit within the context of Christian faith? There are numerous scriptures throughout the Bible that speak against oppression and towards social justice and care for the marginalized. Proverbs 14:31 expresses, "whoever oppresses the poor shows contempt for His maker (NIV), revealing the importance of recognizing ways that we are unintentionally oppressive. Isaiah 1:17 tells us to "seek justice. Defend the oppressed (NIV)." As Christian social workers, we are challenged to to take on our biblical mandate to share the gospel internationally through the use of our social work knowledge and skills. Anti-oppressive practice methods can give us a model to bring "freedom for the oppressed" at the personal, cultural and structural levels of society. My experiences with this process taking place in Romania will provide a case example.

The Case Example of Romania

Romania: A culture between identities

> The history of Romanians is a permanent search for identity, a permanent attempt to define itself. It is a silent drama, which each succeeding generation has lived anew. The country of Romanians does not belong either to Central Europe, or the Balkans, or Western Europe, or the vast Slavic body of the East. It lies at their crossroads. Its history is itself a history of borders; on the outskirts of the Romanian Empire or the Byzantine Empire, as well as the outer limits of the Ottoman, Russian, or later on, Western expansion (Bulei, 2005, p. 5).

Like much of Eastern Europe, Romania has experienced many border changes and struggles for identity. Anti-oppressive social work practice acknowledges the importance of identity and the fact that struggle with identity can act as a source of oppression. Dominelli (2002) discusses how anti-oppressive practice is "integrally involved in the process of contested identities" (p. 39). One's personal sense of identity and how others perceive them can impact the ability to form non-oppressive relationships. The communist era continued to act as a source of oppression for Romania and its people.

Romania is beautiful nation, rich in natural resources and diverse ethnic groups. Unfortunately, much of this wealth was destroyed after World War II during the communist period lasting until 1989 (Bachman, 1991; Bulei, 2005). The final ten years of communism brought the worst of the deprivation under the rule of the final dictator, Nicolae Ceausescu. In 1989, Ceaucescu reported that over the previous ten years he had paid off the national debt by exporting Romania's natural resources . During this time period there were few resources left for the survival of the people. Basic commodities were rationed, leaving people in long lines without the bread they hoped for at the other end. Resources of electricity, heat and gas were also limited. While this was happening, in order to increase the labor force, abortion and birth control were considered illegal and families were given incentive to have more children (Bachman, 1991). This gave rise to increased numbers of children abandoned to the care of the government institutions, similar to the rest of Eastern Europe. The government claimed it could better care for children in institutions, rather than distribute resources to families. (Zamfir, 1997). Individuals, groups, and social classes who did not remain loyal to communist ideals were oppressed, with their employment removed or, in many cases, put in prison. (Zamfir & Ionescu, 1994).

From 1959 to 1990 there were no schools of social work, as the communist government did not recognize the need for solutions to social problems, but believed these problems would resolve themselves (Zamfir and Ionescu, 1994). Like in the Soviet Union and other Eastern European countries, the fall of dictators in the late 1980s brought hope. However, there remained an awareness of the devastating effects that communism had on the country and its people. After the people's revolution in December of 1989, Romania's social problems were revealed to the rest of the world, bringing foreign aid and development efforts into Romania. This included government aid from North American and Europe, grassroots efforts, churches, and secular and faith-based non-governmental organizations (NGOs). It was during this time that the seeds of Veritas took root.

The Development of Veritas, a Faith-Based NGO in Romania

Anti-oppressive practice methods that take a critical approach to policy and practice are very relevant for societies in transition, such as Eastern European nations. As work is done at the structural level, anti-oppressive practice methods can help the voice of the powerless to gain power at the societal level. Alternative service organizations with "bottom up" development efforts are often key in anti-oppressive practice at this level. Veritas is a prime example of a grassroots NGO developed to meet community needs. It became the most active NGO with the widest variety of services within its community.

In the early 1990s American students at Eastern Nazarene College in Quincy, Massachussets who heard about the devastating effects of communism in Romania went there to serve. Their work led Eastern Nazarene College to develop the Romanian Studies Program so that students (including me) could spend semesters in Romania studying and serving the needs of the community. Students and American volunteers were able to develop programs with the aid of Romanian translators, particularly with abandoned and at-risk children. The director of the Romanian Studies Program, Dorothy Tarrant, believed in the community and knew that a legitimate NGO would need to be created for sustainable development and indigenous leadership. Once Veritas was developed as an NGO, Romanian staff could be hired legally to sustain the work.

Romanian leadership did not develop immediately. The history of oppressive structures influenced the local people and a very deliberate anti-oppressive process of empowerment needed to take place; "a process through which oppressed people reduce their alienation and sense of powerlessness and gain greater control over all aspects of their lives and social environment (Fook, p. 179)." As part of this process, I went back to Romania after receiving my MSW degree to coordinate the social services, which had expanded to include children, families, older adults, and people with disabilities. Educational and community development programs were evolving to serve the local community, including small business development and later a program to address domestic violence. Romanian staff were leading these programs, but still hesitant to take on further leadership.

Throughout my time in Romania, I witnessed many other NGO's and Christian ministries developing. I saw both oppressive and anti-oppressive practices within these NGOs, and even within Veritas at times. While many people came with the best intentions, I observed some Westerners putting stipulations on how aid was given, making Romanians more dependent on them. Others were encouraging Romanians to utilize the aid towards sustainability. At the policy level, new social welfare policies were developed after Western models, restricting and sometimes eliminating services that were effectively meeting needs.

These stipulations were not empowering Romanians, but further controlling them. We realized that if Veritas truly believed in the social work and Christian missions values of self-determination, empowerment and indigenization, we must be aware of the unintentional oppression that can take place and deliberately work against process. As Mullaly (2002) suggests, the first step in this process was acknowledging the power that we had as Western social workers and missionaries by the very nature of our cultural history and identity as well as the economic, social and educational opportunities we had experienced. We needed to utilize these opportunities to deliberately empower, rather than unintentionally oppress.

Romanians learned how to be social service workers and leaders through first working alongside American students and volunteers. One method of empowerment throughout history has been education and certainly, as was the case with Veritas employees. Romanian staff developed social work skills that allowed them to take on more and more leadership and become directors of their own programs. Veritas helped them receive formal training by supporting Romanians to get degrees in social work and related fields. Social work was a new profession in Romania and many of our staff did not have university degrees. As Romanians took over as leaders, roles shifted and American students and volunteers began to work alongside Romanians to learn from them.

Many Romanians were satisfied to let foreigners lead them, which I believe was largely due to the cycle of oppression and mistrust they experienced under communism, struggles with their own professional identities, and lack of trust in themselves and their own people. Therefore, in this process it was important that we developed trusting relationships with local Romanians who could freely voice their opinions and see we valued them. These and other small steps showed Romanians we valued their expertise and trusted their leadership. Our confidence in them helped them to trust themselves as leaders and to take on higher levels of leadership.

As this process of trust is developed and the international social worker has the opportunity to utilize skills and theoretical bases of social work, the client systems must be agents of their own change, at the personal, cultural and societal levels. The international social worker can help facilitate this change, but practice must be 'critically reflexive,' allowing the client system to be in control so the pattern of oppression is stopped (Fook, 2002; Mullaly, 2002). During the development of Veritas, a German social worker, Bianca Duemling (2003), came to serve with Veritas as part of her graduate work. She surveyed the Romanian staff to see how they perceived the relationships within a foreign developed NGO and to discover if there were oppressive relations. This was an uncomfortable process at first, but a valuable anti-oppressive practice method.

Results of her study indicated Romanian's appreciation and desire for Western involvement during this time of transition, due to the benefits of training and education, mutual exchange of ideas, and the modeling principles of equality and human rights principles for all members of society. Yet Romanian staff expressed concerns over their dependence on Western funds and the imposition of Western values at times. Interviewees also mentioned the dilemma of Westerners taking away local responsibility, and imposing their own Western values and stereotypes in an oppressive manner. Many, but not all, of their examples, related to short-term involvement of Westerners, but their opinions needed to be taken seriously by long-term Western leadership if we were to act in an anti-oppressive manner. In order to maximize the positive relationships and minimize oppressive tendencies, Romanians suggested that long-term commitment, better communication, and cultural sensitivity were all necessary. The importance of Westerners acting as mentors and allowing Romanians to take over leadership was also mentioned as an important part of the development of Veritas. Duemling's research helped the staff voice some concerns and allowed us to make changes, including a more informative orientation for newcomers and adapting the work schedule to be more culturally sensitive to Romanians expectations. This research and the resulting practice approaches enabled the staff to see that their opinions were valued and respected as part of the process of the development of Veritas.

The opinions of Veritas staff confirm what we know about anti-oppressive practice methods applied to international social work practice. The social worker must not come into the relationship with preconceived ideas of how to help, but in mutual learning, recognize the client system as the expert of its own situation (Mullaly, 2002; Dominelli, 2002). Some degree of withdrawal from the dominant group does need to take place, allowing the client system to know you are available when consultation is needed. As the Romanian leadership was put in place, we foreign leaders took on a behind the scenes role, but made ourselves available as needed. Veritas hired a Romanian director of social services, Petronia Popa, in 2006, who took over completely when the founder of Veritas retired in 2010.

As Mullaly (2002) warns, this process should not be romanticized; it was not simple. Mistakes were made along the way and deliberate steps towards anti-oppressive practice were needed. Although Romanian leadership has taken over at the organizational level, anti-oppressive practice methods must still be applied since much of the funding still comes from outside of Romania. There is an American advisory board that supports this funding and we must still be careful to use deliberate anti-oppressive methods in continuing to support Veritas in its important work.

As Veritas works towards sustainability, it continues to struggle for recognition by local and county governments and often feels oppressed and marginalized in this process. However, as this process takes place, Veritas employees and clients are also being empowered as local leaders to speak for change at the societal level.

Coalition building is also a valuable aspect of anti-oppressive practice. As this has happened between Veritas and other NGO's in Romania, Veritas staff became involved in national coalitions on issues related to child advocacy and were part of creating policies that addressed child welfare and domestic violence at the national level.

Romania became a member of the European Union in 2007. This Europeanization brings new social problems and new struggles for identity. Prices have risen in Romania with little salary increases for the average Romanian. Many Romanians have migrated to other European countries to find work, dividing families and some families leaving children in the care of grandparents or neighbors, causing a new kind of abandonment (Personal Communication, D. Tarrant, May 2008). European Union grants have offered funding for projects that promote Europeanization and democracy building (Schimmelfennig & Sedelmeier, 2005). Healy (2008) suggests that this funding to promote Europeanization is a positive opportunity for professional exchange between the former Eastern bloc and Western Europe, yet admits there are criticisms of this funding as "Eurocentric." This brings about a new challenge for Romania today in its struggle between national identity and Europeanization of its culture (Dragoman, 2007). This presents the question: is Europeanization oppressive to Romanian's development as a democracy and to its continual struggle for identity as a marginalized outgroup on the edge of Europe?

Conclusion

Gray's (2005) words summarize the value of international social work within the paradigm of anti-oppressive practice:

> International social work is not just about the spread of professional social work across the globe, it is also about the development of practices that are relevant in local contexts. As such, different forms of social work emerge and take hold, molded and shaped by the social, political, economic circumstances, the history and culture

of particular contexts, as well as prevailing social work knowledge and values...There is much of value in Western thinking about social work, but this must not stifle the wisdom and experience of local cultures ...International social work, in being responsive to diverse contexts and sensitive to local cultures, must, of necessity, be a flexible entity, open to new forms of social work evolving as it responds to local problems and needs in culturally appropriate and sensitive ways.... (p. 236).

As Christian social workers it is important that we not ignore the need and opportunity for international social work practice both in international contexts and with international populations in the U.S.; however we must take into consideration both Christian faith and social work values that work against oppression and towards culturally empowering partnerships. This often requires cultural humility on the part of the dominant culture in order to develop trusting, empowering relationships that are anti-oppressive at the individual, cultural and societal levels. Without this paradigm of practice, international social workers run the risk of further oppression of people, cultures and societies that have the potential to offer much to the globalized world of social work practice. As international social workers commit themselves to developing the relationships that can allow anti-oppressive methods of practice to develop, not only will the country or culture of focus benefit, but the social work profession as a whole will benefit from this mutual exchange and from newly developed indigenous, culturally relevant practice methods.

References

Addams, J. (1920). Charitable effort. In J. Addams (Ed.), *Democracy and social ethics* (pp. 13-70). NY: Macmillan Company.

Addams, J. (1922). *Peace and bread in time of war.* MacMillan Company: NASW.

Addams, J. (1910). *Twenty years at Hull-Hwith autobiographical notes.* Norwood, MA: The Macmillan Company.

Bachman, R. (Ed.). (1991). *Romania: A country study* (2nd ed.). Washinton, D.C.: U.S. Government Printing Office.

Beauman, K. B. (1996). *Women and the settlement movement.* NY: Radcliffe Press.

Bridge, G. (2004). Social policy and social work in the voluntary sector: the case of Ukraine. *Social Work Education , 23* (3), 281-292.

Bruno, F. J. (1957). *Trends in social work: 1874-1956.* New York: Columbia University Press.

Bulei, I. (2005). *A short history of Romania.* Bucuresti: Meronia Publishers, LTD.

Clifford, D., & Burke, B. (2009). *Anti-Oppressive ethics and values of social work.* NY: Palgrave Macmillan.

Cox, D., & Pawar, M. (2006). *International social work: Issues, strategies, andprograms.* Thousand Oaks, California: Sage Publications.

Darlymple, J., & Burke, B. (2006). *Anti-oppressive practice: Social care and the law.* NY: Palgrave Macmillan.

Dominelli, L. (2002). *Anti-oppressive social work theory and practice.* London: Palgrave Macmillan.

Dominelli, L. (2004). *Social Work: Theory and practice for a changing profession*. Malden, MA: Polity Press.

Dragoman, D. (2007). National identity and Europeanization in post-communist Romania. The meaning of citizenship in Sibiu: European capital of culture. *Communist and Post-Communist Studies , 48*, 63-78.

Duemling, B. (2003). The Dilemma posed by democracy promotion: Shifting the focus from a political to a personal perspective. Experiences of Romanian staff in an international NGO. *Unpublished Master's Thesis* . The Alice Salomon Fachhochschule University of Applied Science, Berlin.

Eitel, K. (1998). "To be or not to be?": The indigenous church question. In J. Terry, E. Smith, & J. Anderson (Eds.), *Missiology: An introduction to the foundations, history and strategies of world missions* (pp. 301-317). Nashville: Broadman & Holman.

Fook, J. (2002). *Social work: Critical theory and practice*. Thousand Oaks, CA: Sage Publications, Inc.

Fox, M. (2010). Post colonist practice: An Australian social worker in rural Zambia. *International Social Work , 53* (5), 720-731.

Friedlander, W. (1975). *International social welfare*. Englewood Cliffs, NJ: Prentice-Hall, Inc.

Gray, M. (2005). Dilemmas of international social work: Paradoxical processes in indigenization, universalism and imperialism. *International Journal of Social Welfare , 14*, 23-28.

Harnack, A., & Hermann, W. (1907). *Essays on the social gospel*. NY: G.P. Putnam's Sons.

Healy, L. M. (2008). *International social work: Professional action in an interdependent world*. NY: Oxford University Press.

Hnik, F. M. (1938). *The philanthropic motive of Christianity: An analysis of the relations between theology and social service*. Oxford: Basic Blackwell.

Holden, A. (1922). *The settlement idea: A vision for social justice*. NY: The Macmillan Company.

Horwath, J., & Shardlow, S. (2004). Drawing back the curtain: Managing learning opportunities accross two linguistic worlds, when the quality of interpretation is poor. *Social Work Education , 23* (3), 253-264.

Ife, J. (2000). Localized need and a globalized economy: Bridging the gap with social work practice. *Candian Social Work, Special Issue: Social Work and Globalization , 2* (1), 50-64.

International Federation of Social Workers. (n.d.). Retrieved December 21, 2011, from http://www.ifsw.org/f38000138.html

Jennissen, T., & Lundy, C. (2011). *One hundred years of social work: A History of the profession in English Canada 1900-2000*. Waterloo: Wilfred Laurier University Press.

Jonsson, J. H. (2010). Beyond empowerment: Changing local communities. *International Social Work , 53* (3), 393-406.

Kendall, K. (1995). Forward. In T. Watts, & D. M. Elliot (Eds.), *International handbook on social work education* (pp. xiii-xvii). Westport, CT: Greenwood Press.

Krehbiel, H. (1937). *Peace war amity*. Newton, KS: H.P. Krehbiel.

Leiby, J. (1978). *A history of social welfare and social work in the United States*. New York: Columbia University Press.

Mackenzie, D. (2010). *A world beyond borders: The history of international organizations*. Toronto: University of Toronto Press.

Magdoff, H. (1978). *Imperialism: From the colonial age to the present*. NY: Monthly Review Press.

Midgley, J. (1997). *Social welfare in a global context*. Thousand Oaks, CA: SAGE Publications.

Mizrahi, T., & Davis, L. (2008). *Encyclopedia of social work.* Washington D.C.: NASW Press.

Morely, C. (2004). Critical reflection in social work: A response to globalization? *International Journal of Social Welfare , 13,* 298-303.

Morse, R. (1918). *My life with young men: Fifty years in the Young Men's Christian Association.* NY: Association Press.

Mullaly, B. (2002). *Challenging oppression: A critical social work approach.* Don Mills, ON: Oxford University Press.

NASW. (2008). Retrieved May 19, 2010, from NASW Code of Ethics: http://www.social-workers.org/pubs/code/code.asp

Parry, J. (1965). *Europe and a wider world: 1415-1715* (13th ed.). London: Hutchinson & Co.

Payne, M., & Askeland, G. A. (2008). *Globalization and international social work: Postmodern change and challenge.* Burlington, VT: Ashgate Publishing Company.

Perry, M., Berg, M., & Krukones, J. (2011). *Sources of European history since 1900* (2nd ed.). Boston: Wadsworth, Cengage Learning.

Queen, S. (1922). *Social work in light of history.* Philadelphia: J. B. Lippincott Company.

Rauschenbusch, W. (1922). *A theology for the social gospel.* Norwood, MA: Berwick & Smith Co.

Rice, A. (1947). *History of the Young WChristian Association.* NY: The Women's Press.

Richmond, M. (1930). Our relation to the churches. In M. Richmond (Ed.), *The longview: papers and addresses* (pp. 115-119). NY: Russell Sage Foundation.

Schimmelfenning, F., & Sedelmeier, U. (2005).. *The Europeanization of Central and Eastern Europe.* Ithaca: Cornell University.

Sims, M. (1936). *Natural history of a social institution-The Y.W.C.A.* NY: J.J. Little and Ives Company.

Smith, E. (1998). Culture: The milieu of missions. In J. Terry, E. Smith, J. Anderson, J. Terry, E. Smith, & J. Anderson (Eds.), *Missiology: An introduction to the foundations, history, and strategies of world missions* (pp. 245-277). Nashville: Broadman & Holman.

Tennent, T. C. (2010). *Invitation to world missions: A trinitarian missiology for the 21st century.* Grand Rapids: Kregel.

Trattner, W. (1994). *From poor law to welfare state: A history of social welfare in America* (5th ed.). NY: Macmillan, Inc.

Valverde, M. (2008). *The age of light, soap, and water: Moral reform in English Canada, 1885-1925.* Toronto: University of Toronto Press.

VanWormer, C. (2004). *Confronting oppression, restoring justice: From policy analysis to social action.* Alexandria, VA: Council of Social Work Education.

Wallace, W. S. (1930). *A history of the Canadian people.* Toronto: The Copp Clark Company, Limited.

Walsch, T., Griffiths, W., McGolgan, M., & Ross, J. (2005). Trans-national curriculum development: Reflection on experiences in Romania. *Social Work Education , 24* (1), 19-36.

Young, A., & Ashton, E. (1956). *British social work in the 19th century.* London: Routledge & Kegan Paul LTD.

Zamfir, E. (1997). Social services for children at risk: The impact on quality of life. *Social Indicators Research , 1,* 41-76.

Zamfir, E., & Ionescu, I. (1994). From the culture of silence to a culture of freedom: New directions in the practice of social work in Romania. In R. Constable, & V. Mehta (Eds.). Chicago: Lyceum Books.

CHAPTER 22

CHRISTIANS RESPONDING TO
GANG INVOLVEMENT

Ronald Carr and Michael S. Kelly

Youth gangs and gang violence continue to be a serious national problem. There are approximately 24,500 gangs in the U.S. In 2008, national experts estimated that the U.S. had 800,000 gang members (Egley, Howell, & Moore, 2010). Of those 800,000 gang members, about 40% are juveniles (under 18); there are roughly 32,000 teenage girls in gangs (Greene & Pranis, 2007).

Almost every large to mid-size city in the U.S. has gang activity and gang activity has been reported in all 50 states in the U.S. (Egley et al., 2010; Howell, 2010). All races are part of the U.S. gang problem, though African-American and Hispanics account for 82% of the gang members in the U.S. (Howell, 2010). Youth gang activity and violence are strongly linked to increases in street drug traffic, illegal gun possession, and delinquent behavior (Braga, 2004). In our home of Chicago, 385 youth from the ages of 10-20 were killed by guns between 2008-2011, most of them due to gang violence (Red Eye, 2011). Gangs have significant and lasting impacts on communities, contributing to unsafe neighborhoods, traumatic stress, and a vicious cycle of impoverished work and housing opportunities that increase incentives for youth to join gangs to earn money and get protection (Glicken & Sechrest, 2003; Greene & Pranis, 2007).

Despite the many environmental factors affecting gang membership, youth join gangs for their own reasons and to meet their own needs. Many get involved for a particular criminal interest; therefore some enjoy theft, some for selling drugs, some, enforcing gang rules through violence and intimidation, and some for the basic fellowship of belonging (Corey, 2008; Howell, 2010). First, we want to share how Ron's own history and faith journey has informed this work to the present day, what the Scriptures and Christian literature say about gangs, and what the research literature says about "what works" to address the challenges of gang-involved youth. Later in this chapter, we will share Ron's process of developing a gang assessment tool to help identify the diverse needs of these youth and how this work has been formed by a culturally-competent, evidence-informed perspective, as well as our calling as Christian helping professionals.

Ron's Story

This is my brief testimony; I grew up on the south side of Chicago in a largely African-American community. My two sisters and brothers were raised as Christian Baptists. I hung out with the gang in the neighborhood, the Conservative Blackstone Rangers, like everyone else did; we were all friends and neighbors. I became a member of the gang gradually, but was a major part of the leadership of the gang by my late teens. I started fighting in school and outside of school by age 12. I was entering the gang life.

I got suspended and arrested several times; finally my mother asked her brother, my uncle, to come over to talk with me about fighting. I didn't know he used to be a pretty good amateur boxer. He arrived one day when I was 13 years old and said he wanted to show me where the "real" tough guys in Chicago hung out.

We went to the Woodlawn Boys Club on East 63rd street. As we entered the two swinging doors I was amazed at what I saw. There were teenagers and young men of all sizes punching on heavy bags, skipping rope, beating the speed bag, in the ring sparring, doing sit-ups and pushups, throwing the medicine ball at each other, and the blast of the three minute timer going off signaling the beginning and end of each round. As I watched the sweat-drenched muscular bodies, I knew I was in the right place. My uncle approached an older gentleman named Mr. Carson, who looked at me and said, "Who do we have here?" My uncle said, "This is my nephew, my sister's boy. He thinks he can fight." Mr. Carson looked at me and smiled, "So you think you can fight, huh?" I told him confidently, "Of course I can fight!"

He smiled again, as he told me, "You know, a man that knows how to fight don't need to fight." I didn't know then what he meant, but I learned he meant that boxing wasn't like fighting in the streets. I had to pace myself and be disciplined. I sat there amazed at the noises and punching techniques and how they all got along with each other in the gym. I started and I got good fast. I won the Golden Glove Championship one year later, at age 14. I was the 147lb. novice champ. That was the first time people thanked me for hitting someone else; it felt good to get applause and a trophy instead of a suspension or court case.

As I continued to box I got less and less interested in the gang life. I had big responsibilities in the leadership of the Conservative Blackstone Rangers as the "Warlord," but that position always was given to the best fighter in the gang anyway, so I wasn't pressured to stop boxing. My homeboys were just as excited about my new boxing reputation as I was. It made me more feared by my rivals in the street. By my sixteenth birthday I was 165lbs; a middle weight. I won the Golden Glove Championship again this time in the open division. I continued to box until I graduated from Hyde Park High School on 63rd and Stony Island, and I knew upon graduation I would leave the gang life and eventually leave Chicago. I had been exposed to other ethnic groups and lifestyles outside of the hood from traveling with the boxing team and my uncle during the summer months. He was an independent trucker and owned three big rigs. He would take me with him all over the country: New York, Philadelphia, Ohio, the Carolinas. Man, I didn't know the country was so big and different! We always went during the summer months when gang banging was at its height. This also was my mother's idea; she was my gang interventionist and my uncle was my mentor. They saved my life.

I recognized through their interventions there was another life outside of gang banging and Chicago, and have spent my adult years bringing those initial life lessons my family gave me to gang members in the Seattle area. After college, I married and began my career in counseling and working with youth in the criminal justice system. My wife and I never had any plans to move to Seattle, but God did, and I have been obedient and doing his will for the past twenty-two years. In the past two decades I have designed and implemented several programs by prayer alone. I started the Seattle Team for Youth (S.T.F.Y.), a gang intervention program consisting of street outreach workers providing intensive case management services to gang-identified youth in Seattle. I started the first Seattle Police Athletic League (P.A.L.) an after-school juvenile crime prevention program with the Seattle Police Department's Gang Unit.

I started my own 501c3 non-profit chapter of P.A.L. in Snohomish County, 30 miles north of Seattle. I also was the lead consultant to the King County Sheriff's Department to expand the Seattle P.A.L. chapter to the greater King County area, which incorporated several southern suburban cities. I mentored and counseled a strong Christian brother, Lydell Spry, on how to establish a P.A.L. chapter in Thurston County 60 miles south of Seattle. Whether I have been receiving community awards and accolades or sharing my perspectives on radio or television shows, I have been clear that my achievements are all about Christ: He put me here to do His will, which is kingdom work and I'm still here because I think He has more for me to do.

God Was Using Me

As an example of what God can do, I want to tell you about a young man named Sam (not his real name) that I worked with for four years. Sam was known on the street as "Big Sam" and was the gang leader of a local Blood set in a small suburb south of Seattle. He was always a big kid; at age fourteen when I first met Sam, he was 5'9" and weighed about 190 lbs. I was the coordinator for the gang unit street outreach program in a nearby town. Sam and his crew used to visit my area quite frequently to conduct illicit activities such as drug sales, give out beat downs, and steal cars. I used to talk to Sam about leadership and his ability to persuade people to follow him and how he could use that in a positive way. He used to just smile as if it was a nice idea, but he had other plans for his influential skills. I also talked to him about the four juvenile prisons that were in Washington State, and I reassured him if he didn't listen to my advice he would definitely end up in one of them. I saw Sam at least once or twice a week.

As he got older, I continued to remind him that the rules would change when he turned eighteen years old. Meanwhile, our division lost the funding for the gang unit's outreach program and I had to take another job. I secured employment with a local school district as the Director of Security at their alternative high school, and learned that Sam was a student there. I had not seen him for about eighteen months and he had grown a great deal, now standing at 6"2" and weighing 250 lbs. His reputation had escalated and he was quite notorious on the school campus.

We reacquainted ourselves and I informed him there was bed space in prison for him. On campus I would get two to three calls a week to escort Sam off school grounds. As we walked off campus, I would emphasize he was headed to prison. After six months or so, Sam was arrested and charged with assault in a gang-related beating and was sentenced to a year in one of our toughest juvenile prisons. He had just turned seventeen and was lucky he was not charged as an adult.

I left the school after two years and took a position as a parole officer in the area. After six months in this position I got a referral from my supervisor and guess whose picture was in the file--"Big Sam!" I telephoned Sam at the institution and he was surprised to find out I would be his parole officer. Sam told me that once he knew I was his parole officer, he knew he was going to succeed. He said, "Man you have been in my life for years saying the same thing and trying to help me; I am finally ready to let you help me. I want to get out of the gang life and go to the Job Corps."

With a silent shout of joy and a hallelujah! I knew God had been using me to help this kid out of the darkness; and now he was finally able to see the light. I informed Sam I would start the paper work and when he was released in the next week I would pick him up and take him out for a tour of the Job Corps campus. The next week we departed early that morning as Job Corps was at least 60 miles north of us. Sam was like a kid in a candy store. He was excited and asking appropriate questions and had a real interest in the construction trade.

Sam was accepted and started two months later in the construction trade. He graduated and joined the local union and is now an apprentice making $17.42 an hour. Once he finishes his three-year apprenticeship, he will be a journeyman starting at $30.50 per hour. Sam has been doing really well: he is working, has a nice girl friend, and is staying away from his former gang banging friends. I truly think God gave me the patience, endurance, and stamina to continue to support, encourage, and motivate Sam to do the right thing with his own God-given skills. He is one of my success stories.

Using the Bible to Help Gang-Involved Youth

I have used numerous Bible verses to get my point across to gangsters, dope dealers, hustlers, and pimps. In my college teaching and work with high school youth, I use Romans 13:1-3. It states: "Let every person be subject to the governing authorities; for there is no authority except from God, and those that exist have been instituted by God. Therefore, whoever resists the authorities resists what God has appointed, and those who resists will incur judgment; for rulers are not a terror to good conduct, but to bad. I have found no God-fearing criminal can argue with this point. In our psycho-education group work with gang members I have used 2 Timothy 2:22-23, which states: "One should flee the evil desires of youth, and pursue righteousness, faith, love, and peace, along with those who call on the Lord out of a pure heart." I emphasize to group members not to have anything to do with foolish and stupid arguments because they produce quarrels. Our work with gang members reveals a perpetual interpersonal and interrelational conflict. When gang members continually engage in sin they will reap the consequences. Foolish chatter occupies their minds with unworthy thoughts that eventually emerge as unworthy actions such as fighting, drive-by shootings, and a litany of criminal behaviors.

Our roles as Christians and citizens are especially clear in a democratic society. The Christian is responsible to honor those in authority and to pray for them (Rom. 13: 1 Tim. 2:2). The Christian is to obey the civil law and authority (Rom. 13:1-10). The Christian is to pay taxes (Rom. 13:6). The Christian is to practice justice and mercy, dealing justly with employees, working to relieve the poor, the minorities (aliens), the oppressed, and the weak, (widows and orphans). Perhaps the strongest passage of all is (Matthew 25:31-46), where we are told in advance the basis of judgment on the last day: We will be judged on the basis of whether we have fed the hungry, given drink to the thirsty, lodged the homeless, clothed the naked, and cared for the sick and imprisoned. As Jesus stated to the Jews that believed (John 8:31), "If you abide in My word, you are My disciples indeed; and you will know the truth and the truth will set you free." I am a servant leader and profound believer in the Lord Jesus Christ; this is truly why I do what I do.

These days, I am a gang interventionist who works primarily as a psycho-educational group facilitator. I work with group members who are relatively well-functioning individuals, but who may have an information deficit in certain areas. In the case of gang involved youth, this deficit is often a lack of knowledge about the laws that govern our society and no regard for the citizenry of their communities. In my groups, I use an integrated approach of civic education, basic concepts in jurisprudence and cognitive reframing, using open-ended questions to generate critical thinking so the kids can see the direct correlation between their ill-informed perceptions about the role of the police. I also focus them on their role as a citizen versus their misguided gang member attitude. Adolescents tend to respond well to group leaders who share relevant information about their circumstances. They respond well if you genuinely respect and enjoy their presence and appropriately reveal your personal experiences and concerns; the reward is reciprocal respect and being Christ-like, demonstrating you have unconditional love for them and are willing to help them understand their brokenness. I have collaborated with another Christian and gang interventionist, Michael Kelly, to further refine and sharpen a program that I developed to address these issues in a structured way.

Developing *Exit Strategies*

We have seen first-hand the cognitive distortions and co-occurring substance abuse and conduct disorders that exist in gang-involved youth. Ron works with youth incarcerated in maximum- to medium-security juvenile correctional facilities in Washington state, and Michael works in therapeutic educational programs for youth in Chicago, first as a school social worker for 14 years and now as a consultant to these districts and researcher on evidence-based strategies for working with their most at-risk youth. Ron started thinking about an assessment tool and psycho-education curriculum called *Exit Strategies* about five years ago; that's what prompted him to go back to school to get a Master's degree in Counseling Psychology. *Exit Strategies* was his thesis project. Ron has witnessed the project evolve from vision, to hypothesis, to accessing funding, to implementation, and to a preliminary evaluation outcome study. Along with Ron's field work and consulting, this research represents his best effort to correct the faulty and irrational thinking patterns of God's misguided children known as gang bangers. The programs Ron helped to develop (and Michael is helping him further refine) are currently in place today throughout Washington state.

Exit Strategies is a multi-pronged gang assessment tool and psycho-education curriculum that seeks to understand and assist at-risk youth in a more culturally competent way. Most of the standardized instruments were not developed specifically for the gang population, but for adolescents with other psychosocial issues that might predispose them to gang involvement (Center for Disease Control, 2005). Additionally, the items contained in some of the standardized instruments may not be culturally relevant for gang-identified youth.

In our work with these youth, we find that this population frequently resorts to cognitive distortions and irrational beliefs. A few of those distortions are: being a gangster is cool, gang brothers support you better than your real family, and gang members will always be there for you. To overcome these self-deceptions, Rational Emotive Behavior Therapy (R.E.B.T.) is regularly utilized to counteract these irrational beliefs. This psychosocial intervention employs active and direct techniques such as thought processing, teaching, suggestion, persuasion, and homework assignments. This model also challenges individuals to learn cognitive restructuring techniques in order to substitute a rational belief system for an irrational one. (Ellis, 2001). Our experiences with these youth show us they find it acceptable to use cognitive distortions, and therefore use them frequently. We also see a pattern in these at-risk youth: they tend to be from hostile and dysfunctional families in which very little emphasis is placed on structure and discipline. There is also an attitude of disdain or rejection of the educational system, established laws, norms, and mores. We realized that an assessment tool that could help us better assess their "civic-resistant attitude" would be beneficial in designing curriculum to effectively address gang-involved youth's attitudes of non-compliance and civic disengagement.

Exit Strategies is a comprehensive behavior clarification curriculum that is delivered in a group format. It utilizes Solution Focused Brief Therapy (SFBT), REBT, and the clinical concepts are integrated with Law Related Education (L.R.E.) and basic concepts in jurisprudence. This psycho-education intervention is designed to challenge the irrational thinking patterns embraced by gang involved youth. This program was designed to counteract the negative influences, nuances, appeal, and allure of various youth subcultures and behavioral lifestyles. [1]

Each youth referred to the program receives the *Exit Strategies* assessment tool, consisting of four sections: (1) initial oral interview, (2) individual questionnaire, (3) six domain category assessments, and (4) re-entry reflective questionnaire. The numeric value of each section is totaled and the individual is placed into an *Exit Strategies* group. This placement not only determines the curriculum content, it also provides information about the depth of gang involvement for each individual.

The categories we identified as high risk for youth recidivism (repeat offending and re-arrest for similar criminal activities) were: (1) new felony charges, (2) recommitted by parole revocation or probation violation, (3) documented ongoing gang activities, (4) documented domestic violence, and (5) documented gang violence. The primary sources used to track our treatment group participants were the statewide Automated Client Tracking system (ACT), the multiple county Juvenile Information System (JVIS), and the Washington State Court System to verify and validate new arrests and new charges. The preliminary results from our pilot project with *Exit Strategies* revealed a dramatic decrease after a 18-month follow-up in the recidivism of youthful offenders (n=85) who completed the program, as compared to demographically similar youth who did not (n=270). The data retrieved from our follow up indicated there was a 42.31% reduction in recidivism in the treatment group of gang involved youth. This gives us tremendous hope for addressing gang involvement.

Hope for the Future

Though the plague of gang involvement and its many damaging impacts have been the main concerns of this chapter, preventing gang involvement and gang violence is in some ways more possible to envision than ever before. We know more about the risk factors for gang involvement, the demographics of current gang members in the U.S., and how communities, schools, and practitioners can all successfully prevent gangs from taking over neighborhoods (Howell, 2010). In many ways, Ron's own story is itself a classic example of what we now know "works" to get gang-involved youth to safety: parental involvement, mentoring, vocational and recreational training, and a change of scene. *Michael Preston, the Executive Director of Central Youth Association declared in his comments to the Seattle Times how much Ron's personal experiences increase his effectiveness:*

> *There's no one like him in Seattle. He's one of the only men who is going straight to the actual gang-involved youth, not just the wannabes and dress-alikes. He deals with the real thing. It takes people like him to be effective. Whatever I can do for Ron (Carr), I'll do. I believe in him."*

While it's tempting to feel overwhelmed by gang activity, a Christian helping professional who wants to help young people "...flee the evil desires of youth, and pursue righteousness, faith, love, and peace, along with those who call on the Lord out of a pure heart" has many spiritual and evidence-based tools at their disposal.

References

Braga, A.A. (2004). *Gun violence among serious young offenders*. Retrieved on August 15, 2011, from http://www.cops.usdoj.gov/files/RIC/Publications/e0507882.pdf

Corey, G. (2008). *Theory and practice of group counseling*. Belmont, CA: Thomson Press.

Center for Disease Control and Prevention (2005). *Measuring Violence-Related Attitudes, Behaviors, and Influences Among Youths: A Compendium of Assessment Tools - Second Edition*. Retrieved on December 10, 2011, from http://www.cdc.gov/ncipc/pub-res/measure.htm

Egley, A., Howell, J. C., & Moore, J.P. (2010, March). *Highlights of the 2008 National Youth Gang Survey*. Retrieved on December 2, 2011, from https://www.ncjrs.gov/pdffiles1/ojjdp/229249.pdf

Ellis, A. (2001). *Overcoming destructive beliefs, feelings, and behaviors*. Amherst, NY: Prometheus Books.

Glicken, D. M. & Sechrest, D.K. (2003). *The role of the helping professions in treating the victims and perpetrators of violence*. Boston, MA: Pearson Education.

Greene, J., & Pranis, K. (2007). Gang wars: The failure of enforcement tactics and the need for effective public safety strategies. Retrieved on December 4, 2011, from http://www.justicepolicy.org/uploads/justicepolicy/documents/07-07_exs_gang-wars_gc-ps-ac-jj.pdf

Howell, J.C. (2010, December). Gang prevention: An overview of research and programs. Retrieved on October 20, 2011, from www.ncjrs.gov/pdffiles1/ojjdp/231116.pdf

Office of Juvenile Justice and Delinquency Prevention (2000). *Comprehensive Approaches to gang problems*. Retrieved January 30, 2009, from http://www.ncjrs.gov/html/ojjdp/summary_2000_8/comprehensive.html

Preston, M. (December 30, 1990) "His Job? Bringing Peace To Gang-Torn Streets." *Seattle Times*.

Red Eye (2011). *Tracking homicides in Chicago*. Retrieved on December 1st, 2011, from http://homicides.redeyechicago.com/

Note

1   The program was designed by Juvenile Rehabilitation Administration Region 3 (J.R.A.), Ronald Carr, and Nick Clovsky.

ABOUT THE EDITORS

Dr. T. Laine Scales is Professor of Higher Education at Baylor University. She served 15 years as a faculty member in social work in three universities. She has published over 40 articles and chapters in the areas of teaching in social work, faith and social work practice, rural social work, and higher education. Her 10 co-authored or co-edited books include *Social Environments & Human Behavior: Contexts for Practice with Groups, Organizations, Communities, & Social Movements*, (Brooks/Cole, 2012) and *Rural Social Work: Building and Sustaining Community Assets* (Brooks/Cole 2004). She is former associate editor of *The Journal of Family & Community Ministries* and *Social Work and Christianity*.

Dr. Michael S. Kelly is Assistant Professor at the Loyola University Chicago School of Social Work. He has written over 30 books, articles, and book chapters on school social work, evidence-based practice, and the intersection of Christianity and social work practice. His most recent book was *School Social Work: An Evidence-Informed Framework for Practice*, published by Oxford University Press. He has served as a Guest Lecturer and consultant to social workers in Chile, Japan, Rhode Island, Wisconsin, and Wyoming. He was a section editor for *The Journal of Family and Community Ministries* and now serves as Assistant Editor of *Social Work and Christianity*.

ABOUT THE CONTRIBUTORS

Tanya Brice earned a BS in Social Work from South Carolina State University, a MSW from the College of Social Work at the University of South Carolina, and a PhD in Social Work from the University of North Carolina at Chapel Hill. She is an Associate Professor at Baylor University's School of Social Work. She has also served as Director of the MSSW program at Abilene Christian University and as an Assistant Professor at the University of South Carolina's College of Social Work. Her research interests include social welfare history, with a particular focus on the contribution of African American women in the development of the profession. She has authored several articles and presented at national conferences on this topic. Her research also includes the impact of race relations on Christianity and the examination of structural oppression and its impact on vulnerable populations.

Ronald Carr, the Founder and Executive Director of the Snohomish County Police Athletic League, is a professional counselor and mental health professional in Washington State. With a BA in Social Science and a Master's degree in Counseling Psychology, he has over thirty five years of experience working with gangs in Chicago, Minneapolis, and the Seattle metropolitan area. Mr. Carr served three years as an Adjunct Professor in Sociology at Puget Sound Christian College and is currently teaching criminal and juvenile justice at Everett Community College.

Rick Chamiec-Case earned a BA in Philosophy from Wheaton College, a MAR in Religion from Yale Divinity School, a MSW from the School of Social Work at the University of Connecticut, and a PhD in Social Work from Fordham University. He has been the Executive Director of the North American Association of Christians in Social Work since 1997, and an adjunct professor of social work at Nyack College in New York City since 2008. He worked for a number of years as Senior Vice President at ARI of Connecticut, whose mission it is to provide homes and jobs for people with disabilities.. Dr. Chamiec-Case has written and presented at conferences on various topics addressing the ethical integration of faith and social work practice, and has research and scholarship interests in the areas of spirituality in the workplace and faith-based social services. He has been the managing editor of *Social Work and Christianity* since 1997.

Diana R. Garland received her BA, MSSW, and PhD degrees from the University of Louisville. She is Professor of Social Work and inaugural Dean of the School of Social Work, Baylor University, Waco, Texas, where she has served on the faculty since 1997. She previously served as Dean of the Carver School of Church Social Work at The Southern Baptist Theological Seminary in Kentucky. She is author, co-author, or editor of 18 books. The most recent are *Inside Out Families; Living the Faith, Together* and *Flawed Families of the Bible: How God Works through Imperfect Relationships.* The second edition of her book *Family Ministry: A Comprehensive Guide* (InterVarsity Press) is forthcoming; previously, it won the 2000 Book of the Year Award of the Academy of Parish Clergy at Princeton Seminary. She has published more than 100 professional articles and book chapters. She has received more than $7 million in research and program grants since coming to Baylor in 1997, from organizations such as Lilly Endowment, Inc, Pew Charitable Trusts, Inc., the Annie E. Casey Foundation, the Henry Luce Foundation, and the Ford Foundation.

Helen Wilson Harris earned a BA from the University of Mary Hardin-Baylor in Belton, Texas, MSW from Our Lady of the Lake University in San Antonio, Texas and Ed.D. from the University of Mary Hardin-Baylor. Presently she is a Senior Lecturer at the Baylor University School of Social Work where she teaches across curriculum. Previously Helen served as Director of Graduate Field Education and Director of Field Education for ten years. Prior to coming to Baylor, Helen was the founding director of the first hospice in central Texas and served for eight years as foster care and independent living director at The South Texas Children's Home. Helen's research and practice interests are children's loss and grief, physical and mental health, end of life care, and faith-based child care and adoptions. She has written in the area of spiritual formation, grief and bereavement and educational administration.

David R. Hodge received his PhD from the Brown School of Social Work at Washington University in St. Louis. Currently, he is a senior nonresident fellow at the University of Pennsylvania's Program for Research on Religion and Urban Civil Society. He is also an Associate Professor in the School of Social Work at Arizona State University, where he teaches graduate courses on spirituality, cultural diversity, and spiritual assessment while overseeing the doctoral program. Dr. Hodge is an internationally recognized scholar on the topic of spirituality and religion. His scholarship has been featured in over 100 peer-reviewed journal articles, encyclopedia entries, book chapters, and conference presentations, as well as in newspapers and other popular media around the world. Forthcoming, is a second edition of his book, *Spiritual Assessment: A Handbook for Helping Professionals* (NACSW, 2003).

Crystal R. Holtrop earned her BSW from Dordt College and her MSW from the University of Iowa. She has 14 years of experience as a Clinical Supervisor and Marriage and Family Therapist at Catholic Charities. A clinical member of the American Association of Marriage and Family Therapy, she has conducted in-service trainings, facilitated workshops, and participated in the redesign of a two-county social service delivery system. Currently, she is enjoying being a stay-at-home mother and homeschooling her two children, Rachel and Esther.

Beryl Hugen received a BA from Calvin College, a MSW from Western Michigan University, and a PhD from the University of Kansas. He is Professor (emeritus) of Social Work at Calvin College in Grand Rapids, Michigan. He has served as a board member and publications editor for the North American Association of Christians in Social Work. He has published papers on mental health, the integration of Christian faith and social work practice, and social work history. He is co-editor of *Spirituality within Religious Traditions in Social Work Practice* (Brooks Cole, 2001) and *Christianity and Social Work: Readings on the Integration of Christian Faith and Social Work Practice*, 3rd Edition, (NACSW, 2008).

Timothy James Johnson received a BS in Bible Social Work from Philadelphia Biblical University, a MSW from the University of Pennsylvania, and a PhD in African American Studies from Temple University. His dissertation research was a study of the Black Church in America. In addition he completed extensive course work toward the PhD in social work and social research at Bryn Mawr College. With close to 32 years of teaching in higher education, he is Emeritus Professor of Social Work at Roberts Wesleyan College. He also served as associate professor of social work at Eastern University, and associate professor of Church Social Work at the Carver School of Church Social Work at The Southern Baptist Theological Seminary in Louisville, KY. A former NACSW board member, Timothy is the author of a number of articles, including NACSW'S 2002 Alan Keith Lucas lecture - "Reconciliation: a Paradoxical Idea and Ideal for Christian Social Work in the 21st Century," also published in the journal *Christianity and Social Work*. His current areas of teaching in social work education are social justice and ethics, macro social work, social work practice theory, human behavior in the social environment, and congregational and community practice theory. He currently serves as Program Director of Johnson Master Consulting, working to bring excellence to human service angencies.

Dennis R. Myers received a BA from Baylor University and a MSSW and PhD from the University of Texas at Austin. He is the Kronzer Professor of Family Studies and Professor of Social Work. He serves on the editorial board of *Social Work and Christianity*. Dr. Myers was recognized as a Distinguished Teacher by the Association for Gerontology in Higher Education and as an expert Gero-Ed Center Expert Trainer by the Council on Social Work Education. He is the principle investigator for the Danny and Lenn Prince Initiative for Quality Long-term Care with Older Adults that provides research, evidence-based practice models, educational programs, and practical resources to strengthen the care environment of residential facilities and to enrich the personal and family life of older persons who reside in them. He is also the co-principal investigator for the Bilingual Mental Health Scholarship Program for Accredited

Social Work Programs, funded by the Hogg Foundation (2008-2013). During the period between 2002 to the present, Dr. Myers authored or co-authored 26 journal articles in the areas of social work practice, educational gerontology, adult caregiving, productive aging, and faith-based community services.

Elizabeth Patterson received her BA in social work from Mount Vernon Nazarene College and her MSW from Roberts Wesleyan College. Presently, she is associate professor and field coordinator at Malone University in Canton, Ohio. Elizabeth is currently working on her dissertation for a PhD in social work at Memorial University of Newfoundland, Canada. Her dissertation research explores how international practicums in social work have influenced participants' career choices and practice approaches. Previously, Elizabeth practiced international social work in a faith-based setting through serving as the coordinator of social services for Veritas in Sighisoara, Romania and as a faculty member for the Romanian Studies Program. Elizabeth has published and presented on various topics related to international social work and study abroad.

Mary Anne Poe earned a BA from Vanderbilt University, a MDiv from The Southern Baptist Theological Seminary in Louisville, Kentucky, and a MSSW from the University of Louisville. Presently she is Professor of Social Work, BSW Director, and Director of the Center for Just and Caring Communities at Union University in Jackson, Tennessee where she has taught since 1996.. She served previously as a congregational social worker in churches in Minnesota and Kentucky. Her research and practice interests are how to engage congregations in effective and culturally sensitive ministry in the community, social and economic justice, and relationships among faith-based organizations, congregations, and other social service providers. She has published case studies and the *Instructors Resources for Christianity and Social Work 3rd Edition*.

Julia Pryce earned at BA in Psychology from Kenyon College, an MSW from the University of Michigan, and a PhD in Social Work from the University of Chicago. Presently, she serves as assistant professor in the School of Social Work, Loyola University, Chicago, She has worked in faith-based services for youth, adolescents, and families impacted by the child welfare system. Her research areas include the use of positive youth development (including mentoring) among system-involved youth, and social work education, particularly as it relates to incorporating social justice into social work pedagogy. Dr. Pryce's research has been funded by the Department of Health & Human Services and the Office of Juvenile Justice & Delinquency Prevention and includes collaboration with an interfaith youth development program in the South of India.

David A. Sherwood, BA, Lipscomb University; MSW, Bryn Mawr; PhD in Social Work from the University of Texas, Austin. He has helped develop BSW and MSW programs at Christian colleges and universities, including Baylor University, Roberts Wesleyan College, Gordon College, and Oral Roberts University. He has written extensively on ethics and topics related to the integration of Christian faith and social work practice. Dr. Sherwood is a co-editor of Spirituality and Religion in Social Work Practice: Decision Cases with Teaching Notes. He has served two terms on the Commission on Accreditation of the Council on Social Work Education, continues to do Commissioner visits with programs in candidacy for accreditation, and consults with social work programs in Christian colleges and universities. Dr. Sherwood has served on the Board and as President of the North American Association of Christians in Social Work and is Editor of the journal Social Work & Christianity.

Jon Singletary received his BA from Baylor University. He then earned an MDiv from the Baptist Theological Seminary at Richmond VA, and his MSW and PhD in Social Work from Virginia Commonwealth University. He currently serves as the Diana R. Garland Endowed Chair of Child and Family Studies and as Associate Dean for Baccalaureate Studies in the Baylor University School ofSocial Work. While at Baylor, he has helped create the Strengthening Congregational Community Ministries Project, the Baylor Interdisciplinary Poverty Initiative and the Texas Hunger Initiative, garnering more than $2 million in external funding. Prior to coming to Baylor, he served as pastor at the Richmond Mennonite Fellowship and as community organizer for the Society of St. Andrew food gleaning program and the Greater Area Richmond Health Care for the Homeless project. Most importantly, he is married and father to four children.

Hope Haslam Straughan earned a BA from Samford University (Alabama), a MSW and Certificate in Theology from the Carver School of Church Social Work at The Southern Baptist Theological Seminary (Kentucky), and a PhD in social work from Barry University (Florida). Presently she is Interim Chair and Associate Professor of Social Work at Wheelock College, and the Director of the MSW program (Massachusetts). Previous social work experience has been as consultant to APERFOSA (Spain) around the establishment of an AIDS hospice, serving as a Volunteer Foster Care Case Reviewer for the Department for Children and Families, and co-leading a dynamic collaborative within the community of Codman Square (Boston) in order to improve the lives of children and families in a diverse, impoverished, and complex neighborhood. Her research interests include spirituality within social work practice with children and families, spiritual development across the lifespan, transracial adoption narratives, and community and organizational collaboration. She is currently working with two other NACSW members to establish a MA Chapter of NACSW, and serving as a board member for FAMILY, Inc.

Allison Tan received her BSW from Taylor University, her MSSA from Case Western Research University, and her PhD in Social Work from Loyola University of Chicago. She worked for more than seven years in the field of HIV, both as a program director at a faith-based community health center and as a consultant. Her dissertation research focused on models of peer-based HIV prevention services. In addition to her academic experience and HIV work, she has also done a number of presentations on faith-based work with the LGBT population, and has served as a consultant to The Marin Foundation in Chicago. She is currently an adjunct instructor of social work at Loyola and Dominican Universities.

James R. Vanderwoerd received a BA from Calvin College, a MSW from Wilfrid Laurier University, and a PhD from Case Western Reserve University. He is currently Professor of Social Work at Redeemer University College, and was formerly the Social Work Program Director at Dordt College. He worked for seven years as a community researcher with the Ontario government's innovative prevention project Better Beginnings, Better Futures. He is the co-author of *Protecting Children and Supporting Families* (Aldine de Gruyter, 1997), and has published articles in *Christian Scholar's Review, Social Work & Christianity, Journal of Baccalaureate Social Work, Critical SocialWork, Nonprofit Management & Leadership,* and *Canadian Social Work.* His research and teaching interests are in prevention of violence against women on college campuses, religion and non-profit organizations in social welfare, and social welfare policy and history.

Gaynor I. Yancey is Professor or Social Work and Associate Dean for Baccalaureate Studies in the School of Social Work, Baylor University, Waco, TX. She received her BA from East Texas Baptist University, the M.R.E. degree from Southwestern Baptist Theological Seminary, the M.S.W. degree from Temple University, and the D.S.W. degree from the University of Pennsylvania. She previously served as Assistant Professor at Eastern University in St. Davids, PA. She worked for over 25 years as a Congregational Community Ministries Director, working with congregations in Philadelphia, PA. She has authored and co-authored numerous professional articles and book chapters, predominantly focused on congregational community ministry. Since coming to Baylor in 1999, she has received more than $3.5 million in research and program grants from organizations such as Pew Charitable Trusts, Inc., Christ is Our Salvation, Bridgeway Charitable Trust, and the Baptist General Convention of Texas. In 1983, Dr. Yancey was the first recipient of the Clovis A. Brantley Award for Outstanding Service in Christian Social Ministries in the United States. In 2004, she received the Marie Mathis Award for Outstanding Life Achievement in Lay Ministry.

APPENDIX A

EPAS CONNECTIONS
ORGANIZED BY CHAPTER

This chart suggests potential connections between specific chapters in this book and competencies listed in the Education Policy and Accreditation Standards of Council on Social Work Education.

Chapter	Chapter Title	Competencies	
Chapter 1	Good News for the Poor	EP 2.1.1	Identify as a professional social worker and conduct oneself accordingly.
		EP 2.1.8	Engage in policy practice to advance social and economic well-being and to deliver effective social work services.
		EP 2.1.9	Respond to contexts that shape practice.
Chapter 2	To Give Christ to the Neighborhoods	EP 2.1.1	Identify as a professional social worker and conduct oneself accordingly.
		EP 2.1.5	Advance human rights and social and economic justice.
		EP 2.1.8	Engage in policy practice to advance social and economic well-being and to deliver effective social work services.
Chapter 3	The Black Church	EP 2.1.1	Identify as a professional social worker and conduct oneself accordingly.
		EP 2.1.4	Engage diversity and difference in practice.
		EP 2.1.9	Respond to contexts that shape practice.
Chapter 4	Accepting a Trust so Responsible	EP 2.1.1	Identify as a professional social worker and conduct oneself accordingly.
		EP 2.1.9	Respond to contexts that shape practice.
		EP 2.1.10	Engage, assess, intervene, and evaluate with individuals, families, groups, organizations, and communities.
Chapter 5	Go in Peace	EP 2.1.1	Identify as a professional social worker and conduct oneself accordingly.
		EP 2.1.4	Engage diversity and difference in practice.
		EP 2.1.8	Engage in policy practice to advance social and economic well-being and to deliver effective social work services.
Chapter 6	The Relationship Between Beliefs and Values	EP 2.1.2	Apply social work ethical principles to guide professional practice.

Chapter	Chapter Title	Competencies	
		EP 2.1.3	Apply critical thinking to inform and communicate professional judgments
Chapter 7	Calling: A Spirituality Model	EP 2.1.1	Identify as a professional social worker and conduct oneself accordingly.
		EP 2.1.7	Apply knowledge of human behavior and the social environment.
Chapter 8	Catholic Social Teaching	EP 2.1.1	Identify as a professional social worker and conduct oneself accordingly.
		EP 2.1.5	Advance human rights and social and economic justice.
Chapter 9	Integrating Christian Faith and Social Work Practice	EP 2.1.1	Identify as a professional social worker and conduct oneself accordingly.
		EP 2.1.9	Respond to contexts that shape practice.
Chapter 10	Fairness Is Not Enough	EP 2.1.2	Apply social work ethical principles to guide professional practice.
		EP 2.1.3	Apply critical thinking to inform and communicate professional judgments
		EP 2.1.5	Advance human rights and social and economic justice.
Chapter 11	Doing the Right Thing	EP 2.1.2	Apply social work ethical principles to guide professional practice.
		EP 2.1.3	Apply critical thinking to inform and communicate professional judgments
Chapter 12	Spiritual Development	EP 2.1.3	Apply critical thinking to inform and communicate professional judgments
		EP 2.1.6	Engage in research-informed practice and practice-informed research.
		EP 2.1.7	Apply knowledge of human behavior and the social environment.
Chapter 13	Social Welfare in a Diverse Society	EP 2.1.5	Advance human rights and social and economic justice.
		EP 2.1.7	Apply knowledge of human behavior and the social environment.
		EP 2.1.8	Engage in policy practice to advance social and economic well-being and to deliver effective social work services.
Chapter 14	Working with LGBT Clients	EP 2.1.4	Engage diversity and difference in practice.
		EP 2.1.7	Apply knowledge of human behavior and the social environment.
		EP 2.1.10	Engage, assess, intervene, and evaluate with individuals, families, groups, organizations, and communities.
Chapter 15	Spiritual Assessment	EP 2.1.6	Engage in research-informed practice and practice-informed research.

Chapter	Chapter Title	Competencies	
		EP 2.1.7	Apply knowledge of human behavior and the social environment.
		EP 2.1.10	Engage, assess, intervene, and evaluate with individuals, families, groups, organizations, and communities.
Chapter 16	The Helping Process	EP 2.1.9	Respond to contexts that shape practice.
		EP 2.1.10	Engage, assess, intervene, and evaluate with individuals, families, groups, organizations, and communities.
Chapter 17	Ethical Integration	EP 2.1.2	Apply social work ethical principles to guide professional practice.
		EP 2.1.10	Engage, assess, intervene, and evaluate with individuals, families, groups, organizations, and communities.
Chapter 18	Moving Mountains	EP 2.1.6	Engage in research-informed practice and practice-informed research.
		EP 2.1.9	Respond to contexts that shape practice.
		EP 2.1.10	Engage, assess, intervene, and evaluate with individuals, families, groups, organizations, and communities.
Chapter 19	Ethically Integrating Faith and Practice	EP 2.1.2	Apply social work ethical principles to guide professional practice.
		EP 2.1.3	Apply critical thinking to inform and communicate professional judgments
		EP 2.1.10	Engage, assess, intervene, and evaluate with individuals, families, groups, organizations, and communities.
Chapter 20	Evidence-Based Practice	EP 2.1.3	Apply critical thinking to inform and communicate professional judgments
		EP 2.1.6	Engage in research-informed practice and practice-informed research.
		EP 2.1.10	Engage, assess, intervene, and evaluate with individuals, families, groups, organizations, and communities.
Chapter 21	International Social Work	EP 2.1.4	Engage diversity and difference in practice.
		EP 2.1.5	Advance human rights and social and economic justice.
		EP 2.1.10	Engage, assess, intervene, and evaluate with individuals, families, groups, organizations, and communities.
Chapter 22	Gang Involvement	EP 2.1.4	Engage diversity and difference in practice.
		EP 2.1.10	Engage, assess, intervene, and evaluate with individuals, families, groups, organizations, and communities.

APPENDIX B

EPAS CONNECTIONS ORGANIZED BY COMPETENCY NUMBER

This chart suggests potential connections between competencies listed in the Education Policy and Accreditation Standards of Council on Social Work Education and specific chapters of this book.

Competency	Competency Details	Chapters Related
EP 2.1.1	Identify as a professional social worker and conduct oneself accordingly.	1, 2, 3, 4, 5, 7, 8, 9
EP 2.1.2	Apply social work ethical principles to guide professional practice.	6, 10, 11, 17, 19
EP 2.1.3	Apply critical thinking to inform and communicate professional judgments	6, 10, 11, 12, 19, 20
EP 2.1.4	Engage diversity and difference in practice.	3, 5, 14, 21, 22
EP 2.1.5	Advance human rights and social and economic justice.	2, 8, 10, 13, 21
EP 2.1.6	Engage in research-informed practice and practice-informed research.	12, 15, 18, 20
EP 2.1.7	Apply knowledge of human behavior and the social environment.	7, 12, 13, 14, 15
EP 2.1.8	Engage in policy practice to advance social and economic well-being and to deliver effective social work services.	1, 2, 5, 13
EP 2.1.9	Respond to contexts that shape practice.	1, 3, 4, 9, 16, 18
EP 2.1.10	Engage, assess, intervene, and evaluate with individuals, families, groups, organizations, and communities.	4, 14, 15, 16, 17, 18, 19, 20, 21, 22